The Language Toolkit

Oxford
Paperback
Reference

The most authoritative and up-to-date reference books for both students and the general reader.

Abbreviations
ABC of Music
Accounting
Archaeology
Architecture
Art and Artists
Art Terms
Astronomy
Better Wordpower
Bible
Biology
British History
Buddhism*
Business
Card Games
Celtic Mythology
Chemistry
Christian Art
Christian Church
Classical Literature
Colour Medical
Computing
Concise Quotations
Dance
Dates
Dynasties of the World*
Earth Sciences
Ecology
Economics
Engineering*
English Etymology
English Folklore
English Grammar
English Language
English Literature
English Place-Names
Everyday Grammar
Finance and Banking
First Names
Food and Nutrition
Foreign Words and Phrases
Geography
Handbook of the World
Humorous Quotations
Idioms
Irish Literature
Jewish Religion
Kings and Queens of Britain
Law
Linguistics
Literary Quotations
Literary Terms
Local and Family History

London Place Names
Mathematics
Medical
Medicines
Modern Design*
Modern Quotations
Modern Slang
Music
Nursing
Opera
Philosophy
Physics
Plant-Lore
Plant Sciences
Pocket Fowler's Modern
    English Usage
Political Biography
Political Quotations
Politics
Popes
Proverbs
Psychology
Quotations
Sailing Terms
Saints
Science
Scientists
Shakespeare
Ships and the Sea
Slang
Sociology
Spelling
Statistics
Superstitions
Synonyms and Antonyms
Theatre
Twentieth-Century Art
Twentieth-Century Poetry
Twentieth-Century World
    History
Weather
Weights, Measures, and Units
Who's Who in the Classical
    World
Who's Who in the Twentieth
    Century
World History
World Mythology
World Religions
Writers' Dictionary
Zoology

*forthcoming

The Language Toolkit

Practical advice on English grammar and usage

Edited by

JONATHAN LAW

Oxford   New York

OXFORD UNIVERSITY PRESS

OXFORD
UNIVERSITY PRESS

Great Clarendon Street, Oxford OX2 6DP
Oxford University Press is a department of the University of
Oxford. It furthers the University's objective of excellence in
research, scholarship, and education by publishing worldwide in
Oxford New York

Auckland Bangkok Buenos Aires Cape Town Chennai
Dar es Salaam Delhi Hong Kong Istanbul Karachi Kolkata
Kuala Lumpur Madrid Melbourne Mexico City Mumbai
Nairobi São Paulo Shanghai Singapore Taipei Tokyo Toronto
with an associated company in Berlin

Oxford is a registered trade mark of Oxford University Press
in the UK and in certain other countries

Published in the United States
by Oxford University Press Inc., New York

First published 2001 as *Oxford Compendium of English Vol. 1.*
First Published as an Oxford University Press paperback 2002

British Library Cataloguing in Publication Data

Data available

Library of Congress Cataloging in Publication Data

Data available

ISBN 019–860615-X

1 3 5 7 9 10 8 6 4 2

Typeset in Kolam Information Services Pvt. Ltd, Pondicherry, India
Printed in Great Britain by Clays Ltd. St Ives Plc

Introduction

Speaking and writing effectively is probably more important today than
everbefore. Yet while the importance of communication skills increases, many
people find it difficult to set about acquiring them. Dictionaries and thesauruses
provide a great deal of information and self-help material, but their greatest
contribution must be restricted to meaning and spelling. For many people today,
the pressing need is a book that augments the detailed but limited guidance
found in dictionaries with more general advice on questions of style, format, and
presentation. *The Language Toolkit* aspires to be that book. Through its
commitment to describing English, Oxford has developed a list of language
reference titles which support and extend the content of its dictionaries. The
present book draws on a wide range of these to provide essential, practical, and
authoritative guidance in all areas of English usage.

The book is divided into nine Sections, each dealing with a particular area of
language use. The earlier Sections deal with the nuts and bolts of language:
Grammar, **Spelling**, **Punctuation**, and **Pronunciation**. These subjects, which
many people find somewhat intimidating, are presented here in a clear,
accessible, and user-friendly style with an emphasis on practical problem-
solving. The next two Sections deal with questions of vocabulary and
construction: **Common Confusables** disentangles those pairs (or sets) of words
that are frequently confused in writing and speech, while **Usage** gives advice on
words or phrases that are problematic for less straightforward reasons (perhaps
the meaning is misunderstood or disputed; perhaps the word is a cliché, or
considered politically incorrect). The question of effective and appropriate style
is then explored more fully in **Style and Format**. This two-part Section
combines detailed guidance on such matters as word choice and sentence
construction, with practical advice on using particular formats, such as the
business letter, the report, or the press release. Attention is also paid to the
wider factors of occasion, audience, and purpose—all of which should guide the
way we write or speak. These matters are particularly relevant to those making
spoken presentations, who have certain practical concerns, too: a separate
Section has therefore been devoted to **Public Speaking**. Finally, there is a short
essay on the ever-more-relevant subject of **World English** – the development of
English as a truly world language with numerous overlapping varieties.

Because of the different nature of the subjects covered, individual Sections
differ quite widely in format, layout, and structure. The aim in each case has
been to present the maximum of useful information in the most user-friendly
form. Some Sections therefore read like an essay or a chapter from a
textbook; others have an alphabetical arrangement, so that the reader can go
straight to particular words or parts of words that cause concern. The Sections
on **Grammar**, **Spelling**, and **Pronunciation** combine these approaches to
make the treatment as comprehensive as possible. Unless it takes the form of
straightforward discursive prose, each Section or part of a Section has its own
introduction, explaining how it may best be used.

Although Sections differ in this way, the underlying philosophy does not.
Three principles have been applied consistently—those of explanation,
exemplification, and recommendation.

Explanation. The explanations given in each Section are intended to be simple and straightforward, even where the subject is inevitably slightly complicated. They take into account the approaches developed by modern linguistic analysis, but employ the traditional terms of grammar as much as possible. (A glossary of all grammatical terms used in this book will be found on pp. 43–53.) Technical symbols and abbreviations, and the International Phonetic Alphabet, are not used at all.

Exemplification. Wherever appropriate, example sentences are given to illustrate the point being discussed. The majority of these are real examples. In the Section on **Usage** and the part of **Grammar** that deals with common grammatical problems, examples have been drawn from some of the best writers of the past 100 years. By contrast, the examples of poor English in the Section on **Style and Format** have been culled from business letters and official documents.

Recommendation. Where usage advice is given, the emphasis is on the degree of acceptability in standard English, rather than on a dogmatic distinction of right and wrong. Much that is condemned as 'bad English' is better regarded as appropriate in informal contexts but inappropriate in formal ones. The appropriateness of usage to context is indicated by the fairly rough categories 'formal' and 'informal', 'standard', 'regional', and 'non-standard', 'jocular', and so on. Some of the ways in which American usage differs from British are also pointed out.

Sources and acknowledgements

As noted, *The Language Toolkit* includes material drawn from a number of published Oxford titles. This has been thoroughly updated to take account of recent changes in the language; it has also been revised and augmented to meet the requirements of the present book.

Grammar: Part I and **Spelling: Part I** are taken with little alteration from *The Oxford Guide to Writing and Speaking* by John Seely (1998); substantial extracts from this book are also used in **Style and Format: Part II** and **Public Speaking**.

The basic format for **Grammar: Part II**, **Spelling: Part II**, and **Pronunciation** is adapted from *The Oxford Dictionary and English Usage Guide*, edited by E. S. C. Weiner (1995), which also supplied a good deal of the content.

Slightly over half the text in **Common Confusables** comes from *The Pocket New Fowler's Modern English Usage*, edited by Robert Allen (1999).

The Section on **Usage** incorporates many of the usage notes given in the *New Oxford Dictionary of English* (1998).

Style and Format: Part I is taken with little alteration from *The Plain English Guide* by Martin Cutts (1996).

Shorter extracts from all these books have been used throughout, as have sections of the following: *The Oxford Dictionary of International Business*, edited by Alan Isaacs and Mark Salad (1998); *Oxford English*, edited by I. C. B. Dear (1986); and *Better Wordpower*, edited by Jane Whitcut (1998).

The Section on **World English** is an entirely new article by Penny Silva.

I would like to thank the authors and copyright holders for permission to use their material, and for reading and commenting on parts of this text.

JONATHAN LAW

Contents

Section 1: Grammar

This Section consists of three Parts, which approach the (to many people) daunting subject of grammar from three different angles:

Part I offers a simple Introduction to Grammar which attempts to answer the basic questions 'What is it all about?', 'How does it work?', and 'How can it be made to work for me?' This Part presupposes no previous formal understanding of the subject and, by design, introduces a minimum of technical vocabulary.

An important aim of Part I is to make the reader more aware of problem areas in writing English but at the same time less alarmed by them. This is taken much further in Part II: Problems of Grammar, which engages head-on with some of the most troublesome and contentious points of English grammar. Although the discussion is necessarily more technical here, the emphasis is firmly practical. The reader is taught to identify certain common difficulties and offered straightforward advice about the best means of evading or surmounting them.

One reason for the grammarphobia that seems so prevalent must be the difficult specialist vocabulary that infests most treatments of the subject. Unfortunately, a certain amount of technical language is unavoidable, for reasons of brevity and precision. With this in mind, Part III: Glossary offers simple definitions of the most commonly used grammatical terms in a single alphabetical list. This can be used as a handy crib for the other Parts of this Section and for the volume as a whole.

PART I: AN INTRODUCTION TO GRAMMAR

To many people grammar appears threatening and even impossible to understand. This is often because of the way in which it has been presented to them, whether at school or later in their lives. The purpose of this Part is to provide a simple introduction to what grammar is and how a basic understanding of it can be used to see how English sentences are constructed.

Grammar is a set of rules which describe how a language works. These are rules in the sense that scientific laws are rules: general statements that describe how things are, not moral regulations like the Ten Commandments. Grammar can be divided into two:

- The rules which describe how words are arranged to make sentences. The technical name for this is **syntax**. Syntax explains why these two sentences have different meanings:

    The cat sat on the mat

    The mat sat on the cat

- The rules which describe how words are changed to fit into sentences. Linguists call this **morphology**. Morphology explains why these two sentences have different meanings:

    The cat sat on the mat

    The cat sits on the mat

Levels

One of the difficulties of grasping grammar is that there seem to be so many things going on at the same time: are we supposed to be looking at the whole sentence, or bits of it? And if the answer is, 'Bits of it,' how do we know which bits to look at?

Grammar answers this by working at a number of different levels. They can be illustrated by this sample sentence:

The cat sat on the mat, while the dog ate its dinner

We can divide this **sentence** into two **clauses**

The cat sat on the mat	*while the dog ate its dinner*
MAIN CLAUSE	SUBORDINATE CLAUSE

Each clause is composed of different **clause elements:**

The cat	*sat*	*on the mat*
SUBJECT	VERB	ADVERBIAL

Each of these can be considered as a **phrase**:

The cat	*sat*	*on the mat*
NOUN PHRASE	VERB PHRASE	PREPOSITIONAL PHRASE

Each phrase in the sentence is made up of words and each word belongs to a particular **word class**:

The	*cat*	*sat*	*on*	*the*	*mat*
ARTICLE	NOUN	VERB	PREPOSITION	ARTICLE	NOUN

So there are all these different levels to think about when talking about grammar:

Sentences

It would seem reasonable at this stage to proceed to a simple definition of each of these levels: 'A sentence is...' and so on. Unfortunately the experts find it difficult (many would say impossible) to give a clear simple definition of what a sentence is. This can give writers about grammar a slightly shifty air, as they try to avoid answering that 'big question'.

The approach in the following pages is as follows. Most people who speak English have in fact got a fairly good working understanding of sentences. Much of the time they have no difficulty in telling you what is and what is not a sentence. Problems arise when they write a sentence that they think may be suspect and they want advice about how it should be put right. The focus here is on just such problem situations. Usually they can be resolved by understanding how the components of the sentence work together. For example, a large proportion of such sentence problems have to do with the relationship between the subject and the verb. So it is important to be able to identify the subject and the verb and to understand a number of key features about them.

In the next six or seven pages we concentrate on simple sentences. These are sentences that consist of one clause, with one subject and one verb. We then look at more complicated constructions and their related problems.

Types of sentence

The sentences we use can be divided into four types, according to their purpose:

- Statements

    Mr Sanderson is leaving the company next month

- Questions

    Why is Mr Sanderson leaving the company next month?

- Directives (sometimes called commands or requests):

    Clear your desk at once

- Exclamations

    What a worker that man was!

All simple statement sentences contain **one subject** and **one verb**.

The Subject

Position and meaning

In a statement sentence, the subject normally comes before the verb. It often (but not always) gives information on what the sentence will be about, or where its focus will be, as in these sentences:

    Success *drives many managers*

    Many of my friends *are unhappy in their work*

This is not always true, however. Sometimes the subject gives little away:

    It *is not always easy to spot a successful product*

The subject of a sentence may be:

- a **noun**

    People are strange

- a **noun phrase**

This is a group of words based on a noun:

    The people in our department *will miss Mr Sanderson*

The noun phrase marked is based on the noun *people*.

- a **pronoun**

This is a word which 'stands for' a noun, a noun phrase, or some other group of words which has recently been mentioned:

    They *say the strangest things*

Warning. The subject does not always come first in the sentence. It is often preceded by other words:

    During the whole of last year I *only went fishing twice*

    Fortunately for the fish my luck *was out*

The subject does not always come before the verb, although this is uncommon:

    Standing in the corner was my old friend Mrs Isaacs

The Verb

The grammatical term 'verb' can be used to refer to a class of words, like *be*, *happen*, and *kill*. It is also used to refer to one part of a clause or sentence (when it is sometimes referred to as the **verb phrase**). This is how it is being used in this section.

Position

In a statement sentence the verb usually comes after the subject:

    Mrs Hart hates *ice cream*

It does not necessarily come immediately after the subject. In this sentence the words in brackets come between the *subject* and the **verb**:

    She [only recently] started to eat *yogurt again*

In exceptional cases, as we have seen, the verb may come before the subject:

Standing in the corner was my old
friend Mrs Isaacs

My old friend Mrs Isaacs was *standing in
the corner*

Meaning

The verb provides important information
about the subject. It usually refers to:

- an action

  The volcano *destroyed* the village

- a state or condition

  I *hate* American football

Or it may act as a **link** between the subject
and the rest of the sentence:

  My father's first name *is* Peter

The form of the verb phrase

The verb in a sentence may be one word or
several:

  I *visited* Paris last week

  I *should have been visiting* my
  grandfather today

When the verb phrase consists of several
words, these are all verbs. They are either:

- **full verbs**

These are verbs that can stand on their own
in a sentence, without reference to any
other verb. They are mostly words with a
'dictionary meaning'. For example:

  collect   make   send   suggest

- **auxiliary verbs**

These are verbs which work with the full
verb. Most auxiliary verbs are of the class
known as **modal verbs**, which includes:

  shall   should   will   would
  may   might   can   could   must etc.

In addition there are three verbs which can
work either as full verbs or as auxiliaries:

  be/is/am/was, etc.   *have/has/had*
  do/does/did, etc.

These are called **primary verbs**.

Parts of a verb. English verbs have the five
forms illustrated in this set of sentences:

Fiona walks [PRESENT TENSE] *a lot. She has
to* walk [STEM + 'TO'] *to the railway station
every day. Yesterday she* walked [PAST
TENSE] *the length of Regent Street looking
for a new coat. While she was* walking
[PRESENT PARTICIPLE] *she met a friend. They
had* walked [PAST PARTICIPLE] *quite a long
way before Fiona found what she wanted.*

In a regular verb, all these forms are based
on the verb stem *walk*; you simply add the
endings *-ing*, *-ed*, and *-s* to create the other
verb forms. Here are the parts of the verb
presented as a table:

STEM	walk
PRESENT TENSE	walk/walks
PRESENT PARTICIPLE	walking
PAST TENSE	walked
PAST PARTICIPLE	walked

Many verbs follow the pattern of *walk*.
These verbs are regular. Other verbs, like *go*
depart from the pattern. So, for example,
instead of saying 'goed' for the past tense,
we say *went*. These verbs are 'irregular'.
There are relatively few irregular verbs, but
they include many of the commonest verbs.
As can be seen from the table, the verb *be*
is very irregular.

STEM	swim	be	have
PRESENT TENSE	swim/ swims	am/is/ are	has/have
PRESENT PARTICIPLE	swimming	being	having
PAST TENSE	swam	was/ were	had
PAST PARTICIPLE	swum	been	had

Tense. English has a wide variety of tenses,
which give information about **when** something happened, and also the **aspect** of the
action we wish to focus on. For example:

SIMPLE PAST

I walked to the office this morning

(Action in the past, attention focused on the fact that it is a single completed action.)

PAST CONTINUOUS

As I was walking I saw a swan

(Action in the past, attention focused on the continuing nature of the action—it was going on when something else happened.)

Agreement. The verb has to agree with the subject in number and person:

SINGULAR	FIRST PERSON	*I walk*
	SECOND PERSON	*you walk*
	THIRD PERSON	*he/she/it walks*
PLURAL	FIRST PERSON	*we walk*
	SECOND PERSON	*you walk*
	THIRD PERSON	*they walk*

Sentence Problems

One of the causes of problems when writing sentences, especially long sentences, is the verb.

Finite verb

A sentence must contain a complete, or finite verb. This is a verb that shows **tense**, **number**, and **person**. If a sentence does not contain a finite verb, then it isn't a sentence:

In late September in Herefordshire, during those last magic days of summer, walking *through the fields down by the river Wye!*

It is typical of sentences like this, that the reader is left waiting for something to happen, but nothing does and then the sentence ends. We want to know **who** the sentence is about and exactly **what** they were doing. It might mean, for example:

In late September in Herefordshire, during those last magic days of summer, I used to love walking *through the fields down by the river Wye!*

But we cannot know what the writer meant, because the sentence does not contain a finite verb.

Lack of agreement

Another possible reason why sentences sometimes don't work is that the subject and verb fail to agree. As we have seen, they should agree in number and person. If the subject is short and simple, there is usually no problem, but when the subject is complicated it becomes more difficult to keep track of exactly what the whole subject is:

Several members of the Royal Family, including the Prince of Wales, has visited the region in the past year

The trick is to ask yourself 'How many: one, or more than one?' In this case the answer is 'More than one', so the verb should be *have visited.*

The question of agreement is particularly vexed where *either* or *neither* are used in the subject. If both items are singular, then there is no problem; the verb is singular:

Either the sales manager or his assistant is the person to take charge of this assignment

If one of the two is plural, then the verb should agree with the one that comes immediately before it:

Either the prime minister or his ministers are to blame

The same applies to the person of the verb:

Either Peter or I am going to look after it

Either you or Peter is going to look after it

Other common problems of agreement are discussed in PART II: PROBLEMS OF GRAMMAR.

Other Sentence Elements

Some sentences only consist of a subject and a verb:

SUBJECT	VERB
Mrs Howard	*has left*
Most of our problems	*are being overcome*
This question	*would have been foreseen*

Many sentences have one or more elements after the verb. These can usually be classified as an **object**, a **complement**, or an **adverbial**.

Object

One definition of the object is that it describes 'what is affected by the action of the verb' and in this example that is clear enough:

> *The dog bit* our visitor

Often, however, there isn't much 'action' involved:

> *I like* ice cream

so it is more accurate, if more complicated, to say:

> An object is a noun, a pronoun, or a noun phrase that follows the verb and usually refers to a different person or thing from the subject.

Some sentences have two objects: **direct** and **indirect**:

Our visitor	*gave*	*the baby*	*a rattle*
SUBJECT	VERB	INDIRECT OBJECT	DIRECT OBJECT

To distinguish these two kinds of object, remember that this kind of sentence can normally be turned round, with the addition of *to*:

Our visitor	*gave*	*the baby*	*a rattle*
Our visitor	*gave*	*a rattle*	*to the baby*

Case

The commonest problem for writers concerns the **case** of the object. Some pronouns in English change according to whether the word is the subject or the object of the sentence:

SUBJECT (SUBJECTIVE CASE)	VERB	OBJECT (OBJECTIVE CASE)
I	*told*	*him*
He	*told*	*me*

The pronouns concerned are:

I/me	*he/him*	*she/her*
we/us	*they/them*	*who/whom*
		(and *whoever* etc.)

Problems can arise when there is a double object:

> *After the accident the chairman visited* my wife and I/my wife and me *in hospital*

If you are in any doubt about which is correct, remove the other part of the object and see if it sounds right.

> *After the accident the chairman visited* I *in hospital*

This can never be correct in standard English (although it is in some dialects); the objective or accusative case, *me*, is what is required:

> *After the accident the chairman visited* my wife and me *in hospital*

You should also use the objective or accusative case after prepositions:

> *The chairman paid several warm compliments to* my wife *and* me

For further discussion, see PERSONAL PRONOUN, CASE OF in PART II.

Complement

A small number of verbs are followed not by an object but by a complement. The verbs, sometimes called **linking verbs**, include:

> *to be*   *to seem*   *to appear*   *to become*

In sentences containing these verbs, the subject and the complement refer to the same person or thing:

SUBJECT	VERB	COMPLEMENT
My uncle	*became*	*Mayor of Sidmouth*

The complement of a sentence can be a noun, pronoun, or noun phrase (just like the object), but it can also be an adjective or adjective phrase:

SUBJECT	VERB	COMPLEMENT
My uncle	*is*	*very happy*

Grammatically the complement should be the same case as the subject; hence the problem people have with:

> *Who's there?—It is I*

Technically this is correct and, in very formal written English, this is what you should use. But if you use *It is I*, rather than *It's me* in everyday conversation people will probably think you are being a bit finicky.

Adverbial

Adverbials are much more varied. They provide information that answers these questions:

- when/how long?

  I met her yesterday

- (to) where?

  He placed a book on the table

- why?

  They did it for my sake

- how?

  The trick was performed very very skilfully

- how much?

  I helped them as much as possible

As these examples show, the adverbial can be:

- a single word, an adverb: *yesterday*

- an adverb phrase (a group of words built up on an adverb): *very very skilfully*

- a prepositional phrase (a group of words that begins with a preposition): *on the table*

Position

The other sentence elements are fairly predictable; there isn't much choice about where you put them in the sentence. Adverbials can turn up anywhere. There is often a choice about where you put them. Both these sentences are possible:

  He placed a book on the table

  On the table he placed a book

The difference is one of emphasis.

Normally the adverbial should come as close as possible to the verb it modifies, though not between the verb and its object. There are, however, occasions when to follow this rule may itself cause confusion. If the object is longer and we place the adverbial after it, the adverbial may become attached to the wrong part of the sentence. This sentence:

  The bricklayer explained his reasons for leaving the site angrily

clearly does not mean the same as this one:

  The bricklayer explained angrily his reasons for leaving the site

Warning. Some common adverbials can cause ambiguity when wrongly placed. All these sentences have different meanings:

(i) Even *the scientists are concerned about traffic fumes*

(ii) *The scientists are* even *concerned about traffic fumes*

(iii) *The scientists are concerned about* even *traffic fumes*

The implication of each sentence is:

(i) Everyone including scientists is concerned

(ii) Scientists are concerned about lots of things, including traffic fumes

(iii) Scientists are concerned about all fumes, including traffic fumes

To avoid ambiguity or wrong emphasis, *even* should be placed next to the word it refers to.

There are sometimes similar problems with *only*, but they are not so great and much of the time it is possible to place *only in its natural place, next to the verb, without causing confusion:*

  I only *read his letter last week*

clearly means 'It was only last week that I read his letter.' No one is likely to understand it to mean 'I could have torn it up or burned it, but all I did was read it.'

Particularly in speech we can make our meaning clearer by tone of voice and emphasis, so normally *only* takes its natural place next to the verb and our voices do the rest. In writing, if there is any possibility of confusion, *only* should be placed next to the word(s) it refers to.

Sentence Length and Variety

Of course, most writing does not consist entirely of simple sentences, containing only one subject and one verb, but there are certain things it is useful to say at this point about written style.

Short sentences

A real strength of simple sentences is that they can be short and punchy. In the right place they can be very powerful. This paragraph contains one short simple sentence right in the middle:

I had seen the collision coming, but when it happened the impact was so abrupt and stunning that it shocked the sense out of me, and for a while I sat quietly among the broken glass of the jeep as though I had been sitting there forever. In any case I found I could not move because of the dead weight of the soldiers on either side of me. We had hit the bus head-on. The front of the jeep was embedded under its bonnet, and the crash must have somehow distorted the wiring apparatus because the first thing I became aware of was a continuous metallic howl from the horn that nobody tried to stop. It seemed as though the machinery itself was screaming in pain, while all the people involved were spellbound and silent.

The first two sentences introduce the situation but by the end of the second we are still not clear exactly what has happened. Then the writer tells us, simply and brutally.

It is important not to overdo it, however. Too many short sentences can make a text seem jerky or immature (young children often write in this way).

Minor sentences

In this Introduction, a sentence has been partly defined as having a finite verb. We often encounter 'sentences' that break this rule. They are particularly common in public notices:

One-way street

Parking for residents only

Fresh stock now in

They also occur in speech:

Lovely weather this morning!

Oh well, easy come, easy go

They make complete sense, but they are grammatically incomplete. Linguists sometimes call them **minor sentences**. They can be used in continuous writing for a particular effect. A good idea? Possibly. Definitely capable of overuse, however. Like most things.

Sentence punctuation

Normally, of course, written sentences are marked off by punctuation, beginning with a capital letter and ending with a full stop. Occasionally writers fail to do this, running sentences together, or separating them with a comma, rather than a full stop:

This type of of writing can be difficult for readers, their eyes are trained to see a comma as marking off parts of one sentence, when they come across writing where this is not done they become confused, it is important to remember this when writing.

This error is sometimes called the **comma splice**, because a comma is used to splice, or join, two sentences. There is, however, a punctuation mark which can be used for this purpose, the **semicolon**.

If you have two sentences which are closely related in meaning, they can be linked in this way:

Writing clearly and simply is not easy; it requires practice

This sentence reads slightly differently from:

Writing clearly and simply is not easy. It requires practice

In the first example we see that the two ideas are closely linked together. In the second they are offered as separate thoughts, one after the other, and the reader is left to make the link from the sense.

Guidelines

1 The **subject** of a sentence can be quite extended. Make sure that your readers do not lose track of the subject before they even reach the verb. This is particularly likely to happen if you put a participle before the subject:

> *Walking down Exhibition Road, just by the old Alhambra Theatre, my old and trusted friend from the good old days and now a wealthy property developer, James McVity, saw ...*

2 Make sure that the **verb** is finite and agrees with the subject in both number (singular/ plural) and person (*she is/we are*, etc).

3 Agreement is particularly tricky in these situations:

- where there is a multiple subject, joined by *and*
- where you are using *either* or *neither*

4 Make sure that pronouns used as **objects** are in the correct, objective, case (*me*, not *I*, *him* not *he*, etc.).

5 In very formal writing, pronouns used as **complements** should be in the subjective case (*It is I*).

6 Make sure that you have placed any **adverbials** in the best position in the sentence. Often this is next to the verb, but sometimes the adverbial must be placed to make the precise meaning clear. This applies particularly to *even* and *only*.

7 Use **short sentences** sparingly for maximum impact.

8 **Minor sentences** can be used in written texts, but again only sparingly and for a particular effect.

9 Make sure that sentences are correctly separated by **punctuation**, normally a full stop and following capital letter. If two sentences are closely linked in sense they can sometimes be joined by a semicolon.

Multiple Sentences

Simple sentences have been defined as having one subject and one verb. Technically such sentences consist of one **finite clause**. A finite clause is a grammatical unit that contains a finite verb; it can stand alone as a simple sentence, or be combined with other clauses into **multiple sentences**. These are of two basic kinds, **compound** and **complex**.

Compound Sentences

The simplest way of joining clauses is by bolting them together like this:

Maybrick Ltd supplies bearings	CLAUSE
and	+
ERICO fits them	CLAUSE

The two clauses are of the same status in the sentence (they are described grammatically as **coordinated**—of the same level) and each could stand on its own as a simple sentence.

Coordinating conjunctions

The commonest conjunctions used to link clauses in this way are:

> *and   but   or   nor   then   yet*

It is important to remember that although they all do the same job grammatically, they have very different meanings.

Then. *Then* is straightforward: the event described by the second clause must follow that described in the first:

> *Maybrick Ltd supplies bearings, then ERICO fits them*

Clearly it wouldn't make sense to have the clauses the other way round.

But/yet. In the example above, *and* simply joins the two clauses, but if it were replaced by *but*, the meaning of the whole sentence would be changed:

> *Maybrick Ltd supplies bearings, but ERICO fits them*

On its own, the sentence does not make clear why the speaker has said *but*, and this is sometimes true even when we know the context. *But* does imply some sort of contrast, conflict, or contradiction, however, even when its exact meaning is unstated. For example, if the speaker is the managing director of Maybrick Ltd he may be implying that once the bearings have left the factory his company has no responsibility for what ERICO does with them.

Yet is used in a similar way to *but*.

Or/nor. These two conjunctions only make sense when the two clauses they link are genuine alternatives. It would, for example, be nonsense to say:

> *Maybrick Ltd supplies bearings, or ERICO fits them*

On the other hand you could say:

> *Maybrick Ltd supplies bearings, or ERICO purchases them from a company in the States*

where it is understood that the first clause means ' ... supplies bearings *to ERICO ...* '

Nor works in a similar way to *or*, but as a negative:

> *I have never met Dominic McGhee, nor do I want to*

It is sometimes said that you should not begin a sentence with a co-ordinating conjunction, because, as its name implies, it must come between the two things it is co-ordinating and should not, therefore, be separated from one of them by a full stop. This 'rule' may appear to be logical but it has cheerfully been ignored by writers across the centuries. Separating the two items being linked by *and* or *but*, for example, can be an effective way of giving additional emphasis to the item that is thus separated. But you should not do it too frequently. Or people will find it irritating. Then they will stop reading.

Complex Sentences

You can only go so far by using compound sentences. Often we need to show more sophisticated relationships between two clauses. Each of the sentences that follows uses the same two clauses, but each expresses a different meaning:

(i) *If Maybrick Ltd supplies bearings, ERICO fits them*

(ii) *Maybrick Ltd supplies the bearings that ERICO fits*

(iii) *ERICO fits the bearings that Maybrick Ltd supplies*

(iv) *Maybrick Ltd supplies bearings so that ERICO can fit them*

Which version is chosen depends on the context and the meaning you wish to convey. In the following paragraphs some of the main kinds of link between clauses are examined.

In grammatical terms, one clause in a complex sentence is more important than the others and is described as the **main clause**. The other clauses, the **subordinate clauses**, are grammatically less important and are nearly always introduced by a **subordinating conjunction**.

A complex sentence works in much the same way as a simple sentence. It contains similar elements: subject, verb, adverbial, object, and complement. In a simple sentence these elements may be single words or phrases. In a complex sentence some of them may also be clauses.

Adverbial clauses

Adverbial clauses are very useful and perform a wide range of different functions. They answer a number of different questions.

When? It is often important to show the relationship in time between two events. Perhaps one was completed before the other began; or one occurred during the period that the other was going on. English is particularly well supplied with ways of showing this.

The commonest conjunctions are:

> after as before since until when while

These words do not do their work on their own, however. They work closely with the verbs in the sentence to convey their meaning. Each of the following sentences uses *when*, but each conveys a very different meaning:

(i) *When she makes the cake she will listen to the radio*

(ii) *When she was making the cake* she listened *to the radio*

(iii) *When she had made the cake* she listened *to the radio*

Where? Time clauses are very common; those indicating place may be less common but can be very important—in instructions and descriptions, for example:

Turn right where the speed limit ends

We parted where three roads meet

The conjunctions used are *where* and *wherever*.

There is one special use of *where* which is worth remembering. It can be used to define conditions under which certain things can happen:

Where it can be shown that the company is negligent ...

Where there is shade and moisture, these plants will flourish

What if? Often we want to say that one thing depends on another happening. We frequently do this by using *if* or *unless*:

(i) *If he comes to the office, the manager will explain the situation*

(ii) *If the company was to blame, then it would pay compensation*

(iii) *If the cheque had bounced, the bank would have told us*

These three sentences all deal with 'one-off' situations: a single event and its possible results. Each suggests a different degree of possibility. Number (i) is open: the '*if*-event' may or may not happen. In number (ii) the *if*-event is unlikely, but if it did happen, then the consequences would follow. These two sentences deal with something that has not yet happened. Sentence (iii) is about something in the past and clearly the speaker believes that it has not happened. (But the bank hasn't told us, so the cheque hasn't bounced.)

There is a different kind of conditional sentence which does not deal with a single event, or a definite number of events, but which concerns 'things in general':

If the company makes a profit, it pays a dividend to the shareholders

If babies are unhappy they cry

As these examples show, it is important to use the correct form of the verb when using *if*. Failure to do so may mean that you do not communicate correctly your own view of the likelihood of the *if*-event—and when dealing with difficult situations, that could cause problems. So, for example, you may want to tell a client in a completely open way that you will help if she has a problem. You mean to say,

If your computer plays up, phone me and I'll come and put it right

Company policy, however, says you should be more formal than this, so you end up saying:

If the product failed to operate properly during the first six months, then the purchaser would be entitled to free on-site service

Not only does this lapse into unnecessary jargon ('on-site service'), but it makes the customer feel that the events described are extremely unlikely. Now that is fine if the machine is very reliable, but it may leave a lingering suspicion in the customer's mind that the home visit is very unlikely—*even if it turns out to be needed.*

Sentence (ii) above can be expressed in two ways that are similar but significantly different:

If the company was to blame, then it would pay compensation

If the company were to blame, then it would pay compensation

The second of these uses a relatively uncommon form of the verb, the **subjunctive**. Its effect is to make the condition *impossible*, rather than just improbable, which is why it is used in sayings such as *If I were you...* (which is clearly impossible). Many people, however, do not observe this distinction; increasingly people say *If I was you...* and it may be that this use of the subjunctive is dying out. For further discussion, see SUB-JUNCTIVE and WAS/WERE in PART II.

For what purpose? Two common

conjunctions enable us to explain the purpose behind an event: *in order that* and *so that* (sometimes abbreviated to *so*):

> The man was executed so that others would be discouraged from imitating him

> We changed the design in order that health and safety regulations would not be broken

Why? 'Never apologize; never explain' may be a popular saying, but we often *do* need to explain the reasons for an event. We do so using *because*, *since*, and *as*:

> As I'm going to be in New York anyway, I thought I'd drop in on her

> We made it of wood because that is the most suitable material

> Since she is responsible for this project, she should be the person to make the presentation

With sentences like these, you can often choose in which order to place the two clauses:

(i) *Since she is responsible for this project, she should be the person to make the presentation*

(ii) *She should be the person to make the presentation, since she is responsible for this project*

The only difference is one of focus. Sentence (i) focuses on the reasoning process; sentence (ii) focuses on 'her' and uses the reason as 'backup'.

With what result? Typical conjunctions here are: *so that*, *so*, and *and so*:

> Some of them have no qualifications in engineering so that they are looked down on by senior management

Sometimes *so* and *that* are separated, with *so* referring to an adjective or adverb. The *that* clause still describes a result:

> It all happened so quickly that I didn't realize what was going on

> He was so fat that he could not get through the door to the dining room

Making concessions. When reasoning or presenting an argument, we may wish to deal with alternative views or other possibilities. We do so using *although*, *though*, *even if*, *whereas*, and *while*:

> Although a pony and trap is an entertaining form of transport, a car is more reliable

> While gas bills may have fallen during the past quarter, our general running costs have remained the same

Noun clauses

Noun clauses can stand as subject or complement in a sentence:

> What I cannot understand is how she got away with it

Here both subject and complement are noun clauses.

The object of a sentence can also be a noun clause:

> He told the Board that he wished to resign

In these examples, noun clauses are introduced by *what*, *that*, and *how*. There are several other words which can introduce them, including *where*, *why*, *whether*, and *when*.

Relative clauses

Relative clauses act like adjectives or adjective phrases:

(i) *I gave her a red scarf* (ADJECTIVE)

(ii) *I gave her a scarf* with a red pattern on it (ADJECTIVE PHRASE)

(iii) *I gave her a scarf* that I bought in Amsterdam (RELATIVE CLAUSE)

Relative clauses can be introduced by the **relative pronoun**s *who*, *whom*, *which*, *that*, *where*, *when* and, confusingly, nothing at all. Sentence (iii) above could be:

> I gave her a scarf I bought in Amsterdam

The relative pronoun is 'understood'.

Restrictive and non-restrictive. Relative clauses do not normally give rise to many problems for the writer. There is, however, one important distinction it is important to make. These two sentences are apparently the same:

(i) *Teachers who work long hours should be paid more*

(ii) *Teachers, who work long hours, should be paid more*

In Sentence (i) the writer has two groups of teachers in mind: those who work long hours and those who do not. The former group should be paid more. In sentence (ii) the writer is making a statement about *all* teachers: they work long hours and so should be paid more. In the first sentence the relative clause restricts or defines the group (a **restrictive**—or **defining**—**relative clause**); in the second it does not (a **non-restrictive**—or **non-defining**—**relative clause**). When we speak we can make the difference in meaning clear by timing and intonation; in writing the difference is made by the punctuation.

It is also argued by some that the relative pronoun *which* is normally used to introduce a non-restrictive clause. If we want to introduce a restrictive clause we should use either *that* or nothing. This is a fairly good general rule, but one with exceptions. For a full discussion see WHICH/THAT in PART II.

Who or whom? The other problem area with relative pronouns is the question of when to use *who* and when to use *whom*. The traditional rule is simple—deceptively so:

(i) *who* is used as the subject of the verb

I had a word with the manager who is looking after the Neasden account

(ii) *whom* is used as the object of the verb

I spoke to our Neasden manager, whom I think you have met

(iii) *whom* is used after prepositions

I spoke to Peter, from whom I received that interesting letter

Modern usage, however, inclines more and more to the use of *who* in all three cases:

(ii) *I spoke to our Neasden manager, who I think you have met*

(iii) *I spoke to Peter, who I received that interesting letter from*

On the other hand, there are still traditionalists out there who object to this and certainly most people would still find

I spoke to Peter, from who I received that interesting letter

rather strange. For a full discussion see WHO/WHOM in PART II.

Problem Areas

Coordinating conjunctions

Many problems associated with conjunctions are linked to the fact that when we use coordinating conjunctions they must link two items that have the same grammatical status (i.e., both clauses—including a finite verb—or both phrases). When writers fail to remember this, the result is poor English:

He told us about the trip and that he had managed to make a number of important new contacts

If you break the sentence down diagrammatically, it is easy to see what is wrong:

He told us

→ *about the trip*   (PHRASE)

→ *that he had managed to make a number of important new contacts*   (CLAUSE)

The sentence needs to be re-cast so that the two items joined by *and* have the same status:

Here *and* is joining two noun phrases:

the trip

the important new contacts

Both. *Both* is used to join two items and not more than two. It is wrong, therefore, to use expressions such as *Both Eleanor and the two girls* … If it works with another conjunction, that conjunction should be *and*, so that this sentence is unsatisfactory:

The company produces both PVA products as well as PVC

It should be:

The company produces both PVA and PVC products

Again, it is important to remember that the pair *both … and* should only be used to join items of equal status.

He both plays in the orchestra and as a soloist

should be rephrased as:

He plays both in the orchestra and as a soloist

Finally, in expressions involving figures, *both* can produce ambiguities like this:

Both books cost £20

Did each book cost £10 or £20? Better to write either *Each book cost £10* or *The two books together cost £40*.

Either...or and **neither...nor.** Like other coordinating conjunctions, *either...or* and *neither...nor* must join items of equal status. It is poor style to write:

This argument neither explains what went wrong nor how it should be put right

It should read:

This argument explains neither what went wrong nor how it should be put right

A simple check is to remove the section of the sentence that begins with *either/neither* and ends with *or/nor*. If the rest of the sentence still works grammatically, then you have got it right. (The sense will have changed, of course.)

This argument explains neither what went wrong nor how it should be put right

For a full discussion, see CORRELATIVE CONJUNCTIONS; NEITHER...NOR; and SUBJECTS JOINED BY OR in PART II.

Subordinating conjunctions

Subordinating conjunctions can cause problems, too, frequently because of ambiguity. Some of the commonest are listed here.

As. This small word can be tricky. It can work as a conjunction or as a preposition. As a conjunction it has a range of meanings, including:

(i) while/when

(ii) because/since

These two meanings can sometimes be confused. For example:

As I was going to the shops, I decided to buy some onions

Does the writer mean 'I made the decision on the way to the shops' or 'Because I was going to the shops'? If the former, then it could be made clearer by writing *While...*; if the latter, then starting the sentence with *Because...* would be clearer.

Another common use of *as* is paired: *as ... as*. This construction can produce ambiguities, too:

I have visited Peter as often as Mary

This could mean:

I have visited Peter as often as I have visited Mary

I have visited Peter as often as Mary has

Because. When it follows a negative statement, *because* can lead to ambiguity, as in this sentence:

He didn't take up the option because he was hard up

This has two possible meanings so it should be rephrased:

Because he was hard up he didn't take up the option

It wasn't because he was hard up that he took up the option

Another possible cause of ambiguity occurs when the reason for coming to a particular conclusion comes *after* the conclusion:

I knew he was lying because I'd spoken to his wife

Here there are two possible meanings:

As I'd spoken to his wife I knew he was lying

I'd spoken to his wife and I knew he was lying because of that

So. *So* can produce ambiguities similar to those of *as*, because it can mean:

(i) as a result

(ii) in order that

This sentence, for example, is ambiguous:

He left home so his parents could get some peace

To make the meaning clear it should be rephrased:

He left home in order that his parents could get some peace

He left home and as a result his parents could get some peace

Guidelines

1 When you use **compound sentences**, co-ordinated with conjunctions such as *and*, *or*, *but*, *nor*, *then*, *yet*, be aware of the limited range of meanings these can convey.

2 Remember that although **complex sentences** can convey a much wider range of meanings, they require more careful construction.

3 When you write *when*-clauses make sure that the order of events you are describing is clear.

4 Remember that **conditional** sentences (usually those beginning *if* or *unless*) require careful handling.

5 **Relative clauses** may be defining or non-defining, and you need to be clear which is which.

6 Take care with **coordinating conjunctions** such as *both … and*: they need to link items that are grammatically similar.

7 Make sure that *either/neither* and *or/nor* are correctly placed and that the verb agrees with the subject.

8 Subordinating conjunctions *as*, *because*, and *so* also need careful use.

PART II: PROBLEMS OF GRAMMAR

This Part deals with specific problems of English grammar in much greater length and technical detail than was possible in PART I. A certain amount of specialized vocabulary is unavoidable here, and the reader is referred to PART III: GLOSSARY for any unfamiliar terms.

*Entries are arranged alphabetically by heading. Wherever possible, the headings chosen are the words or grammatical endings which actually cause problems (e.g. **as**, **-ing**, **-lily**, **none**, **shall/will**). But inevitably many entries have had to be given abstract labels (e.g. **double passive**, **subjunctive**). To compensate for this, a generous number of cross-references are included. The aim throughout is to tackle a particular problem immediately and to give a recommendation as soon as the problem has been identified.*

a(n), the

For advice on whether to omit these, see ARTICLE, OMISSION OF.

adverbial relative clauses

A relative clause often forms parts of a longer adverbial clause expressing time, manner, or place. In such cases the relative clause is generally preceded by preposition + noun (e.g. *on the day* in the example below):

> *On the day* on which the books were opened *three hundred thousand pounds were subscribed* (Lord Macaulay)

It is possible for the relative clause to begin with the same preposition + *which*, as in the example given. However, it is a perfectly acceptable idiom to use a relative clause introduced by *that* without repeating the preposition; this is especially common after the nouns *day, morning, night, time, year*, etc., and *manner, sense, way*, and *place*, e.g.

> *Envy in the consuming sense* that certain persons display the trait (Anthony Powell)

It is also very common for *that* to be omitted in such constructions:

> *If he would take it in the sense* she meant it (L. P. Hartley)

adverbs without -ly

Most adverbs consist of an adjective + the ending *-ly*, e.g. *badly, differently*. Normally the use of the ordinary adjective as an adverb, without *-ly*, is non-standard, e.g.

> *I was sent for* special
>
> *The Americans speak* different *from us*

There are, however, a number of words which are both adjective and adverb and cannot add the adverbial ending *-ly*, e.g.

alone	fast	low
enough	little	much
far	long	still

Some other adjectives can be used as adverbs both with and without *-ly*:

deep(ly)	high(ly)	near(ly)
hard(ly)	late(ly)	

In these cases the two forms have different meanings. The adverbs formed without *-ly* remain close in meaning to the adjectives, as the following examples illustrate:

> *He rode* deep *into the forest*
>
> *He lost his* hard-*earned money*
>
> *It soared* high *above us*
>
> *I will stay up* late *to finish it*
>
> *As* near *as makes no difference*

The forms with -*ly* have meanings that are chiefly figurative or that are otherwise somewhat removed from those of the adjectives:

> Deeply *in love*
>
> He hardly *earned his money*
>
> Highly *amusing*
>
> I *have been very tired* lately
>
> We *are* nearly *there*

The forms with and without -*ly* should not be confused.

See also -LILY, ADVERBS ENDING IN.

and

1 For advice on the use of singular or plural verbs with nouns or noun phrases joined by *and*, see COMPOUND SUBJECTS.

2 For advice on placing the pair *both…and* within sentences, see CORRELATIVE CONJUNCTIONS.

article, omission of

To omit, or not to omit, *a(n)* and *the*?

Omission of the definite or indefinite article before a noun or noun phrase in apposition to a name is a common journalistic device, e.g.

> *Clarissa, American business woman, comes to England*   (*Radio Times*)
>
> *Nansen, hero and humanitarian, moves among them*   (*The Times*)

It is more natural to write *an American business woman*; *the hero and humanitarian*.

Similarly, when the name follows the noun or noun phrase, the effect is of journalistic style, e.g.

> *Best-selling novelist Helen Fielding*
>
> *Unemployed labourer William Smith*

It is better to write *The best-selling novelist*; *An unemployed labourer* (with a comma before and after the name which follows).

After *as* it is possible to omit *a* or *the*, e.g.

> *As manipulator of words, the author reminded me of Joyce*

It is preferable not to omit these words, however.

as, case following

In the following sentences, standard grammar requires the subjective case (*I, he, she, we, they*) because the pronoun would be the subject if a verb were supplied:

> *You are just as intelligent as* he (in full *as he is*)
>
> *He was as apprehensive as* I *about our meeting* (in full *as I was*)   (Janet Frame)

However, informal usage now strongly favours *You are just as intelligent as* him, etc.

> *He seems to be as lonely as* me, *and to mind it more*   (David Lodge)

According to the traditional rules of formal English, the objective case (*me, him, her, us, them*) should only be used when the pronoun would be the object if a verb were supplied:

> *I thought you disliked Andrew's wife, but I see that you like her just as much as* him (meaning *just as much as you like him*)

Note that the modern tendency to use the objective case everywhere can lead to ambiguity here. The sentence quoted could be taken to mean 'I see that you like Andrew's wife as much as he does.' If there is any risk of misunderstanding it is better to rephrase to make one's meaning unmistakable.

See also PERSONAL PRONOUN, CASE OF.

as if, as though

For the tense to use following these, see SECTION 6: USAGE.

auxiliary verbs

There are 16 auxiliary verbs in English, three **primary verbs** (used to make compound tenses of ordinary verbs) and 13 **modal verbs** (used to express mood and, to some extent, tense).

Primary:	be	do	have
Modal:	can	ought (to)	
	could	shall	
	dare	should	

may	used (to)
might	will
must	would
need	

Auxiliaries differ from ordinary (full) verbs in the following ways:

(A) They can precede the negative *not*, instead of taking the *do not* construction, e.g. *I cannot* but *I do not know*.

(B) They can precede the subject in questions, instead of taking *do*, e.g. *Can you?* but *Do you know?*

The modal auxiliaries additionally differ from full verbs in the following ways:

(C) They do not add *-s* for the third person present, and do not form a past tense in *-ed*, e.g. *He must go; He must have seen it.*

(D) They are usually followed by the bare infinitive, e.g. *He will go; He can go* (not 'to go' as with other verbs, e.g. *He intends to go; He is able to go*).

Use of auxiliaries.

In reported speech and some other *that-*clauses *can, may, shall,* and *will* become *could, might, should,* and *would* for the past tense:

> *He said that he* could *do it straight away*
>
> *I told you that I* might *arrive unexpectedly*
>
> *I knew that when I grew up I should be a writer*   (George Orwell)
>
> *Did you think that the money you brought would be enough?*

In clauses of this kind, the auxiliaries *must, need,* and *ought* can also be used for the past tense:

> *This business...meant that I must go to London*   (Evelyn Waugh)
>
> *To go to church had made her feel she need not reproach herself for impropriety*   (V. S. Pritchett)
>
> *She was quite aware that she ought not to quarter Freddy there*   (G. B. Shaw)

Note that this use is restricted to *that-*clauses. It would not be permissible to use *must, need,* or *ought* for the past tense in a main sentence; one could not say *Yesterday I must go.*

For further discussion of the use of auxiliary verbs, see DARE; HAVE; NEED; OUGHT; SHALL/WILL; SHOULD/WOULD.

be

1 For a discussion of e.g. *That must be he at the door* versus *That must be him...*, see PERSONAL PRONOUN, CASE OF.

2 For e.g. *If the truth be told* versus *If the truth is told*, see SUBJUNCTIVE.

3 For e.g. *I wish that were true* versus *I wish that was true*, see WERE/WAS.

between

For *between you and I* versus *between you and me*, see YOU AND I/YOU AND ME.

both...and

For advice on placing the pair *both...and* in sentences, see CORRELATIVE CONJUNCTIONS.

but, case following

The personal pronoun following *but* (meaning 'except') should be in the case it would have if a verb were supplied:

> *No one understands it, no one but I*
> (J. M. Coetzee)
>
> *Our uneducated brethren who have, under God, no defence but us*   (C. S. Lewis)

In the first example *I* is used because it would be the subject of *I understand*. In the second example *us* is used because it would be the object of *who have* (i.e. 'who have us').

See PERSONAL PRONOUN, CASE FOLLOWING.

can/may

For the use of the auxiliary verbs *can* and *may* to express permission, see SECTION 6: USAGE.

collective nouns

Collective nouns are singular words that denote many individuals, e.g. *audience, government, orchestra, the clergy, the public.*

In British English, it is normal for collective nouns to be followed by singular verbs and pronouns:

> The Government is *determined to beat* inflation, *as* it has *promised*

> Their family is *huge:* it consists *of five boys and three girls*

> The bourgeoisie is *despised by self-proclaimed revolutionaries*

The singular verb and pronouns are preferable unless the collective is clearly and unmistakably used to refer to separate individuals rather than to a united body, e.g.

> The Cabinet has *made* its *decision*

> The Cabinet are *resuming* their *places around the table*

The singular should always be used if the collective noun is qualified by a singular word like *this, that, every,* etc.:

> This family is *divided*

> Every team has its *chance to win*

If a relative clause follows, it must be *which* + singular verb or *who* + plural verb, e.g.

> It *was not just the intelligentsia* which was *gathered there*

> The working party who were *preparing the decorations*

Do not mix singular and plural, as (wrongly) in:

> The congregation were *now dispersing.* It *tended to form knots and groups*

comparison of adjectives and adverbs

1 Whether to use **-er, -est** or **more, most**?

The two ways of forming the comparative and superlative of adjectives and adverbs are:

(A) The addition of the comparative and superlative suffixes -er and -est. Monosyllabic adjectives and adverbs almost always require these suffixes, e.g. *big* (*bigger, biggest*), *soon* (*sooner, soonest*), and so normally do many adjectives of two syllables, e.g. *narrow* (*narrower, narrowest*), *silly* (*sillier, silliest*).

(B) The placing of the comparative and superlative adverbs *more* and *most* before the adjective or adverb. These are used with adjectives of three syllables or more (e.g. *difficult, memorable*), participles (e.g. *bored, boring*), many adjectives of two syllables (e.g. *afraid, awful, childish, harmless, static*), and adverbs ending in -ly (e.g. *highly, slowly*).

Adjectives with two syllables vary between the use of the suffixes and of the adverbs. There are many which never take the suffixes, e.g.

antique	breathless	futile
bizarre	constant	steadfast

There is also a large class which is acceptable with either, e.g.

clever	handsome	polite
common	honest	solemn
cruel	pleasant	tranquil

The choice is largely a matter of style.

Even monosyllabic adjectives can sometimes take *more* and *most*:

(i) When two adjectives are compared with each other, e.g.

> More dead than alive

> More well-known than popular

This is standard (we would not say *deader than alive*).

(ii) Occasionally, for reasons of emphasis, e.g.

> This was never more true than at present

2 Whether to use **-er, more** or **-est, most**?

Comparisons between two persons or things require the comparative (-er or more) not the superlative (-est or most):

> I cannot tell which of the two is the elder (not eldest)

> Which of the two is more likely to win? (not most likely)

> Of the two teams, they are the slower-moving (not slowest-moving)

The superlative is used for more than two.

compound subjects

A compound subject is one consisting of two singular nouns or noun phrases joined by **and**. This will normally take a plural verb:

> *My son and daughter* are *twins*
>
> *Where to go and what to see* were *my main concern*

—especially if the compound has a personal noun or pronoun as one or both of its elements:

> *She and Stephen* are *just good friends*
>
> *Do my sister and I look* alike?
>
> *You and I* are *hardly acquainted*

But if the compound represents a single item, it takes a singular verb:

> *The bread and butter* was *delicious*
>
> *The Stars and Stripes* was *flying at half-mast*

And similarly if the two parts of the subject refer to a single individual:

> *My son and heir* is *safe*

A singular verb can also be appropriate when concepts that are distinct in themselves are regarded as a single item in a particular sentence, e.g.

> *A certain cynicism and resignation* comes *along with the poverty of Italian life*

Clearly there will be borderline cases, and then it is what sounds natural that matters:

> *The hurt and disbelief of friends and families is* (or *are*) *already quite real*
>
> *The extent and severity of drug use in the United States has* (or *have*) *been a shock to the medical director*

See also NEITHER…NOR; SUBJECTS JOINED BY OR.

correlative conjunctions

The correct placing of the pairs **both… and**, **neither…nor**, **either…or**, and **not only…but (also)**.

A sentence containing any of these pairs must be so constructed that the part introduced by the first member of the pair 'matches' the part introduced by the second member.

The rule is that if one covers up the two correlative words and all between them, the sentence should remain grammatical. The following sentence illustrates this rule:

> *Candidates will have a background in* either *commercial electronics* or *university research*

Because *in* precedes *either* here, it need not be repeated after *or*. If it had followed *either*, it would have had to be inserted after *or* as well.

In the following example the preposition *of* comes after *either* and must therefore be repeated after *or*:

> *He did not wish to pay the price* either *of peace* or *of war*   (George Orwell)

This conforms with the rule stated above.

It is, however, not uncommon for the conjunctions to be placed so that the two halves are not quite parallel, even in the writings of careful authors, e.g.

> *I end* neither *with a death* nor *a marriage*   (W. Somerset Maugham)

Here, *with* belongs to both halves and needs to be repeated after *nor*.

This is a fairly trivial slip that rarely causes difficulty (except in the case of *not only*: see NOT ONLY in SECTION 6: USAGE). A more serious error is the placing of the first correlative conjunction too late, so that words belonging only to the first half are carried over to the second, e.g.

> *The other bomb was* either *defused* or *blew up*

This should be avoided.

dangling participles

See PARTICIPLES.

dare

The verb *dare* can be used either like a regular verb or like an auxiliary (see AUXILIARY VERBS).

As an ordinary verb it forms such parts as:

I dare	I do not dare	do I dare?
he dares	he did not dare	does he dare?
he dared	I have dared	did he dare?

As an auxiliary verb it forms:

I dare not	he dared not	he dare not
dare he?	dared he?	

The first use, as an ordinary verb, is always acceptably followed by the *to*-infinitive, e.g.

I knew what I would find if I dared to look (Jean Rhys)

But many of the forms can also be followed by the bare infinitive. This sometimes sounds more natural:

Don't you dare put that light on (Shelagh Delaney)

The second use, as an auxiliary, requires the bare infinitive, e.g.

How dare he keep secrets from me? (G. B. Shaw)

double negative

According to standard English grammar, a double negative used to express a single negative, such as *I don't know nothing* (rather than *I don't know anything*), is incorrect.

The rules dictate that the two negative elements cancel each other out to give an affirmative statement, so that *I don't know nothing* would be interpreted as *I know something*.

In practice this sort of double negative is widespread in non-standard usage, and rarely gives rise to confusion as to the intended meaning. Double negatives are standard in certain other languages and did not come to be frowned upon in English until some time after the 16th century, when attempts were made to relate the rules of language to the rules of formal logic.

Thereafter, playwrights and novelists put double negatives into the conversation of vulgar speakers and they are now taken as sure signs of a poor education.

double passive

The construction whereby a passive infinitive directly follows a passive verb is correctly used in the following:

The prisoners were ordered to be shot

The rule is that if the subject and the first passive verb can be changed into the active, leaving the passive infinitive intact, the sentence is correctly formed. The example above (if a subject, say *he*, is supplied) can be changed back to:

He ordered the prisoners *to be shot*

An active infinitive could equally well be part of the sentence, e.g.

The prisoners were ordered to march

The examples below violate the rule because both verbs have to be made active in order to form a grammatical sentence:

The order was attempted to be carried out (active: *He attempted to carry out the order*)

A new definition was sought to be inserted in the Bill (active: *He sought to insert a new definition in the Bill*)

This 'double passive' construction is unacceptable.

The passive of the verbs *fear* and *say* can be followed by either an active or a passive infinitive, e.g.

(i) *The passengers are feared* to have drowned

The escaped prisoner is said to be very dangerous

or:

(ii) *The passengers are feared* to have been killed

The escaped prisoner is said to have been sighted

The construction at (ii) is entirely acceptable. Both constructions occur with other verbs of saying (e.g. *allege, assert, imply*).

either (pronoun)

Either is a singular pronoun and requires a singular verb:

> *Enormous evils, either of which* depends
> *on somebody else's voice* (Louis
> MacNeice)

In the following example the plural verb
accords with the notional meaning 'both
parents were not':

> *It was improbable that either of our
> parents were giving thought to the matter*
> (J. I. M. Stewart)

This is quite common, but better avoided in
formal prose.

either...or

1 For advice on placing the pair *either...or*
within sentences, see CORRELATIVE CONJUNC-
TIONS.

2 For advice on the use of singular or plural
verbs with the construction *either...or*, see
SUBJECTS JOINED BY OR.

-er, -est

For advice on using these to make comparatives and superlatives, see COMPARISON OF
ADJECTIVES AND ADVERBS.

gender of indefinite expres-
sions

For advice on what personal pronouns to
use with expressions of indefinite gender
such as *anyone* or *a person*, see THEY and THEM-
SELF in SECTION 6: USAGE.

group possessive

The group possessive is the construction by
which the ending *-'s* can be added to the
last word of a noun phrase, which is regarded as a single unit, e.g.

> *The king of Spain's daughter*
>
> *John and Mary's baby*
>
> *Somebody else's umbrella*
>
> *A quarter of an hour's drive*

Expressions like these are natural and acceptable. Informal language, however, permits the extension of the construction to
long and complicated phrases:

> *The people in the house opposite's
> geraniums*
>
> *The man who called last week's umbrella is
> still in the hall*

In these, the connection between the words
forming the group possessive is much
looser and more complicated than in the
earlier examples. The effect is often somewhat ludicrous.

Expressions of this sort are better avoided
in serious prose. Substitute:

> *The geraniums of the people in the house
> opposite*
>
> *The umbrella of the man who called last
> week is still in the hall*

have

1 *Have* and *do*.

In some of its uses, the verb *have* can form
its interrogative and negative either with or
without the verb *do*, e.g. *Do you have?* or *Have
you?*; *You don't have* or *You haven't*.

In sentences like those below, *have* is a verb
of event, meaning 'experience'. The interrogative and negative are always formed
with *do*:

> *Do you ever* have *nightmares?*
>
> *We did not have an easy time getting
> here*

In the next pair of sentences, *have* is a verb
of state, meaning 'possess'. When used in
this sense, the interrogative and negative
can be formed without *do*:

> *What have you in common with the child
> of five whose photograph your mother
> keeps?* (George Orwell)
>
> *The truth was that he* hadn't *the answer*
> (Joyce Cary)

In more informal language, the verb *got* is
added, e.g. *What have you got?*; *He hadn't got
the answer*. For a discussion of this construction, see HAVE (1) in SECTION 6: USAGE.

It was formerly usual to distinguish the
sense 'experience' from the sense 'possess'
by using *do* for the first but not for the second (but only in the present tense). Hence *I
don't have indigestion* (meaning, as a rule) was
kept distinct from *I haven't (got) indigestion*

(meaning, at the moment). The use of the *do*-construction when the meaning was 'possess' was considered an Americanism, but it is now quite acceptable in British English.

The use of *do* as a substitute verb for *have*, though common informally, is not recommended in formal prose:

> I had stronger feelings than she did
> (substitute *than she had*)

2 For the double *have* in e.g. *I should have liked to have seen the figures beforehand*, see INFINITIVE, PRESENT OR PERFECT?

3 For the insertion of a superfluous *have* in e.g. *If I'd have known she'd be here…*, see HAVE (2) in SECTION 6: USAGE.

he/him, she/her

1 For a discussion of e.g. *It was he* versus *It was him* or *It's she again* versus *It's her again*, see PERSONAL PRONOUN, CASE OF.

2 He/him who or **she/her who**?

He who and *she who* are correctly used when *he* and *she* are the subject of the main clause, and *who* is the subject of the relative clause:

> He who *hesitates is lost*
>
> She who *was a waif at 20 may find herself a whale at 40*

In these examples *he* and *she* are the subjects of *is lost* and *may find* respectively; *who* is the subject of *hesitates* and *was*.

He who and *she who* should change to *him who* and *her who* if the personal pronouns are not the subject of the main clause:

> The distinction between the man who gives with conviction and him (not *he*) who is simply buying a title

Similarly *who* becomes *whom*—if it is not the subject of its clause:

> I sought him whom *my soul loveth* (Authorized Version)

See also WHO/WHOM.

I/me

1 For a discussion of e.g. *It is me* versus *It is I*, see PERSONAL PRONOUN, CASE OF.

2 For e.g. *between you and me* versus *between you and I* see YOU AND I/YOU AND ME.

-ics, nouns ending in

Nouns ending in -ics denoting subjects or disciplines are sometimes treated as singular and sometimes as plural. Examples are:

apologetics	genetics	optics
classics	linguistics	phonetics
mathematics	physics	dynamics
mechanics	politics	economics
metaphysics	statistics	electronics
obstetrics	tactics	ethics

When used strictly as the name of a discipline they are treated as singular:

> Psychometrics is *unable to investigate the nature of intelligence*　(Guardian)

So also when the complement is singular:

> Mathematics is *his strong point*

When used more loosely, to denote a manifestation of qualities, often accompanied by a possessive, they are treated as plural:

> His politics were *a mixture of fear, greed and envy*　(Joyce Cary)
>
> I don't understand the mathematics of it, which are *complicated*
>
> The acoustics in this hall are *dreadful*

So also when they denote a set of activities or pattern of behaviour, as commonly with words like:

acrobatics	dramatics	heroics
athletics	gymnastics	hysterics

These words usually remain plural even with a singular complement:

> The acrobatics are *just the social side* (Tom Stoppard)

See also -S, NOUNS ENDING IN.

infinitive, present or perfect?

The perfect infinitive is correctly used when it refers to an earlier time than that referred to by the verb on which it depends, e.g.

> *If it were real life and not a play, that is the part it would be best* to have acted
> (C. S. Lewis)
>
> *Someone seems* to have been making *a beast of himself here* (Evelyn Waugh)

In the above examples, the infinitives *to have acted* and *to have been making* relate to actions earlier in time than the verbs *would be best* and *seems*.

Only if both verbs refer to the past, and the infinitive to an earlier past, should a perfect infinitive follow a past or perfect verb, e.g.

> *When discussing sales with him yesterday, I should have liked to have seen the figures beforehand*

In this example *I should have liked* denotes the speaker's feelings during the discussion and *to have seen* denotes an action imagined as occurring before the discussion.

If the state or action denoted by the infinitive occurred at the same time as the other verb, then the present infinitive should be used:

> *She* would have liked to see *what was on the television* (Kingsley Amis)

The 'double past' is often accidentally used informally, e.g

> *I should have liked to have gone to the party*

A literary example is:

> *Mr. McGregor threw down the sack…in a way that would have been extremely painful to the Flopsy Bunnies, if they had* happened to have been *inside it* (Beatrix Potter)

This is better avoided in formal English.

-ing (gerund and participle)

1 The *-ing* form of a verb can in some contexts be used in either of two constructions:

(i) as a gerund (verbal noun) with a possessive noun or pronoun, e.g.

> *In the event of* Randall's *not going* (Iris Murdoch)
>
> *She did not like* his being *High Church* (L. P. Hartley)

(ii) as a participle with a noun or objective pronoun, e.g.

> *What further need would there have been to speak of another* priest arising? (New English Bible)
>
> *Dixon did not like* him doing *that* (Kingsley Amis)

The choice usually arises only when the accompanying word is a proper or personal noun (e.g. *John, father, teacher*) or a personal pronoun.

In formal usage, prefer the possessive construction wherever it is possible and natural:

> *To whom, without its being ordered, the waiter immediately brought a plate of eggs and bacon* (Evelyn Waugh)
>
> *The danger of* Joyce's turning *them into epigrams* (Anthony Burgess)
>
> *Fancy* his minding *that you went to the Summer Exhibition* (A. N. Wilson)

But it is certainly not wrong to use the non-possessive construction if it sounds more natural, as in the New English Bible quotation above. Moreover, there is sometimes a nuance of meaning. *She did not like his being High Church* suggests merely that she did not like the fact that he was High Church, whereas *Dixon did not like him doing that* suggests an element of repugnance to the person as well as to his action.

When using most non-personal nouns (e.g. *luggage*), groups of nouns (e.g. *father and mother*), non-personal pronouns (e.g. *something*), and groups of pronouns (e.g. *some of them*), the possessive would not sound idiomatic at all. Examples are:

> *Travellers in Italy could depend on their* luggage not being *stolen* (G. B. Shaw)
>
> *Due to her* father and mother not being *married*
>
> *The air of* something unusual having happened (Conan Doyle)
>
> *He had no objection to* some of them listening

When the word preceding the *-ing* form is a regular plural noun ending in *-s*, there is no spoken distinction between the two forms. It is unnecessary to write an apostrophe:

> If she knew about her daughters
> attending the party   (Anthony Powell)

2 There is also variation between the two uses of the -ing form after nouns like *difficulty*, *point*, *trouble*, and *use*.

Formal English requires the gerundial use, the gerund being introduced by *in*:

> There was…no difficulty in finding
> parking space   (David Lodge)

Informal usage permits the placing of the -ing form immediately after the noun, forming a participial construction, e.g.

> The chairman had difficulty concealing
> his irritation

However, this is not fully accepted in formal usage.

I who, you who, we who

The verb following a personal pronoun (*I*, *you*, *he*, etc.) + *who* should agree with the pronoun:

> I, who have no savings to speak of, had to
> pay for the work

This remains so even if the personal pronoun is in the objective case (*me*, *us*, etc.):

> They made me, who have no savings at
> all, pay for the work (not who has)

When *it is* etc. precedes *I who* etc., the same rule applies: the verb agrees with the personal pronoun:

> It's I who have done it

> It could have been we who were mistaken

Informal usage sometimes permits the third person to be used (especially when the verb *to be* follows *who*):

> You who's supposed to be so practical!

> Is it me who's supposed to be keeping an
> eye on you?

This is not recommended in formal usage.

However, in constructions which have the form *I am* + noun or noun phrase + *who*, the verb following *who* is always in the third person (singular or plural):

> I am the sort of person who likes peace
> and quiet

> You are the fourth of my colleagues who's
> told me that ('s = 'has')

-lily, adverbs ending in

When the suffix -*ly* is added to an adjective which already ends in -*ly*, the resulting adverb tends to sound odd, e.g. *friendlily*.

Adverbs of this kind are divided into three groups:

(i) Those formed from adjectives in which the final -*ly* is not a suffix, e.g. *holily*, *jollily*, *sillily*. These are the least objectionable and are quite often used.

(ii) Those of three syllables formed from adjectives in which the final -*ly* is itself a suffix, e.g. *friendlily*, *ghastlily*, *lovelily*, *statelily*, *uglily*. These are occasionally found.

(iii) Those of four (or more) syllables formed from adjectives in which the final -*ly* is itself a suffix, e.g. *heavenlily*, *scholarlily*. Such words are deservedly rare.

The adverbs of groups (ii) and (iii) should be avoided if possible, by using the adjective with a noun like *manner* or *way*, e.g. *In a scholarly manner*.

may / might

For advice on which form to use, see SECTION 6: USAGE.

me / I

1 For a discussion of e.g. *It was me* versus *It was I*, see PERSONAL PRONOUN, CASE OF.

2 For e.g. *between you and me* versus *between you and I*, see YOU AND I/YOU AND ME.

measurement, nouns of

There is some uncertainty about when to use the singular form, and when the plural, of nouns of measurement.

(A) These nouns remain singular when compounded with a numeral and used attributively before another noun:

A *six*-foot *wall*   A *five*-pound *note*

A *three*-mile *walk*   A *1,000*-megaton *bomb*

A *ten*-hectare *field* A *three*-litre *bottle*

(B) *Foot* remains in the singular form in expressions such as:

I am six foot   She is five foot two

But *feet* is used where an adjective, or the word *inches*, follows, e.g.

I am six feet tall

She is five feet three inches

Stone and *hundredweight* remain singular, e.g.

I weigh eleven stone

Three hundredweight of coal

Metric measurements always take the plural form when not used attributively (before a noun):

This measures three metres by two metres

Informally, some other nouns of measurement are used in the singular form in plural expressions, e.g.

That will be two pound fifty, please

This is non-standard.

See also QUANTITY, NOUNS OF.

more, most

For advice on using these to make comparatives and superlatives, see COMPARISON OF ADJECTIVES AND ADVERBS.

need

When followed by an infinitive, the verb *need* can be used either like an ordinary (full) verb or like an auxiliary (see AUXILIARY VERBS).

(A) *Need* is used like an ordinary verb in the present tense when the sentence is neither negative nor interrogative, in the past tense always, and in all compound tenses (e.g. the future and perfect):

One needs friends, one needs to be a friend
(Susan Hill)

One did not need to be a clairvoyant to see that war…was coming (George Orwell)

(B) *Need* can be used like an auxiliary verb in the present tense in negative and interrogative sentences. This means that:

(i) The third person singular does not add *-s*:

He need not come

(ii) For the interrogative, *need I* (*you* etc.) replaces *do I need*:

Need I add that she is my bitterest enemy?
(G. B. Shaw)

(iii) The bare infinitive follows instead of the *to*-infinitive:

Fear of expansion that keeps them smaller than they need be
(This is negative in sense, for it implies *They need not be as small as this*)

This auxiliary verb use is optional, not obligatory. The regular constructions are equally correct:

He does not need to…

Do I need to add…

Smaller than they need to be…

It is important, however, to avoid mixing the two kinds of construction, as in the two following examples:

One needs not be *told that…*

What proved vexing, it needs be *said, was…*

neither (pronoun)

Neither is singular, and strictly requires a singular verb:

Neither of us likes to be told what to do

Informal usage permits a plural verb and complement:

Neither of us are good players

Although this is widely regarded as incorrect, it has been an established construction for three or four centuries:

Neither were great inventors
(John Dryden)

One should prefer the singular unless it leads to awkwardness, as when neither *he* nor *she* is appropriate:

Derek and Lucy will have to walk. Neither of them have brought their cars

neither...nor

1 Two singular subjects linked by *neither... nor* can be constructed with either a singular or a plural verb. Strictly and logically a singular verb is required:

> *Neither he nor his wife* has *arrived*
>
> *There* is *neither a book nor a picture in the house*

Informal usage permits the plural:

> *Neither painting nor fighting feed men* (John Ruskin)

When one subject is plural and the other singular, the verb should be plural and the plural subject placed nearer to it:

> *Neither the teacher nor the pupils* understand *the problem*

When one subject is *I* or *you* and the other is a third person pronoun or a noun, or when one is *I* and the other *you*, the verb can agree with the nearer subject. However, this may sound odd, e.g.

> *Neither my son nor I am good at figures*

One can recast the sentence, but this can spoil the effect. It is often better to use the plural:

> *Neither Isabel nor I are timid people* (H. G. Wells)

This is not illogical if *neither...nor* is regarded as the negative of *both...and*.

2 For advice on placing the pair *neither...nor* within sentences, see CORRELATIVE CONJUNCTIONS.

none (pronoun)

It is sometimes held that *none* can only be followed by a singular verb and singular pronouns (not plural ones). In fact, either is acceptable, and the plural tends to be more common.

(Singular)

> *None of them* was *allowed to forget for a moment*

(Plural)

> *None of the fountains ever* play
>
> *None of the authors expected their books to become best-sellers*

None is descended from an Old English word meaning 'not one' and has been used for around a thousand years with both a singular and a plural verb, depending on the context and the emphasis needed. Nevertheless, it is wise to bear in mind that some people find the plural construction objectionable.

not, case following

In the sentence below the pronoun *I* is in the subjective case, because it would be the subject if a verb were supplied:

> *It must be he who is made of india-rubber, not I*   (Angela Carter)

The sense is, *I am not made of india-rubber.*

In the following sentence the objective case is used, because the pronoun would be the object if there were a verb:

> *Helen kissed me, not* him

The sense is, *Helen did not kiss him.*

However, less formal usage tends to prefer the objective case everywhere, e.g.

> *You are the intellectual, not* me

The 'correct' subjective alternative (here *not I*) can sound rather stilted and is rarely heard in speech.

See PERSONAL PRONOUN, CASE OF.

not only...but also

For advice on placing the pair *not only...but also* within sentences, see CORRELATIVE CONJUNCTIONS.

or

1 See SUBJECTS JOINED BY OR.

2 For advice on placing the pair *either...or* within sentences, see CORRELATIVE CONJUNCTIONS.

ought

Which is correct, **oughtn't** or **didn't ought**?

The standard form of the negative of *ought* is *ought not* or *oughtn't*:

A look from Claudia showed me I ought
not *to have begun it* (V. S. Pritchett)

Being an auxiliary verb (see AUXILIARY VERBS),
ought can precede *not* and does not require
the verb *do*. It is non-standard to form the
negative with *do*:

*I hope that none here will say I did
anything I* didn't ought (Michael
Innes)

When the negative is used to reinforce a
question in a short extra clause or 'tag question', the negative should be formed according to the rule above:

You ought to be pleased, oughtn't you?
(not *didn't you?*)

In the same way *do* should not be used as a
substitute verb for *ought*, e.g.

Ought he to go?—Yes, he ought
(not *he did*)

You ought not to be pleased, ought *you?*
(not *did you?*)

participles

A participle used in place of a verb in a subordinate clause must have an explicit subject to qualify. If no subject precedes it, the
participle is understood to qualify the subject of the main clause. In the following
sentences the participles *running* and
propped qualify the subjects *she* and *we*:

Running to catch a bus, she just missed it
(Anthony Powell)

We both lay there, propped on our elbows
(Lynne Reid Banks)

Participles in initial position are acceptable
grammatically but when overdone can produce a poor style, especially when the participial clause bears little relation to the
main one:

*Being blind from birth, she became a
teacher and travelled widely*

A worse error is to begin a sentence with a
participial clause and to continue it with a
subject to which the participle is not related:

*Driving along the road, the church
appeared on our left*
(*We*, not *the church*, is the subject of
driving)

*Having been relieved of his portfolio in
2000, the scheme was left to his successor
at the Ministry to complete*
(*He*, or a proper name, is the subject
of *having been relieved*)

Participles that appear to be attached to the
wrong subject are sometimes known as
dangling (or **unattached** or **hanging**)
participles.

Such sentences must be recast:

*Driving along the road, we saw the
church appear on our left*

As we were *driving along the road, the
church appeared on our left*

Jones *having been relieved of his portfolio
in 2000, the scheme was left to his
successor at the Ministry to complete*

When the participial clause includes a subject it should not be separated by a comma
from the participle:

*Bernadette being her niece, she feels
responsible for the girl's moral welfare*
(not *Bernadette, being her niece, she…*)
(David Lodge)

But if the participle qualifies the subject of
the main sentence, its clause is either
marked off by a pair of commas or not
marked off at all:

*The man, hoping to escape, jumped on
to a bus*

*A man carrying a parcel jumped on to
the bus*

The rule that a participle must have an explicit subject does not apply to participial
clauses whose subject is indefinite ('one' or
'people'). In these the clause comments on
the content of the sentence:

*Judging from his appearance, he has had
a night out*

Roughly speaking, *this is how it went*

The participial clauses here are equivalent
to 'If one judges …' and 'If one speaks …'
Expressions of this kind are entirely acceptable.

See also UNATTACHED PHRASES.

personal pronoun, case of

I, we, they, he, and *she* are **subjective** personal pronouns, which means they are used as the subject of the sentence, often coming before the verb, e.g.

> She *lives in Paris*
>
> We *are leaving*

Me, us, them, him, and *her,* on the other hand, are **objective** personal pronouns, which means that they are used as the object of a verb or preposition, e.g.

> John *hates* me
>
> *His father left* him
>
> *I did it for* her

This explains why it is not correct to say *John and me went to the shops*: the personal pronoun is in subject position, so it must be *I* not *me*. Using the pronoun alone makes the incorrect use obvious: *Me went to the shops* is clearly not acceptable. This analysis also explains why it is not correct to say *He came with you and I*: the personal pronoun is governed by a preposition *(with)* and is therefore objective, so it must be *me* not *I*. Again, a simple test for correctness is to use the pronoun alone: *He came with I* is clearly not acceptable.

However, there is often confusion about which case of a personal pronoun to use when the pronoun appears without the context of a verb or preposition—i.e., when it stands alone or follows the verb *to be*.

(A) When the personal pronoun stands alone, as when it forms the answer to a question, traditional grammar requires it to have the case it would have if the verb were supplied:

> *Who killed Cock Robin?*—I
> (in full *I killed him*)
>
> *Which of you did he approach?*—Me
> (in full *he approached me*)

Informal usage favours the objective case in both kinds of sentence, but this is not always acceptable in formal style, even though the subjective case often sounds stilted. It is then best to avoid the problem by providing the substitute verb *do,* or, if the preceding sentence contains an auxiliary, by repeating the auxiliary, e.g.

> *Who likes cooking?*—I *do*
>
> *Who can cook?*—I *can*

(B) When a personal pronoun follows *it is, it was, it may be, it could have been,* etc., formal usage requires the subjective case:

> *Nobody could suspect that it was* she
> (Agatha Christie)
>
> *What it must have felt like to be* he?

Informal and spoken usage strongly favours the objective case:

> *I thought it might have been* him *at the door*
>
> *Don't tell me it's* them *again!*

However, this is not always acceptable in formal contexts.

When *who* or *whom* follows, the subjective case is required in formal usage and is also quite usual informally:

> *It was* he *who would be waiting on the tow-path* (P. D. James)

The informal use of the objective case often sounds substandard:

> *It was* her *who would get into trouble*

See also AS, CASE FOLLOWING; BUT, CASE FOLLOWING; NOT, CASE FOLLOWING; REFLEXIVE PRONOUNS; THAN, CASE FOLLOWING; YOU AND I/YOU AND ME.

preposition at end

It is a natural feature of the English language that many sentences and clauses end with a preposition, and the alleged rule that forbids this should be disregarded.

In many sentences the preposition cannot be moved to an earlier place, e.g.

> *What did you do that* for?
>
> *What a mess this room is* in!
>
> *The bed had not been slept* in

Where there is a choice, it is very often a matter of style. The preposition has been placed before the relative pronoun in:

> *The present is the only time* in which *any duty can be done* (C. S. Lewis)

But it stands near the end in:

Harold's Philistine outlook, which she had
acquiesced in for ten years   (L. P. Hartley)

Notice, however, that some prepositions
cannot come at the end:

An annual sum, in return for which she
agreed to give me house room
(William Trevor)

During which week will the festival be
held?

One would not write Which she agreed to give
me house room in return for, and Which week will
the festival be held during?

Provided that the meaning is clear, one
should be guided by what sounds natural.
There is no need to alter the position of the
preposition merely in deference to the alleged rule.

quantity, nouns of

The numerals hundred, thousand, million, billion, trillion, and the words dozen and score are
sometimes used in the singular and sometimes in the plural.

(A) They always have the singular form if
they are qualified by a preceding word,
whether it is singular (e.g. a, one) or plural
(e.g. many, several, two, three, etc.), and
whether or not they are used attributively
before a noun or with nothing following:

A hundred days

Three hundred will be enough

I will take two dozen

Two dozen eggs

The use of the plural form here is incorrect:

The population is now three millions
(correctly three million)

Although they are singular, they always
take plural verbs:

There were about a dozen of them
approaching   (Anthony Powell)

(B) They take the plural form when they denote indefinite quantities. Usually they are
followed by of or stand alone:

Are there any errors?—Yes, hundreds

He has dozens of friends

Many thousands of people are homeless

See also MEASUREMENT, NOUNS OF.

reflexive pronouns

These normally refer back to the subject of
the clause or sentence in which they occur,
e.g.

I congratulated myself on outwitting
everyone else

Can't you do anything for yourself?

Sometimes it is permissible to use a reflexive pronoun to refer to someone who is not
the subject, e.g.

It was their success, both with myself and
others, that confirmed me in what has
since been my career   (Evelyn Waugh)

You have the feeling that all their
adventures have happened to yourself
(George Orwell)

To have written me and you respectively in
these sentences would not have been
grammatically incorrect.

A reflexive pronoun is often used after such
words as:

as	but	like
as for	except	than

e.g. For those who, like himself, felt it indeli-
cate to raise an umbrella in the presence of
death   (Iris Murdoch)

It can be a very useful way to avoid the difficult choice between I, he, she, etc. (which
often sound stilted) and me, him, her, etc.
(which are not formally correct) after the
words as, but, and than, e.g.

None of them was more surprised than
myself that I'd spoken   (Lynne Reid
Banks)

Here than I would be strictly correct, while
than me would be informal.

Naturally a reflexive pronoun cannot be
used in the ways outlined above if confusion would result. One would not write

Miles was as surprised as himself that he
had been appointed

but would substitute the person's name, or
he himself was, for himself, or recast the sentence.

relative clauses

A relative clause is a clause introduced by a relative pronoun (*who, which, whose, that,* etc.) and used to qualify a preceding noun or pronoun (called its antecedent), e.g.

> *The visitor* (antecedent) *whom* (relative pronoun) *you were expecting* (remainder of relative clause) *has arrived*

Exceptionally, there are nominal relative clauses in which the antecedent and relative pronoun are combined in one *wh*-pronoun, e.g. *What you need is a drink!* (see WHAT).

Relative clauses can be either **restrictive** or **non-restrictive**. A restrictive relative clause identifies the antecedent, e.g. *A suitcase which has lost its handle is useless.* Here the antecedent *suitcase* is defined by the clause. A non-restrictive relative clause merely adds further information, e.g. *He carried the suitcase, which had lost its handle, on one shoulder.*

Notice that no commas are used to mark off a restrictive relative clause, but when a non-restrictive relative clause comes in the middle of the sentence, it is marked off by a comma at each end. Failure to make use of this distinction can lead to unintentionally comic effects: for example, strictly speaking, the relative clause in

> *If you are in need of assistance, please ask any member of staff who will be pleased to help*

implies contrast with another set of staff who will not be pleased to help. A comma is needed before *who*.

There are two kinds of **relative pronouns**:

(i) The *wh*-type: *who, whom, whose, which,* and (in nominal relative clauses only) *what.*

(ii) The pronoun *that* (which can be omitted in some circumstances: see THAT, OMISSION OF).

When one relative clause is followed by another, the second relative pronoun may or may not be preceded by a conjunction; it also may or may not be omitted.

(A) A conjunction is not required if the second relative clause qualifies an antecedent inside the first relative clause:

> *I found a firm which had some components* for which *they had no use*

Here *for which...use* qualifies *components* which is part of the relative clause qualifying *firm.* And *or* or *but* should not be inserted before *for which.*

But if both clauses qualify the same antecedent, a conjunction is required:

> *Help me with these shelves which I have to take home* but *which will not fit in my car*

(B) The second relative pronoun can be omitted if (i) it qualifies the same antecedent as the first, and (ii) it plays the same part in its clause as the first (i.e. subject or object):

> *George, who takes infinite pains and* (who) *never cuts corners, is our most dependable worker*

Here both *who*'s qualify *George,* and are the subjects of their clauses, so the second can be omitted.

But if the second relative pronoun plays a different part in its clause, it cannot be omitted:

> *George, whom everybody likes but who rarely goes to a party, is shy*

Here *whom* is the object and *who* is the subject of their respective clauses; therefore *who* must be kept.

See also ADVERBIAL RELATIVE CLAUSES; WHICH/ THAT; WHO(M)/THAT; WHO/WHICH; WHO/WHOM; WHOSE/OF WHICH.

-s, nouns ending in

Some nouns, though they have the plural ending -*s*, are nevertheless usually treated as singulars, taking singular verbs and pronouns referring back to them.

(A) *News*

(B) Diseases:

> *measles   mumps   rickets   shingles*

Measles and *rickets* can also be treated as ordinary plural nouns.

(C) Games:

> *billiards   dominoes   ninepins*
> *bowls   draughts   skittles*
> *darts   fives*

(D) Countries:

the Bahamas	*the Philippines*
the Netherlands	*the United States*

These are treated as singular when considered as a unit, which they commonly are in a political context, or when the complement is singular, e.g.

> *The Philippines* is *a predominantly agricultural country*
>
> *The United States* has *withdrawn its ambassador*

The Bahamas and *the Philippines* are also the geographical names of the groups of islands which the two nations comprise, and in this use can be treated as plurals, e.g.

> *The Bahamas* were *settled by British subjects*

See also -ICS, NOUNS ENDING IN.

sentence adverbs

The traditional definition of an adverb is that it is a word that modifies the meaning of a verb, an adjective, or another adverb, e.g.

> *He shook his head sadly*

However, another important function of some adverbs is to comment on a whole sentence, either expressing the speaker's attitude or classifying the discourse. For example, in

> *Sadly, Mark is rather overbearing*

the adverb *sadly* does not mean that Mark is overbearing in a sad manner: it expresses the speaker's attitude to what is being stated.

Traditionalists take the view that the use of sentence adverbs is inherently suspect and that they should always be paraphrased, e.g. using such wording as:

> *It is sad that he is rather overbearing*

A particular objection is raised to the sentence adverbs *hopefully* and *thankfully*, since they cannot even be paraphrased in the usual way. However, there is overwhelming evidence that such usages are well established and widely accepted in everyday speech and writing. See HOPEFULLY; REGRETFULLY; and THANKFULLY in SECTION 6: USAGE.

shall / will

'The horror of that moment,' the King went on, 'I shall never, never *forget!*' 'You *will, though,*' the Queen said, '*if you don't make a memorandum of it.*' (Lewis Carroll)

There is now considerable confusion about when to use *shall* and *will*. Put simply, the traditional rule in standard British English is:

(A) In the first person, singular and plural.

(i) *I shall, we shall* express the simple future, e.g.

> *I am not a manual worker and please God I never* shall *be one* (George Orwell)
>
> *In the following pages we* shall *see good words…losing their edge* (C. S. Lewis)

(ii) *I will, we will* express intention or determination on the part of the speaker (especially a promise made by him or her), e.g.

> I will *take you to see her tomorrow morning*
>
> I will *no longer accept responsibility for the fruitless loss of life* (Susan Hill)

(B) For the second and third persons, singular and plural, the rule is exactly the converse.

(i) *You, he, she, it,* or *they will* express the simple future, e.g.

> *Will it disturb you if I keep the lamp on for a bit?*
>
> *Seraphina* will *last much longer than a car* (Graham Greene)

(ii) *You, he, she, it,* or *they shall* express intention or determination on the part of the speaker or someone other than the actual subject of the verb, especially a promise made by the speaker to or about the subject, e.g.

> *Today you* shall *be with me in Paradise* (Revised Version)
>
> *One day you* shall *know my full story*
>
> Shall *the common man be pushed back into the mud, or* shall *he not?*

The two uses of *will*, and one of those of *shall*, are well illustrated by:

> '*I* will *follow you to the ends of the earth,*' replied Susan, passionately. '*It* will *not be necessary,*' said George. '*I am only going down to the coal-cellar. I* shall *spend the next half-hour or so there.*' (P. G. Wodehouse)

Note also Binyon's lines of 1914, recited every November in memory of the war dead:

> *They* shall *grow not old, as we that are left grow old…We* will *remember them*

There is, too, that old schoolmaster's joke about the drowning swimmer who cried *I* will *drown! No one* shall *save me!* and was therefore left to his fate.

Today such an outcome seems unlikely, as the traditional distinction has weakened considerably in practice. In spoken and informal usage *I will* and *we will* are very often used for the simple future, e.g.

> *I* will *be a different person when I finish this job*

More often the distinction is covered up by the contracted form '*ll*, e.g.

> *I don't quite know when I'll get the time to write again*

However, the use of *will* for *shall* in the first person is still not regarded as fully acceptable in formal usage.

she / her

For a discussion of e.g. *It's she again* versus *It's her again*, see PERSONAL PRONOUN, CASE OF.

should / would

1 When used for the future in the past or the conditional mood:

> *should* goes with *I* and *we*
>
> *would* goes with *you, he, she, it,* and *they*

(A) The future in the past.

First person:

> *Julia and I, who had left…thinking we* should *not return* (Evelyn Waugh)

The person's imagined statement or thought at the time was:

> *We* shall *not return*

—with *shall*, not *will* (see SHALL/WILL).

Second and third persons:

> *He was there. Later, he* would *not be there* (Susan Hill)

The person's statement or thought at the time was:

> *He* will *not be there*

These forms are especially common in reported speech:

> *I said I* should *be late*
>
> *You didn't say you* would *be this late*

(B) The conditional.

First person:

> *I* should *view with the strongest disapproval any proposal to abolish manhood suffrage* (C. S. Lewis)

Second and third persons:

> *If you took 3 ft off the average car, you* would *have another six million feet of road space* (The Times)

In informal usage, *I would* and *we would* are very common in both kinds of sentence:

> *I wondered whether I* would *have to wear a black suit*
>
> *With a small pay rise and better company I* would *have been quite content*

The use of *would* with the first person is understandable, because *should* (in all persons) has a number of other uses, including 'ought to'; sometimes the context does not make it clear whether *I should do* means 'it would be the case that I did' or 'I ought to do', e.g.

> *I wondered whether, when I was cross-examined, I* should *admit that I knew the defendant*

This use of *I would* and *we would* is not, however, regarded as fully acceptable in formal language.

2 There is often uncertainty whether to use *should* or *would* in the first person singular and plural before verbs such as *like* or *think* and before the adverbs *rather* and *sooner*.

(A) *Should* is formally correct before verbs of liking, e.g. *be glad, be inclined, care, like,* and *prefer*:

> *Would you like a beer?—I should prefer a cup of coffee, if you don't mind*

(B) *Should* is likewise formally correct in tentative statements of opinion, with verbs such as *guess, imagine, say,* and *think*:

> I should imagine *that you are right*
>
> I shouldn't have thought *it was difficult*

(C) *Would* is correct before the adverbs *rather* and *sooner*, e.g.

> I would *truly* rather *be in the middle of this than sitting in that church in a tight collar*

Would is always correct with persons other than the first person singular and plural. In practice, however, these distinctions have become very weak, with *would* being used for *should* as a matter of course In spoken and informal contexts the issue rarely arises, owing to the use of the contracted forms *I'd, we'd,* etc.

singular or plural verb?

(A) When subject and complement are different in number (i.e. one is singular, the other plural), the verb normally agrees with the subject, e.g.

(Plural subject)

> *Ships* are *his chief interest*
>
> *Liqueur chocolates* are *our speciality*

(Singular subject)

> *What we need* is *customers*
>
> *Our speciality* is *liqueur chocolates*

(B) A plural subject used as a name counts as singular, e.g.

> Sons and Lovers has *always been one of Lawrence's most popular novels*

(C) A singular phrase that happens to end with a plural word should nevertheless be followed by a singular verb, e.g.

> *One in six* has (not *have*) *this problem*

(D) Nouns joined by quasi-coordinators such as *accompanied by, as well as, not to men-tion, together with,* etc., are followed by a singular verb if the first noun or noun phrase is singular, because the addition is regarded as a parenthesis rather than as part of the grammatical subject:

> *British Telecom, along with many other companies in the UK,* is *not prepared to pay a reasonable amount*
>
> *Daddy had on the hairy tweed jacket which, together with his pipe,* was *his trade mark*

(E) A problem often arises when such words as *number, average, maximum, minimum, handful,* and *total* are used like this:

> *A large number of people wants* (or *want*) *to hear the great tenors*
>
> *An average of 27,000 quotations has* (or *have*) *been sent in each year*
>
> *A worldwide total of 30.6 million cases of HIV has* (or *have*) *been estimated*

Strictly speaking, the verb should agree with the singular noun, but in practice it is often made to agree with the nearest (and in the above examples, plural) noun. This often seems more natural.

(F) If the subject of a relative clause is the same as the antecedent, the verb in the relative clause agrees in number with the antecedent, e.g.

> *It is the children* who *are the first consideration*   (E. M. Forster)

If the relative clause follows *one of the* (or *those*) + a plural noun, either *one* or the noun may be the antecedent. If *one* is the antecedent, the verb should be singular, e.g.

> *One of the most dependable of the older girls, who* was *made responsible* (Flora Thompson)

If the plural noun is the logical antecedent, then strictly speaking the verb should be plural, e.g.

> *He is one of the few businessmen who genuinely* like *journalists*

This can sound slightly awkward and in speech it is quite common to treat *one* as the antecedent:

> *Perhaps you were one of those fellows who sees tricks everywhere*   (Peter Carey)

However, it is important not to mix plural and singular, as in this incorrect sentence:

> *She is one of those people who likes to travel whenever they can*

See also COLLECTIVE NOUNS; COMPOUND SUBJECTS; -ICS, NOUNS ENDING IN; QUANTITY, NOUNS OF; -S, NOUNS ENDING IN; WHAT.

split infinitive

This is the separation of *to* from the infinitive by one or more intervening words, e.g. *He used* to *continually* refer *to the subject*. In this *continually* splits *to refer* into two parts.

The dislike of split infinitives is longstanding but is not well founded, being based on an analogy with Latin. In Latin, infinitives consist of only one word, which makes them impossible to split: therefore, so the argument goes, they should not be split in English either. But English is not the same as Latin. In particular, the placing of an adverb in English is extremely important in giving the appropriate meaning and emphasis. For example, the notorious split infinitive

> *To boldly go where no man has gone before*

conveys a different emphasis from the more strictly 'correct' *To go boldly where…*

Despite this, many people still strongly believe that the split infinitive is an error or (at least) an infelicity. It is therefore a wise general rule to avoid splitting unless the avoidance leads to misplaced emphasis, ambiguity, or clumsiness.

(A) Misplaced emphasis.

Many careful writers habitually avoid splitting the infinitive by placing the adverb before the *to*-infinitive:

> *One meets people who have learned* actually to prefer *the tinned fruit to the fresh*   (C. S. Lewis)

> *He did not want* positively to suggest *that she was dominant*   (Iris Murdoch)

But when an adverb (especially an intensifying adverb such as *actually, even, ever, further, just, quite,* or *really*) belongs with a verb that happens to be an infinitive, it is often better, for reasons of emphasis and rhythm, to place it between *to* and the verb:

> *I want* to really study, *I want to be a scholar*   (Iris Murdoch)

> *In face of all this Patrick managed* to quite like *him*   (Kingsley Amis)

(B) Ambiguity.

When an adverb closely qualifies the infinitive verb it may often be better to split the infinitive. The following example is ambiguous in writing, though in speech stress would make the meaning clear:

> *It fails* completely to carry *conviction*

This either means 'It totally fails …', in which case *completely* should precede *fails*, or it means 'It fails to carry complete conviction', in which case that should be written, or the infinitive should be split.

(C) Clumsiness.

> *It took more than an excited elderly man…* socially to discompose *him* (Anthony Powell)

In this example, *socially* belongs closely with *discompose*: it is not 'to discompose in a social way' but 'to cause social discomposure'. In such cases, it may be better either to split the infinitive or to recast the sentence than to separate the adverb from the verb.

(D) Unavoidable split infinitive.

There are certain adverbial constructions which must immediately precede the verb and therefore split the infinitive, e.g. *more than*:

> *It allowed Fernanda Herford* to slightly more than double *her money*   (Julian Barnes)

And a writer may have sound stylistic reasons for allowing a parenthetic expression to split an infinitive:

> *It would be an act of gratuitous folly* to, as he had put it to Mildred, make *trouble for himself*   (Iris Murdoch)

subjects joined by *or*

When two singular subjects are joined by *or* or *either…or*, the strict rule is that they require a singular verb and singular pronouns:

> *Either Peter or John* has *had his breakfast already*
>
> *A traffic warden or a policeman* is *always on the watch*

However, there is a natural tendency to use the plural with two or more singular subjects when their mutual exclusion is not emphasized, e.g.

> *On which rage or wantonness vented themselves* (George Eliot)

When one subject is plural, it is best to put the verb in the plural, and place the plural subject nearer to the verb:

> *Either the child or the parents* are *to blame*

When personal pronouns are involved, the verb is usually made to agree with the nearer of the two subjects:

> *Either he or you* have *got to give in*
>
> *Either you or your teacher* has *made a mistake*

This form of expression very often sounds awkward:

> *Am I or he going to win?*

It is usually best to recast the sentence by adding another verb:

> *Am I going to win, or is he?*
>
> *Either he has got to give in, or you have*

subjunctive

The subjunctive mood is used to express situations which are hypothetical or not yet realized, and is typically used for what is imagined, hoped for, demanded, or expected. In English the subjunctive mood is fairly uncommon mainly because most of its functions are covered by modal verbs such as *might*, *could*, and *should*.

In fact, the subjunctive is often indistinguishable from the ordinary indicative mood. The present subjunctive form is identical with the indicative, except in the third person singular, which does not end in *-s*. The past subjunctive is identical with the indicative throughout. In the verb *to be*, however, the present subjunctive is *be*, rather than *am*, *are*, or *is*, and the past subjunctive is *were* rather than *was* (see WERE/WAS).

In modern English the subjunctive mood is regarded as optional. Use of the subjunctive tends to convey a more formal tone but there are few people who would regard its absence as actually wrong. Today it survives mostly in a number of fixed expressions which cause no problems:

> Be *that as it may*   Heaven help *us*
>
> Come *what may*   Long live *the Queen*
>
> God bless *you*   So be *it*
>
> God save *the Queen*   Suffice *it to say that*

There are two other uses of the subjunctive that may possibly cause difficulty.

(A) In *that*-clauses after words expressing command, hope, intention, wish, etc. Typical introducing words are:

> *demand that*   *proposal that*
>
> *insist that*   *suggest that*
>
> *be insistent that*   *suggestion that*

Typical examples are:

> *Joseph was insistent that his wishes* be *carried out* (W. Somerset Maugham)
>
> *Your suggestion that I* fly *out* (David Lodge)

The conjunction *that* may often be omitted:

> *It was suggested he* wait *till the next morning* (Michael Ondaatje)

Until recently this use of the subjunctive was restricted to very formal language, where it is still usual, e.g.

> *The Lord Chancellor put the motion that the House* go *into Committee*

It is, however, a usual American idiom, and is now quite common in British English. Nevertheless, *should* or *may*, or (especially in informal use) the ordinary indicative, will do equally well:

> *Your demand that he* should *pay the money back surprised him*
>
> *I insist that the boy* goes *to school this minute*

Beware, however, of constructions in which the sense hangs on a fine distinction between subjunctive and indicative, e.g.

> *The most important thing for Spain is that Britain recognize her sovereignty over Gibraltar*

The implication is that Britain does not recognize it. A change of *recognize* to *recognizes* would drastically reverse this implication. The use of *should recognize* would render the sense unmistakable.

(B) In certain clauses introduced by *though* and *if*, the subjunctive can be used to express reserve about an action or state, e.g.

> *Though he be the devil himself he shall do as I say*

> *The University is a place where a poor man, if he be virtuous, may live a life of dignity and simplicity*   (A. C. Benson)

This is very formal. It should not be used in ordinary prose, where it is preferable to use either the indicative or an auxiliary such as *may*, e.g.

> *Though he may be an expert, he should listen to advice*

> *If this is the case, then I am in error*

than, case following

In the following sentences, the pronoun is in the subjective case, because it would be the subject if a verb were supplied:

> *You are two stone heavier than I* (meaning *than I am*)

> *We pay more rent than they* (meaning *than they do*)

In the sentence below, the objective case is used, because the pronoun would be the object if there were a verb:

> *Jones treated his wife badly. I think that he liked his dog better than her* (meaning *than he liked her*)

Less formal English permits the objective case everywhere, e.g.

> *You do it very well. Much better than me*

The preferred formal alternative, with the subjective, often sounds stilted and unnatural. When this is so, it can be avoided by supplying the verb:

> *We pay more rent than they do*

The pronoun *whom* is always used after *than*, rather than *who*:

> *Professor Smith, than whom there is scarcely anyone better qualified to judge, believes it to be pre-Roman*

See PERSONAL PRONOUN, CASE OF.

that, omission of

1 *That* as conjunction.

(A) The conjunction *that* introducing a noun clause and used after verbs of saying, thinking, knowing, etc., can often be omitted in informal usage:

> *I told him (that) he was wrong*

> *Are you sure (that) this is the place?*

Although the omission of *that* is standard English, it may be inappropriate in formal prose.

That should never be omitted if other parts of the sentence (apart from the indirect object) intervene:

> *I told him, as I have told everyone, that he was wrong*

> *Are you sure in your own mind that this is the place?*

In such cases, omission of *that* makes it difficult to follow the sense in written prose.

(B) When *that* is part of the correlative pairs of conjunctions *so...that* and *such...that*, or of the compound conjunctions *so that*, *now that*, it can be omitted in less formal usage:

> *He walked so fast (that) I could not keep up*

> *I'll move my car so (that) you can park in the drive*

> *Are you lonely now (that) your children have left home?*

It should not be omitted in formal style.

2 *That* as relative pronoun.

The relative pronoun *that* can often be omitted, but in formal contexts the omission is best limited to short clauses which stand next to their antecedents:

> *None of the cars (that) I saw had been damaged*

> *Nothing (that) I could say made any difference*

That cannot be omitted when it is the subject of the relative clause, e.g.

> *Nothing* that *occurred to me made any difference*

> *None of the cars* that *were under cover had been damaged*

See also ADVERBIAL RELATIVE CLAUSES; WAY, RELATIVE CLAUSE FOLLOWING.

the, a(n)

For advice on whether to omit these, see ARTICLE, OMISSION OF.

there is / there are

In a sentence introduced by *there* + part of *to be*, the latter agrees in number with whatever follows:

> *There* was *a great deal to be said for this scheme*

> *There* are *many advantages in doing it this way*

In very informal language *there is* or *there was* is often heard before a plural:

> *There's two coloured-glass windows in the chapel* (Evelyn Waugh)

This is non-standard.

to

The preposition *to* can stand at the end of a clause or sentence as a substitute for an omitted *to*-infinitive, e.g.

> *He had tried not to think about Emma... but of course it was impossible not to* (Iris Murdoch)

This is standard usage.

unattached participles

See PARTICIPLES.

unattached phrases

An adjectival or adverbial phrase, introducing a sentence, must qualify the subject of the sentence, e.g.

> *While not entirely in agreement with the plan,* he *had no serious objections to it*

> *After two days on a life-raft,* the *survivors were rescued by helicopter*

It is a common error to begin a sentence with a phrase of this kind, and then to continue it with a quite different subject, e.g.

> *After six hours without food in a plane on the perimeter at Heathrow,* the flight was cancelled

The phrase *After...Heathrow* anticipates a subject like *the passengers*. Such a sentence should either have a new beginning, e.g.

> *After the passengers had spent six hours...*

or a new main clause, e.g.

> *After six hours...Heathrow,* the passengers learnt that *the flight had been cancelled*

used to

The negative and interrogative of *used to* can be formed in two ways:

(i) Negative: *used not to*
    Interrogative: *used X to?*

Examples:

> *Used you to beat your mother?* (G. B. Shaw)

> *You used not to have a moustache, used you?* (Evelyn Waugh)

(ii) Negative: *did not use to, didn't use to*
     Interrogative: *did X use to?*

Examples:

> *She didn't use to find sex revolting* (John Braine)

> *Did you use to be a flirt?* (Eleanor Farjeon)

Either form is acceptable. On the whole *used you to, used he to,* etc. tend to sound rather stilted and over-formal.

The correct spellings of the negative forms are *usedn't to* and *didn't use to* (not *usen't to* and *didn't used to*).

way, relative clause following

(The) way can be followed by a relative clause with or without *that*:

It may have been the way (that) he
smiled

She couldn't give a dinner party the way
(that) her mother could

There is no need to introduce the relative
clause with *in which*.

we/us

1 For a discussion of e.g. *It was us* versus *It
was we*, see PERSONAL PRONOUN, CASE OF.

2 Expressions consisting of *we* or *us* followed by a qualifying word or phrase, e.g.
we English, us English, are often misused with
the wrong case of the first person plural
pronoun. In fact the rules are exactly the
same as for *we* or *us* standing alone.

If the expression is the subject, *we* should be
used:

(Correct)

Not always laughing as heartily as we
English *are supposed* to *do*
(J. B. Priestley)

(Incorrect)

We all make mistakes, even us editors

If the expression is the object or the complement of a preposition, *us* should be used:

(Correct)

To us English, *Europe is not a very vivid
conception*

(Incorrect)

*The Guardian has said some nice things
about* we in the North-East

were/was

There is often confusion about whether to
use *were* or *was* in the first or third person
singular.

Traditional grammar requires the subjunctive form *were*:

(A) In conditional sentences where the condition is 'unreal', e.g.

If I were younger, I'd travel the world
(The condition is impossible)

If anyone were *to try to save me, I would
refuse*   (Jean Rhys)

(The condition is regarded as
unlikely)

(B) Following *as if* and *as though*, e.g.

It was as if Sally were *disturbed in some
way*   (Anita Brookner)

(C) In *that*-clauses after *to wish*, e.g.

He wishes he were *travelling with you*
(Angus Wilson)

Notice that in all these constructions the
clause with *were* refers to something unreal.

Were may also be used in dependent questions, e.g.

Hilliard wondered whether Barton were
not right after all   (Susan Hill)

In modern English, these uses of *were* are
not regarded as obligatory even in very formal prose. *Was* is acceptable everywhere
except in the fixed expressions *as it were*
and *if I were you*, and in certain inverted constructions, e.g.

*Were I to get drunk, it would help me in
the fight*   (John Updike)

what (relative pronoun)

What can be used as a relative pronoun only
when introducing nominal relative clauses,
e.g.

So much of what *you tell me is strange,
different from* what *I was led to expect*
(Jean Rhys)

Here *what* is equivalent to *that which* or *the
things which*.

What is used to qualify an antecedent only
in non-standard speech, e.g.

The young gentleman what's *arranged
everything*   (Evelyn Waugh)

A *what*-clause used as the subject of a sentence almost always takes a singular verb,
even if there is a plural complement, e.g.

*What interests him is less events...than the
reverberations they set up*   (Frederic
Raphael)

Very occasionally the form of the sentence
may render the plural more natural, e.g.

What once were *great houses* are *now
petty offices*

which/that (relative pronouns)

There is often uncertainty about whether to use *which* or *that* in relative clauses. The general rule is that *which* is used in relative clauses to which the reader's attention is to be drawn, while *that* is used in clauses which do not need special emphasis.

Which is always used in non-restrictive clauses, i.e. those that add further information:

> *The men are getting rum issue,* which *they deserve* (Susan Hill)

The use of *that* in non-restrictive clauses should be avoided. Although it is sometimes employed by good writers to suggest a tone of familiarity, e.g.

> *Getting out of Alec's battered old car* that *looked as if it had been in collision with many rocks, Harold had a feeling of relief* (L. P. Hartley)

it should not be used in ordinary prose.

Both *which* and *that* can be used in restrictive relative clauses, i.e. those that define or restrict the reference to the particular one described. Some guidelines follow:

(A) *Which* preferred:

(i) Clauses which add significant information often sound better with *which*, e.g.

> *Not nearly enough for the social position* which *they had to keep up* (D. H. Lawrence)

(ii) Clauses which are separated from their antecedent, especially by another noun, sound better with *which*, e.g.

> *Larry told her the story of the young airman* which *I narrated at the beginning of this book* (W. Somerset Maugham)

(iii) *Which* after a preposition is often a better choice than *that* with the preposition at the end of the sentence (SEE PREPOSITION AT END), e.g.

> *I'm telling you about a dream* in which *ordinary things are marvellous* (William Trevor)

> (*a dream* that *ordinary things are marvellous* in would not sound natural)

(B) *That* preferred:

(i) When the antecedent is an indefinite pronoun (e.g. *anything*, *everything*) or contains a superlative adjective (e.g. *the biggest car*), English idiom tends to prefer *that* to *which*:

> *Is there nothing small* that *the children could buy you for Christmas?*

> *This is the most expensive hat* that *you could have bought*

(ii) *That* is sometimes a good choice when one is not sure whether to use *who* or *which*:

> *This was the creature, neither child nor woman,* that *drove me through the dusk that summer evening* (Evelyn Waugh)

who

1 For e.g. *It's you who are to blame* versus *It's you who is to blame*, see I WHO, YOU WHO, WE WHO.

2 For e.g. *Let he who did this be punished* versus *Let him who did this...,* see HE/HIM, SHE/HER (2).

who/that (relative pronouns)

Who(m) is always acceptable as the relative pronoun referring to a person.

In non-restrictive relative clauses, i.e. those which add new information, *who(m)* is obligatory, e.g.

> *It was not like Coulter,* who *was a cheerful man* (Susan Hill)

In restrictive (i.e. identifying) relative clauses, *who(m)* is usually quite acceptable:

> *The masters* who *taught me Divinity told me that biblical texts were highly untrustworthy* (Evelyn Waugh)

It is sometimes felt that the relative pronoun *that* is slightly depreciatory if applied to a person. Hence it tends to be avoided in formal usage. However, if

(i) the relative pronoun is the object, and

(ii) the personality of the antecedent is suppressed

that may well be appropriate, e.g.

> *They looked now just like the GIs* that *one saw in Viet Nam* (David Lodge)

Informally *that* is acceptable with any personal antecedent, e.g.

> *Honey, it's me* that *should apologize*
> (David Lodge)

This is better avoided in formal style.

who/which (relative pronouns)

A *wh*-pronoun introducing a relative clause must be *who(m)* if the antecedent is personal, e.g.

> *Suzanne was a woman* who *had no notion of reticence*   (W. Somerset Maugham)

But it must be *which* if the antecedent is non-personal, e.g.

> *There was a suppressed tension about her* which *made me nervous*   (Lynne Reid Banks)

If the relative clause is non-restrictive, i.e. it simply adds new information, the *wh*-type of pronoun *must* be used (as above). If the relative clause is restrictive, i.e. it defines or identifies the antecedent, one can use either the appropriate *wh*-pronoun (as above), or the non-variable pronoun *that*. See WHICH/THAT; WHO(M)/THAT.

who/whom (interrogative and relative pronouns)

Who forms the subjective case and so should be used in subject position in a sentence, e.g.

> Who *decided this?*

> *I* who'*d never read anything before but the newspaper*   (W. Somerset Maugham)

According to formal grammar, when the pronoun is the object of a verb or the complement of a preposition, *whom* should be used:

> *Why are we being served by a man* whom *neither of us likes?*   (William Trevor)

> *The real question is food (or freedom) for* whom   (C. S. Lewis)

The use of *who* as object or complement is very common but regarded as an error (or at best very informal) by traditionalists:

> Who *are you looking for?*

> *The person* who *I'm looking for is rather elusive*

In practice, use of *whom* has retreated steadily and is now restricted to the most formal contexts. The normal practice in modern English is to use *who* instead of *whom* (and, where applicable, to put the preposition at the end of the sentence).

The rarer mistake of substituting *whom* for *who* usually occurs either because the structure of the sentence has misled the writer, or from a misguided belief that *whom* sounds more formal and dignified. The following sentences all require *who*:

> *He never had any doubt about* whom *was the real credit to the family*

> Whom *among our poets could be called the equal of Milton?*

> *J. K. Rowling,* whom *they say is the wealthiest writer in the country*

In this last example confusion has been caused by the parenthetical clause *they say*. A simple rule in such cases is to use *who* if the parenthetical clause can be omitted without damaging the sense (as in the example given). If the parenthetical clause cannot be omitted in this way, use *whom*, e.g.

> *J. K. Rowling,* whom *they believe to be the wealthiest writer in the country*

whose / of which in relative clauses

The relative pronoun *whose* can be used as the possessive of *which* as well as of *who*. The rule sometimes given that *of which* must always be used after a non-personal antecedent should be ignored, as it is by good writers, e.g.

> *The little book* whose *yellowish pages she knew*   (Virginia Woolf)

In some sentences, *of which* would be almost impossible, e.g.

> *The lawns about* whose *closeness of cut his father worried the gardener daily*
> (Susan Hill)

There is, of course, no rule prohibiting *of which* if it sounds natural, e.g.

A little town the name of which I have forgotten (W. Somerset Maugham)

However, *whose* can only be used as the non-personal possessive in relative clauses. The interrogative *whose* refers only to persons, as in *Whose book is this?*

you and I / you and me

When a personal pronoun is linked by *and* or *or* to a noun or another pronoun there is often confusion about which case to use. In fact the situation is exactly as it would be for the pronoun standing alone. (See PERSONAL PRONOUN, CASE OF.)

(A) According to traditional grammar, if the two words linked by *and* or *or* constitute the subject, the pronoun should be in the subjective case, e.g.

Only she and her mother cared for the old house

That's what we'd like to do, John and I

Who could go?—Either you or he

The use of the objective case is common in informal contexts, especially when the pronouns appear without a verb or preposition (as in the second and third examples given above). However, it is not always accept-

able in formal use. The following examples are from the speech of characters in novels:

Perhaps only her and Mrs Natwick had stuck to the christened name

That's how we look at it, me and Martha

Either Mary had to leave or me

(B) If the two words linked by *and* or *or* constitute the object of the verb, or the complement of a preposition, the objective case should properly be used:

The afternoon would suit her and John better

It was time for Sebastian and me to go down to the drawing-room

The use of *I* rather than *me* in such sentences is very common. It probably arises from an exaggerated fear of the error indicated under (A) above:

It was this that set Charles and I talking of old times

Why is it that people like you and I are so unpopular?

Between you and I

This last expression is very commonly heard. *Between you and me* should always be substituted.

PART III: GLOSSARY

This glossary of grammatical terms is intended mainly as a quick-reference guide to be used in conjunction with the other Parts of this Section (and the other Sections of this volume). Its chief function is to provide simple definitions of the terms used in this book as they are used in this book. To enhance its value as a general reference aid, other terms in general use have been added to the core glossary, but there has been no attempt at complete or systematic coverage. The glossary adheres to no particular system of analysis or nomenclature – terms from the newer forms of descriptive linguistic analysis rub shoulders indiscriminately with those from traditional schoolroom grammar. Cross-references to other terms in the glossary are indicated by SMALL CAPITALS.

absolute adjective See NON-GRADABLE ADJECTIVE.

abstract noun See NOUN.

accusative 1 Denoting a noun or pronoun that is governed by a verb or preposition, e.g.

> Then we saw the house
>
> The house stood right in front of us

2 Another name for the OBJECTIVE case.

active The VOICE of a verb in which the subject of the verb performs the action and the object is affected by the action, e.g. *France beat Brazil in the final.* Compare PASSIVE.

adjective A word that names an attribute, used to describe a noun or pronoun, e.g.

> A small *child*   She is very small

An alternative term is **modifier**, which also covers the grey area of ATTRIBUTIVE nouns, e.g. *city* in *city council* and *table* in *table lamp.* An adjective has three forms, traditionally called a positive (e.g. *hot, splendid*), a COMPARATIVE (e.g. *hotter, more splendid*), and a SUPERLATIVE (e.g. *hottest, most splendid*).

adjective phrase A PHRASE based on an adjective and functioning as an adjective within the clause or sentence, e.g.

> She wore a dress with a red pattern on it

adverb A word that (typically) qualifies the meaning of a verb, adjective, or another adverb. The principal adverb uses answer the questions 'how?' or 'in what manner?', many of these being formed by the addition of the suffix -ly to adjectives (e.g. *carefully, quickly, steadily, well*); 'when?' or 'how often?' (e.g. *soon, regularly, yesterday*); 'where?' (e.g. *downstairs, here, outside*); and 'to what extent?' (e.g. *extremely, hardly, somewhat*). The term covers a wide variety of words, and is the least satisfactory of the conventional word classes applied to English.

adverbial Part of a clause which modifies the verb and provides information in answers to questions such as 'when?', 'where?', 'how?', and 'why?' It often takes the form of a prepositional phrase, e.g.

> She arrived after lunch
>
> She arrived in a very strange mood

adverbial clause A subordinate CLAUSE in a complex sentence that functions in a similar way to an ADVERBIAL but contains a FINITE VERB, e.g.

> I met her when we had both finished work

adverbial relative clause A RELATIVE CLAUSE that functions as part of an ADVERBIAL CLAUSE, e.g.

> On the day that I turned 30, I felt strangely relieved

It is almost always preceded by preposition + noun (*on the day* in the sentence quoted above).

affix A PREFIX or SUFFIX.

agent noun A noun denoting a person or thing that performs the action of a verb, e.g. *builder*, *accelerator*. It is usually formed using the **agent suffix** *-er* or *-or*.

agreement (also called **concord**) The correct relation to each other of different parts of a sentence, so that e.g. the form of the verb corresponds to its subject:

> *The house* was *small, and its walls* were *painted white*

The gender and number (singular or plural) of a pronoun conforms to that of the person or thing it refers to:

> *He had never been close enough to a girl to consider making* her *his* wife

antecedent A noun or phrase to which a RELATIVE PRONOUN refers back, e.g.

> *The book that I left on the train*

> *I gave the key to* Sue*, who lives next-door*

apposition The placing of a word, especially a noun, syntactically parallel to another, e.g.

> *William the Conqueror*

> *Our old friend David Jones*

article In English, *a(n)* or *the*. The **indefinite article**, *a(n)*, is used to introduce a noun phrase not previously mentioned or non-specific in its reference, e.g.

> A *man I once met*   *She gave me a CD*

The **definite article**, *the*, is used to introduce a noun phrase that has already been or is about to be defined, e.g.

> The *man who called yesterday*

> *She gave me* the *latest Madonna CD*

aspect The form of the verb in a sentence that tells us whether the action is SIMPLE (*she eats*), CONTINUOUS (*she is eating*), or PERFECT (*she has eaten*).

attributive Denoting a word, normally an adjective or noun, that is put before another word, normally a noun, to qualify or describe it in some way, e.g. *brown* in *brown*

shoes and *table* in *table lamp*. Compare PREDICATIVE.

auxiliary verb A verb that is used with another verb to form a particular TENSE or MOOD, e.g.

> *We* were *pleased*   *They* have *gone*

Sometimes more than one auxiliary verb is used to form a tense, e.g.

> *We* will be *going*   *You* have been *warned*

Auxiliary verbs are either MODAL VERBS or PRIMARY VERBS.

bare infinitive See INFINITIVE.

case The function of a noun, pronoun, etc. in a sentence, as reflected in its ending or some other aspect of its form. In English the chief cases are (i) the SUBJECTIVE (or nominative) case, in which the word functions as the subject of a verb or sentence, e.g.

> *The* house *was on fire*   I *watched him*

(ii) the OBJECTIVE (or accusative) case, in which the word functions as object, after a transitive verb or preposition, e.g.

> *Look* it *up in the book*   *He watched* me

and (iii) the POSSESSIVE (or genitive) case, in which the word shows possession or ownership, e.g.

> Jane's *umbrella is in* my *car*

Most English speakers now think of cases chiefly in connection with other, more inflected, languages such as Latin and German. In English, case-endings and case-forms have become restricted over many centuries to plurals and possessives of nouns (*books, children, boy's, girls'*, etc.) and to the pronouns (*I/me, who/whom, we/our, etc.*).

clause A group of words normally containing a FINITE VERB and its SUBJECT. A MAIN CLAUSE makes sense by itself and can constitute an entire sentence, e.g.

> *The train arrived at 6 o'clock*

A SUBORDINATE CLAUSE is one that qualifies a main clause, e.g.

> *The train arrived at 6 o'clock* when it was already dark

A clause can have the status of another part of speech; for example it can be an adverbial clause (as in the sentence just given), an adjectival or RELATIVE CLAUSE, e.g.

> The train which left London this morning *arrived at 6 o'clock*

or a noun clause, e.g.

> The train *arrived at* what we thought was 6 o'clock

collective noun A noun that is singular in form and denotes a number of individuals, for example *audience, choir, committee, flock, multitude.* Apart from the names of individual animals, birds, etc. (*deer, grouse, sheep, trout*) and names of institutions, firms, and teams (*BBC, Marks & Spencer, Tottenham Hotspur,* etc.), there are some 200 collective nouns in common use in English.

combining forms A word form that is only used in combination with other elements. The normal linking vowel is *-o* (e.g. *Anglo-, electro-*) or *-i* (*alti-, horti-*). Combining forms can also occur at the ends of words (e.g. *-imeter, -ology*).

common noun See NOUN.

comparative The form of an adjective or adverb expressing a higher degree of a quality, e.g. *braver, worse, more regularly.*

complement 1 A noun phrase or adjective phrase that follows a verb and has the same reference as the subject, e.g.

> I *am* his brother   She *looked* lovely

or the same reference as the object, e.g.

> He *called his mother* a fool

2 A noun phrase that is governed by a preposition, e.g.

> He put it *on* the table   She felt *over* the moon

complex preposition (or **compound preposition**) Two or more words together having the function of a preposition, e.g. *according to, apart from, in accordance with, with regard to.*

complex sentence A sentence which contains a MAIN CLAUSE and one or more SUBORDINATE CLAUSES.

compound noun Two or more words together having the function of a noun, e.g. *boy scout, forget-me-not, governor general.*

compound sentence A sentence which contains two or more MAIN CLAUSES joined by coordinating CONJUNCTIONS, e.g.

> First she went to Waterstones, *then* she visited the bank, *and* finally she had a coffee in Costa

Here the three clauses are of equal status and are joined by the coordinating conjunctions *then* and *and.*

compound subject A SUBJECT consisting of two or more noun phrases joined by *and*, e.g. *You and I, fish and chips, thunder and lightning.*

compound verb A verb formed by adding an AUXILIARY VERB to a full verb to express tense, aspect, or mood, e.g.

> We *shall go* tomorrow
>
> *Do* you *come* here often?

A tense formed in this way (in English, every tense except the simple past and simple present) is a **compound tense**.

concessive Denoting a clause or phrase introduced by a conjunction such as *although, but,* or *though,* or by a preposition such as *despite* or *in spite of,* which expresses a sense that is contrary to what is expected in the rest of the statement.

concord See AGREEMENT.

concrete noun See NOUN.

conditional 1 A clause or sentence which expresses a condition, typically one introduced by *if* or *unless.* **2** A MOOD of the verb used in the consequential clause of a conditional sentence, e.g.

> If he had come, I *should have seen* him

conjunct An ADVERBIAL which helps to relate one part of a text to another through a relationship of meaning, e.g.

> Peter and I had planned to go into business. When it came to the crunch, *however,* he lacked the necessary capital

Here the word *however* shows the relationship between the second sentence and the first; in this case, one of contrast. Conjuncts are often used to make the link between two paragraphs.

conjunction A word such as *and, because, but, for, if, or,* and *when* which is used to connect words, phrases, clauses, and sentences. **Coordinating conjunctions** join like with like, e.g.

> The room is large and bright
>
> You can come in but you cannot stay long
>
> Would you like tea or coffee?

Subordinating conjunctions join a subordinate clause to a main clause, e.g.

> I shan't go if you won't come with me
>
> I was late because I missed the train

Pairs of conjunctions such as *either…or* and *neither…nor* are called CORRELATIVE CONJUNCTIONS.

continuous (also called **progressive**) An ASPECT of a verb that expresses prolonged or continuous activity, e.g. *I am staying, they were going,* etc., as contrasted with the simple aspect *I stay, they went,* etc.

contraction The shortening or running together of words that is common in speech. In writing, it is often shown by the use of apostrophes, so that e.g. *I shall not* becomes *I shan't.*

coordination The linking of two or more parts of a COMPOUND SENTENCE that are equal in importance, normally by means of a coordinating CONJUNCTION, e.g.

> He sang and she played the piano

copular verb See LINKING VERB.

correlative conjunctions A pair of words used to link corresponding parts of a sentence, e.g. *both…and, either…or, not only…but also.* Correlatives that involve a subordinate clause include *hardly…when* and *if…then.*

countable nouns Nouns that refer in the singular to one and in the plural to more than one, e.g. *ship, crisis, attitude, lexicographer.* They can be qualified by *a, one, every,* etc. and *many, two, three,* etc. In all these respects they differ from MASS NOUNS.

dangling participle (also called **hanging** or **unattached participle**) A PARTICIPIAL CLAUSE that is not related to the subject of the main clause, e.g.

> Walking down the road, *my hat fell off*
>
> Educated privately, *his early works include several plays*

This is a common error in written English.

defining clause See RESTRICTIVE CLAUSE.

definite article See ARTICLE.

demonstrative A DETERMINER or PRONOUN used to indicate the particular thing or person referred to, e.g.

> That *carpet looks good there*
>
> Give me those *at once*

descriptive grammar The type of grammar which is based on the analysis of a body of carefully selected spoken and written texts and leads to a set of statements which describe how language actually works rather than how the writer thinks it should. It is commonly contrasted with PRESCRIPTIVE GRAMMAR.

determiner A word that goes before a noun and determines its status in some way, such as *a, the, this, all,* and *such.* A **predeterminer** occurs before another determiner (e.g. *all* in *all the time*) and a **postdeterminer** occurs after another determiner (e.g. *only* in *the only one*).

directive A clause or sentence expressing command, request, or exhortation, e.g.

> Give it to me, please
>
> Stop being ridiculous!

The verb is in the IMPERATIVE mood and the implied subject (*you*) is generally omitted.

direct object The noun or pronoun or phrase that is directly affected by the action of a transitive verb, e.g.

> They bought a new house

Here the phrase *a new house* is the direct object of the verb *bought.* Compare INDIRECT OBJECT.

distributive Denoting words that refer separately to each individual of a number or class. Distributive adjectives and pronouns are words such as *each, every, either, neither.* A distributive plural is one that corresponds to individuals separately rather than jointly, as in *The students wear gowns on formal occasions*, meaning that each student wears one gown.

ditransitive Denoting a verb that appears to have two objects, as in *He gave the baby a bottle* and *They envied him his good fortune*. It often involves the suppression of a preposition, as in the first example here (which means 'He gave a bottle *to* the baby'). See also INDIRECT OBJECT.

double negative A construction in which two negatives are used where standard English requires one, e.g.

I don't *know* nothing *about it*

double passive The construction in which a PASSIVE verb is followed by a passive infinitive, e.g.

The hostages are thought to have been killed

double subject A construction in which a noun subject is followed by a supporting pronoun, as in Longfellow's

The skipper he *stood beside the helm*

It is common in ballads and folk songs and in literary representations of working-class or rural speech.

ellipsis The omission from a sentence of words which are normally needed to complete the grammatical construction or meaning. It occurs most often in everyday speech, in expressions such as *Told you so* (meaning 'I told you so') and *Sounds fine to me* (meaning 'That sounds fine to me'), but also occurs regularly in written English.

ergative A type of verb of action or movement in which the object of the verb can become the subject of the same verb used intransitively (without an object), as in *They closed the door | The door closed*. There are many verbs of this type, including *change, close, cook, finish, move, open, shut, slide*.

feminine The gender to which words referring to female beings usually belong.

final clause A clause that states a purpose, especially when introduced by a formula such as *to, in order to, in order that, in the hope that*, etc.

He turned on the radio in order to hear the traffic controller

Clerks double-book their barristers in the hope that one of the cases will be settled before getting to court

finite verb A verb that agrees with a subject in person and number, e.g. *I am*, *They come*. A clause containing a finite verb is sometimes called a **finite clause**.

full verb Any ordinary verb that can stand on its own in a clause without an AUXILIARY VERB.

future The TENSE of a verb referring to an event yet to happen, e.g.

I shall go   She will arrive *tomorrow*

The tense known as **future in the past** refers to an event that was yet to happen at a time prior to the time of speaking, e.g.

He said he would come *later*

genitive See POSSESSIVE.

gerund (also called **verbal noun**) The form of a verb that ends in *-ing* and can be used like a noun, e.g.

Smoking *damages your health*

What is the use of my scolding *him?*

govern (of a verb or preposition) To determine the function of a noun or pronoun within a clause and therefore its CASE. The object or complement in a clause is said to be governed by the verb or preposition that (usually) precedes it.

gradable adjectives Adjectives that can vary in the intensity of their meaning, have COMPARATIVE and SUPERLATIVE forms, and can be qualified by adverbs such as *very, too, fairly*, etc. *Greedy, large, patient*, and *rich* are all gradable, whereas *dead, female, married*, and *rectangular* are NON-GRADABLE ADJECTIVES.

group possessive A construction in which the possessive ending *-'s* can be added to the last word of a noun phrase, e.g.

The dean of geography's office

Simon and Sharon's car

historic present The use of the present tense to describe events in the past. It is mainly used for dramatic effect, e.g.

Yesterday I'm walking *down the road and a man* comes *up to me...*

imperative The MOOD of a verb expressing command, e.g. *Come here!*; *Don't answer back!*

impersonal verb In English, a verb used in the third person singular with indefinite *it* as subject, e.g. *It is snowing; It seems to me that something has gone wrong.*

indefinite article See ARTICLE.

indefinite pronoun A PRONOUN that does not specify any person or thing in particular, e.g. *someone, anything, none.*

indicative The MOOD of a verb used to make ordinary statements rather than to form expressions of wish, commands, questions, etc. Compare SUBJUNCTIVE.

indirect object A person or thing named as the recipient of the DIRECT OBJECT of a transitive (or more strictly, DITRANSITIVE) verb, e.g.

I gave my sister *a book*

I gave him *a good talking-to*

infinitive The basic form of a verb that does not indicate a particular tense or number or person. There are two forms: the **to-infinitive**, used with preceding to, e.g. *I want to know*, and the **bare infinitive**, without preceding to, e.g. *Help me pack; I had better wait.*

inflection The process by which words change their form (by the addition of suffixes etc.) in accordance with their grammatical role. Inflection of nouns usually involves the addition of *-s* or *-es* to form plurals; of verbs, the addition of *-s* or *-es*, *-ed*, and *-ing* to express person, number, and tense; and of adjectives, the addition of *-er* and *-est* to form comparative and superlative forms.

intensifier A class of adverbs that amplify or add emphasis to a GRADABLE ADJECTIVE, e.g. *extremely, greatly, highly*, and *very*. Some adjectives are also classed as intensifiers, e.g. *complete (a complete fool)*, *single (not a single word)*, *sure (a sure sign)*, and *whole (a whole month)*.

interjection An exclamation or expletive that conveys emotion rather than any particular meaning, e.g. *um, oh!, shit!* It usually stands alone syntactically.

interrogative A word used to frame questions, such as *who?, whose?, what?, which?*, etc. An interrogative may function as a PRONOUN, a DETERMINER, an ADJECTIVE, or an ADVERB, e.g.

Who goes there?   How did you get on?

Which dress shall I wear?

intransitive Designating a verb that does not take a direct object, e.g.

I must think   The sun rose in the sky

Some verbs are always or predominantly intransitive (especially verbs of motion such as *arrive, come, go*, etc.), whereas others are sometimes TRANSITIVE and sometimes intransitive.

inversion The process by which the normal order of words, with the subject followed by the verb and then by the object or complement (if any), is broken. The two main types are when the subject is placed after the verb, as in questions, e.g.

Do you play football on Saturdays?

and when the complement (or part of it) is placed first in the sentence, often for emphasis, e.g.

On Saturdays we play football

irregular (of a verb or other word) Having INFLECTIONS that do not follow the usual pattern. Compare REGULAR.

linking verb (or **copular verb**) A verb, such as *be, become, feel, get*, etc., that links the subject and COMPLEMENT of a sentence, e.g.

He is a pilot   She felt rather annoyed

They look hungry

living Denoting a PREFIX or SUFFIX that can be freely used to create new words.

main clause The most important CLAUSE or clauses of a sentence. Unlike a SUBORDINATE CLAUSE, a main clause could stand alone as a grammatically complete short sentence with little or no alteration.

masculine The gender to which words referring to male beings usually belong.

mass noun A noun that refers to something that cannot be counted, such as a quality or indivisible substance. Mass nouns do not form a plural and are never qualified by *a*, *those*, *many*, *two*, *three*, etc. Examples include *luggage*, *oxygen*, *china*, *welfare*, *kudos*, etc. This type of noun is also called an **uncountable noun**. The term **mass noun** is sometimes extended to include things that can only be counted when the reference is to different units or types of the thing, e.g. *water* (*We stock several different mineral waters*) or *tea* (*I ordered two teas*). Compare COUNTABLE NOUN.

minor sentence A sentence without a FINITE VERB. Such utterances have a clear and complete meaning but they are grammatically incomplete, e.g. *No entry*; *Car park for customers only*.

modal verbs A class of AUXILIARY VERBS that are used to express the MOOD of other verbs. The principal verbs of this type are *can*, *could*, *may*, *might*, *must*, *ought*, *shall*, and *will*. These verbs behave in special ways, of which the most important are: (i) they can form questions and negatives without the use of *do*, and (ii) their third-person singular forms do not add *-s*. A group of other verbs that share some of these features, such as *dare* and *need*, are sometimes called **semi-modal verbs**.

modifier See ADJECTIVE.

mood The form of a verb that identifies utterances as being statements, expressions of wish, commands, questions, etc. In English, moods are expressed by means of an auxiliary verb (*can*, *may*, etc.) called a modal verb, or by the subjunctive mood.

morphology The study of the forms of words, especially of the regular patterns of INFLECTION etc. that may be observed in a language.

multiple sentence A sentence that consists of more than one CLAUSE. Multiple sentences can be categorized as either COMPOUND or COMPLEX SENTENCES.

nominal Denoting a phrase or clause that is used like a noun, e.g.

What you need *is a drink*

I *don't know* how she does it

nominative 1 Denoting a noun or pronoun that is the subject of a verb or sentence, e.g.

The house *stood on a hill*

I *walked up to the house*

2 Another name for the SUBJECTIVE case.

non-defining clause See RESTRICTIVE CLAUSE.

non-finite Designating a part of a verb not limited by person and number, e.g. the INFINITIVE, GERUND, or PARTICIPLE. Compare FINITE VERB.

non-gradable adjectives Adjectives that are not normally used in COMPARATIVE or SUPERLATIVE forms and cannot be qualified by adverbs such as *fairly*, *largely*, *more*, *rather*, or *very*. These are classifying adjectives such as *dead*, *rectangular*, *scientific*, or descriptive adjectives with a meaning that does not usually permit gradability, such as *equal*, *impossible*, *supreme*, *total*, *unique*.

non-restrictive clause See RESTRICTIVE CLAUSE.

noun A word that names a person, place, thing, or idea. **Common nouns** name persons or things which are not peculiar to one example, i.e. are of a general nature (*bridge*, *girl*, *sugar*, *unhappiness*), whereas **proper nouns** name persons or things of which there is only one example (*Asia*, *Dickens*). **Concrete nouns** refer to physical things (*bread*, *woman*), and **abstract nouns** to concepts (*greed*, *unhelpfulness*).

noun clause A CLAUSE which functions like a noun and forms the subject, object, or complement of a complex sentence, e.g.

What I want to know *is the answer to my first question*

You still haven't told me what I want to know

That is what I want to know

noun phrase A PHRASE based on a noun and functioning within the clause or sentence as a noun, e.g.

The one over there *is mine*

Mt Blanc is the highest mountain in Europe.

Noun phrases can form the subject, object, or complement of a clause.

number Denoting the status of words as singular or plural.

object A noun, pronoun, or noun phrase governed by an active transitive verb or preposition, e.g.

> *I will have* a coffee   *She asked for* me
>
> *I lost* what I treasured more than anything

See also DIRECT OBJECT; INDIRECT OBJECT.

objective The CASE of a pronoun typically used when the pronoun is the object of a verb or governed by a preposition, e.g.

> *She told* me *everything*
>
> *I walked ahead of* him

objective genitive A construction like *the boy's murder*, in which the genitive (possessive) form *boy's* denotes not possession (as in *the boy's dog*) but the object of the noun *murder*.

participial clause A subordinate clause in which a PARTICIPLE appears in place of a finite verb, e.g.

> Coming out of the meeting, *I felt suddenly tired*

participle The part of a verb used like an adjective in e.g. *working mothers* or *chopped liver* and to form certain compound tenses. There are two kinds of participle in English: the **present participle** ending in *-ing*, as in *We are going*, and the **past participle**, ending in *-d* or *-ed* for regular verbs, as in *Have you decided?*

parts of speech See WORD CLASSES.

passive The VOICE of a verb illustrated by the sentence:

> *Brazil were beaten by France in the final*

Here the logical object of the sentence (*Brazil*) has become the grammatical subject of a passive verb, and the logical subject (*France*) is expressed as an agent introduced by the preposition *by*.

Passive verbs are formed with *be* + the past participle. Other verbs are used to form so-called **semi-passives**, in which the past participle is at least partly adjectival, e.g. *He got changed*; *They seem bothered*. Compare ACTIVE.

past Any TENSE of a verb expressing past action or state, e.g.

> *I arrived yesterday.*

past participle See PARTICIPLE.

past perfect A TENSE expressing action already completed prior to the time being spoken or written about, e.g.

> *I had arrived by then*

In English it is formed with *had* + the past participle.

perfect A TENSE expressing completed action or action viewed in relation to the present. In English it is formed with *have* + the past participle, e.g.

> *I have finished now*

perfect infinitive The construction *to have been, to have said*, etc., used to refer to an earlier time than that described by the main verb in a clause. It occurs most commonly after the verbs *appear* and *seem*, e.g.

> *She appeared* to have encouraged *him*
>
> *It seems* to have been *an isolated incident*

person One of the three classes of PERSONAL PRONOUNS or verb-forms, denoting the person speaking (**first person**), the person spoken to (**second person**), and the person or thing spoken about (**third person**).

personal pronouns The pronouns *I, we, he, she, it, we, you*, used to refer back to a definite person or thing and to express differences of person, number, and gender. They are also inflected to show CASE, having the objective forms *me, us, him, her, it, them, you*.

phrasal verb A combination of verb + adverb or preposition (or both), such as *come about, draw up, put up with*, and *work out*. Phrasal verbs have meanings that cannot be directly deduced from the individual words, and in some cases they have several meanings, e.g.

> *She* ran up *the road*   *She* ran up *the flag*
>
> *She* ran up *huge debts*

phrase A group of words which forms a part of a clause, but which, unlike a clause, does not contain a FINITE VERB. Phrases can be classed as noun, verb, adjective, adverb, or prepositional phrases, according to their function within the clause.

plural Denoting more than one.

possessive The CASE of a noun or a pronoun indicating possession, e.g.

> Britain's *oldest man*
>
> *The* Johnsons' *house*
>
> Theirs *not to reason why*

The **possessive pronouns** are *my, your, his/hers/its, our, their*; the forms *mine, yours, ours,* and *theirs* are used predicatively (i.e. after a verb).

postdeterminer See DETERMINER.

predeterminer See DETERMINER.

predicate The part of a clause consisting of what is said of the SUBJECT, including verb + complement or object.

predicative Designating a word, normally an adjective, that occurs in the PREDICATE of a clause, e.g.

> *The dog is* old   *She seems* unhappy

Compare ATTRIBUTIVE.

prefix A word or element added at the beginning of another word to adjust or qualify its meaning, e.g. *ex-* (*ex-husband*), *non-* (*non-smoking*), and *super-* (*supermodel*). Compare SUFFIX.

preposition A word such as *after, in, to,* and *with,* which usually precedes a noun or pronoun and establishes its relation to what goes before, e.g.

> *The man* on *the platform*
>
> *She came* after *dinner*
>
> *What did you do that* for?

prepositional phrase A PHRASE consisting of a preposition and its complement, e.g.

> *I am surprised* at *your reaction*
>
> *She vanished* behind *the green baize door*

prescriptive grammar Grammar which sets out rules about how language should be used, rather than simply describing how it is used. Compare DESCRIPTIVE GRAMMAR.

present A TENSE of a verb expressing action now going on or habitually performed in past and future, e.g.

> *The door is* open   *He commutes* daily

present participle See PARTICIPLE.

primary verbs The three essential English verbs *be, have,* and *do.* They can be used as FULL VERBS in their own right and as AUXILIARY VERBS to form various COMPOUND VERBS, e.g.

> *I* am *going to work*
>
> *We* have *seen it all before*
>
> *She* did *visit regularly but no longer does*

progressive See CONTINUOUS.

pronoun A word used instead of a noun or noun phrase that has already been mentioned or is known, especially in order to avoid repetition, e.g.

> *We invited the Jones family to our party because we like* them
>
> *When Jane saw what had happened* she *laughed*

Pronouns include the PERSONAL PRONOUNS (*I, you, he,* etc.); the POSSESSIVE pronouns (*my, your, his,* etc.); the REFLEXIVE PRONOUNS (*myself, yourself,* etc.); the DEMONSTRATIVE pronouns (*this, that, these, those*); the RELATIVE PRONOUNS (*that, which, who,* etc.); the INTERROGATIVE pronouns (*what?, which?, who?,* etc.); the INDEFINITE PRONOUNS (*all, any, both,* etc.); and the so-called extended pronouns (*whatever, whoever, each other, one another,* etc.).

proper noun See NOUN.

qualify (of an adjective or adverb) To attribute some quality to a noun, adjective, or verb.

quantifier A DETERMINER or PRONOUN used to indicate quantity, e.g.

> *She ate* all *the cake*   *I ate* some *too*

reflexive pronouns The PRONOUNS *myself, herself, ourselves,* etc., which are chiefly used when the subject of the verb and the object are the same person or thing, e.g.

> *We enjoyed* ourselves *very much*
>
> *Make* yourself *at home*

regular (of a verb or other word) Having INFLECTIONS that follow the usual pattern. Compare IRREGULAR.

relative clause A clause used to qualify a noun, pronoun, or noun phrase earlier in the sentence; it is usually connected to the main clause by means of a RELATIVE PRONOUN (*who, which, whose,* or *that*). For the two types of relative clause, see RESTRICTIVE CLAUSE.

relative pronouns The pronouns *that, which, who(m), whose,* which link a RELATIVE CLAUSE to a main clause by referring back to a noun phrase (the ANTECEDENT) in the main clause.

restrictive clause (or **defining clause**) A RELATIVE CLAUSE that gives essential information about the noun or noun phrase that comes before, e.g.

She held out the hand *that was hurt*

Here *the hand* is defined or identified as 'the one that was hurt'. By contrast, in

She held out her hand, *which I clasped in both of mine*

the information in the relative clause could be left out without affecting the core meaning of the sentence; this is called a **non-restrictive** (or **nondefining**) **clause**.

semi-modal verbs See MODAL VERBS.

semi-passives See PASSIVE.

sentence adverb An adverb that qualifies or comments on the whole sentence, not one of the elements in it, e.g.

Unfortunately, he missed his train

Frankly, I don't care

Adverbs that have this special role include *actually, basically, clearly, normally,* and *regrettably.*

simple sentence A sentence consisting of a single CLAUSE containing one subject and one verb.

simple tense A TENSE formed without an AUXILIARY VERB, e.g. *He drank* as opposed to *He was drinking.* In English there are two simple tenses, the **simple past** (*I went, He was, We had*) and the **simple present** (*I go, He is, We have*). See also COMPOUND VERB.

singular Denoting a single person or thing.

split infinitive The separation of *to* from the INFINITIVE by an intervening word or words (normally an adverb), e.g.

I had come *to really love him*

It is traditionally regarded as an error, but is often unavoidable or better than the available alternatives.

stem The essential part of a word to which inflections and other suffixes are added, e.g.

unlimited eaten

subject The element in a clause (usually a noun or its equivalent) about which something is stated. Compare PREDICATE.

subjective The CASE of a pronoun typically used when the pronoun is the subject of a clause, e.g.

She loves to go out dancing

You are as tall as *I*

subjunctive The MOOD of a verb used to express what is imagined, wished, demanded, proposed, and so on, rather than what is real. In modern English it is distinguishable from the ordinary INDICATIVE mood only in the third person singular present tense, and in the forms *be* and *were* of the verb *to be.*

subordinate clause A clause dependent on the MAIN CLAUSE and functioning like a noun, adjective, or adverb within the sentence, e.g.

He said *that you had gone*

As I was going that way, *I gave her a lift*

subordinating conjunction See CONJUNCTION.

substitute verb The verb *do* used in place of another verb, e.g.

He likes chocolate—*Does he?*

suffix A word or element added at the end of another word to adjust or qualify its meaning, such as *-ation* (*confirmation, privatization*), *-ing* (*driving, soldiering*), and *-itis* (*appendicitis*). Compare PREFIX.

superlative The form of an ADJECTIVE or adverb expressing the highest or a very high degree of a quality, e.g. *bravest, worst, most interesting.* See COMPARATIVE.

syntax The set of rules that describes how words and phrases in a language are arranged to make grammatical sentences.

tag question A question added at the end of a statement and acting as a reinforcer rather than seeking an answer, e.g.

You will do this for me, won't you?

She hasn't been to America, has she?

In each case the verb in the main statement has been changed into an equivalent question; if the statement is positive the tag is negative, and vice versa.

tense The location in time of the state or action expressed by a verb. In the strictest sense of the word, English verbs have only two tenses, the SIMPLE PRESENT (*I am*) and SIMPLE PAST (*I was*). However, the verb phrase can take a variety of other forms to show time. The FUTURE is formed with *shall* or *will* and other ASPECTS are formed with auxiliary verbs (*I have been, I was being,* etc.). See also COMPOUND TENSE.

to-infinitive See INFINITIVE.

transitive Designating a verb that takes a DIRECT OBJECT, e.g.

I said nothing

Michael gave her a strange look

Some verbs are always or predominantly transitive, (e.g. *assure, bury, deny, put*), whereas others are sometimes transitive and sometimes INTRANSITIVE. See also DITRANSITIVE.

uncountable noun See MASS NOUN.

unreal condition In a CONDITIONAL sentence, a condition which will not be or has not been fulfilled, e.g. *If I were prime minister.* It is sometimes expressed by the SUBJUNCTIVE MOOD.

verb A word or phrase that describes the action or state which the sentence seeks to convey, e.g.

She locked *the door*   *He* was *very angry*

The water had risen *alarmingly*

A verb is normally an essential element in a clause or sentence. See also INTRANSITIVE; TRANSITIVE.

verbal noun See GERUND.

verb phrase A PHRASE that functions as a verb in a clause or sentence; it may be a single FULL VERB or a COMPOUND VERB containing one or more AUXILIARY VERBS.

voice A category of the verb that expresses whether the subject of a clause is the agent or the recipient of the action described. See ACTIVE; PASSIVE.

wh-question word A convenient term for the INTERROGATIVE and RELATIVE PRONOUNS, most beginning with *wh-*: *what, when, where, whether, which, who, whom, whose, why, how.*

word classes The traditional word classes (also called **parts of speech**) that have been in use for English since the 16th century are NOUN, VERB, ADJECTIVE, ADVERB, PRONOUN, PREPOSITION, CONJUNCTION, and INTERJECTION. These categories were taken over from those used to describe Latin grammar and often barely suit the word functions and sentence structure of English. For general purposes, however, the traditional names remain in use despite their inadequacies, and they are used in this book rather than the more specialized terms that have been adopted in modern linguistics.

Section 2: Spelling

For complex historical reasons, English has evolved a system of spelling that is notorious for its multiple irregularities. As a result, many educated professional people in the English-speaking world have little confidence in their ability to spell and cling ever more desperately to the false security offered by the computer spellcheck. Like SECTION 1: GRAMMAR, this Section approaches a subject that many people find rather daunting from three directions at once:

PART I offers a brief INTRODUCTION TO SPELLING. This sets out and accounts for some of the difficulties of English spelling and goes on to suggest a general strategy for coping with them, based on the recognition of patterns and an awareness of certain rules. PART II follows with a detailed presentation of the most important RULES OF SPELLING AND WORD FORMATION. These address the systematic problems that arise with words of certain kinds (e.g. adjectives ending in -y or -ey, such as **bony** or **gluey**) and in the inflection of words (e.g. the -ed and -ing forms of verbs such as **benefit** or **unravel**). The numerous exceptions to the rules are also noted.

Although the rules are one important key to better spelling, many English words give rise to particular difficulties of their own, not covered by these or any other guidelines. Examples include the spelling of **embarrass** with two rs but **harass** with one, and **millionaire** with one n and **questionnaire** with two. Troublemakers of this kind figure prominently in the list of DIFFICULT SPELLINGS that makes up PART III.

To add to the confusion, English is remarkable for the number of words that can have more than one correct spelling. This latitude is something of a mixed blessing, because it works in unpredictable ways: **accessary/accessory** and **judgement/judgment** are all permitted spellings, for example, whereas **accomodation** is not a permitted variant of **accommodation** nor **millenium** of **millennium**. Although the following pages are chiefly concerned with distinguishing correct from from incorrect spellings, preferences between permitted variants are also stated in many cases.
Recommendations of this kind are made only where current usage shows a clear bias and there is marked agreement among the best modern authorities. In the absence of such a consensus, no attempt has been made to impose Oxford University Press house style (or any other).

PART I: AN INTRODUCTION TO SPELLING

Why *is* English spelling so much of a problem for so many people? There are two answers to this question. The first is that actually it is not as much of a problem as many people think. Wrong spelling rarely leads to mistakes of understanding; much more frequently it just annoys sticklers for accuracy. This is not, however, to justify a deliberate policy of letting things slip. It is much easier for everyone if we all spell words in the same way.

The second answer is a matter of linguistic history. Unlike Italian and other so-called 'phonetically spelt' languages, English cannot easily have a direct correspondence between sounds and letters. There are over 40 sounds in English, far more than in Italian, and we only have the same 26 letters in the alphabet. So we have to combine letters in different ways to represent the 'missing' sounds. To do this we rely on a series of conventions. These developed over a period of history during which the vocabulary of English and its pronunciation were both also developing. Words came into English from many other languages and many retained their original spelling but changed their pronunciation. Other imports came from languages with a different writing system and were written down by travellers and merchants in the best way they could.

In all this richness of vocabulary and linguistic vitality there has never been a consistent attempt to reform the whole spelling system and, given the worldwide status of English, probably never will be.

So we are stuck with a spelling system that is far from ideal and the best we can do is to devise workable strategies to help us spell better. There is no doubt that some people find spelling much easier than others. But even so it *is* possible for even the worst speller to make big strides towards much greater accuracy. There are ways of getting a grip on spelling generally and there are specific rules that can be learned.

Looking for Patterns

The key to a generally more positive approach to spelling is to look constantly for **patterns**. There are two kinds of pattern which are helpful:

- patterns of sound/letter relationship
- patterns of letter/letter relationship

Sound/letter patterns

At first sight looking for correspondences between the sounds and letters of English seems a daunting task. The first sound in the name *George* can be spelt in eight different ways:

> *j* as in *jug*
>
> *g* as in *gesture*
>
> *dg* as in *judge*
>
> *gg* as in *suggest*
>
> *dj* as in *adjust*
>
> *de* as in *grandeur*
>
> *di* as in *soldier*
>
> *ch* as in *sandwich* (as pronounced by some speakers)

Vowels cause even more difficulty. The vowel in *me* is commonly spelt in seven different ways:

> *e* as in *me*
>
> *ee* as in *beet*
>
> *ea* as in *beat*
>
> *ie* as in *fief*
>
> *ei* as in *receive*
>
> *ey* as in *key*
>
> *i* as in *routine*

In addition it occurs in these words:

> *quay*   *people*

Leaving the latter two 'exceptions' on one side, however, it is easy to see patterns of sound/letter correspondence:

beet	*beat*	*fief*
feed	heap	thief
feet	leap	piece
feel	real	field
peep	heal	siege
etc.	etc.	etc.

When children are taught to read by sounding letters (the **phonic method**), this is how they are taught. *The cat sat on the mat* follows just such an approach.

Letter/letter patterns

The other broad approach to teaching children to read is often called **look-and-say**. This works on the belief that the human brain looks for visual (and other) patterns and that when children are learning to read they often perceive a whole word as a pattern. This accounts for the fact that very early on in the process children will learn to recognize quite long words, provided they have a clearly distinguishable visual pattern, with ascenders and descenders (bits of letters that stick up or down), like *elephant* or *aeroplane*.

As we learn to read we also take on board the combinations of letters that are typical of English. For example, given a small amount of time, most people could think of words that contained these letter combinations:

    -igh-   *-ugh-*

It is much more difficult to think of words that contain the combination *-egh-*. There are some, but they are fairly obscure.

The other way in which we habitually use patterning is in the recognition of word stems, prefixes, and suffixes: once you understand and can spell *psychology* you should not have too much trouble spelling the first part of psych*iatry* and psycho-*analysis* or the endings of *geology* and *histology*.

Finally, and most important, write it down. If you wish to remember a visual pattern it is important that you should see it. When you are trying to learn a spelling that causes problems, a well-known method is **look—cover—write—check**:

- **Look** at the correct spelling on the printed page so that you 'print' it on your brain. Spell the word out loud.

- **Cover** it up.

- **Write** it down from memory, spelling it out loud as you do so.

- **Check** against the printed version that you have got it right.

With a problem word this process should be repeated at increasing intervals until you are confident that it is fixed in your mind. Also, when in doubt about a spelling it is always worth trying to write down its various possible forms on scrap paper to see which looks right.

Rules Based on Patterns

Spelling patterns and the rules that describe them fall into two broad categories:

- those that cover the spelling of certain **sounds** which can be written in two or three different ways

- those that explain how adding to a word changes the spelling of the original stem (rules of **word formation**)

An example of the first type is the most famous spelling rule:

    i before *e* except after *c*, when the sound is long 'ee'

This rule works because it is easy to remember, has very few exceptions, and only causes trouble when people forget the second half of it.

Another example is the rule '*c* noun, *s* verb', which lets you know whether to write

practice	or	*practise*
prophecy	or	*prophesy*

in a particular context.

The rule is easily remembered because the initial letters are in alphabetical order: *C-N-S-V.*

A somewhat different example is the linguistic knowledge that can help you choose correctly between the suffixes *-able* and *-ible* in forming words like *acceptable* and *ac-*

cessible. Here the key is knowing that *-ible* is reserved for words borrowed from Latin and that the list of 180 or so words spelt in this way is now 'closed'—no new words spelt in this way are being created. Words derived from Old English words and all new words (e.g. *networkable*, *unclubbable*, *windsurfable*) are spelt *-able*.

A quick check, which works most of the time, is that if you remove *-able* from a word, you are usually still left with a complete word. If you do the same with *-ible*, generally you are not.

These examples, and many others, are dealt with in much greater detail in PART II: RULES OF SPELLING AND WORD FORMATION.

The other group of rules or patterns covers how we spell words when we add bits to them. These rules are generally quite complicated and cannot usually be reduced to simple mnemonic form. For example, the comparative and superlative forms of many adjectives are formed by adding the suffixes *-er* and *-est*:

> great   greater   greatest

The suffixes are normally added without further change, but there are four groups of exceptions:

(i) Words that end in a consonant followed by *-y*, change the *-y* to an *-i* before adding the suffix:

> happier   happiest

(ii) Words with one syllable which contain a long vowel sound and which end with *-e* (e.g., *late*); remove the *-e before adding the suffix*:

> later   latest

(iii) Words of one syllable containing a short vowel sound and ending in a single consonant letter (e.g., *sad*); double the final consonant before adding the suffix:

> sadder   saddest

(iv) Words ending in *-l* normally just add the suffix, but there is one exception:

> cruel   crueller   cruellest

For many other useful rules of this kind, see PART II.

Developing a personal strategy

If you wish to develop a positive strategy based on rules and patterns, you need to begin by analysing the nature of the mistakes you make. It is then necessary to attach your problem words to words that you *can* spell.

A typical problem area is the double or single letters that occur in words like *accommodation*, *imitate*, and *professional*. You could try to learn the whole list of problem words by heart. An approach more likely to succeed, however, is to group the words according to a series of patterns and thus relate problem words to others that have the same pattern:

No double letters

fulfil	*imitate*	*marvel*	*omit*
patrol	*pedal*	*transmit*	

One pair of double letters

abbreviate	*accelerate*	*accident*
accomplish	*accurate*	*allergy*
appropriate	*approximate*	*assist*
beginning	*brilliant*	*caterpillar*
collapse	*collect*	*commemorate*
commit	*corridor*	*desiccated*
disappear	*disappoint*	*dissatisfied*
discuss	*exaggerate*	*excellent*
gorilla	*hallelujah*	*happen*
harass	*illustrate*	*immediate*
millionaire	*necessary*	*occasion*
occur	*paraffin*	*parallel*
proceed	*procession*	*professional*
questionnaire	*scissors*	*sheriff*
succeed	*sufficient*	*terrible*
tomorrow	*tranquillity*	

Two pairs of double letters

accommodation	*accidentally*	*address*
commission	*committed*	*embarrass*
guerrilla	*happiness*	*mattress*
millennium	*possess*	*successful*
unnecessary	*woollen*	

You could develop a similar approach to problems of sound/letter correspondence and word formation based on the rules set out in PART II (some of which have already been alluded to).

Finally, some words just cause problems which cannot be solved by learning rules. The only thing to do is to learn them by heart. Words of this kind are listed (with brief comments) in PART III: DIFFICULT SPELLINGS.

A Note on Computer Spellchecks

But surely, some readers will object, the advent of the computer spellcheck makes all this learning of patterns, rules, and exceptions quite obsolete—an optional diversion for those who find such matters interesting? Unfortunately not. The computer spellcheck is really just that—a useful check: it cannot guarantee accurate spelling, only inform you that certain words you have written do not appear in its dictionary and suggest plausible alternatives.

Reliance on this facility has two main drawbacks. One is that any unfamiliar words—scientific or technical terms, proper names, abbreviations not in general use—will register as errors and throw up alternative suggestions (often deeply absurd). This is not usually very harmful but can be a nuisance for someone writing on technical subjects or in some other specialized field. It is usually possible to augment the spellcheck dictionary to include any other terms that you require. The second drawback is much more serious. This is that the computer will fail to recognize a genuine error, however ridiculous or damaging, if it corresponds to the correct spelling of a different word. So, for instance, if I wrote:

> The computer spellcheck is a handy tool but should not be used as a crotch (meaning crutch)

the error would pass undetected. It should also be pointed out that many spellchecks will automatically operate on the basis of American (rather than British) spelling unless they are altered accordingly.

PART II: RULES OF SPELLING AND WORD FORMATION

The following pages provide ground rules for spelling English words and word elements, including inflected forms, compound forms, and forms created by adding prefixes and suffixes. Little space has been given to meaning or use.

Some notes are added where the conventions of American spelling differ: these are indicated by a bullet •. Cross-references are indicated by the use of SMALL CAPITALS.

-able, -ible

Adjectives ending in *-able* generally owe their form to the Latin termination *-abilis* or the Old French *-able* (or both), and words in *-ible* to the Latin *-ibilis*. The suffix *-able* is also added to words of distinctly French or English origin, and as a living element to English roots. Nouns ending in *-ability, -ibility* undergo the same changes.

(A) Words ending in **-able**. The following alterations are made to the stem:

(i) Silent *-e* is dropped, e.g. *adorable, imaginable*.

Exceptions: words whose stem ends in *-ce, -ee,   -ge, -le*, and the following:

blameable	rateable*
dyeable	ropeable*
giveable	saleable
(but *forgivable*)	shareable*
hireable	sizeable*
holeable	tameable*
likeable*	tuneable*
liveable	unshakeable*
nameable	

Although these are the preferred spellings in current use, the words marked * can also be spelt without the *-e-*.

• American spelling tends to omit *-e-* in all the words above.

(ii) Final *-y* becomes *-i-*, e.g. *deniable* (see -Y TO -I AT END).

Exception: *flyable*.

(iii) A final consonant may be doubled, e.g. *clubbable*.

Exceptions:

inferable	referable
preferable	transferable
(but *conferrable*)	

(iv) Most verbs of more than two syllables ending in *-ate* drop this ending when forming adjectives in *-able*, e.g. *alienable, calculable, demonstrable*, etc. Verbs of two syllables ending in *-ate* form adjectives in *-able* regularly, e.g. *creatable, debatable, dictatable*, etc.

(B) Words ending in **-ible.** These are fewer, since *-ible* is not a living suffix (i.e. it cannot be freely used to form new words). Below is a list of the commonest. Almost all form their negative in *in-, il-*, etc.; the exceptions are indicated by (*un*).

accessible	fusible
adducible	gullible
admissible	incorrigible
audible	indelible
avertible	(un)intelligible
collapsible	irascible
combustible	legible
compatible	negligible
comprehensible	ostensible
contemptible	perceptible
convertible	perfectible
corruptible	permissible
credible	persuasible
defensible	plausible
destructible	possible

digestible reducible
dirigible reprehensible
discernible repressible
divisible reproducible
edible resistible
exhaustible responsible
expressible reversible
extensible risible
fallible sensible
(un)feasible (un)susceptible
flexible tangible
forcible visible

ae, oe

In words derived from Latin and Greek, these are now always written as separate letters, not as the ligatures æ, œ, e.g. *aeon, gynaecology; amoeba, Oedipus*. The simple *e* is preferable in several words once commonly spelt with *ae* or *oe*, especially *medieval* and *ecology, ecumenical*.

• In American spelling, *e* replaces *ae, oe* in many other words, e.g. *gynecology, diarrhea*.

-ant / -ent

-ant is the noun ending, -ent the adjective ending in the following:

dependant dependent
descendant descendent
pendant pendent
propellant propellent

The spelling *dependent* (noun) was formerly American only but is now accepted in British English. *Independent* is both adjective and noun; *dependence, independence* are the abstract nouns.

The following are correct spellings:

ascendant, -nce, -ncy relevant, -nce
attendant, -nce repellent
expellent superintendent, -ncy
impellent tendency
intendent, -ncy transcendent, -nce

-ative / -ive

Correct are:

(i) authoritative qualitative
exploitative quantitative
interpretative

(ii) absorptive preventive
assertive supportive

The forms *exploitive, interpretive* (which has a special computing meaning), and *preventative* also occur.

-c at end to -ck

Words ending in -c interpose k before suffixes which would otherwise indicate a soft c, chiefly -ed, -er, -ing, -y, e.g.

bivouacker, -ing panicky
colicky picnicked, -er, -ing
frolicked, -ing plasticky
mimicked, -ing trafficked, -ing

Exceptions: *arced, -ing, zinced, zincify, zincing*.

Before -ism, -ist, and -ize, c remains and is pronounced soft, e.g. *Anglicism, physicist, domesticity, italicize*.

-ce / -se

Advice, device, licence, and *practice* are nouns; the related verbs are spelt with -se: *advise, devise, license, practise*. Similarly *prophecy* (noun), *prophesy* (verb).

• American spelling favours *licence, practice* for both noun and verb; but the nouns *defence, offence, pretence* are spelt with c in British, s in American English.

-cede / -ceed

Exceed, proceed, succeed are correct; the other verbs similarly formed have -cede, e.g. *concede, intercede, recede*.

Note also *supersede*.

doubling of final consonant

(A) Before certain suffixes beginning with a vowel, the final consonant of the stem word is doubled:

if the preceding vowel is written with a single letter (or single letter preceded by *qu*), and

if that vowel bears the main stress (hence all monosyllables are included)

So *bed*, *bedding* but *head*, *heading*; *occúr*, *occúrred* but *óffer*, *óffered*; *befit*, *befitted* but (preferably) *bénefit*, *bénefited*.

Suffixes which cause this doubling include:

(i) The verb inflections *-ed*, *-ing*, e.g.

begged, *begging*   *revved*, *revving*

bussed, *bussing*   *trekked*, *trekking*

(ii) The suffixes *-able*, *-age*, *-en*, *-er*, *-ery*, *-est*, *-ish*, *-y*, e.g.

clubbable	*waggery*
tonnage	*saddest*
sadden	*priggish*
trapper	*shrubby*

(B) Words of more than one syllable, not stressed on the last syllable, do not double the final consonant, unless it is *l*, when a suffix beginning with a vowel is added, e.g.

biased	*gossipy*	*turbaned*
blossoming	*lettered*	*wainscoted*
faceted	*pilotage*	*wickedest*
focusing	*targeted*	*womanish*

Exception: *worship* makes *worshipped*, *-ing*. The forms *biassed*, *focussing*, *turbanned*, and *wainscotted* are also acceptable.

Note that some other words in which the final syllable has a full vowel (not obscure *e* or *i*) also double this consonant, e.g.

format	*horsewhip*	*leap-frog*
handicap	*humbug*	*sandbag*
hobnob	*kidnap*	*zigzag*

• American spelling sometimes has *kidnaped*, *kidnaping*, *worshiped*, *worshiping*.

(C) Consonants that are never doubled are *c*, *h*, *w*, *x*, *y*.

(D) When endings beginning with a vowel are added, *l* is *always* doubled after a single vowel wherever the stress falls, e.g.

controllable	*flannelled*
jeweller	*panelling*

Note also *woollen*, *woolly*.

Exceptions: *parallel* makes *paralleled*, *-ing*; *devil* makes *devilish*.

• In American spelling *l* obeys the same rules as the other consonants (except *c*, *h*, *w*, *x*, *y*), e.g. *traveler*, but *pally*.

Note also American *woolen* (but *woolly*).

(E) A silent final consonant is not doubled. Endings are added as if the consonant were pronounced, e.g.

crocheted, *-ing*	*rendezvouses*
pince-nezed	(third person singular)
precised	*rendezvousing*

dropping of silent -e

(A) When a suffix beginning with a vowel (including *-y*) is added to a word ending in silent *-e* (including *e* following another vowel), the *-e* is dropped; e.g.

braver, *bravery*	*hoed*
dyed, *dyer*	*issued*
freer, *freest*	*manoeuvred*
adorable	*imaginable*
analysable	*manoeuvrable*
bribable	*usable* (preferred)
cleavage	*dotage*
centring	*housing*
gluing	*queuing* (preferred)
whitish	*mousy* (preferred)

Exceptions:

(i) Words ending in *-ce* and *-ge* retain the *e* to indicate the softness of the consonant, e.g. *bridgeable*.

(ii) In a number of *-able* adjectives, *e* is retained. See -ABLE/-IBLE.

(iii) The few *-able* adjectives formed on verbs ending in consonant + *-le*; e.g. *handleable*.

(iv) *acreage*, *mileage*.

(v) Unless the suffix begins with *e*, final *ee*, *oe*, and *ye* remain, e.g.

agreeing	dyeing	hoeing
canoeing	eyeing	shoeing

(vi) *blueing, cueing*.

(vii) *routeing, singeing, swingeing* are distinguished from *routing* ('putting to flight'), *singing*, and *swinging*.

(viii) *moreish, ogreish* (preferred).

(ix) See -Y/-EY, ADJECTIVES ENDING IN. Both *stagy* and *stagey* are acceptable.

For change of *ie* to *y* in *dying, lying*, etc., see -IE AT END TO -Y.

(B) When a suffix beginning with a consonant is added to a word ending in silent *-e*, the *-e* is retained, e.g.

awesome	houseful
definitely	whiteness

Exceptions: *argument, awful, duly, eerily, eeriness, fledgling* (preferred), *truly, wholly*.

• In American spelling *e* is dropped after *dg* and before a suffix beginning with a consonant, e.g. *abridgment, acknowledgment, judgment*, In British English the spellings with *-e-* are all preferred (but *judgment* is often used in legal works).

• Final silent *-e* is often omitted in American spelling, and so is final silent *-ue* in the endings *-gogue, -logue*, e.g.

ax	adz	program
analog	epilog	pedagog

-efy/-ify

The chief words with *-efy* (*-efied, -efication*, etc.) are:

liquefy	rubefy	tumefy
putrefy	stupefy	
rarefy	torrefy	

All the others have *-ify* etc. See also -IFIED/ -YFIED.

ei/ie

(A) The rule '*i* before *e* except after *c*' holds good for nearly all words in which the vowel-sound is long 'ee':

Aries	hygienic	yield

but

ceiling	deceit	receive

(B) The following words which are, or can be, pronounced with the 'ee'-sound are exceptions:

caffeine	Madeira	seize
casein	neither	seizure
codeine	peripeteia	specie
counterfeit	plebeian	species
either	prima facie	superficies
heinous	protein	weir
inveigle	seise	weird

Note also *forfeit, surfeit*, and many proper names, e.g. *Keith, Leith, Neil, Reid, Sheila*.

-er/-est

For changes to the stem required by these suffixes of comparison, see DOUBLING OF FINAL CONSONANT; DROPPING OF SILENT -E; Y TO I.

-erous/-rous

The ending *-erous* is normal in adjectives related to nouns ending in *-er*, e.g. *murderous, slanderous, thunderous*. The exceptions are:

ambidextrous	leprous	slumbrous
cumbrous	meandrous	wondrous
disastrous	monstrous	

-f at end to -v

Certain nouns that end in *f* (or *f* followed by silent *e*) change this to *v* (or *-ve*) in some derivatives. Most are familiar, but in a few cases there is variation or uncertainty:

beef: plural *beeves* 'oxen', but *beefs* 'kinds of beef'

calf (young animal): *calfish* 'calflike'; *calves-foot jelly*

calf (of leg): (*enormously*) *calved* 'having (enormous) calves'

corf (basket): plural *corves*

dwarf: plural usually *dwarfs* but *dwarves* is increasingly found

elf: *elfish* and *elvish* are both acceptable; *elfin* (figure etc.) but

sometimes *elven* in fantasy
writings

handkerchief: plural *handkerchiefs*

hoof: plural usually *hooves* but the
historic form *hoofs* is also
common; adjective *hoofed* or
hooved

knife: verb *knife*

leaf: *leaved* 'having leaves' (*broad-
leaved* etc.) but *leafed* as past of *leaf*
(*through a book* etc.)

life: *lifelong* 'lasting a lifetime' but
livelong (*day* etc.); the plural of *still
life* is *still lifes*

oaf: plural *oafs*

roof: plural *roofs*; *rooves* is commonly
heard but should be avoided in
writing

scarf (garment): plural *scarves*; *scarfed*
'wearing a scarf'

scarf (joint of timber etc.): plural and
verb keep *f*

sheaf: plural *sheaves*; verb *sheaf* or
sheave; *sheaved* 'made into a sheaf'

shelf: plural *shelves*; *shelvy* (of seas,
lakes, etc.) 'having sandbanks'

staff: plural *staffs* but archaic and
musical *staves*

turf: plural *turfs* or *turves*; verb *turf*;
turfy

wharf: plural *wharves* or *wharfs*

wolf: *wolfish* 'of or like a wolf'

final vowels before suffixes

(A) For treatment of final *-e* and *-y* before
suffixes see DROPPING OF SILENT -E; -Y AT END
TO -I.

(B) For treatment of final *-o* before *-s* (suffix), see PLURAL FORMATION; -S.

(C) In nearly all other cases, the final vowels *-a*, *-i*, *-o*, and *-u* are unaffected by suffixes
and do not affect them:

skier	*vetoer*
cameras	*(he) rumbas*
corgis	*(she) skis*
emus	*taxis*

echoing	*skiing*
radioing	*taxiing*
baaed	*radioed*
concertinaed	*subpoenaed*
echoed	*taxied*
mascaraed	*tiaraed*
mustachioed	

The *-ed* spelling is preferable for this last
group, but a *-'d* spelling is often acceptable,
especially after the letter *a*, e.g. *rumba'd*,
idea'd.

(D) Final *-é* in words taken from French is retained before all suffixes; the *e* of *-ed* is
dropped after it, e.g.

appliquéd	*chasséing*
attachés	*émigrés*
canapés	*soufflés*

for- / *fore-*

The prefix *for-* means 'away, out, completely', or implies prohibition or absten-
tion. *Fore-* means 'beforehand, in front'.

Note especially:

forbear 'refrain'	*forebear* 'ancestor'
forfeit	*foreclose*
forgo 'abstain from'	*forego* 'precede' (especially in *foregoing*, *foregone*)

-ful (suffix)

For changes that may be required by the
adjectival suffix *-ful*, see -Y AT END TO -I; L,
SINGLE OR DOUBLE?

-ie at end to *-y*

When the suffix *-ing* is added to words
(chiefly verbs) that end in *-ie*, *e* is dropped
(see DROPPING OF SILENT -E), and *i* becomes *y*,
e.g.

dying   *tying*

Exceptions: *hie*, *sortie*, make *hieing*, *sortieing*.
Both *stymieing* and *stymying* are acceptable.

-ified/-yfied

-ified is usual, whatever the stem of the preceding element, e.g.

citified	gentrified
countrified	sissified
Frenchified	yuppified

Note, however, the exception ladyfied.

in-/un- (negative forms)

There is no comprehensive set of rules, but the following guidelines are offered. Note that in- takes the form of il-, im-, or ir- before initial l, m, or r.

(A) in- properly belongs to words derived from Latin, whereas un- combines with any English word. Hence:

(i) un- may be expected to spread to words originally having in-. This has happened when the in- word has developed a sense more specific than the mere negative of the stem word:

unartistic	inartistic
unhuman	inhuman
unmaterial	immaterial
unmoral	immoral
unreligious	irreligious
unsolvable	insoluble

(ii) It is always possible to coin a nonceword with un-:

A small bullied-looking woman with unabundant brown hair (Kingsley Amis)

(B) Adjectives and participles ending in -ed and -ing rarely accept in-.

Exception: inexperienced.

(C) in- seems to be preferred before ad-, co-(col-, com-, con-, cor-), de-, di(s)-, ex-, per-.

Important exceptions are:

unadventurous	undeniable
uncommunicative	undesirable
unconditional	undetectable
unconscionable	unexceptionable
unconscious	unexceptional

uncooperative	unpersuasive
undemonstrative	

(D) un- is preferred before em-, en-, im-, in-, inte(r)-.

(E) Adjectives ending in -able usually take in- if the stem preceding the suffix -able is not, by itself, an English word:

palpable   stem palp-   negative im-

Exceptions: unamenable, unamiable, unconscionable.

They usually take un- if the stem is a short English word:

unbridgeable   unreadable

Exceptions: incurable, immovable, impassable ('that cannot be traversed': but impassible 'unfeeling').

But no generalization covers those with a longer English stem:

illimitable	undeniable
invariable	unmistakable

Note: rule (B) overrides rule (C) (e.g. uncomplaining, undisputed, unperturbed) and rule (C) overrides rule (E) (unconscionable).

-ize/-ise

Both spellings are common in Britain, but -ize is more usual in North America. Where both are in use, different publishing houses, businesses, and individuals will have their own preference; the important thing is to be consistent.

(A) The choice arises only where the ending is pronounced 'eyes', not where it is 'ice', 'iss', or 'eez'. So precise, promise, expertise, remise must all be spelt -ise.

(B) The choice applies only to the verbal suffix added to nouns and adjectives with the sense 'make into, treat with, or act in the way of (the stem word)'.

Hence are eliminated:

(i) nouns ending in -ise:

compromise	exercise	revise
demise	franchise	surmise

disguise   *merchandise*   *surprise*

enterprise

(ii) verbs corresponding to a noun which has -*is*- as part of the stem (e.g. in the syllables -*vis*-, -*cis*-, *mis*-), or identical with a noun ending in -*ise*.

advertise	*despise*	*incise*
advise	*devise*	*merchandise*
apprise	*disguise*	*premise*
arise	*emprise*	*prise* (open)
chastise	*enfranchise*	*revise*
circumcise	*enterprise*	*supervise*
comprise	*excise*	*surmise*
compromise	*exercise*	*surprise*
demise	*improvise*	*televise*

(C) In most cases, -*ize* verbs are formed on familiar English stems, e.g. *authorize*, *familiarize*, *symbolize*; or with a slight alteration to the stem, e.g. *agonize*, *dogmatize*, *sterilize*. A few words have no such immediate stem: *aggrandize* (noun *aggrandizement*), *appetize* (noun *appetite*), *baptize* (noun *baptism*), *catechize* (noun *catechism*), *recognize* (noun *recognition*), and *capsize* (noun *capsizal*). See also -IZE in SECTION 6: USAGE.

l, single or double?

Knowing whether to write a single or double *l* can sometimes be a problem.

(A) For cases in which a suffix is added to single final *l*, see DOUBLING OF FINAL CONSONANTS.

(B) *l* is single when it is the last letter of the following verbs:

annul	*enrol*	*fulfil*
appal	*enthral*	*impel*
distil	*extol*	*instil* (preferred)

These double the *l* before a vowel, e.g. *annulled*, *fulfilling*, but not before -*ment*:

enrolment   *distillation*   *enthralling*

• In American spelling *l* is usually double here except in *annul*(*ment*), *extol*.

(C) Final -*ll* usually becomes *l* before a consonant, e.g.

almighty, *almost*, etc.   *skilful*

chilblain   *thraldom*

dully   *wilful*

Exception: Before -*ness*, -*ll* remains in *dullness*, *fullness*.

• In American spelling *ll* is usual in *skillful*, *thralldom*, *willful*.

-*ly*

The suffix -*ly* forms adjectives and adverbs, e.g. *earth*, *earthly*; *sad*, *sadly*. One of the following spelling changes may be required:

(A) If the word ends in double *ll*, add only -*y*, e.g. *fully*, *shrilly*.

(B) If the word ends in consonant + *le*, change *e* to *y*, e.g. *ably*, *singly*, *subtly*, *supply*, *terribly*.

(C) If the word ends in consonant + *y*, change *y* to *i* and add -*ly*, e.g. *drily*, *happily*.

Exceptions: *shyly*, *slyly*, *spryly*, *wryly*.

(D) Unstressed *ey* changes to *i*, e.g. *matily*.

(E) If the word ends in -*ic*, add -*ally*, e.g. *basically*, *scientifically*.

Exceptions: *politicly* (from *politic*, distinguished from *politically*, from *political*), *publicly*.

(F) Final -*e* is dropped before -*ly* in *duly*, *eerily*, *truly*, *wholly*.

(G) Final -*y* changes to *i* before -*ly* in *daily*, *gaily*.

-*ness*

Addition of this suffix may require the change of -Y AT END TO -I.

-*or* / -*er*

Both suffixes mean 'person or thing that performs (a verb)'. However:

(A) -er is the living suffix, forming most agent nouns; but -or is common with words of Latin origin, e.g.

chopper	producer	avenger
counsellor	carburettor	conqueror

(B) -or follows -at- to form -ator, e.g. duplicator, incubator.

Exception: debater.

Note: nouns ending in -olater, e.g. idolater, do not contain the agent suffix -or/-er.

(C) Both suffixes are very common after -s-, -ss-, and -t- (apart from -at-). So supervisor, prospector, but advertiser, perfecter. Only rough guidelines can be given: -tor usually follows -c, unstressed i, and u, e.g. actor, compositor; -ter usually follows f, gh, l, r, and s, e.g. drifter, fighter.

(D) A functional distinction is made between -or and -er in the following:

accepter 'one who accepts'	acceptor (in electronics
adapter 'one who adapts'	adaptor (in electronics)
conveyer 'person who conveys'	conveyor 'machine that conveys'
sailer 'ship of specified power'	sailor 'seaman'

See also CASTER/CASTOR; CENSER/CENSOR/CENSURE; and RESISTER/RESISTOR in SECTION 5: COMMON CONFUSABLES.

(E) A number of words have -er in normal use but -or in law:

abetter	mortgager
accepter	settler
granter	

(F) A few words have the suffix -ar, the commonest being:

beggar	burglar	liar

-oul-

• In mould, moulder, moult, and smoulder, American spelling favours o alone instead of ou.

-our/-or

(A) In agent nouns, only -or occurs as the ending (see -OR/-ER), e.g. actor, counsellor.

Exception: saviour.

(B) In abstract nouns, -our is usual, e.g. colour, favour, humour. Only the following end in -or:

error	pallor	terror
horror	squalor	torpor
liquor	stupor	tremor

• In American English -or is usual in all cases except glamour.

(C) Nouns ending in -our change this to -or before the suffixes -ation, -iferous, -ific, -ize, and -ous, e.g.

coloration	humorous
soporific	vaporize.

Exception: colourize.

But -our keeps the u before other suffixes, e.g.

armourer	behaviourism	colourful
favourite	honourable	

Exceptions: humorist, rigorist.

past of verbs, formation of

(A) Regular verbs add -ed for the past tense and past participle. For other spelling changes that may be required, see DOUBLING OF FINAL CONSONANT; DROPPING OF SILENT -E; -Y AT END TO -I.

Note laid, paid, and said from lay, pay, and say.

(B) A number of verbs vary between -ed and -t (and in some cases change the vowel-sound in the stem):

burned, burnt	learned, learnt
dreamed, dreamt	smelled, smelt
kneeled, knelt	spelled, spelt
leaned, leant	spilled, spilt
leaped, leapt	spoiled, spoilt

The -t form tends to be favoured when the past participle is used like an adjective, e.g. spilt milk but I spilled the milk.

• The *-d* form is usually retained in American English.

Bereave is regular when the reference is to the loss of relatives by death; *bereft* is used for loss of possessions.

Cleave is a rare word with two opposite meanings: (i) 'stick' and (ii) 'split'. Sense (i) is regular in the past, e.g. *They cleaved together*. In sense (ii) *clove*, *cleft*, and *cleaved* are all permissible, but *cleaved* is usual in scientific and technical contexts; *clave* is now archaic. The past participle varies in certain fixed expressions: *cloven-footed*, *cloven hoof*, *cleft palate*, *cleft stick*.

(C) A number of verbs vary in the past participle only between the regular form and one ending in *-(e)n*:

hew	mow	saw
sew	shear	show
sow	strew	swell

In most of these the latter form is to be preferred; in British English it is obligatory when the participle is used as an attributive adjective. So *new-mown hay*; *a sawn-off shotgun*; *shorn of one's strength*; *a swollen gland*. *Swelled head* (implying conceit) is a colloquial exception.

(D) The past tense has *-a-*, the past participle *-u-*, in:

begin	shrink	stink
drink	sing	swim
ring	sink	

It is an error to use *begun*, *drunk*, etc. for the past tense.

(E) The following verbs can cause difficulty:

abide (*by*) makes *abided* (not 'abode')

alight makes *alighted* (not 'alit')

bet: *betted* is increasingly common beside *bet*

bid ('make a bid') is unchanged in past tense and past participle

bid ('command'; *bid goodnight* etc.): *bid* is usual, *bade*, *bidden* are archaic

broadcast is unchanged in past tense and past participle

chide: *chided* is now usual, but older texts may have *chid*

forecast is unchanged in past tense and past participle

hang: *hanged* for capital punishment, otherwise *hung*

highlight makes *highlighted*

knit: *knitted* is usual, but *knit* is common in metaphorical uses

light makes *lit* but *lighted* before a noun, e.g. *a lighted match*

quit makes *quit*, but *quitted* is also found

reeve (nautical) makes *rove*

rid is unchanged in past tense and past participle (not 'ridded', 'ridden')

speed makes *sped*, but *speeded* in the sense 'travel at illegal speed'

spit makes *spat* (but *spit* in American usage)

spotlight makes *spotlighted* (preferred to *spotlit*)

stave ('make a hole in') makes *staved* or *stove*

stave ('ward off') makes *staved*

sweat makes *sweated* (but *sweat* in American usage)

thrive: *thrived* is now more common than *throve*, *thriven*

plural formation

Most nouns simply add *-s*, e.g. *cats*, *dogs*, *horses*, *cameras*.

(A) The regular plural suffix *-s* is preceded by *-e-*:

(i) After sibilant consonants, i.e. after

ch: e.g. *benches*, *coaches*, *matches*

(but not *lochs*, *stomachs* where the *ch* has a different sound)

s: e.g. *buses*, *gases*, *pluses*, *yeses*

(single *s* is not doubled)

sh: e.g. *ashes*, *bushes*

ss: e.g. *grasses*, *successes*

x: e.g. *boxes*, *sphinxes*

z: e.g. *buzzes, waltzes*

(note *quizzes* with double *z*)

Proper names follow the same rule, e.g. *the Joneses, the Rogerses, the two Charleses.*

(ii) After *-y* (not preceded by a vowel), which changes to *i*, e.g. *ladies, soliloquies, spies.*

Exceptions: proper names, e.g. *the Willoughbys, the three Marys*; also *lay-bys, stand-bys, zlotys* (Polish currency).

(iii) After *-o* in certain words:

buffaloes	*mosquitoes*
calicoes	*noes*
dominoes	*potatoes*
echoes	*stuccoes*
embargoes	*tomatoes*
goes	*torpedoes*
heroes	*vetoes*

Words not in this list add only *-s*. Some words (e.g. *cargo, grotto, halo, innuendo, mango, memento, motto, peccadillo, portico, tornado, volcano*) are found with either plural form.

It is helpful to remember that *-e-* is never inserted:

(a) when the *o* follows another vowel, e.g. *cuckoos, ratios.*

(b) when the word is an abbreviation, e.g. *hippos, kilos.*

(c) with proper names, e.g. *Lotharios, Figaros, the Munros.*

(iv) With words that change *-F* AT END TO *-V*, e.g. *calves, scarves.*

(B) Plural of compound nouns.

(i) Compounds made up of a noun followed by an adjective, prepositional phrase, or adverb attach *-s* to the noun, e.g.

courts martial   *heirs presumptive*
poets laureate

(But *brigadier-generals, lieutenant colonels, sergeant-majors*)

sons-in-law   *tugs of war*
hangers-on   *passers-by*

In informal use the type noun + adjective (e.g. *court martial*) often pluralizes the second word.

(ii) Compounds which contain no (apparent) noun add *-s* at the end:

forget-me-nots   *will-o'-the-wisps*
pullovers   *sit-ups*

So also do nouns formed from phrasal verbs and compounds ending in *-ful*, e.g.

handfuls   spoonfuls

(iii) Compounds containing *man* or *woman* make both elements plural, as usually do those made up of two words linked by *and* e.g.

menservants   *women priests*
pros and cons   *ups and downs*

(C) The plural of these nouns ending in *-s* is unchanged:

biceps	*means*	*species*
congeries	*mews*	*superficies*
forceps	*series*	*thrips*
innings		

The following are mass nouns, not plurals:
bona fides ('good faith')   *kudos*

Although sometimes seen, the singulars *bona-fide* (as a noun), *congery*, and *kudo* are erroneous.

(D) Plural of nouns of foreign origin. The terminations that may form their plurals according to a foreign pattern are given in alphabetical order below; to each is added a list of the words that normally follow this pattern, although some of these (marked *) may also take *-s* or *-es*. It is recommended that the regular plural (*-s*) should be used for all the other words with these terminations.

(i) *-a* (Latin and Greek) becomes *-ae* (or *-as*):

alga   *lamina*   *nebula**
alumna   *larva*   *papilla*

Note: *formula* has *-ae* in mathematical and scientific use.

(ii) *-eau, -eu* (French) add *-x* (or *-e(a)us*)

*beau**   *château*   *plateau**
*bureau**   *milieu**   *tableau*

(iii) *-ex, -ix* (Latin) become *-ices*:

appendix   *cortex*   *matrix*
codex   *helix*   *radix*

Note: *index* and *vortex* have *-ices* in mathematical and scientific use; *appendixes* is common for the internal organ.

(iv) *-is* (Greek and Latin) becomes *-es* (pronounced 'eez'):

amanuensis	*hypothesis*
analysis	*metamorphosis*
antithesis	*oasis*
axis	*parenthesis*
basis	*synopsis*
crisis	*thesis*
ellipsis	

(v) *-o* (Italian) becomes *-i* (or **-os*):

concerto grosso (*concerti grossi*)

graffito	*ripieno**
maestro*	*virtuoso**

Note: *solo* and *soprano* may have *-i* in technical contexts.

(vi) *-on* (Greek) becomes *-a* (or **-ons*):

automaton*	*parhelion*
criterion	*phenomenon*

(vii) *-s* (French) is unchanged in the plural (it is silent in the singular but pronounced *-z* in the plural):

chamois	*corps*	*fracas*
chassis	*faux pas*	*patois*

Also (not a noun in French): *rendezvous*.

(viii) *-um* (Latin) becomes *-a* (or **-ums*):

addendum	*effluvium*
bacterium	*emporium**
candelabrum	*epithalamium**
compendium*	*erratum*
corrigendum	*maximum**
cranium*	*minimum**
crematorium*	*quantum*
curriculum	*scholium*
datum spectrum	
desideratum	*speculum*
dictum*	*stratum*

Note: *medium* has the plural *-a* in scientific use and in the sense 'means of communication'; the collective plural of *memorandum* 'things to be noted' has *-a*; *rostrum* has *-a* in technical use.

(ix) *-us* (Latin) becomes *-i* (or **-uses*):

alumnus	*bronchus*	*calculus**
bacillus	*cactus**	*fungus**
gladiolus	*nucleus*	*stimulus*
locus	*radius**	*terminus**
narcissus		

Note: *focus* has the plural *-i* in scientific use; *genius* has the plural *genii* when used to mean 'guardian spirit'; *genus* becomes *genera*, while *corpus* becomes *corpora* or *corpuses*, and *opus* becomes *opera* or *opuses*.

The following words of foreign origin are plural nouns; they should normally not be construed as singulars.

bacteria	*phenomena*
insignia	*regalia*
criteria	*strata*

See also AGENDA; CANDELABRA/CANDELABRUM; DATA/DATUM; GRAFFITI; and MEDIA in SECTION 6: USAGE.

(E) There is no need to use an apostrophe before *-s*:

(i) After figures: *the 1990s.*

(ii) After abbreviations: *KOs, MPs, SOSs.*

But it is needed in: *dot the i's and cross the t's, do's and don'ts.*

possessive case

To form the possessive:

(A) Normally, add *-'s* in the singular and the apostrophe alone in the plural, e.g.

Bill's book	*the Johnsons' dog*
his master's voice	*a girls' school*

Plural nouns that do not end in *-s* add *-'s* to the plural form, e.g.

children's books   *women's liberation*

(B) Most nouns ending in *s* add *-'s* for the singular possessive, e.g.

my boss's	*Hicks's*
St James's Square	*Father Christmas's*

To form the plural possessive, they add an apostrophe to the *s* of the plural in the normal way, e.g.

> *my bosses' strategy* *the octopuses'*
> *the Joneses' dog* *tentacles*

French names ending in silent *s* or *x* add -*'s*, which is pronounced as *z*, e.g.

> *Dumas's* *Crémieux's*

Names ending in -*es* pronounced 'iz' are treated like plurals and take only an apostrophe (following the pronunciation, which is 'iz', not 'iziz'), e.g.

> *Bridges'* *Moses'*

Polysyllables not accented on the last or second last syllable can take the apostrophe alone, but the form with -*'s* is equally acceptable, e.g.

> *Barnabas'* or *Barnabas's*
> *Nicholas'* or *Nicholas's*

It is customary to use the apostrophe only, irrespective of pronunciation, for ancient classical names ending in -*s*, e.g.

> *Ceres'* *Herodotus'* *Venus'*

Jesus' is the usual liturgical form, but in other contexts *Jesus's* is acceptable.

Before the word *sake*, be guided by the pronunciation, e.g.

> *for goodness' sake* *for God's sake*
> *for conscience' sake* *for Charles's sake*

After -*x* and -*z*, use -*'s*, e.g. *Berlioz's music*, *Lenz's law*.

For further discussion, see APOSTROPHE in SECTION 3: PUNCTUATION.

-re / -er

The list below gives the principal words in which the ending -*re* has the unstressed 'er' sound (there are others with the sound 'ruh', e.g. *macabre*, or 'ray', e.g. *padre*):

accoutre	*metre* (but note *meter*
*acre	the measuring device)
amphitheatre	*mitre*
*cadre	*nitre*
calibre	*ochre*
centre	**ogre*
*euchre	*philtre*
fibre	*reconnoitre*
goitre	*sabre*

litre	*sceptre*
louvre	*sepulchre*
*lucre	*sombre*
lustre	*spectre*
manoeuvre	*theatre*
*massacre	*titre*
meagre	**wiseacre*
mediocre	

• All but those marked * are spelt with -*er* in American English.

-s (suffix)

(A) For the use of -*s* to make the plural of nouns, see PLURAL FORMATION.

(B) As the inflection of the third person singular present indicative of verbs, -*s* requires the same changes in the stem as the plural ending, namely the insertion of -*e*-:

(i) After sibilants (*ch, s, sh, x, z*), e.g. *catches, tosses, pushes, fixes, buzzes*; note that single *s* and *z* are subject to doubling of final consonant, though the forms in which they occur are rare, e.g. *gasses, nonplusses, quizzes, whizzes.*

(ii) After the change of -Y AT END TO -I, e.g. *cries, flies, carries, copies.*

(iii) After *o*: *echo, go, torpedo, veto*, like the corresponding nouns, insert -*e*- before -*s*.

-xion / -ction

Complexion, crucifixion, effluxion, fluxion all have -*x*-; *connection, deflection, inflection, reflection* all have -*ct*-; both *genuflection* and *genuflexion* occur.

-y / -ey, adjectives ending in

When -*y* is added to a word to form an adjective, the following changes in spelling occur:

(A) DOUBLING OF FINAL CONSONANT, e.g. *shrubby.*

(B) DROPPING OF SILENT -E, e.g. *bony, chancy.*

Exceptions:

(i) After *u*:

bluey gluey tissuey

(ii) In words that are not well established in the written language, where the retention of -*e* helps to clarify the sense:

 cottagey dikey

 dicey   villagey

Note also *holey* (distinguished from *holy*); *phoney*.

(C) Insertion of -*e*- when -*y* is also the final letter of the stem:

 clayey skyey

 wheyey sprayey

Also in *gooey*.

(D) Adjectives ending in unstressed -*ey* change this -*ey* to -*i*- before the comparative and superlative suffixes -*er* and -*est* and the adverbial suffix -*ly*, e.g.

 dicey: dicier   gooey: gooier

 pacey: pacier   phoney: phonily

 matey: matily

Before -*ness* there is variation, e.g.

 clayey: clayeyness phoney: phoniness

 wheyey: wheyiness

-*y*, -*ey*, -*ie*, nouns ending in

The diminutive or pet form of nouns can be spelt -*y*, -*ey*, or -*ie*. Most nouns which end in the sound of -*y* are so spelt, e.g.

 aunty baby nappy

The following are the main diminutives spelt with -*ey* (-*ey* nouns of other kinds are excluded from the list):

goosey	matey
housey-housey	nursey
Limey	Sawney (Scotsman)
lovey-dovey	slavey

The following list contains the diminutives ending in -*ie*, and many similar nouns. Most Scottish diminutives are spelt with -*ie*, e.g. *corbie*, *kiltie*.

beanie (hat)	junkie
birdie	Kewpie (doll)
bookie	laddie
brownie	lassie
budgie	mealie (ear of maize; but note adjective mealy)
chappie	
charlie	
clippie	Mountie
cookie	movie
coolie	nightie
dearie	oldie
doggie (noun; but note adjective doggy)	pinkie (little finger) pixie quickie
genie (spirit; but note plural genii)	rookie sheltie
Geordie	softie
gillie	walkie-talkie
girlie	zombie
goalie	

See also BOGEY/BOGIE/BOGY and CADDIE/CADDY in SECTION 5: COMMON CONFUSABLES.

y/*i*

There is often uncertainty about whether *y* or *i* should be written in the following words:

Write *i* in:	Write *y* in:
cider	dyke (*dike* is also found)
cipher (*cypher* is also found)	Gypsy (*Gipsy* is also found)
Libya	
lich-gate (*lych-* is also found)	lyke-wake
linchpin (*lynchpin* is also found)	lynch law
	pygmy (*pigmy* is also found)
sibyl (classical)	Sybil (as Christian name)
siphon (*syphon* is also found)	stymie
siren	
stile (in fence)	style (manner)
	stylus

syllabub (*sillabub* is also found)

sylvan (*silvan* is also found)

syrup

timpani (drums; *tympani* is also found)

tympanum (eardrum)

tyre (of wheel)

tyro (*tiro* is also found)

witch-hazel (*wych-hazel* is also found)

wych-elm

-y at end to -i

(A) Words that end in -*y* after a vowel retain the -*y* before certain suffixes.

enjoyable   conveyed   gayer   coyly

donkeys   buys   joyful

Exceptions: *daily*, *gaily*, and adjectives ending in unstressed -*ey* (see -Y/-EY, ADJECTIVES ENDING IN).

(B) If the -*y* follows a consonant (or silent *u* after *g* or *q*), it changes to -*i*- before:

(i) -*able*, e.g. *deniable*, *justifiable*.

Exception: *flyable*.

(ii) -*ed*, e.g. *carried*, *denied*.

(C) -*er*, -*est*, e.g. *carrier*, *driest*, *happier*.

Exceptions: *fryer*, *shyer* (one that shies). Both *flyer* and *flier* occur, as do *drier* (one that dries) and *dryer*.

(D) -*es*, e.g. *ladies*, *carries*.

(E) -*ful* (adjectives), e.g. *beautiful*, *fanciful*. (*Bellyful* is not an adjective.)

(F) -*less* (adjectives), e.g. *merciless*, *remediless*.

Exceptions: some rare compounds, e.g. *countryless*.

(G) -*ly* (adverbs), e.g. *drily*, *happily*, *plaguily*.

Exceptions: *shyly*, *slyly*, *spryly*, *wryly*.

(H) -*ment* (nouns), e.g. *embodiment*, *merriment*.

(I) -*ness* (nouns), e.g. *happiness*, *cliquiness*.

Exceptions: *dryness*, *flyness*, *shyness*, *slyness*, *spryness*, *wryness*, *busyness* (distinguished from *business*).

-yse, -yze

This verbal ending (e.g. in *analyse*, *catalyse*, *paralyse*) is not a suffix but part of the Greek stem -*lyse*. It should not be written with *z* in British English (though *z* is normally used in such words in North America).

PART III: DIFFICULT SPELLINGS

The list below contains words which occasion difficulty or uncertainty in spelling. In each case the form given in bold as a headword is the standard or preferred spelling in contemporary British English. Inflections and derivatives are sometimes given (in bold) when these are irregular or otherwise problematic. If there are permissible variants (American forms, older spellings still in use, special legal or technical spellings), these are given in italic type. Incorrect spellings are also indicated (in roman type and within quotation marks) when these are particularly common. Where a rejected variant is widely separated alphabetically from the recommended spelling, the former appears in the main headword list accompanied by the mark • and a cross-reference to the preferred form.

For reasons of length, priority has been given in this Part to spellings that are exceptions to, or are simply not covered by, the rules set out in PART II: RULES OF SPELLING AND WORD FORMATION. However, to enhance the value of the list as a general reference tool, a good deal of overlap has been allowed; such troublesome customers as **accessible, skilful, surprise,** *etc. are therefore listed here despite earlier coverage. For similar reasons a handful of proper nouns (chiefly place names) have also been included.*

Where the problem is less one of spelling per se, and more one of choosing between similarly spelt words denoting different things, the reader is referred to SECTION 5: COMMON CONFUSABLES.

A

abattoir has single *b*, double *t*.

abductor is spelt -*or*, not '-er'.

aberration has double *r*.

abetter has double *t* and ends -*er* (but -*or* in legal terminology).

abridgement is the preferred British spelling; *abridgment* is the usual American form.

abrogate

abscess has -*sc*- in the middle.

abysmal

accelerate has double *c*, single *l*.

accessible has double *c*, double *s*, and ends -*ible*, not '-able'.

accessory is now preferred to *accessary* in all meanings (but -*ary* is still sometimes used for the legal sense).

accommodate, accommodation are among the most commonly misspelt words in English: there are two *c*s and two *m*s.

accrue

acknowledgement is to be preferred in British English, although *acknowledgment* is the more usual American form.

acolyte

acquaintance

acquiesce

acrylic

acumen

adaptor is the preferred spelling for the electrical device; **adapter** is preferred in more general contexts.

adenoids

adieu can have the plural **adieus** or **adieux**.

adjourn

adjudicator has a *d* near the beginning and ends -*or*.

admissible is spelt -*ible*, not '-able'.

adolescence not 'adolesense' etc.

advantageous has an *e*.

advertise is always spelt *-ise*, not '-ize'.

advice is the correct spelling of the noun, **advise** of the verb.

adviser is still the more common spelling in British English, although the American form *advisor* has gained ground.

•**aerie:** see EYRIE.

aegis

aeon ('long period of time') is spelt with initial *ae-* in British English (American *eon* or *aeon*).

aerial not 'airial'.

aesthete, aesthetic are spelt with initial *ae-* in British English; in American English they are often spelt *esthete, esthetic*.

affidavit has double *f*.

aficionado has single *f*.

ageing is preferable to *aging*, although both are in use.

aggressor has double *g*, double *s*, and ends *-or*, not '-er'.

aghast

agitator is spelt *-or*, not '-er'.

agoraphobia

aisle (of a church) not 'isle'.

ait ('small river island') is preferable to *eyot*.

align, alignment Do not be misled by the word *line* to write 'aline', 'alinement'.

alimentary

allege

allegiance

•**alleluia:** see HALLELUJAH.

alliteration has double *l*, single *r*.

almanac is now spelt *-ac* except in traditional titles such as *Whitaker's Almanack*.

aluminium is the usual British spelling. The American spelling *aluminum* (stressed on the second syllable) is the one adopted by its discoverer, Sir Humphrey Davy, in about 1812.

amanuensis has no double letters (and plural **-ses**).

ambidextrous not '-terous'.

ambience is preferable to *ambiance*.

amoeba is the British spelling (American *ameba*). The usual plural is **amoebas** (American *amebas*); *amoebae* is only used in technical contexts.

amok is better than *amuck*.

amphibious

anachronism

anaemia, anaemic are spelt *-ae-* in British English and *-e-* or *-ae-* in American English.

anaesthetic is spelt *-ae-* in British English (American *anesthetic*).

analgesic

analyse is spelt *-yse* in British English (American *analyze*).

ancillary The misspelling (and mispronunciation) 'ancilliary' is common.

androgynous

anemone The sequence of consonants is *n-m-n*, not (as is sometimes heard) *n-n-m*. The word comes from Greek *anemos* 'wind' and is therefore akin to the English word *animated*.

annex, annexe In British English the verb is *annex* and the noun *annexe*; in American English the noun is usually spelt *annex* too.

annihilate has double *n*.

anomalous has no double letters.

antecedent not 'anti-'.

antechamber not 'anti-'.

antediluvian not 'anti-'.

antirrhinum (flower) has double *r*.

any time is always written as two words.

Apennines (Italian mountain range) has single *p*, double *n*.

apophthegm has *-phth-* in the middle (American *apothegm*).

apostasy not '-acy'.

appal is the British spelling (American *appall*), with inflections **appalled, appalling**.

appreciate has double *p*.

apprise is always spelt *-ise*, not '-ize'.

appurtenance

aqueduct

archaeology is the British spelling (American *archeology*).

archetype

archipelago

ardour is spelt *-our* in British English (American *ardor*).

armour is spelt *-our* in British English (American *armor*).

arpeggio has single *p* and double *g*.

artefact is the usual British spelling (American *artifact*).

ascendancy, ascendant are now the preferred spellings, although *ascendency* and *ascendent* are still sometimes found.

asinine has only one *s*.
asphalt not 'ash-'.
asphyxiate
aspidistra
assassin has two double *ss*.
asthma has -*th*- in the middle.
attendant has double *t* and ends -*ant*, not '-ent'.
aubergine
aubrietia is the correct form, but 'aubretia' and 'aubrieta' are now so common that they may soon rank as acceptable alternatives.
aught ('anything') not 'ought'.
authoritative not 'authoritive'.
auxiliary has single *l*.
avocado has single *c*.
aye ('yes', 'always') is never written 'ay'.

B

bacillus
baguette
banjos is the recommended plural for the instrument, although *banjoes* is also found.
barbecue not 'barbeque'.
baroque
battalion has double *t* and one *l*.
baulk (noun and verb) is the usual British spelling; *balk* is chiefly American.
Beelzebub (devil)
behove is the British spelling (American *behoove*).
benefited, benefiting are preferable to the spellings with double *t*.
beret (hat)
besiege like *siege*, is spelt -*ie*-.
biased The spelling with one *s* is preferred.
bitumen
bivouac (noun and verb) has no *k*. But the inflected forms **bivouacked, bivouacking** are spelt -*ck*-.
blameable has an *e* in the middle.
blancmange
bouillabaisse (stew)
bourgeois
brand-new not 'bran new'.
Brittany (in France) not 'Britany' or 'Britainy'.
broccoli has double *c*, single *l*.
budgerigar
burglary not 'burglery'.

C

cadaver
caffeine is an exception to the '*i* before *e*' rule.
calibre is the British spelling (American *caliber*).
caliph is preferred to *khalif*.
calligraphy has double *l*.
caliper is now more common than *calliper*.
calypso
camellia is spelt with double *l*, despite its pronunciation with long 'ee'.
capercaillie (wood-grouse) This is now the normal spelling, not the Scottish Gaelic form *capercailzie*.
carburettor is the preferred spelling in British English (American *carburetor*).
carcass is the preferred form (rather than *carcase*) and has the plural **carcasses**.
Caribbean is spelt with one *r* and double *b*.
cataclysm
catarrh
caviar is preferable to *caviare*.
cemetery
chameleon
chancellor is spelt -*or* (but note the correct spelling **chancellery**).
changeable is spelt with an *e* in the middle to preserve the soft sound of the *g*.
charismatic
Charollais (breed of cattle)
chastise is always spelt -*ise*, not '-ize'.
chauffeur has double *f*.
chauvinism
cheque ('order to a bank') is the British spelling; the American form *check* also means 'bill' (in a restaurant etc.)
chequer is the British spelling (American *checker*).
chiaroscuro ('contrasted light and shadow')
chihuahua
chilblain not 'chill-'.
chilli (pepper) is the preferred British form; *chili* is the usual American spelling.
chimera (mythological being, 'illusory thing or idea') is the recommended spelling, not *chimaera*.
chivvy has inflections **chivvies, chivvied**.
chlorophyll
cholesterol
choosy not '-ey'.
chromosome not '-one'.
chrysalis
chrysanthemum

chukker (polo term) is the British spelling (American *chukka*).

cipher is the recommended spelling, not *cypher*.

circumcise is always spelt *-ise*, not '-ize'.

clarinettist is the British spelling (American *clarinetist*).

clue is the normal spelling. *Clew* is an archaic variant now mainly confined to nautical uses.

coalesce

coconut not 'cocoa-'.

coleslaw is spelt *cole-*, not 'cold-' (from Dutch *kool* 'cabbage').

colloquial has double *l*.

colonnade has single *l*, double *n*.

colossal has double *s* and two single *l*s.

colourize is the British spelling (American *colorize*). But **coloration** is standard in both varieties.

commemorate has double *m* then single *m*.

commissionaire has double *m*, single *n*.

commit, commitment have double *m*.

committee has double *m* and double *t*.

comparative

competent

concede not '-sede'.

conjuror is preferred to *conjurer*.

connoisseur has double *n* and double *s*.

conscientious has two *i*s.

consensus not '-census'.

convertible is spelt *-ible*, not '-able'.

cookie is the established spelling, not 'cooky'.

coolly (adverb) has double *l*.

coolie (Asian labourer) has single *l* and ends *-ie*.

corollary has double *l* and two single *r*s.

corpuscle

corrector ('person who points out faults') is spelt *-or*, not '-er'.

correspondence has double *r*.

corrupter ('person or thing that corrupts') is spelt *-er*, not '-or'.

cosy is the British spelling (American *cozy*).

crueller(-est), cruelly have double *l*.

•**czar:** see TSAR.

curtsy not 'curtsey' or 'courtsy'. Its plural is **curtsies**, and as a verb it has inflected forms **curtsies, curtsied, curtsying**.

D

dachshund not '-sund' (German *-hund*, 'dog').

dahlia

datable not 'dateable'.

debatable not 'debateable'.

debonair has no *e* on the end.

definite

dependant (noun) is the preferred spelling in British English; *dependent* was previously American only, but is now an accepted variant in Britain. The adjective is always **dependent** and the abstract noun is **dependence** (not '-ance').

descendant (noun) not '-dent'.

desperate not 'despar-'.

•**despatch:** see DISPATCH.

desiccated has single *s*, double *c* (from Latin *siccus* 'dry').

destructible is spelt *-ible*, not '-able'.

deteriorate not 'deteriate'.

devise is always spelt *-ise*, not '-ize'.

dialogue is the British spelling (American *dialog*).

diaphragm has a *g*.

diarrhoea is the British spelling (American *diarrhea*).

dietitian is the recommended spelling, not *dietician*.

dilemma

dilettante has single *l*, double *t*, single *t*.

diphtheria is spelt with *-ph-* (and should be pronounced 'dif-', not 'dip-').

diphthong is spelt with *-ph-*.

dirigible (adjective or noun) is spelt *-ible*, not '-able'.

disappoint has single *s* and double *p*.

disastrous not '-erous'.

disc, disk In general senses *disc* is the usual British spelling, while *disk* is the preferred American form. However, for senses relating to computers (*disk drive* etc.), *disk* is nearly always used.

discernible is spelt *-ible*, not '-able'.

discussible is spelt *-ible*, not '-able'.

dismissible is spelt *-ible*, not '-able'.

dispatch is the preferred form, not *despatch* (first recorded, probably in error, by Dr Johnson).

dispensable is spelt *-able*, not '-ible'.

disposable is spelt *-able*, not '-ible'.

dissect has double *s*.

dissipate has double *s*, single *p*.

dissociate not 'disassociate'.

distil is spelt with single *l* in British English and with double *l* in American English. The inflections in both varieties are **dis-**

tilled, **distilling**, and the noun derivatives are **distillation**, **distiller**, and **distillery**.

disyllable

doh (musical note) is preferable to 'do'.

doily not 'doyley'.

duly not 'duely'.

dungeon The archaic variant *donjon* now refers only to part of a castle.

dyeable has an *e* in the middle.

dysentery

E

ebullient has single *b* and double *l*.

eccentric has double *c*.

ecstasy is spelt -*asy*, not '-acy'. The drugs meaning is spelt with a capital initial.

ecumenical

eighth is spelt *eight* + *h*.

•**eikon:** see ICON.

effervescence has double *f* and -*sc*- in the middle.

eisteddfod has three *d*s altogether.

elegiac not 'elegaic'.

eligible is spelt -*ible*, not '-able'.

embarrass has double *r*, double *s*.

embed not 'im-'.

embryo

enclose, enclosure are the usual spellings, except with reference to the 18th century *inclosure* movement (e.g. *Inclosure Acts*).

encyclopedia is now preferred to *encyclopaedia*.

endeavour (noun and verb) is the British spelling (American *endeavor*).

enforceable not 'enforcable'.

enrol is spelt with single *l* in British English and inflected with double *l* in **enrolled**, **enrolling**; but there is only one *l* in **enrolment**. In American English, there are two *l*s in all these forms, including *enroll* itself.

enthral is spelt with single *l* in British English and inflected with double *l* in **enthralled, enthralling**; but there is only one *l* in **enthralment**. In American English, there are two *l*s in all these forms, including *enthrall* itself (and there is a variant *inthrall*).

entrench is spelt *en*-, not 'in-'.

envelop (verb) but **envelope** (noun).

•**eon:** see AEON.

epitome

eraser is spelt -*er*, not '-or'.

erogenous has no double letters.

erroneous has double *r*.

erupt

espresso is preferable to *expresso*.

ethereal is preferable to *etherial*.

eucalyptus

evenness has double *n*.

evilly (adverb) has double *l*.

exaggerate has double *g*.

exercise (noun and verb) is always spelt -*ise*, not '-ize', and has single *c*.

exhaustible is spelt -*ible*, not '-able'.

exhilarate has *a* in the middle (not *e*).

expatriate not 'expatriot'.

expedite

expressible is spelt -*ible*, not '-able'.

extol is spelt -*ol* and has inflected forms **extolled, extolling**.

extrovert is now the usual spelling; the older form *extravert* is still found in technical use in psychology.

•**eyot:** see AIT.

eyrie is the British spelling; *aerie* is an American variant.

F

facetious

faecal, faeces are the British spellings (American *fecal, feces*).

Fahrenheit

fallible

fascia ('board or panel') is preferable to *facia*.

February has an *r* in the middle.

fee'd (verb 'paid a fee') is better than *feed*.

feldspar is preferable to *felspar*.

fetid is now more common than *foetid*.

fetal, fetus In technical uses the spelling *fetus*, previously regarded as an Americanism, is now standard throughout the English-speaking world. It is also increasingly displacing *foetus*, until recently the standard British spelling, in non-technical contexts.

fiasco

fiery not 'firey'.

fiord, fjord are equally acceptable spellings.

flavour is spelt -*our* in British English (American *flavor*). The derivatives (**flavouring, flavoursome**, etc.) are also spelt -*our* except **flavorous**.

fledgling is the recommended spelling, not *fledgeling*.

florescence ('flowering') has two *c*s.

flotation not 'float-'.

flunkey is the preferred spelling, not *flunky*. The plural is **flunkeys**.

fluorescence has two *c*s.

flyer is the preferred spelling in all meanings of this agent noun formed from the verb *fly*. *Flier* is more common in American English.

focused, focusing are preferable to the spellings with double *s*.

•**foetal, foetus:** see FETAL, FETUS.

•**foetid:** see FETID.

fogey *Fogy* (plural *fogies*) was formerly dominant but the spelling with -*ey* (plural **fogeys**) is now more common.

font ('typeface') was formerly regarded as an Americanism but is now more common in British English than *fount*.

forbade not 'forbad'.

forebode not 'for-'.

foreign

foresight not 'for-'.

forestall not 'for-'.

foretell not 'for-'.

forty not 'fourty'.

frolicked, frolicking with -*ck*- are inflected forms of *frolic*.

fryer is the preferred spelling for the agent noun meaning 'a person or thing that fries', not *frier*.

fuchsia

fulfil is the British English spelling; in American English it alternates with *fulfill*. The inflections in both varieties are **fulfilled, fulfilling**.

fulsome not 'fullsome'.

furore is the British spelling (American *furor*).

fuselage

fusilier

fusillade has double *l*.

G

•**gaol:** see JAIL.

garrotte (verb and noun) is the customary British spelling. In American English the dominant spelling is *garrote* (with inflections *garroted*, *garroting*).

gases

gauge is the usual British spelling; *gage* is American and has special nautical meanings.

gazpacho (soup)

gazump not 'gazoomph' etc.

gelatin is the customary form in chemical use and the standard American spelling; the British variant *gelatine* is common in contexts to do with food preparation.

generator is spelt -*or* in all its meanings, not '-er'.

geriatric

gherkin

ghoul

gibe ('to jeer, mock') is preferable to *jibe*.

gigolo

glycerine is the British spelling (American *glycerin*).

gnome

gormandize ('eat greedily') but note **gourmand** ('glutton').

gormless

goulash not 'ghoulash'.

gourmet

government has an *n* in the middle.

gram is now the preferred spelling for the metric unit of mass; the variant *gramme* is British only.

grandad has single *d* in the middle.

granddaughter has double *d*.

grayling (fish, butterfly) not 'greyling'.

greenness has double *n*.

grey is the dominant form in British English (American *gray*).

grievance

guardian

guerrilla is preferred to the common variant *guerilla*.

guillotine

gullible is spelt -*ible*, not '-able'.

Gurkha

gymnasium

gynaecology is the British spelling (American *gynecology*).

gypsy is the recommended spelling, not *gipsy*. The capitalized form *Gypsy* is used to emphasize ethnic status.

H

habeas corpus

haemoglobin is the British spelling (American *hemoglobin*).

haemorrhage is the British spelling (American *hemorrhage*); both forms have -*rrh*- in the middle.

haemorrhoids is the British spelling (American *hemorrhoids*); both forms have *-rrh-*.

hallelujah is the version that comes direct from Hebrew, and the usual spelling in general contexts; **alleluia**, from ecclesiastical Latin, is more common in the Christian liturgy and church music. Both are acceptable but mixed spellings such as 'alleluja' should be avoided.

hara-kiri

harangue

harass has single *r*, double *s*.

harbour is spelt *-our* in British English (American *harbor*).

harum-scarum ('reckless')

hashish not 'hashhish'.

hausfrau (German 'housewife')

hearken not 'harken'.

heinous

hello is the preferred spelling; *hallo* is more common in British than in American English; and *hullo* is now uncommon. The noun has the plural form **hellos** and the verb ('to say hello') has inflected forms **helloes, helloed, helloing**.

herbaceous

heterogeneous ('of different kinds') is commonly misspelt 'heterogenous'.

hiccup is preferable to *hiccough*, formed by false association with *cough*. The verb has inflected forms **hiccuped, hiccuping**.

Hindu The spelling 'Hindoo' is now archaic.

hingeing is better spelt this way to clarify the sound of the soft *g*.

hirsute

holocaust

homeopathy

homogeneous ('of the same kind') is commonly misspelt 'homogenous'. A word *homogenous* exists, but only as a technical term in biology (now rarely used).

honorific not 'honourific'.

•**hooping cough:** see WHOOPING COUGH.

honour, honourable are the British spellings (American *honor, honorable*).

humour is spelt *-our* in British English (American *-or*). But note **humorist, humorous** in both varieties.

hurrah, hurray are preferable to *hoorah, hooray*.

hyacinth

hydrangea

hyena is spelt *-e-*, not (as formerly) '-ae-'; the plural is **hyenas**.

hypochondria

hypocrisy not 'hypocracy'.

hysteria

I

ichthyosaurus has *-chth-*.

icicle has no *e* in the middle.

icon is preferable to *ikon* or *eikon*.

idiosyncrasy should not be spelt '-cracy', as if it were connected with words such as *democracy* and *autocracy*.

idyll

ignoramus and plural **ignoramuses** (no double *s*).

illegible has double *l* and ends *-ible*, not '-able'.

•**imbed:** see EMBED.

immovable is spelt without an *e* in the middle.

impeccable

impostor is the recommended spelling, not *imposter*.

impromptu

improvable is spelt without an *e* in the middle.

inadvisable has no *e* in the middle.

•**inclose, inclosure:** see ENCLOSE, ENCLOSURE.

incandescent ends *-ent*, not '-ant'.

incise is always spelt *-ise*, not '-ize'. The noun derivative is **incisor** (usually meaning a front tooth), not '-er'.

incubator is spelt *-or*, not '-er'.

incur has only one *r*.

indefatigable is spelt *-able*, not '-ible'.

indefensible is spelt *-ible*, not '-able'.

independent (noun and adjective) is never spelt '-ant'.

indict (charge with crime) has a *c*.

indigenous

indigestible ends *-ible*, not '-able'.

indispensable is spelt *-able*, not '-ible'.

indistinguishable is spelt *-able*, not '-ible'.

indivisible is spelt *-ible*, not '-able'.

infer has one *r* but inflected forms **inferred, inferring**.

inflexible is spelt *-ible*, not '-able'.

inheritor is spelt *-or*, not '-er'. It can be used of both a man and a woman.

initial

innocuous has double *n*, single *c*, and two *us*.

innovate has double *n*.

inoculate has no double letters.

inputting spelt with double *t*, is the present participle of *input* (computer data). The past and past participle is either **input** or **inputted** (double *t*).

in so far is written as three separate words.

insomuch is written as one word.

inspector is spelt *-or*, not '-er'.

install has double *l* (likewise **installed, installing**). However, **instalment** is spelt with one *l* in British English; *installment* is an American variant.

instil is preferable to *instill* but has inflected forms **instilled, instilling**.

instructor is spelt *-or*, not '-er'.

intercede not '-sede'.

interceptor (fighter aircraft) is spelt *-or*, not '-er'.

interchangeable is spelt with an *e* in the middle to preserve the soft sound of the *g*.

intermittent is spelt *-ent* not '-ant'.

internecine

inure

inveigle is spelt *-ei-*.

investigator is spelt *-or*, not '-er'.

investor is spelt *-or*, not '-er'.

invincible is spelt *-ible*, not '-able'.

invisible is spelt *-ible*, not '-able'.

Iraqi (noun and adjective) has no *u* after *q*.

irascible is spelt *-ible*, not '-able'.

iridescent is spelt with single *r*, being derived from the Latin word *iris* 'rainbow'.

irreducible has double *r* and is spelt *-ible*, not '-able'.

irreplaceable has double *r*, an *e* in the middle to preserve the soft sound of the *c*, and ends *-able*.

irrepressible has double *r*, and ends *-ible*, not '-able'.

irresistible has double *r* and ends *-ible*, not '-able'.

irresponsible has double *r* and ends *-ible*, not '-able'.

irreversible has double *r* and ends *-ible*, not '-able'.

irrupt ('enter violently') has double *r*.

J

jail, jailer are now more common than *gaol*, *gaoler* in British English as well as being the dominant American spellings. Prefer the *j*-spellings except in historical contexts in which the *g*- forms might be more appropriate.

jamb ('door-post')

•**jibe:** see GIBE.

jardinière ('pot or stand for plants')

jeopardy not 'jeoprady' as it is often mispronounced.

jewellery is the British spelling (American *jewelry*); also **jeweller, jewelled** (American *jeweler, jeweled*).

jihad ('holy war undertaken by Muslims') is preferable to *jehad*.

jodhpurs has an *h*.

judgement is the spelling in general use in British English; *judgment* is dominant in legal contexts and in American English.

juggernaut

ju-jitsu (Japanese system of unarmed combat) is preferable to *jiu-jitsu*.

juxtapose

K

kaleidoscope

ketchup

•**khalif:** see CALIPH.

khaki

kilogram not '-gramme'.

kilometre is spelt *-metre* in British English (American *-meter*).

kleptomania

knowledgeable has an *e* in the middle.

Koran is normally spelt this way in English contexts, although the form *Quran* or *Qur'an* is a closer transliteration of the Arabic original.

L

labour is the British spelling (American *labor*).

labyrinth

lachrymal ('of tears') is the usual spelling in general contexts but **lacrimal** (*ducts* etc.) is preferred in physiology (likewise **lacrimate, lacrimatory,** etc.)

lachrymose ('tearful', 'inducing tears') is always spelt this way.

lackadaisical

lacquer

languor is spelt *-uor*.

laryngitis

lascivious has a *c*.

latish ('somewhat late') is normally spelt without an *e* in the middle.

-leaved In combinations such as *broad-leaved* and *four-leaved*, *-leaved* is preferred to *-leafed* in current use.

leisure

leprechaun

leukaemia is the British spelling (American *leukemia*).

liaison has two *i*s.

library has two *r*s.

licence, license In British English, the noun is spelt *licence* and the verb *license* (and so *licensed premises*, *licensing hours*, *licensee*, etc.) In American English, both the noun and the verb are spelt *license*.

•**licorice**: see LIQUORICE.

lich-gate ('roofed gateway to a churchyard') is more often spelt *lich-*, than *lych-*. It is derived from the Old English word līc meaning 'corpse', because the gateway was formerly used at burials for sheltering a coffin until the clergyman's arrival.

lightning (with thunder) has no *e*.

likeable is the preferred form, not *likable*.

linchpin is preferred to *lynch-*.

lineage ('ancestry')

lineament ('facial feature')

liquefy is spelt *-efy*, not *'-ify'*. Its inflected forms are **liquefies**, **liquefied**, **liquefying**.

liqueur ('flavoured alcoholic liquor')

liquorice is the British spelling (American *licorice*).

•**litchi**: see LYCHEE.

literature has no double letters.

litre is the British spelling for the metric unit (American *liter*).

littérateur (French 'literary person')

littoral ('on the shore of a sea or lake')

liveable is the preferred form, not *livable*.

llama (mammal)

loathsome has no *e* in the middle.

lodestar, lodestone are the preferred spellings, not *load-*.

longevity

longitude not 'longtitude'.

loofah

loquacious

lour ('frown, look angry') is preferable to *lower*.

louvre ('set of overlapping slats for ventilation') is spelt this way in British English (American *louver*).

lovable is the preferred spelling, not *loveable*.

luncheon has an *e*.

Luxembourg has an *o*.

lychee is preferable to *litchi*.

M

Mac, Mc (prefix to surnames) Spelling depends on the custom of the person bearing the name; in alphabetical arrangement, treat as *Mac* however spelt.

macabre

mackintosh (waterproof coat) is spelt with a *k*, although the inventor's name was Charles *Macintosh*. But the shortened form is **mac** not 'mack'.

maelstrom

maestro

maharaja is preferable to *-jah*.

maharani ('wife of a maharaja') is preferable to *-nee*.

•**Mahomet**: see MUHAMMAD.

mandolin is the only spelling for the musical instrument and the preferred spelling for the kitchen utensil (also *mandoline*).

mangy is preferred to *mangey*.

manila (type of hemp or paper) has one *l*.

manoeuvrable has no *e* before the *-able* suffix in British spelling (American *maneuverable*).

manoeuvre is the British spelling, with inflected forms **manoeuvred**, **manoeuvring**. The American spelling is *maneuver*, with inflected forms *maneuvered*, *maneuvering*.

maraschino (cherry liqueur).

marijuana is preferable to *marihuana*.

marriageable has an *e* in the middle.

marshal (noun and verb) has one *l* but inflected forms **marshalled**, **marshalling** (American *-led*, *-ling*).

marten (mammal)

martial (adjective 'of war')

Marylebone (in London)

massacre

matey is preferred to *maty*.

matins has one *t*.

matt is the British spelling (American *matte* or sometimes *mat*).

mayonnaise has double *n*, single *s*.

mbaqanga (South African musical style) has *q* without *u*.

meagre is the British spelling (American *meager*).

medicine

medieval is now preferred to *mediaeval*.

mediocre

Mediterranean is spelt with one *d*, one *t*, and double *r*, as its derivation from the Latin words *medius* 'middle' and *terra* 'land' reminds us.

mellifluous

memento ('souvenir') should not be converted into the dubious formation 'momento'. The plural form is **mementoes**.

merchandise (noun and verb) is always spelt *-ise* in British English. In American English, the verb is often spelt with a final *-ize*.

meringue

metre is the British spelling for the unit of length and the meaning 'rhythm in poetry' (American *meter*).

mezzanine has double *z* and two single *ns*.

migraine has an *e* on the end.

mileage is the recommended spelling, not *milage*.

milieu has plural forms **milieux** or **milieus**.

millenarianism ('belief in the Second Coming') has double *l*, single *n*.

millenary ('thousandth anniversary') has double *l*, single *n*.

millennium has double *l*, double *n*, as does the related adjective **millennial**.

milli- (prefix 'one-thousandth') has double *l*.

millionaire has single *n*.

millipede is preferable to *millepede*.

milometer is preferable to *mileo-*.

mineralogy is spelt *-alogy*, not '-ology'.

miniature has an *a* in the middle.

minuscule The incorrect spelling 'miniscule' has arisen by analogy with other words beginning with *mini-*, where the meaning is similarly 'very small'.

mischievous not '-ious' as often mispronounced.

misdemeanour is spelt *-our* in British English (American *misdemeanor*).

misogynist

misspell has double *s*.

Mississippi (in the US) has two double *ss* and double *p*.

mistakable has no *e* in the middle.

mistle thrush is preferable to *missel*.

mitre is the British spelling (American *miter*).

mnemonic starts with silent *m*.

moccasin has double *c*, single *s*.

moneyed ('affluent') not 'monied'.

moneys is preferable to *monies*.

•**Moslem:** see MUSLIM.

mould, moulder are the British spellings (American *mold-*).

moult is the British spelling (American *molt*).

moustache is the normal British spelling but *mustache* (pronounced with stress on the first syllable) is more usual in American English.

mouth (verb) not 'mouthe'.

mucus is the noun, **mucous** the adjective.

Muhammad is the preferred spelling, not *Mohammad* or 'Mahomet'.

Muslim is now the preferred spelling, not *Moslem*.

myrrh has double *r*.

myxomatosis has no double letters.

N

naive, naivety are now preferred to *naïve*, *naïvety*.

necessary has single *c*, double *s*.

negligee without accents is now preferred to *negligée*, or *négligé*.

negligible is spelt *-ible*, not '-able'.

neighbour is spelt *-our* in British English (American *neighbor*).

nerve-racking is better than *-wracking*.

net ('not subject to deduction') is now preferred to *nett*.

neuralgia

niece is one of the most commonly misspelt words in English.

noes is the plural of *no*.

nonplussed, nonplussing have double *s*.

nonsuch ('unrivalled person or thing') is preferable to *nonesuch*.

no one is always written as two words and without a hyphen.

nosy ('inquisitive') is preferable to *nosey*.

noticeable has an *e* in the middle.

nuptial

O

O not 'Oh' is used to form a vocative in archaic or liturgical English (*O Caesar, O Lord hear us*, etc.)

oasis has two single *ss* (and plural **oases**).

obeisance

objector is spelt *-or* not '-er'.

obsequious has six vowels.

occasionally has double *c* and double *l*.

occurred, occurring, occurrence have double *c* and double *r*.

ochre is the British spelling; *ocher* is an American variant.

odour is spelt *-our* in British English (American *odor*). The corresponding adjective is **odorous** in both varieties.

odyssey has double *s* and ends *-ey*.

oesophagus is the British spelling (American *esophagus*).

oestrogen is the British spelling (American *estrogen*).

offence is spelt *-ence* in British English (American *offense*).

omelette is the British spelling; *omelet* is more common in American English.

ophthalmic has *-phth-* in the middle.

oppressor has double *p* and double *s*.

opprobrium has double *p*.

orangeade has *e* in the middle.

orang-utan is now preferred to *orang-outang*.

orator is spelt *-or*, not '-er'.

originator is spelt *-or*, not '-er'.

orthopaedic is the British spelling (American *-pedic*).

oscillate has double *l*.

overrun has double *r*.

oyez! (call of public crier) is preferable to *oyes!*

P

paediatric is the British spelling (American *pediatric*).

paedophile is the British spelling (American *pedophile*).

paid not 'payed'.

palaeo- (prefix 'ancient') Words of the type *palaeography, palaeolithic*, etc., are normally spelt with *-ae-* in British English, although the American form *paleo-* is beginning to influence British practice.

pallor is spelt *-or* in both British and American English.

panellist is the British spelling (American *panelist*).

paparazzo has single *p*, double *z*. The plural (more often used) is **paparazzi**.

papaya (fruit) is now preferred to *papaw* or *pawpaw*.

papier mâché

paraffin has single *r*, double *f*.

parakeet

parallel has inflected and derivative forms **paralleled, paralleling, parallelism, parallelogram**. The final *-l* is never doubled.

paralyse is the usual British spelling; the variant *paralyze* is chiefly American.

paraphernalia has a second *r* towards the end.

parenthesis and plural **-ses**.

pariah

parliament has *-ia-* in the middle.

parlour is the British spelling (American *-or*).

paroxysm

parquet

partisan is now preferred to *partizan*.

pastille (sweet) ends *-ille*.

pavilion has single *l*.

•**pawpaw**: see PAPAYA.

peaceable has an *e* in the middle and ends *-able*, not '-ible'.

peccadillo has double *c*, double *l*.

peddler, pedlar Although formerly regarded as an Americanism, *peddler* is now used increasingly for *pedlar* in British English; it is the form most likely to be used when the sense is 'drug dealer'. The verb forms **peddling, peddled** are always spelt with double *d*.

pederast is now preferred to *paederast*.

pedigreed

pejorative

Peloponnese (in Greece) has single *l*, single *p*, double *n*.

pencilling, pencilled are the British spellings (American *penciling, penciled*).

pendant is the noun form, **pendent** the adjective.

penicillin has single *n*, double *l*.

peninsula has no double letters. The adjective is **peninsular**.

peony

perceive

perennial has double *n*.

perfectible is spelt *-ible*, not '-able'.

periphery

permanent has no double letters.

permissible has double *s* and ends *-ible*, not 'able'.

personnel has double *n*.

pettifogging not 'petty-'.

pharaoh is spelt *-aoh*, not '-oah'.

pharmacopoeia is spelt *-poeia* in British English and *-poeia* or *-peia* in American.

Philippines has single *l* and double *p*. The inhabitants are called **Filipinos**.

phlegm has silent g.

phlox

phonetic

phosphorescence has two cs.

phosphorus is the correct spelling for the chemical element; the correct spelling for the adjective meaning 'containing phosphorus' is **phosphorous**. A common mistake is to use the -ous spelling for the noun.

physique

Piccadilly (in London) has double c, double l.

picnicking, picnicked are inflections of picnic.

pidgin (language)

pigeon (bird)

piggyback not 'pickaback'.

pilau (spiced dish of rice) is normally spelt in this way in British English, but the American variants pilaf or pilaff are now increasingly common.

pizazz (slang 'verve, sparkle') has several variant spellings but this seems the most common.

playwright not '-write'.

plebeian is an exception to the 'i before e' rule.

plenitude not 'plentitude'.

plimsoll (shoe) is preferable to plimsole. The **Plimsoll line** (or **mark**) is always spelt this way.

plough is the British spelling (American plow).

politician

polythene

pommel (part of a sword or saddle) has double m, single l. See also PUMMEL.

Portuguese (noun and adjective) has two us; the plural noun is the same.

possession has two double ss.

posthumous

practice, practise In British spelling, practice is used for the noun and practise for the verb, whereas in American English practice is used for both.

precede ('come before')

precipice

precis is now generally written without an accent. The plural is **precises**.

predecessor has double s.

predominant not 'predominate'.

preferred, preferring are inflected forms of prefer. But note single r in **preferable**, **-ably**.

premises ('building etc. used by business') has no double letters.

pretentious

preventable is the preferred spelling, not -ible.

primeval is now the dominant spelling, not primaeval.

prise ('force open') is the British spelling (American prize or pry).

privilege not 'privelege'.

privy counsellor is the preferred spelling for a member of the **Privy Council**.

proceed ('go on, continue')

program, programme In general uses the standard spelling is programme in British English and program in American. However, in the context of computing program is universal. The verb has inflected forms **programmed, programming** (with the variants **programed, programing** also available in American English).

promiscuous

promissory ('conveying a promise') has double s and no e.

promontory

promoter not '-or'.

pronounceable has an e in the middle.

pronunciation not 'pronounce-'.

propeller has double l and ends -er, not '-or'.

prophecy is the noun (plural **prophecies**) and **prophesy** the verb (inflections **prophesies, prophesied, prophesying**).

proprietor is spelt -or not '-er'. But note **proprietary** (right, name, etc.)

prosecutor is spelt -or, not '-er'.

protector is spelt -or, not '-er'.

protein is an exception to the 'i before e' rule.

protester is spelt -er, not '-or'.

protractor (instrument used in geometry) is spelt -or, not '-er'.

provable is spelt without an e in the middle.

provenance ('origin, place of origin') is the usual British form; provenience is mainly American.

pseudonym

psychedelic

pukka ('genuine, excellent') is preferable to pukkah.

pummel ('pound with fists') is preferable to pommel and has inflected forms **pummelled, pummelling** (American pummeled, pummeling).

pupillage not 'pupilage'.
pursue
purveyor is spelt *-or*, not '-er'.
pusillanimous has double *l*, single *n*.
putrefy is spelt *-efy*, not '-ify'.
putt (in golf)
pyjamas is the standard spelling in British English (American *pajamas*).

Q

Qatar (country) has no *u* after *q*.
qawwali (Muslim devotional music) has no *u* after *q*.
quadraphony, quadraphonic are preferable to *quadro-*.
quarrel has double *r*, single *l*, but inflected forms **quarrelled, quarrelling** (American *quarreled, quarreling*).
quatercentenary not 'quarter-'.
questionnaire has double *n* and terminal *e*.
•**Qur'an:** see KORAN.
queue has two *us* and two *es*; the preferred spelling for the present participle is **queuing** (one *e*).
quotient

R

racket (for ball games) is preferred to *racquet*. The game is always spelt **rackets**.
radioes, radioed, radioeing are the inflected forms of *radio*. But note the plural noun **radios** (no *e*).
raja (Indian prince) is better than *rajah*.
rarefy is spelt *-efy*, not '-ify'.
rarity has no *e*.
rateable is the preferred spelling, not *ratable*.
raze ('destroy completely') is better than *rase*.
recede
receipt has silent *p*.
recommend has double *m*.
recompense not '-pence'.
recondite
reconnoitre is the British spelling (American *reconnoiter*). Both forms have double *n*.
reducible is spelt *-ible*, not '-able'.
reflector is spelt *-or*, not '-er'.
relevant
reminiscence has two *cs* in the last syllable.
Renaissance has double *s*; the older variant *Renascence* is now rare.

renege not 'renegue'.
repellent has double *l*.
repertory
replaceable is spelt with an *e* in the middle to preserve the soft sound of the preceding *c*.
reprehensible is spelt *-ible*, not '-able'.
reprieve
reproducible is spelt *-ible*, not '-able'.
rescind
resistible is spelt *-ible*, not '-able'.
resplendent is spelt *-ent*, not '-ant'.
responsible is spelt *-ible*, not '-able'.
restaurateur not 'restaurant-'.
resuscitate has *-sc-* in the middle.
reversible is spelt *-ible*, not '-able'.
revue (musical entertainment)
rhetoric
rheumatism
rhinoceros
rhododendron
rhubarb
rhyme (in poetry) not 'rime'.
rhythm has two *hs*.
ribbon is now the usual form; the older variant *riband* is used only in heraldry and the titles of certain sporting contests.
rickety is spelt *-ety*, not '-etty'.
ricochet
rigorism, rigorist not 'rigour-'.
rigor mortis not 'rigour'.
rigour is generally spelt *-our* in British English and *-or* in American. The corresponding adjective is **rigorous** in both varieties. Note, however, the British spelling *rigor* for the medical sense 'sudden feeling of cold and shivering'.
rille ('channel on the moon's surface')
riveted, riveting have single *t*.
roguish has no *e*.
role The spelling 'rôle' is no longer used.
Romania is the official spelling. *Roumania* and *Rumania* will be found in older writing.
roofs not 'rooves'.
rotisserie has double *s*.
rumba is preferable to *rhumba*.
rumbustious is spelt *-ious*, not '-uous'.
rumour is the British spelling (American *rumor*).

S

sabre is the British spelling (American *saber*).

sacrilegious is formed from the noun *sacrilege* and is spelt with the first *i* and the *e* in the order shown, not (by confusion with *religious*) the other way round.

saleable is preferred to *salable*.

sanatorium is the British form (plural **-oriums** or **-oria**). The American form is *sanitarium*.

sanctimonious

sari is preferred to *saree*. The plural form is **saris**.

sarsaparilla (plant, drink)

saucisson (French sausage)

sauerkraut not 'sour-'.

scallop (mollusc, shell) not 'scollop'. The verb ('to decorate with scallop designs') has inflected forms **scalloped**, **scalloping**.

scallywag is the British form; *scalawag* is an American variant.

scaly not '-ley'.

sceptic is the British spelling (American *skeptic*).

sceptre is the British spelling (American *scepter*).

schizophrenic

schnapps

sciatica

scimitar

scurrilous has double *r*, single *l*.

scythe

sear (verb) not 'sere'.

secateurs

secede

secrecy not '-esy'.

secretary not '-ery'.

seize is an exception to the '*i* before *e*' rule.

selvedge ('edge on woven fabric') is the usual British spelling; the variant *selvage* is mainly American.

senator is spelt *-or*, not '-er'.

separate not (as commonly misspelt) '-erate'.

sepulchre is the British spelling (American *sepulcher*).

sergeant is the normal spelling in the context of the police, army, and airforce; *serjeant* is usually restricted to the titles of certain ceremonial offices (e.g. *serjeant-at-arms*).

serviceable is spelt with an *e* in the middle, to preserve the soft sound of the *c*.

sett ('earth of a badger')

Shakespearean now tends to be preferred to *Shakespearian*.

shareable is preferred to *sharable*.

sharia (Muslim law) is generally preferred to *shariah* or *shariat*.

sharif (Muslim leader) is now preferred to *sherif* or *shereef*.

sheath is the noun form, **sheathe** the verb.

sheikh is preferred to *shaikh*, *shaykh*, or *sheik*.

Shia (branch of Islam) is generally preferred to *Shi'a*.

shibboleth has double *b*.

show not 'shew'.

sibyl (female oracle) but note **sibylline** ('prophetic, mysterious').

siege

sienna (brown pigment) is spelt with two *ns* despite being derived from the name of *Siena* (one *n*) in Italy.

simultaneous

singeing ('burning lightly') is spelt like this to distinguish it from *singing* (formed from the verb *sing*).

Sinhalese (people and language of Sri Lanka) is preferred to *Singhalese* or *Sinhala*.

sizeable with an *e* in the middle is preferred to *sizable*.

skied, skiing are preferable to *skid*, *ski-ing*.

skilful is the usual British spelling; the variant *skill-* is mainly American.

slavish is spelt without an *e*.

slimy is spelt without an *e*.

smart alec is preferable to *aleck*, but the adjective is **smart-alecky**.

smoky is spelt without an *e*.

smooth The verb is spelt the same as the adjective, not 'smoothe'.

smoulder is the British spelling; *smolder* is an American variant.

snaky is spelt without an *e*.

snorkel not 'schnorkel'.

sobriquet ('nickname') is preferable to *soubriquet*.

solemness has one *n*.

soliloquy has no double letters.

sombre is the British spelling (American *somber*).

somersault not 'summer-'.

soufflé has an acute accent.

soupçon has a cedilla.

spectator is spelt *-or*, not '-er'.

spectre is the British spelling (American *specter*).

speculator is spelt *-or*, not '-er'.

splendour is the British spelling (American *splendor*).

spontaneous

sprightly not 'spritely'.

spurt not 'spirt'.

squalor is spelt *-or* in both British and American English.

squeegee (cleaning or scraping implement)

squirearchy has an *e* in the middle.

staunch The verb ('stop a flow of blood etc.') is spelt this way in British English with *stanch* as a possible American variant. The adjective ('loyal') is always spelt *staunch*.

stoep (African veranda)

storey ('level of building') is the British spelling: *story* is an American variant.

stoup (for holy water etc.) not 'stoop'.

strait-jacket not 'straight-'.

strait-laced not 'straight-'.

strategy

strychnine

stupefy is spelt *-efy* not '-ify'.

sty The word meaning 'a pen for pigs' has the plural form **sties**. The word for 'an inflamed swelling on the eyelid' is better spelt *sty* but can be spelt *stye*; the plural form is **sties** or **styes**.

stymie ('hinder') is spelt this way, not 'stimy'; the present participle is **stymying** or **stymieing**.

subtly not 'subtlely'. But note **subtlety**.

succeed has double *c*, double *e*.

succinct has double *c*.

sufficient has double *f* and an *i* in the last syllable.

suitor is spelt *-or*, not '-er'.

sulphur remains the standard British spelling (American *sulfur*). The related words **sulphuric**, **sulphurous**, etc. are likewise spelt with *f* in American English.

summons (noun and verb 'order to appear in court') The noun has the plural **summonses** and the verb has the past **summonsed**.

sumptuous has three *us*.

supercilious not '-silious'.

superintendent ends *-ent*, not '-ant'.

supersede is the standard spelling, not 'supercede'. However, owing to the influence of *intercede*, *accede*, etc., the *c* spelling is now very common; it has

been entered without comment in some modern dictionaries.

supervise is always spelt *-vise*, not '-vize'.

suppressor (electrical device) is spelt *-or*, not '-er'.

surgeon

surmise is always spelt *-ise*, not '-ize'.

surprise is always spelt *-ise*, not '-ize'.

surreptitious has double *r* and an *i* in the last syllable.

surveillance has double *l*.

suspicious

swap not 'swop'.

sycamore not 'syco-'.

sycophant

syllabus

symmetry has double *m*.

syncopation

synthesis

synthesize is preferable to *synthet-*.

T

tacit

targeted, targeting have single *t*.

tattooed, tattooing

taxiing is preferable to *taxying*.

teasel is preferable to *teazel* or *teazle*.

tee-hee (laugh)

teetotaller is spelt with two ls in British English, but has an American variant *teetotaler*. **Teetotal** and **teetotalism** are always spelt with single *l*.

televise As a back-formation from *television*, this is always spelt *-ise*, not '-ize'.

temperament not 'tempra-'.

template is preferable to *templet*.

tenant not 'tennant'.

tendentious

tenet

Tennessee (in the US) has double *n*, double *s*.

tête-à-tête requires accents.

thank you is written as two words (but hyphenated in *thank-you letter*).

theatre is the British spelling (American *theater*).

thesaurus

thief

threshold

thyroid

tic ('spasmodic contraction of muscles')

tick (parasite)

titbit is the usual spelling in British English (American *tidbit*). The first element is probably derived from an English dialect word *tid* meaning 'tender, nice, special'.

toboggan has double *g*. The verb forms and other derivatives do not double the *n*.

today, tomorrow, tonight are never hyphenated or written as two words.

tonsillitis has double *l*.

tormentor is spelt *-or*, not '-er'.

torpor is spelt *-or* in both British and American English.

toupee is preferable to *toupet*.

tourniquet

trade union not 'trades'. But **Trades Union Congress**.

traipse

tranquillity, tranquillize, tranquillizer are spelt with two *l*s in British English, but usually with one *l* in American. The adverb is **tranquilly** in both varieties.

transcendent not '-dant'.

transferred, transferring are inflected forms of *transfer*. But note one *r* in **transferable**.

transgressor is spelt *-or*, not '-er'.

transistor is spelt *-or*, not '-er'.

transonic ('close to the speed of sound') is preferable to *trans-sonic*.

transsexual is preferable to *transexual*.

trans-ship ('transfer from one ship etc. to another') is preferable to *tranship*.

traveller is the British spelling (likewise **travelled, travelling**); all three words can be spelt with one *l* in American English.

triptych

trolley

troupe (of performers)

trousseau has five vowels and double *s*.

truly not 'truely'.

truncheon has an *e*.

tsar is the preferred spelling in British English, not *tzar* or *czar*.

T-shirt is preferred to *tee-shirt*.

tumour is the British spelling (American *tumor*).

tunnelled, tunnelling are spelt with double *l*.

Turco- is the combining form of *Turkish*, not 'Turko-'.

tyranny has double *n*.

tyre (wheel's rubber covering) is the British spelling (American *tire*).

U

ubiquitous

umbrella

unctuous

under way not 'underway' or 'under weigh' (even in nautical contexts).

unguent ('ointment')

unwieldy not '-wieldly'.

V

vaccination has double *c*.

vacillate has single *c*, double *l*.

vacuum has double *u*.

vainness is spelt with two *n*s.

valorize ('ascribe validity to') not 'valour-'.

valour is the British spelling (American *valor*). But the adjective is spelt **valorous** in both varieties.

valuable has no *e* in the middle.

vapour is the British spelling (American *vapor*). Derivatives such as **vapourless** and **vapourish** follow the spellings of the root forms, but **vaporous** (adjective) and **vaporize** (verb) are spelt *-or-* in both British and American English.

variegated has *e* in the middle.

vehicle

veld is preferred to *veldt*.

vendor is the usual British spelling; *vender* is a mainly American variant, sometimes used in the sense 'vending machine' in Britain.

venereal has three *e*s.

veranda is now the usual spelling, not *verandah*.

verger (church official) is spelt as shown, except that the spelling *virger* is used of St Paul's Cathedral in London and Winchester Cathedral.

vermilion has no double letters.

verruca has double *r*.

veterinary

vibrator is spelt *-or*, not '-er'.

vice (tool) is the British spelling (American *vise*).

vichyssoise (French soup)

vicissitude

victuals

vigour is the British spelling (American *vigor*). But the adjective **vigorous** is spelt *-or-* in both varieties.

vinaigrette not 'vineg-'.

violoncello not 'violin-'.

Virgil is the preferred spelling of the name of the Roman poet, not *Vergil* (despite the Latin form *Publius Vergilius Maro*).

viscous

visitor is spelt *-or*, not '*-er*'.

visor is the preferred spelling, not *vizor*.

vocal cord not 'chord'.

voluptuous has two *o*s and three *u*s.

W

wagon is generally preferred to *waggon*.

Wahhabi (member of Muslim sect) usually has double *h*.

Waitangi Day (New Zealand holiday)

waive ('forego voluntarily')

wantonness is spelt with two *n*s.

warranty

wastable not 'waste-'.

Wednesday

weir is an exception to '*i* before *e*'.

weird is an exception to '*i* before *e*'.

welfare not 'well-'.

werewolf

whisky is the spelling for Scotch, but Irish **whiskey**.

Whitsun

wholly not 'whole-'.

whooping cough not 'hooping'.

wilful is the British spelling, but *willful* is also used in America.

wisteria is preferred to *wistaria*.

withhold is spelt with two *h*s.

woebegone, woeful

woodenness is spelt with two *n*s in the middle.

woollen, woolly are the British spellings (American *woolen*).

wrath is the spelling for the noun, **wroth** for the adjective.

X

Xhosa (Bantu people and language)

Y

yashmak

yogurt is preferred to *yoghurt* or *yoghourt*.

Yom Kippur

Section 3: Punctuation

The purpose of punctuation is to mark out strings of words into manageable groups and to show how these groups are related to each other. Correct punctuation clarifies both the meaning of the individual words and the construction of the sentence as a whole, so that even quite complex sentences can be understood at first reading, without stumbling or backtracking. To some extent, therefore, punctuation acts as a substitute for the devices we all use in speech, such as pausing and altering pitch; however, the differences between written and spoken language mean that the parallel should not be pushed too far.

Punctuation shouldn't cause as much fear as it does. Only about a dozen marks need to be mastered and the guidelines are fairly simple. The marks most commonly used to divide a piece of prose are the **full stop***, the* **semicolon***, and the* **comma***, with the strength of the dividing or separating role diminishing from the full stop to the comma. The full stop therefore marks the main division into sentences; the semicolon joins sentences (as in this sentence); and the comma, which is the most flexible in use and causes most problems, separates smaller elements with the least loss of continuity.* **Brackets** *and* **dashes** *also serve as separators—often more strikingly than commas (as in this sentence).*

You can see these marks being well applied every day in the serious newspapers, where 99 per cent of the punctuation will accord with the advice given here. Study of press punctuation also reveals the full range of marks, as journalists—especially the star columnists—use far more **colons***, semicolons, and dashes than business and official writers. The current trend towards using the minimum of necessary punctuation in business reports, government information, etc. should not mislead anyone into thinking that a concern for proper punctuation is pedantic or old-fashioned. A command of the full range of punctuation marks helps you to say more, and to say it more interestingly and effectively. Punctuation is an essential part of the tool-kit—as important as choosing the right words.*

apostrophe '

The apostrophe is now so widely misused that its eventual death seems inevitable. This would be a pity, as the correct use of apostrophes conveys meaning and prevents ambiguity. For example, this surreal apostrophe-free message has been seen roaming Britain on a fleet of lorries:

COLLECTING TOMORROWS

DELIVERIES TODAY

The mystery only becomes clear when an apostrophe is placed between the *w* and the *s*, to show that *tomorrow's* is a possessive rather than a common plural. Gratuitous or misplaced apostrophes can be equally distracting. This article deals first with the straightforward uses and abuses of the apostrophe, and then looks at some disputed areas:

(A) The main use of the apostrophe is to indicate the possessive case, as in *John's book*, etc. It comes before the *s* in singular and plural nouns not ending in *s*, as in *the boy's games* and *the women's games*. It comes after the *s* in plural nouns ending in *s*, as in *the boys' games*.

In singular nouns ending in *s* practice differs between (for example) *Nicholas'* and *Nicholas's*. For a fuller discussion and detailed guidelines, see POSSESSIVE CASE in PART II of SECTION 2: SPELLING.

(B) The apostrophe is also used to indicate a contraction, e.g. *he's*, *wouldn't*, *bo's'n*, *o'clock*. However, the use of an apostrophe at the start of *bus*, *phone*, *flu*, *cello*, etc. is old-fashioned and unnecessary, as these are now the usual forms.

(C) Apostrophes should not be used in straightforward plurals. Refuse to be led astray by the notorious 'grocer's plural' in such shop notices as:

Shrimp's, prawns', pears', orange's, and sandwich'es

An exception to the rule is the occasional use of an apostrophe to form plurals of individual letters or numbers:

mind your p's and q's

a list of do's and don'ts

However, this use is diminishing and should be avoided unless there is a risk of ambiguity or unclearness. The apostrophe is helpful in *cross your t's* but unnecessary in *MPs* and *1990s*.

(D) The possessive pronouns *his*, *hers*, *ours*, *yours*, *theirs*, *its*, and *whose* never take apostrophes: no letters are missing and the idea of possession is built into the word. (The only exception here is *one's*.)

The form *it's* means *it is* or *it has*; *who's* means *who is* or *who has*. There are no words *her's*, *our's*, *their's*, *your's*.

(E) Such expressions of measurement and time as *a fortnight's holiday*, *a pound's worth*, *at arm's length*, contain possessives and should have apostrophes correctly placed. Strictly speaking, this applies equally to the plural forms *two weeks' holiday* etc. but in these cases the apostrophes are now routinely dropped in much everyday writing (presumably because they make no real difference to the sense and are undetectable in speech). Although the apostrophe here

may one day become extinct, at present it is safer to retain it in more formal writing.

(F) In *I'm going to the butcher's, grocer's*, etc. there is a possessive with ellipsis of the word 'shop'. The same construction is used in *I'm going to Brown's, Green's*, etc., where a business calls itself *Brown, Green*, or the like.

However, many businesses and other concerns now omit the apostrophe from their official name, e.g. *Debenhams, Barclays Bank, Citizens Advice Bureau, Farmers Guardian*. Although sometimes disapproved of, this practice can be justified as an attributive rather than possessive use of the noun (i.e. the advice bureau is for the use of citizens rather than their possession). As a result of this trend, it can be difficult to know whether to write e.g. *I bought it in Smiths/Smith's/W. H. Smith* or *I have a Barclays/Barclay's/Barclays' account*, and so on. In formal writing, it is doubtless best to use the correct name of the company concerned; in everyday use, however, the variants above should be considered equally acceptable in each case.

Note also that it is unnecessary to use an apostrophe in e.g. *I'm going to the cleaners*, as the plural *cleaners* could be a common noun rather than a possessive.

bracket ( ) [ ]

The types of brackets used in normal punctuation are **round brackets** or **parentheses ( )** and **square brackets [ ]**.

(A) **Round brackets.**

(i) The main use is to enclose an explanation, comment, or piece of information that is relatively unimportant to the main text:

He is (as he always was) a rebel.

Zimbabwe (formerly Rhodesia)

They talked about Machtpolitik (*power politics*).

(ii) They are used to give references and citations:

Thomas Carlyle (1795–1881)

integrated circuits (see p. 38)

(iii) They are used to enclose reference letters or figures, e.g. *(1)*, *(a)*.

(iv) They are used to enclose optional words:

There are many (apparent) difficulties.

In this example, the difficulties may or may not be only apparent.

(v) Brackets can also be used to prevent the meaning of a particularly complicated sentence from disintegrating:

Many plans have been studied but the agreed solution is a system of river mattressing (to avoid breaches) and embankment raising (to avoid exceptionally high-tide flooding).

(B) **Square brackets** are used less often.

(i) The main use is to enclose an explanation or comment by someone other than the writer or speaker of the surrounding text:

At this point she [Mrs Patel] asked her to leave the shop.

(ii) In some contexts they may be used to convey special kinds of information, especially when round brackets are used for other purposes: for example, in dictionaries they are often used to give the etymologies at the end of entries.

(C) If a sentence begins within a bracket, it should end with a full stop inside the bracket: otherwise the stop should come after the bracket. (For examples of cases in which a final stop outside the bracket may be omitted, see FULL STOP.) A comma should rarely if ever precede a bracket but there is no harm in putting one after the closing bracket if this aids meaning.

capital letters

Capital letters (upper case) are used to signal special uses of words, either to mark a significant point in written or printed matter (especially the beginning of a sentence), or to distinguish names that identify particular people or things from those that describe any number of them. Practice varies when people and things do not always fit neatly into one or other of these two categories. This article deals with the elementary uses first, and then with the less straightforward ones.

In general, the modern trend is to use capitals sparingly and to err on the side of lower case.

(A) A capital is used for the first letter of the word beginning a sentence:

He decided not to come. Later he changed his mind.

This includes sentences that form quoted speech:

The assistant turned and replied, 'There are no more left.'

But not those contained in brackets within a larger sentence:

I have written several letters (there are many to be written).

(B) By convention, it is used for the pronoun *I* (but not for *me, my, mine*).

(C) It is used in personal and proper names, e.g. *Paris, Africa, Tony Blair, the Cutty Sark, the Taj Mahal.*

(D) It is used in names of peoples and languages and in related adjectives, e.g. *Englishman, Austrian, French.*

(E) It is used for names of days and months, e.g. *Tuesday, March, Boxing Day,* but not usually for those of seasons, e.g. *spring.*

(F) It is used for names of historical events and periods, e.g. *the Middle Ages, the Enlightenment, the Vietnam War.*

(G) It is used in titles of books, newspapers, plays, films, television programmes, etc.:

A Tale of Two Cities

The Good, the Bad, and the Ugly

Insignificant words such as *of* and *the* are not usually capitalized. Note that foreign-language titles follow the conventions of the language in question: this usually involves a more sparing use of capitals than would be normal in English:

Les Enfants du paradis

La dolce vita

(H) It is used in references to the Deity, e.g. *God, the Almighty, the Lord showed His strength.* The use of capitalized *He, Him,* and *His* in references to Jesus Christ is now much less common than it was, even in writings by and for believing Christians.

(I) It is used in designations of rank or relationship when used as titles, e.g. *Prince Charles, Aunt Mabel, Mr President, His Holiness*.

The tendency to capitalize *the Prince, the President, the Pope*, etc. when referring to particular holders of these offices is now less common than it was (although the reigning monarch is always *the Queen* or *King* in the UK). There is now considerable diversity of practice in this area. For example, *The Sunday Times* prints *home secretary* and *chancellor of the exchequer*, whereas *The Times* has *Home Secretary* and *Chancellor of the Exchequer*. Titles which include a place name tend to retain their capitals, e.g. *Archbishop of Canterbury*, as do those that look odd in lower case, e.g. *Master of the Rolls, Lord Chief Justice*.

(J) A capital letter is used for names of institutions, when these are regarded as identifying rather than describing, e.g. *Christianity, Islam, Marxism, the (Roman) Catholic Church, the Labour Party, the House of Lords*. Organizations, government departments, and acts of parliament generally take initial capitals only when their full name or something similar is used. Thus *Metropolitan Police* but *the police; County Court* and *Court of Appeal* but *the court; the Health and Safety at Work Act* but *the act; Legal Aid Fund* but *legal aid*. A newspaper would print *Blankshire District Council* but *the council*. The council itself, however, might prefer to use a capital *c* whenever it referred to itself.

The word *Church* is often capitalized when it refers to an institution (or the Church as a whole, considered theologically), so as to distinguish it from the use of the word to mean a building or local body. The similar use of *State* with a capital letter is now uncommon (except in the phrase *Church and State*).

(K) Capitalization often indicates that a word is being used in a specific and limited (rather than a more general) sense. Particular care may be required in this area:

a *Conservative voter* but *conservative tastes*

a *Roman Catholic* but *catholic sympathies*

an *Irish Republican* but e.g. *Australian republicans*

a *Christian Scientist* (i.e. follower of Mrs Eddy) but a *Christian scientist*

(L) Words derived from proper names use a small initial letter when connection with the proper name is indirect or allusive, e.g. *jersey, platonic love, pasteurized milk*. However, when the connection of a derived adjective or verb with a proper name is felt to be alive, use a capital, e.g. *Platonic philosophy, Shakespearean drama*.

Adjectives of nationality usually retain the capital even when used in transferred senses, e.g. *Dutch courage, Turkish delight, French windows*. The chief exceptions are *arabic numeral, roman numeral*, and *roman type*.

(M) The name of a product or process, if registered as a trade mark, is a proprietary name, and should be given a capital initial, e.g. *Coca-Cola, Hoover, Xerox*. However, if the name becomes established as a generic term this is often ignored in everyday use, e.g. *biro*.

(N) For points of the compass use small initials except:

(i) When part of the name of a country, province, or town, e.g. *South Africa, Northern Ireland, West Bromwich*.

(ii) When denoting a recognized region, e.g. *South Wales, East Africa, the Far North of Sweden*.

(iii) When abbreviated, e.g. *NNE* for *north-north-east*.

(iv) In bridge.

(O) Many abbreviations consist partly or entirely of the initial letters of words in capital letters: *BBC, DfEE, M.Litt*. Acronyms that can easily be spoken as words need only have an initial capital: *Nato, Unicef, Unesco*.

(P) The current trend is to use capitals very sparingly in titles, section headings, captions, etc. A common practice now is to capitalize only the first word of the heading and any other words that would normally require it.

(Q) Block capitals are rarely used in ordinary prose. Their main function is to highlight statements that must on no account be overlooked:

WARNING: DO NOT EXCEED THE STATED DOSE

(R) Lines of verse often begin with a capital letter.

colon :

The colon is the punctuation mark that is least used and least well understood in ordinary writing. It has several distinct functions that make it different from the full stop, the comma, or the semicolon.

(A) The main role of the colon is to separate main clauses when there is a step forward from the first to the second, especially from introduction to main point, from general statement to example, from cause to effect (or vice versa), and from premise to conclusion:

> *There is something I want to say: I should like you all to know how grateful I am.*

> *It was not easy: to begin with I had to find the right house.*

> *The weather was bad: so we decided to stay at home.*

In the third example, a comma could be used, but the emphasis on cause and effect would be much reduced.

(B) It is also used to introduce a list of items where the sense requires a pause before the list:

> *The following were present: J. Smith, J. Brown, M. Jones.*

> *She has several positive characteristics: charm, dignity, and stickability.*

Here the colon should not be followed by a dash, although this practice is sometimes seen in older printing.

(C) It is used to introduce, more formally and emphatically than a comma would, speech or quoted material:

> *I told them last week: 'Do not in any circumstances open this door.'*

(D) It can be used to separate two sharply contrasting and parallel statements:

> *During Wimbledon, television is like someone with a reserved ticket: radio is the enthusiast who has queued all night to get in.*

A weaker contrast might be signified by a semicolon (there is some overlap in meaning between the two marks here).

(E) As an extension of these uses, a colon is often placed at the end of a printed paragraph to introduce a long quotation, an example or examples, a set of numbered points, or the conclusion of an argument. In these cases it is often preceded by *for example, namely, the following, to sum up*, etc.

(F) In American English a colon usually follows the initial greeting in a letter (*Dear Ms Jones:*), where in British English a comma is customary. A colon also separates hours and minutes in notation of time in American English (*10:30 a.m.*)

comma ,

There is much variation in the use of the comma in print and in everyday writing. Essentially, its role is to give detail to the structure of sentences, especially longer ones, and to make their meaning clear by marking off words that either do or do not belong together. Too many commas can prevent the reader from grasping the construction of the sentence as a whole; too few can make a piece of writing difficult to read or, worse, difficult to understand.

(A) The comma is widely used to separate the main clauses of a compound sentence when they are not sufficiently close in meaning or content to form a continuous unpunctuated sentence, and are not distinct enough to warrant a semicolon. A conjunction such as *and, but, yet*, etc. is normally used:

> *The road runs through a beautiful wooded valley, and the railway line follows it closely.*

It is sometimes said that commas should be inserted between main clauses that have different subjects (as in the sentence quoted above), but omitted when the clauses have the same subject, e.g.

> *The road runs through a beautiful wooded valley and then crosses the railway line.*

Although not bad as a rule of thumb, this is clearly too simple. For example, the clauses in the following sentence have different

subjects but are too closely linked to require a comma:

> *Do as I tell you and you'll never regret it.*

By the same token, an 'unnecessary'
comma can create special effects, such as
suspense:

> *They crept into the room, and found the*
> *body.*

(B) It is considered incorrect to join the
clauses of a compound sentence without a
conjunction (the so-called 'comma splice').
In the following sentence, the comma
should either be replaced by a semicolon,
or be retained and followed by *and*:

> *I like swimming very much, I go to the pool*
> *every week.*

(C) It is also considered incorrect to separate
a subject from its verb:

> *Those with the smallest incomes and no*
> *other means, should get most support*

or a verb from an object that is a clause:

> *They believed, that nothing could go*
> *wrong.*

(D) The comma is used in pairs to separate
elements in a sentence that are not part of
the main statement:

> *I should like you all, ladies and gentlemen,*
> *to raise your glasses.*

> *There is no sense, as far as I can see, in this*
> *suggestion.*

> *It appears, however, that we were wrong.*

Readers can, if they wish, leapfrog over the
cordoned-off area and still make sense of
what is said.

(E) It is also used to separate a relative clause
from its antecedent when the clause is not
serving an identifying function (see RELA-
TIVE CLAUSE in PART II of SECTION 1: GRAMMAR):

> *The girls, who will join the team next week,*
> *are fine players.*

In the above sentence, the information in
the *who* clause is incidental to the main
statement; without the commas, it would
form an essential part of it in identifying
which girls are being referred to:

> *The girls who will join the team next week*
> *are fine players.*

Particular care is needed here, as the presence or absence of commas can change the
whole sense of what is being said.

(F) A single comma usually follows adverbs
(including so-called sentence adverbs) in
initial position in a sentence:

> *Quickly, she ran upstairs.*

> *Thankfully, it was soon over.*

The same applies to sentence connectors
(such as *however*, *moreover*, or *nevertheless*) in
initial position:

> *However, it was not to be.*

(G) Similarly, a comma is often used to separate an adverbial clause in initial position
from the main clause in a sentence:

> *If the current plan turns out to be*
> *unworkable, we will obviously reconsider.*

> *As I'm in the area tomorrow afternoon, I*
> *might as well drop in.*

The comma is particularly common after
concessive clauses beginning with *although*,
despite, *while*, etc.

> *Although greatly admired abroad, she is*
> *still little known in her homeland.*

(H) A comma is particularly necessary after
a participial or verbless clause:

> *Having had breakfast, I went for a walk.*

> *The sermon over, the congregation filed*
> *out.*

(I) It should also follow a salutation or vocative:

> *James, it's been ages!*

> *Ladies and gentlemen, I give you a toast.*

(J) A comma is used to separate complementary clauses in sentences of this kind:

> *Parliament is not dissolved, only prorogued.*

> *She is from New Zealand, not Australia.*

> *Spoken prayer can be powerful, as can*
> *silence.*

(K) A comma is generally used to introduce
direct speech:

> *He then asked, 'Do you want to come?'*

It is also used to introduce the implied direct speech in sentences of this kind:

> *The question is, what can be done?*

> *My first thought was, let's just go home.*

(L) An important role of the comma is to prevent ambiguity or (momentary) misunderstanding, especially after a verb used intransitively where it might otherwise be taken to be transitive:

> With the police pursuing, the people shouted loudly.

Other examples follow:

> He did not want to leave, from a feeling of loyalty.
>
> In the valley below, the houses appeared very small.
>
> In 2000, 1940 seems a long time ago.
>
> Mr Douglas Hogg said that he had shot, himself, as a small boy.

(M) Commas are usually inserted between adjectives coming before a noun:

> an enterprising, ambitious person
>
> a cold, damp, badly heated room

But the comma is omitted when the last adjective has a closer relation to the noun than the others:

> a distinguished foreign politician
>
> a little old lady

(N) Commas are used to separate items in a list or sequence. Usage varies as to the inclusion of a comma before and in the last item; the practice in this *Compendium* (and in other books published by the Oxford University Press) is to include it:

> The following will report at 9.30 sharp: Jones, Smith, Thompson, and Williams.

A final comma before and, when used regularly and consistently, has the advantage of clarifying the grouping at a composite name occurring at the end of a list:

> We shall go to Smiths, Boots, Woolworths, and Marks and Spencer.

(O) There is no need for a comma between nouns when one is put before the other to qualify or describe it in some way:

> my friend Tom
>
> the Labour MP Sarah Jackson

But insert a comma when the second noun is a parenthesis:

> His father, Humphrey V. Roe, was not so fortunate.

(P) A comma follows *Dear Sir, Dear John*, etc. in letters, and *Yours sincerely*, etc. at the end.

(Q) Commas are used in numbers of four or more figures (in some house styles, five or more figures), to separate each group of three consecutive figures starting from the right, e.g. 14,236,681.

(R) No comma is needed between month and year in dates, e.g. *May 2000*, or between number and road in addresses, e.g. *12 Acacia Avenue*.

dash – —

There are, in formal printing at least, two types of dash: the **en-rule** (–) and the **em-rule** (—). An en-rule is twice the length of a hyphen, and an em-rule is twice the length of an en-rule. Most word-processing programs are able to distinguish the two lengths of rule, but in ordinary writing no distinction is usually made (and many people are not even aware of one).

(A) The shorter **en-rule** is used to join two or more items together. In contradistinction to the hyphen, it is used where movement or opposition, rather than co-operation or unity, is felt between these items. Its meaning therefore resembles *to* or *versus*:

> the 1914–18 war
>
> the London–Horsham–Brighton route
>
> the Marxist–Trotskyite split
>
> the France–Germany match

But note *the Marxist-Leninist position* and *the Franco-Prussian War* with hyphens.

The en-rule is also used for joint authors or the like, e.g. *the Lloyd–Jones hypothesis. The Lloyd-Jones hypothesis* with a hyphen would indicate a single author with a double-barrelled name.

(B) The longer **em-rule** is the more familiar in everyday use, and corresponds to what most people understand by the term 'dash'.

(i) A single dash is used to indicate a pause, generally to introduce an explanation or expansion of what comes before it:

We then saw the reptiles—snakes, crocodiles, that sort of thing.

Smokers argue that if their illnesses are self-inflicted, well, so are most people's— look at traffic accidents, look at potholers.

It can also add emphasis:

He shot big game for status, pleasure—and greed.

(ii) A pair of dashes is used to indicate asides and parentheses, forming a more distinct break than commas would:

Visitors may stay overnight—or for as long as they wish—in the hostelry run by the friars.

People in the north are more friendly—and helpful—than those in the south.

In practice dashes tend to draw attention to the phrase they enclose, whereas brackets usually have the opposite effect.

There is no rule against using more than one pair of dashes in a sentence but take care that meaning and syntax do not disintegrate. The following sentence by a newspaper columnist comes close to collapse:

Volkswagen is in trouble—terrible trouble—very terrible trouble, and we can sit on the sidelines—entry free—and bask in somebody else's trouble for hours on end.

Multiple dashes often indicate that a sentence is poorly constructed and needs redrafting.

(iii) Dashes can be useful in rendering the hesitations, repetitions, and looser syntax typical of direct speech:

'I think you should have—you should have at least told me,' he replied.

Paired dashes can be used to show the interruption of one speaker by another:

'I didn't—' 'Speak up, boy!' '—hear anything.'

(iv) The use of a dash to stand for a coarse word (e.g. *f—*) in reported speech is much less common than it used to be, because public acceptance of these words spelt out is that much greater.

ellipsis ...

This is used to show that material is missing, perhaps from a quotation:

We shall fight on the beaches, we shall fight on the landing grounds...We shall never surrender

It can also indicate suspense:

'And the winner is...Sydney, Australia!'

Or an unfinished statement left hanging in the air:

Unless, of course, she is the murderer after all...

There should be three dots in the ellipsis, not two, five, or seven. Some publishers insert a letter space before and after the ellipsis, or before and after each dot (. . .) Others add a fourth dot when a sentence ends with an ellipsis, the fourth dot being set tight on the third to show its different character (. ...)

exclamation mark !

In ordinary writing, the exclamation mark should be used sparingly (and always singly). In particular, it should not be used to add a spurious sense of drama or sensation to writing that is otherwise undramatic or unsensational, or to signal the humorous intent of a comment whose humour might otherwise go unrecognized. There are a number of established uses:

(A) To make a command or warning:

Go to your room!   Be careful!

(B) To indicate the expression of a strong feeling of absurdity, surprise, approval, dislike, pain, etc., especially after *how* or *what*:

What a suggestion!	*How awful!*
Aren't they beautiful!	*What a good idea!*
That's revolting!	*I hate you!*
Ouch!	*That hurts!*
God!	*Shit!*

(C) To express a wish or feeling of regret:

I'd love to come!

If only I had known!

(D) To indicate someone calling out or shouting:

> Outside Edith's house, someone knocked. 'Edith!'

> 'You're only shielding her.' 'Shielding her!' His voice rose to a shriek.

full stop .

(A) A full stop (also called **point, full point,** and **period**) is used to mark the end of a sentence when it is a statement (and not a question or exclamation). This applies even to sentences that are not complete grammatical units:

> Well, yes. Her family. Loaded, of course, but talk about dysfunctional.

In prose, sentences marked by full stops normally represent a discrete or distinct statement; more closely connected or complementary statements are joined by a semicolon (as here).

(B) The full stop is also used to mark abbreviations and contractions, although this use is diminishing, partly as a matter of printing style and partly because many abbreviations have become more familiar and no longer need identification.

It is sometimes argued that abbreviations proper (e.g. I.o.W. = Isle of Wight) should take a stop, whereas contractions in which the last letter of the word is retained (e.g. Dr = Doctor) should not. Although this may once have been a useful distinction, it has been eroded by the tendency to print shortenings of every kind without stops, e.g. BBC, DPhil, etc, ie, Mr, Ms, J K Smith, 8 am, p 38, etc. This trend is particularly marked in contemporary business writing.

The style preferred here is somewhat more conservative. It is recommended that full stops should be dropped:

(i) In initialisms that are all capital letters, e.g. BBC, TUC, five miles SW, AD, CD

(ii) In acronyms that are pronounced as words, whether written as capitals or not, e.g. Nato, TESSA

(iii) In such titles as Mr, Mrs, Ms, Mme, Mlle, Dr, Revd, St

(iv) With C, F (of temperature), chemical symbols, and measures of length, weight, time, etc., e.g. cm, ft, cwt, lb, kg

In scientific and technical writings stops should never appear with SI units.

(v) In such everyday abbreviations as p (= pence), St (=Street), Rd (= Road).

(vi) In colloquial abbreviations, especially when these have become the usual form of a word e.g. gym, pub, bike

On the other hand, they are better retained:

(i) In lower-case initialisms such as a.m., e.g., and i.e.

(ii) In mixed styles such as D.Phil. and M.Sc.

(iii) In military ranks, e.g. Gen., Lieut., Brig.

(iv) In shortened words such as Oct. (= October) and Tues. (= Tuesday). This may be particularly necessary with unfamiliar or foreign words, e.g. rall. (= rallentando).

(v) In personal names, e.g. T. S. Eliot, George W. Bush.

The important point, however, is to achieve consistency within a particular piece of writing or printing. Note, too, that some shortenings have a greater need of full stops to avoid possible ambiguity with other words in some contexts, e.g. a.m. (= ante meridiem), no. (= number).

(C) If an abbreviation with a full stop comes at the end of a sentence, another full stop is not added when the full stop of the abbreviation is the last character:

> Bring your own pens, pencils, rulers, etc.

In more conservative styles, a full stop is added when the abbreviation is followed by a parenthesis or quotation marks:

> Bring your own things (pens, pencils, rulers, etc.).

However, this extra stop is omitted in much current practice.

(D) When a sentence concludes with a quotation which itself ends with a full stop, question mark, or exclamation mark, no further full stop is needed:

> He cried, 'Get off!'

When the sentence ends with a question mark or exclamation mark within parentheses, conservative practice favours a final full stop:

I just didn't believe him (would you?).

However, this is now frequently omitted.

(E) Full stops are routinely used between units of money (£11.99, $27.50), before decimals (10.5), and between hours and minutes (10.30 a.m.; the usual American style is 10:30 a.m.)

(F) For the use of three stops (…) to indicate an omission or pause, see ELLIPSIS.

hyphen -

Hyphens are used to connect words and word elements that are more closely linked to each other than to the surrounding syntax. Unfortunately their use is not consistent. Some pairs or groups of words are written as a single word (e.g. *motorcycle, payslip, oilfield*), others, despite their equally close bond, as separate words (e.g. *motor car, pay day, oil rig*); very similar pairs may be found with a hyphen (e.g. *pay-off, oil-press*).

There are no hard and fast rules that will predict whether a group of words should be written as one, with a hyphen, or separately. However, the following generalizations have some force as a guide to current practice.

(A) The use of the hyphen to connect two nouns to form a compound word is diminishing in favour of one-word forms, especially when the elements are of one syllable and present no problems of form or pronunciation, as in *birdsong, eardrum*, and *playgroup*; this also applies to some longer formations such as *figurehead*, and even (despite the clash of vowels) *radioisotope*. However, a hyphen is often necessary to separate two similar consonant or vowel sounds in a word, e.g. *breast-stroke, sword-dance*.

In the area of choice between spelling as one word with hyphen and as two words, the second option is now widely favoured, especially when the first noun acts as a straightforward modifier of the second, as in *filling station* and *house plant*. Different house styles in publishing and journalism have different preferences in many of these cases.

(B) Phrasal verbs such as *spell out, build up, come about*, etc. rarely require hyphens. However, to avoid any ambiguity nouns derived from such verbs are usually either hyphenated or written as one, e.g. *play-off, lay-off, turn-on*; *playback, layout, turnover*. Phrases consisting of *-er* + adverb are generally hyphenated, e.g. *runner-up, lookers-on*.

Note, however, that phrases consisting of *-ing* + adverb tend to be left as two words, e.g. *Your going over to France surprised me*, unless they have become a unit with a special meaning, e.g. *She gave him a real going-over*.

(C) Many phrases and compounds which are not otherwise hyphenated are given hyphens when used attributively (before a noun). Some common collocations of this type are:

(i) Adjective + noun

> *a common-sense argument* (but *This is common sense*)

> *an open-air restaurant* (but *eating in the open air*)

(ii) Preposition + noun

> *an out-of-date aircraft* (but *This is out of date*)

> *an in-depth interview* (but *interviewing him in depth*)

(iii) Participle + adverb

> *a longed-for departure* (but *a departure greatly longed for*)

(iv) Other syntactic groups

> *an all-but-unbearable strain*

Note, however, that capitalized noun compounds are not usually hyphenated when they appear attributively:

> *a World War I hero*

> *a West Country accent*

(D) Adjectival phrases consisting of adjective + participle are nearly always hyphenated, whether they appear before a noun or in some other position:

a red-blooded male

She was left red-faced with embarrassment.

But phrases consisting of adverb + participle are not usually hyphenated, wherever they appear:

a rapidly growing economy

his prose is carefully crafted

A grey area occurs with those adverbs that do not end in *-ly*, most of which double as adjectives. These are usually hyphenated in attributive position, and sometimes in other positions too:

a well-known scientist

her long-awaited first novel

His story seemed rather far-fetched.

The distinction is not clear-cut.

Collocations of adverb + adjective are usually written as two words:

a less interesting topic

an amazingly good performance

but occasionally take a hyphen to avoid misunderstanding:

She had impressed several more-discerning judges.

(this does not mean 'several additional discerning judges').

(E) Verb phrases sometimes need to be hyphenated when the first word of the phrase is not itself a verb, e.g. *court-martial*, *second-guess*, *fast-forward*.

(F) Hyphens are used to represent a common second element in all but the last word of a list:

two-, three-, or fourfold

gas- or oil-related issues

(G) A group of more than two words forming a syntactic unit normally has hyphens, e.g. *happy-go-lucky*, *good-for-nothing* (adjectives), *stick-in-the-mud*, *ne'er-do-well* (nouns).

(H) With most prefixes and suffixes it is normal to write the whole compound as a single word; the use of the hyphen is exceptional, and the writing of prefix or suffix and stem as two words virtually unknown.

The hyphen is most likely to be used in the following cases:

(i) After the prefixes *ex-* (e.g. *ex-wife*) and *self-* (e.g. *self-destructive*).

Exceptions: *selfsame*, *unselfconscious*.

(ii) When the use of a hyphen aids recognition of the second element, e.g. *anti-g*, *co-respondent* (as against *correspondent*).

(iii) When the hyphen distinguishes the compound from another word identically spelt, e.g. *un-ionized* (as against *unionized*), *re-form* (as against *reform*).

(iv) Between a prefix ending with a vowel and a stem beginning with the same vowel, e.g. *de-escalate*, *pre-empt*, *co-opt* (but usually *cooperate*, *coordinate*).

(v) Between a prefix and a stem beginning with a capital letter, e.g. *anti-Darwinian*, *hyper-Calvinism*, *Pre-Raphaelite*.

(vi) With specially coined or irregularly formed compounds, e.g. *Mickey Mouse-like*, *confidence-wise*, *unget-at-able*.

(vii) With the suffix *-like* after a stem ending in *l*, e.g. *eel-like*, and when attached to a word of two or more syllables, e.g. *cabbage-like*.

Exception: *businesslike*.

(viii) With the suffix *-less* after a stem ending in double *l*, e.g. *bell-less*, *will-lessness*.

(I) There is no entirely satisfactory way of dealing with phrases like *ex-prime minister* or *Booker Prize-winning novel*, in which both elements are compounds; one can only rely on the tendency of readers to choose the natural meaning. A second hyphen, e.g. *ex-prime-minister*, is not recommended unless there is real danger of misunderstanding.

(J) Above and beyond all these guidelines, hyphens are sometimes required to clarify meanings in groups of words when the associations are not clear, or when several possible associations may be inferred. This is the area of usage that involves the greatest initiative and discretion on the part of the writer. The best way of offering guidance is to give examples in which careful hyphenation prevents misunderstanding:

> *The library is reducing its purchase of hard-covered books.*

> *Twenty-odd people came to the meeting.*

> *The group was warned about the dangers of extra-marital sex.*

> *the non-German-speakers at the conference*

> *Police want to interview a black-cab driver.*

> *a big bust-up on the fifth floor*

(K) The hyphen is also used to divide a word that comes at the end of a line and is too long to fit completely. The principle here is a different one, because the hyphen does not form a permanent part of the spelling. This type of hyphenation occurs mainly in print, where the text has to be accurately spaced and the margin justified; in handwritten and typed or word-processed material it can be avoided altogether.

In print, words need to be divided carefully and consistently, taking account of the appearance and structure of the word. Typesetters and printers therefore have sets of rules about where to divide words; for example, between consonants as in *splen-dour* and between vowels as in *appreci-ate*; words of one syllable should not be divided at all, even quite long ones such as *queues*. Detailed guidance on word-division may be found in the *Oxford Spelling Dictionary* (1986) and similar publications.

parentheses See BRACKETS.

period See FULL STOP.

question mark ?

This is used in place of the full stop to show that the preceding sentence is a question:

> *Do you want another piece of cake?*

Although its use is generally straightforward, the following areas may cause uncertainty:

(A) A question mark is necessary—indeed, it may be particularly necessary—when the question takes the form of a statement:

> *He really is her husband?*

(B) It is used after most types of rhetorical question, including so-called 'tag' questions:

> *Do you want to lose your job?*

> *She's lost weight, hasn't she?*

However, in rhetorical questions that are really exclamations it may be replaced by an exclamation mark:

> *What kind of bastard are you!*

(C) It is not used when the question is implied by indirect speech:

> *I asked you whether you wanted another piece of cake.*

(D) Nor is it required if the question is really a polite demand:

> *Will you please let me have your reply by noon tomorrow.*

(E) It is used (often in brackets) to express doubt or uncertainty about a word or phrase immediately following or preceding it:

> *Thomas Tallis, ?1505–85*

quotation marks ' ' " "

The main use of quotation marks (also called **quotes**, **speech marks**, or **inverted commas**) is to indicate direct speech or quoted material. In writing it is common to use double quotation marks (" "), while in printing practice varies between the double and single style (' '). Single marks are commonly associated with British practice (as in the Oxford and Cambridge styles) and double marks with American practice, but the distinction in usage is not always so clear-cut. Some house styles, for instance, specify that double marks should be used for quotations proper and single marks for citations, titles, etc.

The main roles of practice in British English follow, with indications of any variant practice in American English.

(A) In direct speech and quotations, the closing quotation mark normally comes after a final full stop:

> *She said, 'I have something to ask you.'*

It should come after any other punctuation mark (such as an exclamation mark) which is part of the matter being quoted:

They shouted, 'Watch out!'

(the final full stop is omitted after an exclamation mark in this position).

(B) When the end of a quotation is followed by words such as *he said, she replied*, etc., a comma is used in place of a full stop:

'That is nonsense,' he said.

When these words interrupt the quotation, traditional British usage places the commas outside the quotation marks:

'That', he said, 'is nonsense.'

But the first comma goes inside the quotation marks if it would be part of the uninterrupted utterance:

'That, my dear fellow,' he said, 'is nonsense'.

In most American practice the commas are placed inside the quotation marks in all these cases; this style is becoming increasingly common in Britain, too.

(C) When quoting a single word or a short unpunctuated phrase, the traditional British practice is to place the punctuation that belongs to the sentence as a whole outside the quotation marks:

What do you mean, you're 'not satisfied'?

No one should 'follow a multitude to do evil', as the Scripture says.

In American English, however, it is usual to place quotation marks outside the sentence punctuation, and this style is becoming quite common in Britain:

No one should "follow a multitude to do evil," as the Scripture says.

(D) Quotation marks are also used around cited words and phrases that are not quotations or direct speech:

What does 'integrated circuit' mean?

His writing has been associated with the so-called 'New Puritan' movement.

They may be used to clothe a word in irony or, usually unnecessarily, to apologize for some clumsy or supposedly colloquial usage:

As for this government's much-heralded 'realism'...

At this time I also 'touched base' with many other interested people.

(E) Quotation marks are used when citing titles of articles in magazines, chapters of books, shorter poems, and songs.

Titles of books, magazines, and long poems are usually printed in italic: titles of books of the Bible are printed in roman without quotation marks.

(F) When a quotation occurs within a quotation, the inner quotation is put in double marks if the main quotation is in single marks (and vice versa, especially in American practice):

'Have you any idea,' he asked, 'what a "gigabyte" is?'

If there is a third quotation within the second quotation (and so on), the process of alternating single and double marks continues.

semicolon ;

The semicolon is probably the least confidently used of the regular punctuation marks in ordinary writing. This is surely a pity: when used correctly, and in moderation, it can be an important aid to effective communication. Its role is to mark a grammatical separation that is stronger in effect than a comma but less strong than a full stop.

(A) The semicolon unites main clauses of similar importance that are closely related in subject matter. It is especially appropriate when the two clauses complement or parallel each other in some way:

In the north of the city there is a large industrial area with little private housing; further east is the university.

To err is human; to forgive, divine.

When one clause leads on from the other as a conclusion, example, result, etc., a colon is usually more suitable.

(B) It is often used as a stronger division in a sentence that already includes divisions by means of commas:

> He came out of the house, which lay back from the road, and saw her at the end of the path; but instead of continuing towards her, he hid until she had gone.

(C) It is used in a similar way in long, catalogue-type lists of names or other items, to indicate a stronger division:

> Target audiences for the new manual will include other companies in our group, both European and US-based; business leaders, top politicians and other leading opinion-formers; consultants of proven expertise; and local schools and colleges.

To use merely commas as dividers would produce chaos here, because commas already exist within some of the listed items.

square brackets See BRACKETS.

Section 4: Pronunciation

The Section is in two Parts, which can be used either separately or in tandem. PART I:
GENERAL POINTS OF PRONUNCIATION *offers ground rules to cover some of the more
troublesome points of English pronunciation. Most of these concern the way or ways in
which letters or groups of letters are sounded in different words, but guidance on
word stress and the use of reduced forms in rapid speech is also given. This is followed
by* PART II: DIFFICULT PRONUNCIATIONS, *a list of some 600 individual words that cause
widespread uncertainty or dispute. The various possible pronunciations are given,
together with brief advisory comments; although sloppy, erroneous, or widely disliked
pronunciations are pointed out, the general approach is flexible and undogmatic.*

*Giving one pronunciation rather than another implies the existence of a standard.
There are many varieties of spoken English but the treatment here is based upon
Received Pronunciation (RP), the accent taken as standard by British dictionaries and
taught to foreign students. Historically, RP was based upon the speech habits of upper-
and middle-class speakers in London and the southeast of England, which were usually
assumed to be superior to those of other regions and classes. Today's RP is less socially
exclusive (indeed, many characteristics of upper-class speech are now regarded as non-
standard) and more tolerant of regional variation, American forms, and the inevitable
processes of linguistic change. In this modified form, RP (or something fairly close to it)
is spoken by a greater proportion and a wider cross-section of the British population
than ever before. It also has the important advantage of being intelligible throughout
the English-speaking world. Although still sometimes regarded as the 'best' way of
pronouncing English, the standard provided by RP is now essentially one of
convenience rather than correctness.*

*To make this Section as user-friendly as possible, pronunciations are described mainly
by analogy to other well-known words, e.g. 'with a as in* calm', 'with the first
syllable like *bourgeois*', 'to rhyme with *bailiff*'. *Where this is not possible, a form
of approximate phonetic spelling is used, e.g. 'a-fiss-eon-ah-do' for* aficionado,
'*frack-ah*' for fracas, *with italics to show the stressed syllables. In other cases, acute
(´) and grave (`) accents have been used to show primary and secondary stresses in a
word, e.g.* secretárial, cáterpìllar. *The International Phonetic Alphabet has not been
used.*

PART I: GENERAL POINTS OF PRONUNCIATION

It is impossible to lay down hard and fast rules here, since pronunciation is continually changing, and at any time there is bound to be considerable variation within RP. The following pages provide a clear but undogmatic guide to certain problem areas in contemporary British speech.

Uncertainty about pronunciation arises mainly from the irregularity of English spelling. Individual letters, or sequences of letters, that repeatedly cause difficulty are therefore listed in alphabetical order below, with comments on their pronunciation in particular words or classes of words. Problems also arise from the inconsistent and gradually shifting patterns of word stress in English. A note on this subject (which can arouse extraordinary feeling) has therefore been added at the end of the main alphabetical sequence. Finally, there is a short note on the reduction of common words in rapid speech.

Where the American pronunciation of forms and words listed below differs significantly from the British, this is usually indicated. However, no general or systematic account of the differences between British and American speech has been attempted.

a

(A) Pronunciation of *a* varies between the sound heard in *calm*, *father* and that heard in *cat*, *fan*, in the following:

(i) The suffix *-graph* (in *photograph*, *telegraph*, etc.) Here the sound of *calm* is preferred except where *-ic* is added (e.g. in *photographic*); in these cases only the *a* of *cat* is used.

(ii) The prefix *trans-* (as in *transfer*, *translate*, etc.) Here either kind of *a* is acceptable.

(B) The word endings *-ada*, *-ade*, and *-ado* occasion difficulty.

(i) In *-ada* words, *a* is pronounced as in *calm*, e.g. *armada*, *cicada*.

(ii) In most *-ade* words, *a* is pronounced as in *made*, e.g. *barricade*.

Exceptions: *a* is pronounced as in *calm* in the following:

aubade	*façade*	*promenade*
ballade	*gambade*	*roulade*
charade	*pomade*	*saccade*

It is also pronounced this way in loan-words from French, e.g. *oeillade*.

(iii) In most *-ado* words, *a* is pronounced as in *calm*, e.g. *bravado*.

Exceptions: *tornado* (*a* as in *made*) *bastinado* (*a* as in *made* or *calm*).

(C) *a* in the suffix *-alia* is pronounced like *a* in *alien*, e.g. in *marginalia*.

(D) In many words the pronunciation of *a* before *ls* and *lt* varies between *aw* in *bawl* and *o* in *doll*. Examples include:

> *alter*   *palsy*   *waltz*

The same variation occurs with *au* in *assault*, *fault*, *somersault*, *vault*.

Note: in several words *a* before *ls* and *lt* can only be pronounced like *a* in *sally*, e.g.

Alsatian	*contralto*	*peristalsis*
alto	*Malthusian*	*saltation*

(E) The *a* in *-ata*, *-atum*, and *-atus* is usually pronounced as in *mate*, e.g. in *apparatus*.

Exceptions: *cantata, cassata, chipolata, desideratum* (plural *desiderata*), *erratum* (plural *errata*), *serenata, sonata, toccata* all with *a* as in *calm*; *stratum, stratus* with the *a* of *calm* or *mate*.

-age

The standard pronunciation of the following words ending in -*age* is with stress on the first syllable, *a* as in *calm*, and *g* as in *regime*.

> barrage   dressage   persiflage
> camouflage   garage   sabotage

This is also the preferred pronunciation of *collage, massage*, and *mirage*, although these words can be stressed on the second syllable too. *Montage* is usually stressed on the second syllable.

Arbitrage can be pronounced in two ways: with the stress on the first syllable and the last syllable rhyming with *bridge*, or with the stress on the last syllable which is pronounced to rhyme with *barrage* etc. *Garage* can be pronounced in both these ways but neither is recommended. *Fuselage* can rhyme with *barrage* or *bridge* but is always stressed on the first syllable.

It is also acceptable to use the sound of *g* as in *large* in *dressage, garage*, and *massage*.

-arily

In a few five-syllable adverbs ending with -*arily*, there is a tendency to stress the *a* for ease of pronunciation. Some in common use are:

> arbitrarily   ordinarily
> momentarily   temporarily
> necessarily   voluntarily

Probably under the influence of American English, rapid colloquial speech has adopted a pronunciation with the *a* sounding like *e* in *verily*; it would be pedantic (and futile) to censure this.

The case of the word *primarily* is more controversial. It contains only four syllables, which can be reduced to the easily pronounced spoken form 'prim'rily'. It could therefore be argued that there is no need to pronounce the word with stress on the second syllable. However, the pronunciations 'pri-*mare*-ily' and 'pri-*merr*-ily' are now well established.

-ed

(A) In the following adjectives the ending -*ed* is pronounced as a separate syllable:

> accursed   naked   wicked
> cragged   rugged   wretched
> deuced   sacred

Note: *accursed* and *deuced* can also be pronounced as one syllable.

(B) The following words have different meanings according to whether -*ed* is pronounced as a separate syllable or not. In most cases the former pronunciation indicates an adjective, the latter part of a verb.

-*ed* as separate syllable	not as separate syllable
aged	
= 'very old' (*he is very aged, an aged man*)	= 'having the age of' (*a boy aged three*); past of *to age* (*he has aged greatly*)
beloved	
used before noun (*beloved brethren*); = 'beloved person' (*my beloved is mine*)	used as predicate (*he was beloved by all*)
blessed	
= 'fortunate', 'holy, sacred' (*blessed are the meek, the blessed saints*)	part of *to bless*; sometimes also in senses listed in left-hand column
crabbed	
= 'ill-humoured', 'hard to follow', etc.	past of *to crab* (= 'fish for crabs')
crooked	
= 'not straight', 'dishonest'	= 'having transverse handle' (*crooked stick*); past of *to crook* (*a finger etc.*)

cursed

  before noun   past of *to curse*
  = 'damnable'

dogged

  = 'tenacious'   past of *to dog*

jagged

  = 'serrated'   past of *to jag*
                       (= 'stab, pierce')

learned

  = 'erudite'   past of *to learn*
                       (usually *learnt*)

ragged

  = 'rough, torn', etc. past of *to rag*
                             (= 'make fun of')

-edly, -edness

When the further suffixes *-ly* and *-ness* are added to adjectives ending in *-ed*, an uncertainty arises about whether to pronounce this *-ed-* as a separate syllable. Such cases can be divided into three kinds:

(A) Those in which *-ed* is already a separate syllable – either because it is preceded by *d* or *t* (e.g. *belated, wicked*) or because the adjective is one of those discussed in the entry for -ED above (e.g. *naked, blessed*).

When either *-ly* or *-ness* are added, *-ed-* remains a separate syllable, e.g.

(i) *belatedly*   *nakedly*
     blessedly   *wickedly*

(ii) *belatedness*   *nakedness*
     blessedness *wickedness*

(B) Those in which the syllable preceding *-ed* is unstressed, e.g. *embarrassed, self-centred*. When either *-ly* or *-ness* are added, *-ed-* remains non-syllabic, e.g.

(i) *abandonedly*   *self-centredly*
     embarrassedly *variedly*

(ii) *self-centredness* *studiedness*

(C) Those in which the syllable preceding *-ed* is stressed or is a monosyllable, e.g. *assured, fixed*.

(i) When *-ly* is added *-ed* becomes an extra syllable, e.g.

   advisedly   *fixedly*
   allegedly   *markedly*
   assuredly   *professedly*
   deservedly   *unfeignedly*

There are a few exceptions to this rule, e.g. *subduedly, tiredly* (*-ed* is not a separate syllable here). Some words show variation, e.g. *shamefacedly*.

Note that some adverbs formed from adjectives ending in *-ed* sound awkward whether *-ed-* is pronounced as a separate syllable or not. Because of this, some authorities discourage the formation of words like *boredly, discouragedly*.

(ii) When *-ness* is added, there is greater variation. The *-ed-* can be sounded as an extra syllable in the following:

   concernedness   *mixedness*
   deservedness   *preparedness*
   fixedness   *unashamedness*
   markedness

However, in all these words it is acceptable *not* to make *-ed-* a separate syllable.

-ein(e)

The ending *-ein(e)* is now pronounced like *-ene* in *polythene* in:

   caffeine   *codeine*
   casein   *protein*

Note: *casein* can also be pronounced with *-ein* disyllabic.

-eity

Traditionally, the *e* in this termination has been pronounced as in *me*, examples being:

   contemporaneity *homogeneity*
   deity   *simultaneity*
   heterogeneity   *spontaneity*

However, the modern tendency is to substitute the sound of *e* in *café, suede*. Some speakers pronounce the first two syllables of *deity* like *deer*, and so with the other words.

The same variation is found in the sequence *-ei-* in the words *deism, deist, reify, reification* (but not *theism, theist*).

-eur

This termination (occurring in words originally taken from French) normally carries the stress and sounds like *er* in *deter, refer*. Examples are:

agent provocateur	*raconteur*
coiffeur	*restaurateur*
connoisseur	*saboteur*
entrepreneur	*secateurs*
masseur	

Stress is usually on the first syllable in *amateur* (and *amateurish*) and *chauffeur*.

Feminine nouns can be formed from some of these words by the substitution of *-se* for *-r*: the resulting termination is pronounced like *urze* in *furze*, e.g. *coiffeuse, masseuse, saboteuse*.

liqueur is pronounced 'li-*cure*' (but American 'li-*cur*').

g

(A) In certain less familiar words there is uncertainty as to whether g preceding *e, i*, and (especially) *y* is pronounced hard as in *get* or soft as in *gem*.

(i) The prefix *gyn(o)-* meaning 'woman' now always has a hard g, as in *gynaecology, gynoecium*.

(ii) The element *-gyn-* with the same meaning, occurring inside the word, usually has a soft g, as in *androgynous, misogynist*.

(iii) The elements *gyr-* (from a root meaning 'ring') and *-gitis* (in names of diseases) have a soft g, as in:

gyrate	*gyro* (*-scope, -compass*,
laryngitis	etc.)

The poetic word *gyre* (= 'gyrate', 'gyration') can be pronounced with either a soft or a hard g.

(iv) The following, among many other words, have a hard g:

gibbous (of the moon)	*gill* (fish's organ)
	gingham
gig (all senses)	

The g should be hard in *analogous*.

(v) The following have a soft g:

gibe	*gypsophila*
gill (measure)	*gypsum*
gillyflower	*gyrfalcon*
giro (payment system)	*longevity*
gybe	*panegyric*

(vi) The following can vary, but usually have a hard g:

demagogic, -y   *pedagogic, -y*

(vii) The following can vary, but usually have a soft g:

gibber	*gibberish*
hegemony	*longitude*

(B) For words of the type *arbitrage, barrage, garage*, etc., see -AGE.

-gm

In the sequence *gm* at the end of a word g is silent:

diaphragm   *phlegm*

But the g is pronounced between vowels:

enigma   *phlegmatic*

h

(A) Initial h is silent in *heir, honest, honour, hour*, and their derivatives; also in *honorarium*. It is sounded in *habitué*.

(B) Initial h used commonly to be silent if the first syllable was unstressed, as in *habitual, hereditary, historic, hotel*. This pronunciation is now old-fashioned and rarely heard.

-ies

The ending *-ies* is usually pronounced as one syllable (like *ies* in *diesel*) in:

caries	*rabies*
congeries	*scabies*
facies	

The reduction of this ending to a sound like the ending of *armies*, *babies*, etc., is better avoided in careful speech.

Exceptions: *series* and *species* can have either pronunciation.

-ile

The ending *-ile* is normally pronounced like *isle*, e.g. in:

docile   missile   sterile

The usual American pronunciation in most words of this kind is with the sound of *il* in *daffodil* or *pencil*.

The pronunciation is like *eel* in:

automobile   -mobile (suffix)

imbecile

-ile forms two syllables in *campanile* (rhyming with *Ely*), *cantabile* (pronounced can-*tah*-bi-ly), and *sal volatile* (rhyming with *philately*).

ng

The sequence *ng* can represent either a single sound or a compound consisting of this sound followed by the sound of hard *g*.

(A) The single sound is the only one to occur at the end of a word, e.g. in *song*, *writing*.

(B) Although the single sound also occurs in the middle of words, these are usually compounds of a word ending in *-ng* + suffix, e.g.

bringing   kingly   stringy

hanged   longish   wrongful

(C) The compound sound, 'ng + g', is otherwise the norm in the middle of words, e.g. in *hungry*, *language*.

As an exception to (B) above, it also occurs in *longer*, *-est*, *prolongation*, *stronger*, *-est*, *younger*, *-est*.

(D) It is considered non-standard:

(i) To pronounce *bringing*, *writing*, etc. as 'bringin', 'writin'.

(ii) To use 'n' for 'ng' in *length*, *strength*. (The pronunciation 'lenkth', 'strenkth' is acceptable.)

(iii) To use 'nk' for 'ng' in *anything*, *everything*, *nothing*, *something*.

(iv) To use 'ng + g' in all cases covered by rules (A) and (B). This pronunciation is, however, normal in certain regional forms of English.

o

(A) In many words the 'u'-sound as in *butter* is spelt with *o*, e.g. *come*. There is an increasing tendency to pronounce a few such words with the sound of *o* in *body*.

(i) The following are usually pronounced with the 'u'-sound:

accomplice   constable   mongrel

accomplish   frontier

(ii) The following are usually pronounced with the 'o'-sound:

combat   dromedary   pomegranate

comrade   hovel   pommel (noun)

conduit   hover   sojourn

(B) There was formerly a variety of RP in which *o* was pronounced like *aw* in *law* before *ff*, *ft*, *ss*, *st*, and *th* in certain words, so that *off*, *often*, etc. sounded like *orf*, *orphan*, etc. This pronunciation is now non-standard.

(C) Before double *ll*, *o* has the long sound (as in *pole*) in some words, and the short sound (as in *Polly*) in others.

(i) The following have the long sound:

boll	stroll
droll	swollen
knoll	toll
poll (vote, head)	troll
roll	wholly
scroll	

(ii) The following have the short sound:

doll   loll   moll   poll (parrot)

and most words in which another syllable follows, e.g.

collar   holly   pollen

(D) Before *lt*, *o* is pronounced long in RP, e.g. *bolt*, *revolt*.

The substitution of short *o* in these words is common but non-standard.

(E) Before *lv*, *o* is pronounced short, e.g.

absolve	*involve*	*revolver*
dissolve	*resolve*	*solve*

The substitution of long *o* in these words is non-standard.

ough

Although most words with *ough* are familiar, difficulties may arise with the following:

brougham (type of carriage)	'*broo*-am' or 'broom'
chough (bird)	'chuff'
clough (ravine)	'cluff'
hough (animal's joint)	'hock'
slough (swamp)	rhymes with *plough*
slough (snake's skin)	'sluff'
sough (sound of wind)	usually rhymes with *bough* but can also rhyme with *tough*

phth

This sequence should sound like *fth* (in *fifth*, *twelfth*) in e.g. *diphthong*, *monophthong*, *naphtha*, *ophthalmic*. It is common but non-standard to pronounce these 'dip-thong' etc. However, 'dip-theria' is now easily the most common pronunciation of *diphtheria*, so this must be regarded as standard.

Initially, as in the words *phthisical*, *phthisis*, the *ph* can be silent; it is also usually silent in *apophthegm*.

pn-, ps-, pt-

In these sequences at the beginning of words, it is normal not to pronounce the *p-*. The exception is *psi* (name of the Greek letter *ψ*).

r

(A) When *r* is the last letter of a word (or precedes 'silent' final *e*), it is normally silent in RP—e.g. in *four*, *here*, *runner*.

But when another word, beginning with a vowel sound, follows in the same sentence, it is normal to pronounce the final *r*—e.g. in *four hours*, *here it is*, *runner-up*. This is called the 'linking *r*'.

It is standard to use linking *r* and unnatural to try to avoid it.

(B) A closely connected feature of the spoken language is what is called 'intrusive *r*'. This occurs when an 'r'-sound is introduced where there is no letter *r* in the spelling. The most common occurrences are:

(i) After a word such as *villa*, ending with the obscure 'a'-sound:

a villa-r in Italy

Here it is acceptable in rapid, informal speech.

(ii) After the sounds of *ah* and *aw*, and the *eu* of *milieu*, both between words and before endings:

a milieu-r in which…

law-r and order   draw-r-ing with a pencil

The use of intrusive *r* here is widely considered unacceptable; it is therefore better avoided in formal speech.

(C) There is a tendency in certain words to drop *r* if it is closely followed (or in a few cases, preceded) by another *r* at the beginning of an unstressed syllable. Examples include:

deteriorate pronounced 'deteriate'

February pronounced 'Febuary'

honorary pronounced 'honary' (prefer 'hon'rary')

itinerary pronounced 'itinery'

library pronounced 'lib'ry'

secretary pronounced 'seketry' or 'seketerry'

temporary pronounced 'tempary' (prefer 'temp'rary')

In formal speech this is generally better avoided (although the pronunciation 'Febuary' is now more or less accepted).

(D) In most forms of American English it is usual to pronounce r wherever it occurs in the spelling.

s, sh, z, and zh

In certain kinds of word, where the spelling is *ci*, *si*, or *ti*, or where it is *s* before long *u*, there is variation between two or more of these sounds:

'␣s' as in *sun*   'z' as in *zone*

'sh' as in *ship*   'g' as in *regime*

'zh' representing the sound of *s* in *leisure*

(A) There is variation between 's' and 'sh' in words such as:

appreciate	negotiate
associate	sociology
glacial	

This variation does not occur in all words with a similar structure: only *s* is used in *glaciation*, *pronunciation* (= '-see-ay-shon'), and only *sh* in *partiality* ('par-shee-*al*-ity'). Only *sh* occurs in *initial*, *racial*, *sociable*, *spatial*, *special*, etc.

(B) There is variation between 's' and 'sh' in *sensual*, *sexual*, *issue*, *tissue*, and between 'z' and 'zh' in *casual*, *casuist*, *visual*.

(C) There is variation between 'sh' and 'zh' in *aversion*, *equation*, *immersion*, *version*.

Either variant is acceptable in each of these kinds of word, although in all of them 'sh' is the traditional pronunciation.

(D) In the names of some countries and regions ending in *-sia* (and in the adjectives derived from them) there is variation between 'sh' and 'zh'; in some cases there is variation between 'z(i)' and 's(i)' as well. So:

Asian	= 'A-shan' or 'A-zhan'
Asiatic	= 'A-shi-*at*-ic' or 'A-zhi-*at*-ic' or 'A-zi-*at*-ic' or 'A-si-*at*-ic'
Australasian	= 'Austral-*a*-zhan' or '-shan'
Indonesian	= 'Indo-*nee*-shan' or

	'-zhan' or '-zi-an' or '-si-an'
Persian	= 'Per-shan' or 'Per-zhan'

The pronunciation with 'sh' is the most widely acceptable. The pronunciation with 'zh' is also generally acceptable.

(E) There is variation between 'zh' and 'z(i)' in *artesian* (*well*), *Cartesian*, *Caucasian*, and *Friesian*.

Either variant is acceptable.

t

(A) In rapid speech, *t* is often dropped from the sequence *cts*, so that *acts*, *ducts*, *pacts* sound like *axe*, *ducks*, *packs*. This should be avoided in careful speech.

(B) In older forms of RP the *t* is not sounded in *often* (which is pronunced to rhyme with *soften*); however, the pronunciation of the *t* is perfectly acceptable.

th

(A) Monosyllabic nouns ending in *-th* after a vowel sound (or vowel + *r*) form the plural by adding *-s* in the usual way. The resulting sequence *ths* may be voiceless as in *myths*, or voiced as in *mouths*.

(i) The following are pronounced like *myths*:

berths	fourths	moths
births	girths	sleuths
breaths	growths	sloths
deaths	hearths	smiths
faiths	heaths	wraiths

(ii) The following are usually pronounced like *mouths*:

oaths	sheaths	wreaths
paths	truths	youths

baths, *cloths*, *laths*, *swath(e)s* vary, but are now commonly pronounced like *myths*.

(B) Note that final *th* is like *th* in *bathe*, *father* in:

bequeath	booth
betroth	mouth (verb)

betroth and *booth* can also be pronounced with *th* as in *truth*.

u

The sound of long *u*, as in *cube, cubic, cue, use* is also spelt *eu, ew,* and *ui,* as in *feud, few, pursuit.* It is properly a compound of two sounds, the semivowel '*y*' followed by the long vowel elsewhere written *oo.* Hence the word *you* (= '*y*' + '*oo*') sounds like the name of the letter *U, ewe,* and *yew.*

After some consonants the '*y*' is lost, leaving only the '*oo*'-sound. This occurs mainly:

(A) After *ch, j, r,* the sound of *sh,* and *l* following a consonant. So *brewed, chews, chute, Jules, rude,* sound like *brood, choose, shoot, joules, rood,* and *blew, glue,* etc. sound as if they were spelt 'bloo', 'gloo', etc.

(B) In a stressed syllable after *l.* The words *lubricate, lucid, ludicrous,* etc. therefore have a simple 'oo' pronunciation; although some older speakers use the 'yoo'-sound in e.g. *lewd, allude, interlude* this now sounds rather affected. It is, however, the preferred pronunciation of *lieu* and *voluminous.*

In *unstressed* syllables, however, the 'yoo'-sound is the only one possible, e.g. in

> *deluge*   *soluble*   *value*
>
> *prelude*   *valuable*   *volume*

Contrast *solute* (= 'sol-yoot') with *salute* (= 'sa-loot').

(C) After *s,* although there is some variation here. Most people now use 'oo' in *Susan* and *Sue,* and where another vowel follows, as in *sewer* and *suicide,* but 'yoo' in *pseudo-, assume,* and *pursue.*

In an unstressed syllable, the '*y*'-sound is kept:

> *capsule*   *consular*   *peninsula*

(D) After *d, n,* and *t.* Here, however, the loss of the '*y*'-sound is non-standard, e.g. in *due, new, tune.*

Note: in American English loss of the '*y*'-sound is normal after these consonants.

(E) The tendency to make *t* and *d* preceding long *u* in stressed syllables sound like *ch* and *j* (e.g. *Tuesday, duel* as if *Chooseday, jewel*)

should be avoided in careful speech. In unstressed syllables (e.g. in *picture, procedure*) it is normal.

ul

After *b, f,* and *p,* the sequence *ul* sounds like *ool* in *wool* in some words (e.g. in *bull, pull*) and like *ull* in *hull* in others (e.g. in *bulk, pulp*). In a few words there is uncertainty or variation.

(i) Pronounced with *u* as in *hull*:

> *Bulgarian*   *effulgent*   *pulmonary*
> *catapult*   *pullulate*   *pulverize*

(i) With *u* as in *bull*:

> *bulwark*   *fulmar*   *fulsome*

(ii) With variation:

> *ebullient*   *fulminate*
> *fulcrum*   *fulvous*

urr

In Standard English the stressed vowel of *furry* and *occurring* is like that of *stirring,* not that of *hurry* and *occurrence.*

The two sounds are identical in normal American English.

wh

In some regions *wh* is preceded or accompanied by an 'h'-sound.

This pronunciation is not standard in RP, but is acceptable to most RP-speakers.

stress

(A) The position of the stress accent is the key to the pronunciation of many English polysyllabic words, since unstressed vowels are subject to reduction in length, obscuration of quality, and, quite often, complete elision. Compare the sound of the stressed vowel in the words on the left with that of the same vowel, unstressed, in the words on the right:

> a: *humánity*   *húman*
>   *monárchic*   *mónarch*

practicálity   práctically ('-ic'ly')
secretárial   sécretary ('-t'ry')

e: presént (verb)   présent (noun)
protést   protestátion
mystérious   mýstery (= 'myst'ry')

i: satírical   sátirist
combíne   combinátion
anxíety   ánxious
       (= 'anksh'ous')

o: ecónomy   económic
oppóse   ópposite
histório   hístory (= 'hist'ry')

u: luxúrious   lúxury
indústrial   índustry

Many of the most hotly disputed questions of pronunciation centre on the placing of the stress.

(B) It is impossible to formulate rules accounting for the position of the stress in every English word, but two very general observations can be made.

(i) Although the stress can fall on any syllable, more than three unstressed syllables cannot easily be uttered in sequence. Hence, for example, five-syllable words with stress on the first or last syllable are rare. Very often in polysyllabic words at least one syllable bears a secondary stress, e.g. cáterpillar, còntrovèrtibílity.

(ii) Some patterns of stress are clearly associated with spelling or with grammatical function (or, especially, with variation of grammatical function in a single word). For example, almost all words ending in -ic and -ical are stressed on the syllable immediately preceding the suffix. There is only a handful of exceptions: Arabic, arithmetic (noun), arsenic, catholic, choleric, heretic, lunatic, politic(s), rhetoric.

Some general tendencies will now be described, and related to the existing canons of acceptability.

(C) **Two-syllable words**

There is a fixed, although not invariable, pattern, by which nouns and adjectives are stressed on the first syllable, and verbs on the second, e.g.

accent   import   torment
conflict   present   transfer
fragment   suspect

nouns: climate   primate
verbs: create   dictate

This pattern has exercised an influence over several other words not originally conforming to it. The words

ally   defect   rampage
combine   intern

were all originally stressed on the second syllable; as nouns, however, they are all now usually stressed on the first. Exactly the same tendency has affected

dispute   research
recess   romance

but in these words, the stressing of the noun on the first syllable is rejected by many people. The following nouns and adjectives (not corresponding to identically spelt verbs) show the same transference of stress: adept, adult, chagrin, supine.

In the verbs combat, contact, harass, and traverse, a tendency towards stress on the second syllable is now discernible, but the new stress has been fully accepted only in the word traverse. The pronunciation of harass with the stress on the second syllable is so common that it must now be considered standard, yet it continues to arouse strong disapproval in many people.

(D) **Three-syllable words**

Of the three possible stress patterns in three-syllable words, that with stress on the first syllable is the best established.

(i) Words with stress on the final syllable are rare. In some, a stress on the first syllable is acceptable in RP, e.g. artisan, commandant, confidant, partisan, promenade; in others it is not, e.g. cigarette, magazine.

(ii) Many words originally having stress on the second syllable now commonly have stress on the first, e.g.

abdomen   precedent
albumen   remonstrate

composite (noun)   *secretive*

obdurate   *subsidence*

In some other cases the pronunciation with stress on the first syllable is common but controversial, e.g.

Byzantine   *contribute*

clandestine   *distribute*

However, in all these cases except *Byzantine* the newer pronunciation is now effectively part of the standard language.

(iii) There is a tendency in a few words to move the stress from the first to the second syllable. This has prevailed in *aggrandize*, *chastisement*, *conversant*, *doctrinal*, *environs*, *pariah*, *urinal*, while *exquisite* and *stigmata* can now be stressed in either way.

However, stressing *combatant*, *deficit*, and *patina* on the second syllable is still definitely non-standard.

(E) Four-syllable words

While it has been traditional in RP to favour stress on the first syllable of these, recent decades have seen a general shift to the second syllable.

Words that have been, or are being, adapted to the antepenultimate stress pattern include:

centenary   *miscellany*

despicable   *nomenclature*

explicable   *pejorative*

hospitable   *peremptory*

metallurgy   *transferable*

migratory

This tendency has been strongly resisted in some cases, e.g.

applicable   *demonstrable*

aristocrat   *formidable*

controversy   *kilometre*

Dislike for the newer pronunciation is particularly strong in the cases of *contrversy*, *formidable*, and *kilometre*. Nevertheless, this pronunciation of all the above words must now be regarded as a standard variant.

Putting the stress on the second syllable remains non-standard in the following cases:

adversary   *participle*

comparable   *preferable*

momentary   *promissory*

In standard English these should be stressed on the first syllable with one of the two middle unstressed syllables elided.

For *primarily*, see -ARILY.

(F) Five-syllable words

Five-syllable words originally stressed on the first syllable have been affected by the difficulty of uttering more than three unstressed syllables in sequence. The stress has been shifted to the second syllable in *laboratory*, *obligatory*, whereas in *veterinary* the fourth syllable is elided, and usually the second as well.

For *arbitrarily*, *momentarily*, etc., see -ARILY.

(G) The main difference between the patterns of stress in British and American English is as follows. In words of four syllables and over, in which the main stress falls on the first or second syllable, there is a strong secondary stress on the last syllable but one in American English, e.g. *cóntemplàtive*, *térritòry*. The vowel in the penultimate syllable is fully enunciated.

reduced forms

In rapid speech, many shorter lightly stressed words tend to be reduced either by the obscuring of their vowels or the loss of a consonant or both. They may even be attached to one another or to more prominent words. Similarly, some such words are in rapid speech omitted altogether, while longer but common words are shortened by the elision of unstressed syllables. Typical examples are:

gonna, wanna	= 'going to', 'want to'
kinda, sorta	= 'kind of', 'sort of'
gimme, lemme	= 'give me', 'let me'
'snot	= 'it's not'
innit, wannit	= 'isn't it', 'wasn't it'
doncher, dunno	= 'don't you', 'I don't know'
'spect or *I'xpect*	= 'I expect'
(I) spose	= 'I suppose'

cos, course	= 'because', 'of course'
on'y	= 'only'
praps, probly	= 'perhaps', 'probably'

Note also the reduction or omission of *do, does, did* in e.g. *What's he say?*, *Where d'you find it?*, *What you want it for?*, and that of *have, had*, in e.g. *We done it before.*

Most of these reduced forms (with the possible exception of *innit, wannit*) are natural in informal RP, but should be avoided in formal contexts.

PART II: DIFFICULT PRONUNCIATIONS

The entries in this list are of three kinds. Some are words, mainly unusual ones, that have only one current pronunciation, which cannot be deduced with certainty from the spelling. Others have one pronunciation, which is slurred in rapid speech; these reduced forms are noted, with comments on their acceptability in formal speech. The third and largest group is of words with two or more current pronunciations. Both (or all) are given, with any advice or comment that seems pertinent. Pronunciations that cause particular dislike are pointed out, even where the feeling seems irrational. The approach throughout is fairly flexible.

Where American pronunciations differ significantly from the British, these are noted and labelled accordingly. The distinction is not always clear-cut, however, this being one area of usage that is constantly changing. Many pronunciations formerly regarded as American only are now accepted as standard variants within British English; others are in the process of becoming so, despite passionate resistance from some speakers.

Proper nouns have not generally been included, but an exception has been made for a few troublesome place names.

A

abdomen is stressed on the first syllable in general use, but on the second by many members of the medical profession.

accomplice, accomplish The pronunciation with the second syllable as *come* (rather than as in *comma*) is now predominant.

acoustic The second syllable is pronounced *coo*, not *cow*.

acumen is now usually stressed on the first syllable (not, as formerly, on the second).

adept The adjective can be stressed on the first or the second syllable; the noun is stressed on the first syllable only.

adult (adjective and noun) can be stressed on the first or the second syllable, although the former is preferred in British English.

adversary is stressed on the first syllable.

aficionado is pronounced 'a-fiss-eon-*ah*-do'.

ague has two syllables.

albumen, albumin are stressed on the first syllable (with a 'y'-sound before the *u*).

ally The noun is stressed on the first syllable; the verb can be stressed on either syllable. Before a noun **allied** is stressed on the first syllable.

almond The *l* is often silent.

analogous The *g* is pronounced as in *log* (not 'a-*na*-lo-jus').

Antarctic The first *c* is pronounced in careful speech.

anti- (prefix) rhymes with *shanty* in British English (the pronunciation 'ant eye' is American).

Apache (American Indian) rhymes with *patchy*; the sense '(Parisian) street ruffian' rhymes with *cash*.

apartheid The preferred pronunciation is with the third syllable like *hate*. The anglicized 'apart-hide' is, however, acceptable.

apophthegm is pronounced 'a-po-them'.

apparatus is pronounced with the third syllable like *rate* (not 'appar-*ah*-tus').

applicable can be stressed either on the first syllable or on the second.

apposite The third syllable should sound like that of *opposite*.

arbitrarily Although traditionally stressed on the first syllable, this word is much easier to say with the stress on the third: the latter pronunciation can now be regarded as standard.

Arctic The first *c* is pronounced in careful speech.

Argentine The third syllable is pronounced as in *turpentine*.

argot rhymes with *cargo*.

aristocrat Stress on the first syllable is preferred in British English. American 'a-*rist*-ocrat' is, however, common and acceptable.

artisan is traditionally stressed on the third syllable in Britain; American pronunciation with stress on the first syllable is now common, however.

aspirant can be stressed either on the first syllable or on the second.

asthma The familiar pronunciation is 'ass-ma'; to sound the *th* is pedantic (American 'ax-ma').

ate can rhyme with *bet* or *bate*.

audacious The *au* is pronounced as in *audience*, not as in *gaucho*.

auld lang syne The third word is pronounced like *sign*, not *zine*.

auxiliary is pronounced 'awg-*zil*-yer-ri'.

azure is now usually pronounced '*az*-yoor'.

B

banal The second syllable can sound like that of *canal* or *morale*. Pronunciation to rhyme with *anal* is American only.

basalt The first *a* is pronounced as in *gas*, the second as in *salt* or the *u* in *difficult*.

bathos The *a* is pronounced as in *paper*.

bestial The first syllable should sound like *best*, not *beast*.

blackguard is pronounced '*blagg*-ard'.

bolero (dance) is stressed on the second syllable; the sense 'jacket' is sometimes stressed on the first.

booth can rhyme with *smooth* or *tooth*.

bouquet The first syllable is pronounced as *book*, not as *beau*.

Bourbon The dynasty and the biscuit are usually pronounced with the first syllable as *bourgeois*; the US whisky with the same syllable as *bur*.

breeches can rhyme with *pitches* or *peaches*.

brochure can be stressed on either syllable.

brusque can be pronounced 'broosk' or 'brusk'.

bureau is stressed on the first syllable.

burgh (in Scotland) sounds like *borough*.

Byzantine is stressed on the second syllable in British English (American '*biz*-en-teen').

C

cadaver can rhyme with *waver* or *lava*.

cadaverous The second syllable is pronounced like the first of *average*.

cadre is usually pronounced to rhyme with *harder*; the sense 'group of revolutionaries' is sometimes pronounced with the *a* as in *cake*.

caliph usually rhymes with *bailiff*; the first syllable can also be pronounced as in *pal*.

camellia usually rhymes with *Amelia* but sometimes with *smellier*.

canine The first syllable may be pronounced as *cane* or *can*.

canton (subdivision of country) is usually stressed on the first syllable. The second syllable is pronounced as the first of *tonic*.

cantonment (military camp) is stressed on the second syllable, which may be pronounced like that of *canton* or that of *cartoon*.

capitalist is stressed on the first syllable.

Caribbean The pronunciation stressing -*be*- is traditional in British English, but that stressing -*rib*- has gained ground recently. The latter is the usual pronunciation in the US and the Caribbean itself.

carillon usually rhymes with *trillion* (American '*carry*-lon').

caryatid is stressed on the second *a*.

catacomb The third syllable can be pronounced as *comb*, or rhyming with *tomb*.

catechumen is stressed on the third syllable ('catty-*cue*-men').

Celt, Celtic The standard pronunciation is with the first syllable like *Kelly*, not *sell* (except in the case of the Glaswegian football team).

centenary is pronounced 'sen-*tee*-nary' (American '*sen*-te-nary').

cento is pronounced with *c* as in *cent*, not *cello*.

centrifugal, centripetal were originally stressed on the second syllable, but now usually on the third.

certification The preferred stress is on the first and the fourth syllables (not the second and the fourth).

cervical can be stressed either on the first syllable (with last two syllables as in *vertical*) or on the second (rhyming with *cycle*). The first pronunciation was formerly American only but is now the most common pronunciation in Britain, too.

chaff can rhyme with *staff* or *naff*.

chagrin is usually stressed on the first syllable in British English and on the second in American. The second syllable is pronounced as *grin*.

chamois (antelope) is pronounced 'shamwah'; the sense 'leather' can also be pronounced 'shammy'.

chastisement can be stressed on the first or the second syllable.

chimera The *ch* is pronounced 'k', not 'sh'; the first vowel can be pronounced as in *eye* or *it*.

chiropodist The *ch* should strictly speaking be pronounced as 'k', but as 'sh' is common.

choleric The first two syllables are pronounced like *collar*.

chutzpah ('cheek, audacity') The first syllable rhymes with *puts*; the initial sound should be pronounced like the *ch* in *loch* or the *h* in *hut* (not like *ch* in *chutney*).

cigarette is stressed on the third syllable in British English (often on the first in American).

clandestine Stress on the second syllable is preferred.

clangour rhymes with *anger*.

clientele is pronounced 'kleeon-*tell*'.

clique rhymes with *leak*, not *lick*.

colander The first syllable can be pronounced as *cull* or as in *Colin*.

combat (verb), **combatant**, **combative** are stressed on the first syllable in British English (on the second in American).

combine (noun) is stressed on the first syllable.

commandant was formerly stressed on the third syllable, but now often on the first.

communal is stressed on the first syllable.

commune The noun is stressed on the first syllable, the verb on the second.

comparable is stressed on the first syllable, not on the second.

compensatory The older (and American) pronunciation has stress on the second syllable, but stress on the third is now more common in Britain.

compilation The second syllable is pronounced as *pill*.

composite is stressed on the first syllable in British English (on the second in American). The third syllable is pronounced like that of *opposite*.

conch was originally pronounced 'conk', but now often with *ch* as in *lunch*.

conduit The last three letters were formerly pronounced like those of *circuit*, but now often 'con-dew-it'.

confidant(e) can be stressed on the first or the last syllable.

congener can be stressed on the first or the second syllable; *g* as in *gin*.

congeries ('jumble') is pronounced 'con-*jeer*-eez'.

congratulatory can be stressed on the second or the fourth syllable.

conjugal is stressed on the first syllable.

consuetude is stressed on the first syllable, with *sue* like *swi* in *swift*.

consummate The verb is stressed on the first syllable, with the third syllable as *mate*. The adjective can be stressed on the second or the first syllable, with the third syllable as in *climate*.

contact The noun is stressed on the first syllable; the verb can be stressed on either.

contemplative is stressed on the second syllable.

contrarily In the sense 'perversely' this is usually stressed on the second syllable; in the sense 'on the contrary' it is usually stressed on the first.

contribute The older pronunciation is with stress on the second syllable. Pronunciation with stress on the first syllable is very common but disliked by some people.

controversy The traditional pronunciation is with stress on the first syllable. Pronunciation with stress on the second is now very common but strongly disapproved of by some people.

contumacy is stressed on the first syllable in British English (on the second in American).

contumely can have three syllables or four, with stress on the first in both cases.

conversant is now usually stressed on the second syllable.

courier is pronounced with *ou* as in *could*.

courteous is pronounced with the first syllable like *curt*.

courtesan is pronounced with the first syllable like *court*. Either the first or the last syllable can be stressed.

courtesy The first syllable is pronounced like *curt*.

covert In British English the first syllable is usually pronounced like that of *cover*. The pronunciation '*co*-vert' is chiefly American.

cul-de-sac The first syllable may rhyme with *dull* or *full*.

culinary The *cul-* is now pronounced as in *culprit* (formerly as in *peculiar*).

cyclical The first syllable can be pronounced like *cycle* or like *sick*.

D

dais was originally one syllable, but is now usually two.

data The first syllable is pronounced as *date*.

decade was formerly stressed on the first syllable only, but stress on the second is now accepted as standard.

defect (noun) Stress on the first syllable is now usual.

deficit is stressed on the first syllable.

deify, deity were traditionally pronounced with *e* as in *me*; pronunciation with *e* as in *suede, fête* is now more usual and accepted as standard.

delirious The second syllable is pronounced as the first of *lyrical*, not *Leary*.

demesne (manorial lands) The second syllable can sound like *main* or *mean*.

demonstrable is now usually stressed on the second syllable.

deprivation The first two syllables are pronounced like those of *deprecation*.

derisive, derisory The second syllable can be pronounced like *rice* or *rise*.

despicable is now usually stressed on the second syllable (formerly on the first).

desuetude The *sue* is pronounced as *swi* in *swift*.

desultory is stressed on the first syllable.

deteriorate The pronunciation 'deteri-ate' should be avoided in formal speech.

detour is pronounced '*dee*-tour' not '*day*-tour' (American 'de-*tour*').

deus ex machina The final word is pronounced '*mak*-ina', not 'ma-*shee*-na'.

dilemma The first syllable can be pronounced like *dill* or *die*.

dinghy can be pronounced either '*ding*-gy' or rhyming with *stringy*.

diphtheria is now usually pronounced 'dip-theria' (formerly 'dif-').

diphthong is pronounced 'dif-thong' not 'dip-'.

disciplinary The older (and American) pronunciation has stress on the first syllable, but it is now usually stressed on the third.

disputable is stressed on the second syllable.

dispute (noun) is traditionally stressed on the second syllable; pronunciation with the stress on the first is now common but rejected by many speakers.

dissect The first syllable was formerly pronounced 'diss' but pronunciation to rhyme with *bisect* is now more usual.

distribute was formerly stressed on the second syllable only. Pronunciation with stress on the first is now very common but is still considered incorrect by some people.

doctrinal is stressed on the second syllable, with *i* as in *mine*.

dolorous, dolour In British English the first syllable is pronounced like *doll* (in American like *dole*).

dour The older and preferred pronunciation rhymes with *lure* rather than *lower*.

dubiety The last three syllables sound like those of *anxiety*.

ducat (coin) The first syllable is like *duck*, not *duke*.

dynastic, dynasty In British English the first syllable is like *din* (American like *dine*).

E

ebullient The *u* can be pronounced like that in *dull* or *bull*.

economic The *e* can be pronounced as in *extra* or as in *equal*.

e'er ('ever') sounds like *air*.

efficacy is stressed on the first syllable, not the second.

ego The first syllable is usually pronounced like that of *eager* (but sometimes like *egg*).

egocentric, egoism, etc. The pronunciation with the first syllable like *eager* was once chiefly American but is now common in British English.

either In British English the *ei* can be sounded as in *height* or *seize* (in American only the second).

elixir is stressed on the second syllable and can rhyme with either *mixer* or *Mick's ear*.

enclave is pronounced with *en-* as in *end*, *a* as in *slave*.

entirety is now pronounced 'entire-ety' (formerly 'entire-ty').

envelope The noun is pronounced with *en-* as in *end* or *on*, although the latter is disliked by some older speakers. The verb is pronounced with *en-* as in *in* or *end* (and with stress on the second syllable).

environs rhymes with *sirens*.

epoxy (resin) is stressed on the second syllable.

equerry The older pronunciation is with stress on the second syllable, but stress on the first is now common and generally accepted.

espionage is now usually pronounced with *-age* as in *camouflage* (formerly to rhyme with *cabbage*).

et cetera is pronounced 'etsetera' not 'ek-setera'.

explicable The stress was originally on the first syllable, but is now usually on the second.

exquisite The stress was originally on the first syllable, but is now often on the second.

extraordinary The first *a* can be pronounced but this is unusual and widely disliked.

F

fakir The first syllable can sound like *fake* or that in *factory*.

falcon The first vowel can be pronounced like that in *fork* or *folly* (but not as in *alcove*).

fascia ('board or panel') rhymes with *Alsatia*; the anatomical sense is usually pronounced like *fashion*.

fascism, fascist The first syllable is like that of *fashion*.

February In rapid or informal speech it is common and acceptable to drop the first *r* ('feb-yoo-erry'), although more conservative speakers consider this incorrect.

fetid The *e* can be pronounced as in *fetter* or as in *feet*.

fifth In careful speech, it is better not to drop the second *f*.

finance can be stressed on the first syllable (with *i* as in *fine*) or on the second (with *i* as in *fin* or *fine*).

flaccid can be pronounced to rhyme with *acid* or with *cc* as in *accident*.

forbade The second syllable can be sounded like *bad* or *bayed*.

formidable was once stressed on the first syllable only, but now often on the second. Both are acceptable, but the second is strongly disliked by some people.

forte The sense 'one's strong point' was originally pronounced like *fort*, but this is now mainly American; in British English the preferred pronunciation is like *forty* or the musical term *forte* ('for-tay').

foyer is now pronounced 'foy-ay', not 'fwah-yay' (American 'foy-er').

fracas The singular is pronounced 'frack-ah', the plural 'frack-ahz' (American 'frake-us', 'frake-us-es').

fulminate The *u* can be pronounced as in *dull* or *bull*.

fulsome is now always pronounced with *u* as in *full*.

furore In British English this can have two syllables or three, being stressed on the second in both cases (American **furor** with two syllables, stressed on the first).

G

Gaelic The first syllable can be pronounced like *gale* or *gal*.

gala In British English this is now usually pronounced with the first *a* as in *calm*. The older pronunciation with *a* as in *gale* is still used in northern England and the US.

gallant The sense 'brave' is stressed on the first syllable; the sense 'polite to women' can be stressed on either syllable (as can the noun).

garage The preferred pronunciation is with stress on the first syllable and *age* as in *camouflage* (or rhyming with *large*). Pronunciation to rhyme with *carriage* or with stress on the second syllable is disapproved of by many RP speakers.

garrulity is stressed on the second syllable, which sounds like *rule*.

garrulous is stressed on the first syllable.

gaseous The first vowel can be pronounced like that in *gas* or that in *gaze*.

genuine The *ine* is pronounced as in *engine*, not as in *wine*.

genus can be pronounced with *e* as in *genius* or as in *general*; the plural **genera** has the second pronunciation only.

gibber, gibberish usually have *g* as in *gin*.

glacier can be pronounced with *a* as in *glad* or *glade*; **glacial** has the second pronunciation only.

golf has *o* as in *got*. The pronunciation 'goff' is old-fashioned.

gone has *o* as in *on*. The pronunciation 'gawn' is non-standard.

government In formal speech, do not drop the first *n* (or the whole of the second syllable).

gratis The pronunciations 'graytis', 'grahtis', and 'grattis' are all acceptable.

greasy The *s* may be as in *cease* or *easy*.

grievous does not rhyme with *previous*.

guacamole (vegetable dish) is pronounced 'gwark-er-*mole*-i'.

gunwale is pronounced 'gunn'l'.

H

half-past In formal speech, avoid saying 'hah past' or 'hoff posst'.

hara-kiri is pronounced as written, not 'harry-carry'.

harass, harassment were formerly stressed on the first syllable, but now often on the second. Both are acceptable, although the latter pronunciation is considered incorrect by some people.

have In rapid speech, weakly stressed *have* sounds like weakly stressed *of*. When stress is restored to it, it should become *have*, as in 'You couldn't 've done it'—'I could have' (not 'I could of').

hectare The second syllable is usually pronounced like *tare* (less commonly, *tar*).

hegemony is now usually pronounced in the American way, with *g* as in *gem* not *get*. It is stressed on the second syllable.

Hegira (in Islam) is stressed on the first syllable, which is like *hedge*.

heinous was formerly pronounced with *ei* as in *rein* only, but now often to rhyme with *Venus*. Both are acceptable, but the newer pronunciation is disliked by many RP speakers. That rhyming with *genius* is erroneous.

homeopathy The first syllable can rhyme with *tome* or *Tom*.

homogeneous The last three syllables can sound like *genius*, or 'jenny-us', but the *e* should not be dropped.

homosexual, homosexuality The first syllable can be pronounced to rhyme with *tome* or *Tom*.

honorarium The *h* is silent, the *a* as in *rare*.

hospitable can be stressed on the first or the second syllable.

hotel The *h* should be pronounced.

housewifery is stressed on the first syllable, with *i* as in *whiff*.

hovel, hover are usually pronounced with *o* as in *hot*. Pronunciation with *o* as in *love* is now chiefly American.

I

idyll, idyllic have *i* as in *idiot*.

illustrative is stressed on the first syllable in British English (on the second in American).

imbroglio rhymes with *folio*, the *g* being silent.

impious was formerly stressed on the first syllable, but now often on the second. **Impiety** is always stressed on the second syllable.

importune is stressed on the third syllable.

inchoate was formerly stressed on the first syllable, but now more often on the second.

indict rhymes with *incite*, the *c* being silent.

indisputable is stressed on the third syllable.

inexplicable is usually stressed on the third syllable, but sometimes on the second.

infamous is stressed on the first syllable.

inherent The first *e* can be pronounced as in *here* or as in *error*.

intaglio has silent *g*; the *a* can be pronounced as in *pal* or *pass*.

integral can be stressed on the first or the second syllable, although the latter is considered incorrect by some people. The pronunciation '*int*-re-gal' is erroneous.

intern (verb) is stressed on the second syllable; the noun sense 'trainee' (chiefly American) is stressed on the first.

internecine is stressed on the third syllable with the last syllables like *knee sign*.

interstice is stressed on the second syllable.

intestinal Traditionally pronounced with stress on the second syllable and the third like *tin*; now commonly with stress on the third, pronounced *tine*.

intricacy is stressed on the first syllable.

invalid ('sick person') is stressed on the first syllable with the second *i* as in *lid* or *machine*; the adjectival sense 'not valid' is stressed on the second syllable with the final *i* short.

inveigle The second syllable can be pronounced as in *vague* or rhyming with *beagle*.

inventory is pronounced like *infantry* with *v* instead of *f*.

irrefragable ('indisputable') is stressed on the second syllable.

irreparable is stressed on the second syllable.

irrevocable is stressed on the second syllable.

issue is usually pronounced with *ss* as in *mission* but sometimes to rhyme with *miss you*.

isthmus In rapid or informal speech the *th* often becomes *t* or disappears completely. This is acceptable.

J

January The usual British pronunciation is 'jan-yoor-y' (American 'jan-yoo-erry').

jejune is stressed on the second syllable.

jewellery is pronounced 'jewel-ry' or 'jewl-ry', not 'jool-ery'.

joule (unit of work) rhymes with *fool*.

jubilee was formerly stressed on the first syllable, but now often on the third.

jugular The first syllable is now pronounced like *jug* and not as in *conjugal*.

junta is usually pronounced as written in British English. 'Hoonta', an attempt to reproduce the Spanish, is the standard American pronunciation.

K

karaoke The first two syllables are properly pronounced like those of *caramel*, but (to avoid the awkward hiatus) more often like *carry*.

kilometre was formerly stressed on the first syllable, but now very often on the second. Both are acceptable, but the latter is considered incorrect by many people.

knoll has *o* as in *no*.

L

laboratory is usually stressed on the second syllable. The former pronunciation, with stress on the first, is now chiefly American (with *ory* as in *Tory*).

lamentable should be stressed on the first syllable.

languor is pronounced to rhyme with *anger*.

lasso is usually stressed on the second syllable, with *so* as *sue* (but sometimes on the first syllable, with *so* as *sew*).

lather can rhyme with *rather* or *gather*.

leeward is pronounced 'lee-ward' in general use, but like *lured* in nautical contexts.

leisure rhymes with *pleasure* in British English (with *seizure* in American).

length The preferred pronunciation is with *ng* as in *long*; 'lenkth' is acceptable but 'lenth' is non-standard.

levee ('reception') is stressed on the first syllable, with the final vowel like *lee* or *lay*; the sense 'embankment' (chiefly American) may be stressed on the second syllable (with the final syllable always as in *levy*).

library In formal speech it is better to avoid dropping the second syllable ('li-bry').

lichen The first syllable can be pronounced as *like* or as in *Lichfield*.

lieutenant In British English the first syllable is pronounced like *left* (American like *loot*).

liquorice can be pronounced 'licker-iss' or 'licker-ish'.

longevity has *ng* as in *lunge*.

longitude The *ng* can be pronounced as in *lunge* or as in *linger*, but 'longtitude' is an error.

lour rhymes with *hour*.

lugubrious is pronounced 'loo-*goo*-brious'.

M

machete rhymes with *Betty*; the *ch* can be sounded as in *machine* or as in *attach*.

machination was formerly pronounced with *ch* as in *mechanical*, but now often as in *machine*.

machismo The *ch* can be pronounced as in *attach* or as in *mechanical*. But **macho** can only be pronounced in the first way.

magazine is stressed on the third syllable in British English (often on the first in American).

mandatory is stressed on the first syllable.

margarine is usually pronounced with *g* as in *Margery* (but sometimes with *g* as in *magazine*).

marital is stressed on the first syllable.

massage In British English the preferred stress is on the first syllable (in American on the second).

matrix, matrixes have *a* as in *mate*.

medicine can be pronounced with two or three syllables. The latter pronunciation is normal in Scotland and the US, but is disapproved of by some users of RP.

mediocre The first syllable is pronounced like *mead*.

metallurgy, metallurgist are now usually stressed on the second syllable. The older pronunciation with stress on the first is now chiefly American.

metamorphosis can be stressed on the third or the fourth syllable.

metope (architectural term) can have two syllables or three: in either case it is stressed on the first.

midwifery is stressed on the second syllable, with *i* as in *whiff*.

mien sounds like *mean*.

migraine can be pronounced with the first syllable like *me* or *my*. The latter was originally American but is now widespread in Britain.

migratory was formerly stressed on the first syllable only, but now often on the second.

millenary can be stressed on the second syllable, which is like *Len*, or on the first.

miscellany is stressed on the second syllable in British English (on the first in American).

mischievous is stressed on the first syllable. The pronunciation rhyming with *previous* is an error.

misericord (in a church) is stressed on the second syllable.

mnemonic is stressed on the second syllable, with the first like *nimble* not *Newman*.

mocha sounds like *mocker* in British English (but rhymes with *coca* in American).

momentary, momentarily are stressed on the first syllable.

mullah can be pronounced with *u* as in *dull* or as in *bull*.

municipal is stressed on the second syllable.

N

nadir was formerly pronounced '*nay*-dear' in British English, but now often with the first vowel as in *nag*.

naive is now usually pronounced 'nigh-*Eve*', but sometimes 'nah-*Eve*'.

naivety has three syllables.

nascent The *a* was formerly pronounced as in *fascinate*, but now often as in *nation*.

necessarily For ease of pronunciation this is often stressed on the third syllable (rather than on the first like *necessary*). This is acceptable but disliked by some people.

neither In British English the *ei* can be sounded as in *height* or *seize* (in American only the second).

nephew was formerly pronounced with *ph* like *v*, but now usually '*neff*-you'.

nicety has three syllables.

niche is now usually pronounced 'neesh' (but sometimes 'nitch').

nomenclature is usually stressed on the second syllable in British English. The pronunciation with stress on the first and third syllables is now chiefly American.

nonchalant is stressed on the first syllable, with *ch* as in *machine*.

nuclear is pronounced '*newk*-lee-er'. The pronunciation 'nucular', famously used by Presidents Eisenhower and Carter, is an error in both British and American English.

nucleic is stressed on the second syllable, which can be sounded as *clee* or *clay*.

O

obdurate is stressed on the first syllable.

obeisance is stressed on the second syllable, which sounds like *base*.

obligatory is stressed on the second syllable.

obscenity has *e* as in *scent*.

occurrence The second syllable is pronounced like the first in *current* (not like *cur*).

oche (in darts) rhymes with *hockey*.

o'er ('over') now usually rhymes with *goer*.

of In rapid speech, weakly stressed *of* sounds like weakly stressed *have*. When *of* is stressed, it should sound like *of*, not *'ve*.

often Traditionally, this has a silent *t*, as in *soften*; the sounding of the *t* is, however, acceptable.

ominous The first syllable is pronounced like that of *omelette*.

ophthalmic The *ph* should be pronounced like *f* not *p*.

opus The *o* can be pronounced as in *open* or *operate*.

ormolu is pronounced 'orm-o-loo', with the second *o* weak as in *Caroline*.

P

p (abbreviation for 'penny', 'pence') In formal contexts, it is better to say *penny* (after *one*) or *pence* rather than 'pee'.

pace ('with all due respect to') can be pronounced with the first syllable like *parch* or *pacy*.

paella is pronounced 'pie-*ell*-a' rather than 'pah-*ell*-a'.

panegyric is stressed on the third syllable, with *g* as in *gin* and *y* as in *lyric*.

paprika is usually stressed on the first syllable in British English (on the second in American).

pariah The pronunciation rhyming with *carrier* (rather than with *Isaiah*) is now old-fashioned.

participle is stressed on the first syllable (the first *i* may be dropped). The stressing of the second syllable is common but not yet standard.

particularly In formal speech, it is better to avoid saying 'particuly'.

partisan is traditionally stressed on the third syllable in Britain; American pronunciation with stress on the first syllable is now common, however.

pasty (pie) has *a* as in *lass* (not as in *pastry*).

patent can be pronounced with the first syllable like *pat* or *pate*.

pathos The *a* is pronounced as in *paper*.

patina is stressed on the first syllable.

patriarch The first *a* is pronounced as in *paper*.

patriot, patriotic can have *a* as in *pat* or *paper*.

patron has *a* as in *paper*.

patronal ('of a patron saint') is stressed on the second syllable, which rhymes with *toe*.

patronage, patronize usually have *a* as in *pat* but sometimes as in *patron*.

pejorative is stressed on the second syllable. The pronunciation with stress on the first syllable is now old-fashioned.

peremptory is usually stressed on the second syllable in British English (on the first in American).

perhaps In formal speech, this is better pronounced as two syllables with *h*, not *r*, sounded. 'Praps' is common informally.

pharmacopoeia is stressed on the *oe*; *-poeia* rhymes with *idea*.

philharmonic Traditionally, the second *h* was silent; it is now more often sounded.

phthisis (wasting disease) has silent *ph*; the first syllable is usually pronounced like *thigh*, but sometimes like *tie*.

pianist is stressed on the first *i*, with *ia* as in *Ian*.

piano (instrument) has *a* as in *man*; the sense 'softly' has *a* as in calm.

piazza The *zz* is pronounced 'ts'.

pistachio has *a* as in *calm* or *cat*, *ch* as in *machine*.

plaid, plait rhyme with *lad, flat*.

plastic now rhymes with *fantastic*, rather than having the sound of *plaster*.

plenty The pronunciation 'plenny' is nonstandard.

pogrom is stressed on the first syllable.

pomegranate The pronunciation 'pommy-gran-it' is now usual, rather than 'pom-gran-it' or 'pum-gran-it'.

porpoise The *oise* was formerly pronounced like *ose* in *purpose*, but now often like *poise*.

posthumous has silent *h*.

pot-pourri The traditional pronunciation is with stress on the second syllable (American on the third) and *pot-* like *Poe*. However, the *t* in *pot* is now often sounded.

precedence is usually stressed on the first syllable (mostly sounded like *press*, but sometimes with the vowel like *priest*).

precedent The noun is stressed on the first syllable, the adjective usually on the second.

predilection should not be pronounced as if spelt 'predeliction'.

preferable is stressed on the first syllable. The pronunciation stressing the second syllable is widespread but not yet standard.

premise The noun ('statement assumed to be true') is pronounced as in *premises*; the verb ('based') is stressed on the second syllable, rhyming with *surmise*.

prestige is stressed on the second syllable, with *i* and *g* as in *regime*.

prestigious has three syllables only, rhyming with *religious*.

prima facie is pronounced 'pry-ma *fay*-shee'.

primarily is traditionally stressed on the first syllable. The pronunciation with stress on the second is well established but widely disliked.

privacy can be pronounced with *i* as in *privet* or *private*; the latter is the older pronunciation.

probably In formal speech, all three syllables should be sounded; informally often 'probbly'.

proboscis is pronounced 'pro-*boss*-iss'.

process (noun) has *o* as in *probe*. (The older pronunciation with *o* as in *profit* is now only American.) The verb meaning 'to subject to a process' is pronounced like the noun but the verb 'to walk in procession' is stressed on the second syllable.

promissory is stressed on the first syllable.

pronunciation The second syllable is pronounced like *nun* (not as in *pronounce*).

prosody The first syllable is like that of *prospect* (not like *prose*).

protean was stressed originally on the first syllable, now commonly on the second.

protégé In British English the first syllable is usually like *protestant* (in American like *protest*).

proven has *o* as in *prove*, but pronunciation like *woven* is widespread.

proviso The second syllable is as that of *revise*.

puissance ('power') may be pronounced 'pew-iss-ance', 'pwees-ance' or 'pwiss-ance'. (The word is mainly found in poetry, where the pronunciation will depend on scansion.) The showjumping sense is often pronounced with approximation to French, i.e. with *pui* as 'pwi' and the *a* nasalized.

pursuivant (in heraldry) is pronounced 'Percy-vant'.

pyramidal is stressed on the second syllable.

Q

quaff rhymes with *scoff*.

quagmire The *a* was originally as in *wag*, now usually as in *quad*.

qualm rhymes with *calm*; to rhyme with *shawm* is now rare.

quandary is stressed on the first syllable.

quasi- The final consonant may be pronounced as *s* or *z*: in the former case, the vowels are pronounced as those in *crazy*; in the latter, they may also be pronounced as in *wayside*.

quatercentenary may be pronounced 'kwatt-er-' or 'kwayt-er-', but not 'quarter-'.

questionnaire The first syllable is usually pronounced like *quest*; the pronunciation 'kest-' is acceptable but widely disliked.

R

rabid The first syllable is pronounced like that of *rabbit*.

rabies In formal speech the second syllable is best pronounced like *bees*, not as in *babies*.

rampage The verb is stressed on the second syllable, the noun usually on the first.

rapport is stressed on the second syllable, which sounds like *pore* in British English (like *port* in American).

ratiocinate The first two syllables are usually like *ratty*, with stress on the third. The first syllables may also be pronounced as in *rashy*.

rationale has *ale* as in *morale*.

really rhymes with *ideally*, *clearly*, not with *freely*.

recess (noun and verb) is traditionally stressed on the second syllable; the noun is now very often stressed on the first, but this is disliked by some people.

recognize In formal speech, it is better not to drop the *g*.

recondite may be stressed on the first or the second syllable.

recuperate The second syllable is now pronounced as *coop* and not like the first of *Cupid*.

referable is stressed on the second syllable.

remediable, remedial are stressed on the second syllable, with *e* as in *medium*.

remonstrate is stressed on the first syllable.

Renaissance is stressed on the second syllable in British English, with *ai* as in *plaice*.

renege can rhyme with *plague* or *league*.

reportage is usually pronounced with -*age* as in *camouflage*, but stressed. Pronunciation to rhyme with *cabbage* (and stress on -*port-*) is also acceptable.

research (noun and verb) is traditionally stressed on the second syllable. American pronunciation of the noun with stress on the first syllable is now quite widespread in Britain, but is considered incorrect by some people.

respite is stressed on the first syllable; in British English the second syllable is usually pronounced like *spite* (American like *spit*).

restaurant Pronunciation with the final *t* silent and the second *a* nasalized is preferred by some, but that with *ant* as 'ont' is now more common. In rapid speech the second syllable is often elided.

revanchism has *anch* as in *anchovy*.

ribald can be pronounced with the first syllable like *rib* and the second like that of *gambled*; or with the first like *rye* and the second like *bald*.

risible rhymes with *visible*.

risqué can be pronounced 'riss-*kay*', '*riss*-kay', or '*rees*-kay'.

romance Traditionally, the stress is on the second syllable. Pronunciation with stress on the first (usually in the sense 'love affair, love story') is widespread but disliked by some people.

Romany The first vowel can be pronounced as that of *romp* or *rope*.

rotatory can be stressed on the first or the second syllable.

rowan has *ow* as in *low* or *cow*.

rowlock rhymes with *Pollock*.

S

sacrilegious now always rhymes with *religious* (despite the difference in spelling).

sahib has silent *h* and sounds like *Saab* in rapid speech.

salsify (root vegetable) is pronounced '*sal*-si-fee'.

salve (noun and verb) now rhymes with *valve* in British English (with *have* in American). Pronunciation to rhyme with *halve* is now old-fashioned.

satiety The last syllables are pronounced like *anxiety*.

Saudi can rhyme with *rowdy* or *bawdy*.

scabies In formal speech the second syllable is best pronounced like *bees*, not as in *babies*.

scabrous can have *a* as in *skate* or *scab*.

scallop can rhyme with *wallop* or with *gallop*.

scarify ('to cut or scratch') can rhyme with *clarify* or be pronounced '*scare*-ify'. The informal word *scarify* meaning 'terrify' is pronounced in the second way only.

scenario has *sc* as in *scene*, *ario* as in *impressario* (American pronunciation has *a* as in *Mary*).

schedule traditionally has *sch* as in *Schubert*; the American pronunciation with *sch* as in *school* is now quite common in Britain.

schism The older pronunciation is 'siz'm' with silent *ch*; 'skiz'm' is widespread and acceptable.

schist (rock) has *sch* as in *Schubert*.

schizo- is pronounced 'skitso' in senses to do with psychology (e.g. *schizophrenia*) but usually 'shy-zo' in senses to do with biology (e.g. *schizogony*).

scilicet ('namely') can be pronounced with the first syllable like *sigh* and the rest like *licit*; or the first like *ski* and the rest like *lick it*.

scone can rhyme with *on* or *own*. The second pronunciation now tends to be associated with pretentious pseudo-gentility, so is perhaps better avoided.

second (verbs) The sense 'to support or endorse' is stressed on the first syllable; the sense 'to transfer' on the second.

secretary is pronounced 'sek-re-try', not 'sek-e-try' or 'sek-e-terry'; 'sek-re-terry' is American only.

secretive is stressed on the first syllable.

segue ('uninterrupted transition') is pronounced 'seg-way'.

seisin (in law) has *ei* as in *seize*.

seismic has the first syllable like *size*.

seraglio has silent *g* and *a* as in *ask*.

shaman The first syllable was formerly pronounced like *sham*, but now often like *shame*.

sharia (Islamic law) rhymes with *arrear*.

sheikh can sound like *shake* or *chic*. (The former is the older British pronunciation.)

simultaneous In British English the *i* is pronounced as in *simple* (American as in *Simon*).

sinecure is traditionally pronounced with *i* as in *sign*, but *i* as in *sin* is common and acceptable.

Sinhalese (people and language of Sri Lanka) is pronounced 'sin-(h)al-ese'.

Sioux is pronounced 'soo'.

sisal (cactus, fibre) The first syllable is like the second of *precise*.

sixth The pronunciation 'sikth' is avoided in careful speech.

slalom has *a* as in *spa*.

slaver ('dribble') can be pronounced with *a* as in *have* or *slave*.

sleight sounds like *slight*.

sloth rhymes with *both*.

slough The noun meaning 'bog' rhymes with *bough*; the verb meaning 'to cast a skin' with *tough*.

sobriquet ('nickname') The first syllable is like that of *sober*, the last like that of *croquet*.

sojourn The first vowel is pronounced as in *sob* (American as in *sober*), the second as in *bludgeon* or *adjourn*.

solder can have *o* as in *sold* or *sob* (American pronunciation is 'sodder' or 'sawder').

solecism has *o* as in *sob*.

solenoid (magnetic coil) is stressed on the first syllable, with *o* as in *sober* or as in *sob*.

sonorous is usually stressed on the first syllable, with the first *o* as in *sob* (but sometimes on the second syllable, with the second *o* as in *orb*).

soporific The first *o* is now pronounced as in *sob*.

sough (wind sound) can rhyme with *plough* or *tough*.

sovereignty is pronounced 'sov'renty' (not 'sov-rain-ity').

Soviet can have *o* as in *sober* or *sob*.

species The older pronunciation is 'spee-sheez'; 'spee-seez' is now generally accepted but disliked by some people.

spinet (keyboard instrument) may be stressed on either syllable.

spontaneity was traditionally pronounced with *e* as in *me*; pronunciation with *e* as in *suede*, *fête* is now more usual and accepted as standard.

stalwart The first syllable can be pronounced like *stall*, or as in *stallion*.

status In British English the first syllable is pronounced like *stay*.

stigmata was formerly stressed on the first syllable, but is now more often pronounced like *sonata*.

strafe can rhyme with *staff* or *safe*.

stratosphere has *a* as in *Stratford*.

stratum, strata The *a* of the first syllable can be pronounced like that in *ate* or *art*.

strength The preferred pronunciation is with *ng* as in *strong*; 'strenkth' is acceptable but 'strenth' is non-standard.

suave, suavity have *a* as the first *a* in *lava*.

subsidence was stressed originally on the second syllable with *i* as in *side*; now often with stress on the first syllable and *i* as in *sit*.

substantial The first *a* is pronounced as in *ant*, not *aunt*.

substantive ('separate, permanent') is now usually stressed on the second syllable; the grammatical sense 'noun' is stressed on the first.

suffragan (bishop) has *g* as in *get* (not as in *suffrage*).

suit is now usually pronounced with 'oo', rather than 'yoo'.

supererogation is stressed on the fifth syllable, but **supererogatory** on the fourth syllable.

superficies is pronounced 'super-*fish*-(i)eez'.

supine is stressed on the first syllable in British English (on the second in American).

suppose should be given two syllables in formal speech.

surety is now usually pronounced '*sure*-et-y' (originally '*sure*-ty').

surveillance The older pronunciation is 'sur-*vey*-lance'; the *l* is now often dropped but some people consider this incorrect.

suzerain ('sovereign') has *u* as in *Susan*.

swathe The sense 'broad strip or area' is pronounced with *th* as in *cloth* and *a* as in *water* or *wash*; the sense 'wrap in layers of fabric' rhymes with *bathe*.

syndrome is now always pronounced with two syllables (originally three).

T

Taoiseach (Irish prime minister) is pronounced '*tee*-sh'kh', with the last sound as *ch* in *loch*.

taxidermy is stressed on the first syllable but **taxidermist, taxidermal**, and **taxidermic** on the third.

temporarily For ease of pronunciation this is often stressed on the third syllable (rather than on the first like *temporary*). This is acceptable but disliked by some people.

tirade is pronounced 'tie-*raid*' or with the *i* as in *tin*.

tissue is usually pronounced with *ss* as in *mission* but sometimes to rhyme with *miss you*.

tonne sounds like *ton*. To avoid misunderstanding, *metric* can be prefixed; but in most spoken contexts the slight difference between the weights will not matter.

tortoise The *oise* was formerly pronounced like *ose* in *purpose*, but now often like *poise*.

tourniquet In British English the first syllable is pronounced like *tour* or *turn* and the third like *croquet* (American 'turn-a-*kit*').

towards The form with two syllables is now more common than 'twords' or 'tords'.

trachea ('windpipe') is usually stressed on the *e* in British English (on the first *a*, pronounced as in *trade*, in American).

trait Traditionally, the second *t* is silent in British English; however, the American pronunciation, in which *t* is sounded, is now widespread as well.

trajectory can be stressed on the second syllable or the first.

transferable can be stressed on the second or the first syllable.

transition is now pronounced 'tran-*zish*-on' not 'tran-*sizh*-on'.

transparent The last two syllables can sound like *apparent* or *parent*.

trauma, traumatic can be pronounced with *au* as in *cause* or as in *gaucho*.

traverse The noun is usually stressed on the first syllable and the verb on the second.

trefoil (plant) is stressed on the first syllable, with *e* as in *even* or as in *ever*.

triumvir The first two syllables are like those of *triumphant*.

troth formerly rhymed with *both* in British English, but now also with *cloth* (as in American).

trow ('believe') rhymes with *know*, not *now*.

truculent now has the first *u* as in *truck* (formerly as in *true*).

turquoise can be pronounced 'tur-*kwoyz*' or 'tur-*kwahz*'.

U

ululate is pronounced '*yool*-yoo-late' or '*ull*-yoo-late'.

umbilical can be stressed on the second syllable or on the third sounded as *like*.

unprecedented has the second syllable like *press*.

untoward Pronunciation with stress on the third syllable is now usual (the older pronunciation rhymed with *lowered*).

Uranus can be stressed on the first or the second syllable.

urinal can be stressed on the first or the second syllable.

usual In formal speech, it is better to avoid complete loss of the second *u* ('*yoo*-zh'l').

uvula (in anatomy) is pronounced '*yoo*-vyoo-la'.

uxorious The first *u* is pronounced as in *Uxbridge*.

V

vacuum is now pronounced as two (not three) syllables.

vagary is now stressed on the first (rather than the second) syllable.

vagina, vaginal are stressed on the second syllable, with *i* as in *china*.

valance (drapery for bed) rhymes with *balance*.

valence, valency (in chemistry) have *a* as in *ale*.

valet Those who employ them sound the *t*.

Valkyrie can be stressed on the first or the second syllable.

vase In British English this has *a* as in *dance* (in American it rhymes with *face* or *phase*).

veld rhymes with *felt*.

venison is usually pronounced 'ven-i-z'n' or 'ven-i-s'n'.

veterinary is stressed on the first syllable and generally reduced to 'vet-rin-ry' or 'vet-in-ry'. The form 'vet-nary' is erroneous, while 'vet-rin-ery' is American only.

vice versa The first word can be pronounced to rhyme with *spice* or like the first two syllables of *bicycle*.

victualler, victuals sound like 'vitt-ell-er', 'vittles'.

viola The musical instrument is stressed on the second syllable, with *i* as in *Fiona*; the flower (and woman's name) is stressed on the first syllable, with *i* as in *vie*.

vitamin The traditional British pronunciation is with *i* as in *hit*; however, American pronunciation as in *vital* is now also widespread.

viz. ('namely') In speech, it is customary to say *namely*.

voluntarily For ease of pronunciation this is often stressed on the third syllable (rather than on the first like *voluntary*). This is acceptable but disliked by some people.

W

waistcoat was formerly pronounced 'wesskot' (with the second syllable like *mascot*), but now usually as spelt.

walnut, walrus The *l* should not be dropped.

werewolf The first syllable can sound like *weir* or *wear*.

whooping cough The first syllable is pronounced *hoop*.

wrath rhymes with *cloth* or *north* in British English (with *hath* in American).

wroth formerly rhymed with *both* in British English, but now also with *cloth* (as in American).

Y

yoghurt The usual British pronunciation is 'yogg-urt' (American 'yoh-gurt').

Z

zoology was formerly pronounced with the first *o* as in *zone*, but now more often 'zoo-ol-ogy'. The second pronunciation is considered incorrect by some people.

Section 5: Common Confusables

This Section lists pairs (or larger sets) of English words that are frequently confused in speech or writing. These 'confusables' appear here in a single alphabetical sequence, accompanied by brief descriptions and examples to clarify the correct use of each.

Why are some words so frequently mistaken in this way? The most obvious cause is a similarity of sound or spelling, as with the familiar stumbling blocks **draft/draught, forbear/forebear, stationary/stationery,** *and* **who's/whose,** *etc. In other cases, the forms of the words have little or no resemblance, but the things or concepts signified are similar enough to cause confusion (while remaining properly distinct); examples include* **allegory** *and* **fable, creole** *and* **pidgin,** *and* **strategy** *and* **tactics.** *Finally, and inevitably, there is a large number of cases in which the problems overlap, as with the eminently confusable pairs* **concave/convex, derisive/derisory, epigram/epigraph, inequity/iniquity,** *and* **stalactite/stalagmite.** *Here, often because the words are etymologically related, both form and reference are confusingly similar—a combination that can mislead even the most practised and sophisticated users of the language.*

By design, this Section deals only with those (relatively) straightforward cases in which one word tends to usurp the place and function of another. Cases in which there is more to be said—generally because the distinction between the words is contentious, subtle, or less than absolute—are dealt with at greater length in SECTION 6: USAGE.

In a nutshell, this Section should keep you from using the wrong word, whereas that Section will help you to find the best word.

A

abjure / adjure Abjure means 'to renounce on oath' or more generally 'to abandon or abstain from', e.g. *He had abjured all religious belief.* By contrast, **adjure** means 'to command by exacting an oath' or more commonly now 'to request earnestly', e.g. *They were all shouting at once, adjuring each other to have another pint.*

abrogate/arrogate Abrogate means 'to repeal, annul, or cancel' and is used with reference to laws, rules, treaties, and other formal agreements, e.g. *The new regime abrogated the constitution.* **Arrogate** means 'to lay claim to without justification' often in the structure 'arrogate (something) to oneself', e.g. *The regime arrogated to itself whatever powers it chose.*

abysmal / abyssal Abysmal has the meaning 'immeasurable, bottomless' whether applied literally to gorges, outer space, etc., or used figuratively in such phrases as *abysmal ignorance.* The use of **abysmal** to mean simply 'very bad', as in *The film was abysmal* is widespread but somewhat informal. **Abyssal** is limited to technical usage in oceanography, where it means 'belonging to one of the deepest levels of the ocean'.

activate / actuate See SECTION 6: USAGE.

adjacent / adjoining Adjacent means 'near or close' but does not necessarily imply contact; an *adjacent room* can be across a corridor, and *adjacent tables* are next to each other, but with a space between. **Adjoining** invariably denotes contact, and is therefore preferable when this meaning is unambiguously required.

adopted/adoptive In correct use, a child is **adopted** and its acquired parents are **adoptive**. The distinction has become eroded in recent usage, especially in extended uses with reference to countries, homes, etc.

adverse / everse Adverse means 'unfavourable or harmful' and is normally used of conditions and effects rather than people, e.g. *adverse weather conditions*. **Averse**, on the other hand, is used of people, always with 'to' or 'from', and means 'having a strong dislike or opposition to something', e.g. *I am not averse to helping out.* A common error is to use **adverse** instead of **averse** in such constructions as *He is not adverse to making a profit.*

affect/effect Effect is most common as a noun meaning 'a result or consequence', e.g. *Regular exercise has a generally beneficial effect*, while **affect** is most common as a verb meaning 'to have an effect on', e.g. *Exercise indirectly affects all the organs of the body.* As a noun, **affect** survives only as a technical term in psychology, meaning 'mood, mental state, emotion'. As a verb, **effect** means 'to bring about, cause, accomplish', e.g. *Growth in the economy can only be effected by stringent controls.*

albumen/albumin Albumen specifically denotes egg white or the protein found in egg white. **Albumin**, on the other hand, denotes the more general category of protein which is soluble in water and which coagulates on heating, of which **albumen** is just one type.

Algonquin / Algonquian Algonquian refers to a large family of American Indian languages, of which **Algonquin** is a specific member. **Algonquin** is also the term used for the American Indian people speaking the Algonquin language.

allegory / fable / parable / symbolism All four words are used of a narrative or story in which the characters and events have a meaning beyond the literal one. **Allegory**, which flourished mainly in medieval and Renaissance literature, usually makes a religious or moral point and involves characters who stand for such abstract qualities as Death or Pride; the best-known example in English is Bunyan's *Pilgrim's Progress* (1678, 1684). An example of a political allegory, in which the characters stand for historical figures, is Dryden's *Absalom and Achitophel* (1681). In allegory the correspondence between characters or events and their deeper meaning is fixed and explicit; a tale in which various deeper meanings are suggested but never pinned down (such as Melville's *Moby Dick*, 1851) is more properly described in terms of its **symbolism**. A **parable** is a particular kind of allegory in which a moral point is made from a brief everyday story; the most famous are the parables attributed to Jesus Christ in the New Testament. A **fable** also makes a moral point, but is usually couched in terms of fictional characters who are made to do impossible things (e.g. animals speak).

all ready/already Already means 'before a stated, implied, or expected time'; **all ready** means 'all prepared'. Correct usage is illustrated by the sentence *'Are we all ready?'* she asked, already beginning to get flustered.

all together / altogether All together means 'all at once' or 'all in one place or in one group', e.g. *They came all together; We managed to get three bedrooms all together* (i.e. near each other). **Altogether** means 'in total', e.g. *The hotel has twenty rooms altogether.*

allusion/illusion An allusion is an indirect reference to something or someone, e.g. *a veiled allusion to his illegitimacy*; an **illusion** is a deception or misapprehension about the true state of affairs, e.g. *The idea of total freedom is always an illusion.* See also DELUSION/ILLUSION in SECTION 6: USAGE.

alternate/alternative In British English alternate means 'every other', e.g. *There will be a dance on alternate Saturdays*, or 'following in turn', e.g. *alternate joy and misery*: **alternative**, however, means 'available as another choice or possibility', e.g. *They chose an alternative route.* In North American usage, **alternate** can also be used to mean 'available as another choice'.

ambivalent / ambiguous Ambivalent means 'inconsistent, contradictory' and applies to feelings and attitudes or those who have them, e.g. *Many women today feel* *ambivalent about marriage.* **Ambiguous**, means 'having more than one possible meaning' and refers to things subject to interpretation, such as statements and events, e.g. *She gave a cleverly ambiguous reply.*

amend / emend To **amend** something is to change it for the better; the word is applied mainly to personal behaviour, e.g. *He resolved to amend his life,* and to the process of revising an act of parliament or other formal document, e.g. *an opposition amendment.* **Emend** is a more technical word meaning 'to remove errors or faults from (something written)'; it is applied mainly to the activity of textual scholars, e.g. *The poems have been collected, arranged, and emended.*

amoral/immoral While **immoral** means 'not conforming to accepted standards of morality', **amoral** implies 'not concerned with or ignorant of morality'. The difference is illustrated in the following examples: *The prosecution denounced his conduct as callous and immoral; The client pays for the amoral expertise of the lawyer.*

amyl nitrate/amyl nitrite Amyl nitrite, a street drug that is inhaled and used as a stimulant, is often referred to mistakenly as **amyl nitrate**, which is a distinct substance used in medicine (as a vasodilator) and in perfumes.

ante-/anti- These two prefixes need to be distinguished, if only to ensure correct spelling. The first means 'before, preceding' and forms words such as *antenatal* and *antechamber.* The second, which is much more common, means 'opposite, opposed to, against', and forms words such as *anti-aircraft, anti-American,* and *anti-hero.*

antisocial / unsociable / unsocial Although there can be some overlap in meaning, these words are used differently. In general, **antisocial** is used to describe behaviour which is offensive to other people or harmful to society, while **unsociable** refers to a person who dislikes being in the company of others; **unsocial** is used almost exclusively in the phrase *unsocial hours* meaning 'hours outside normal working hours'.

apiary / aviary Both are structures in which tame or captive creatures are kept: an **apiary** for bees, and an **aviary** for birds.

appraise / apprise Appraise means 'assess (someone or something)', e.g. *a need to appraise existing techniques,* while **apprise** means 'inform (someone)', e.g. *Psychiatrists were apprised of his condition.* **Appraise** is frequently used incorrectly for **apprise**, in such constructions as *Once appraised of the real facts, there was only one person who showed any opposition.*

apprehend / comprehend The two words denote different aspects of understanding. **Apprehend** means 'to grasp or perceive' and is applied to general ideas, concepts, or situations, whereas **comprehend** means 'to understand' and is applied to arguments or statements. Correct use is illustrated by these examples: *She was slow to apprehend the strength of his feelings; Owing to the language barrier I failed to comprehend the point he was making.*

arbiter / arbitrator These related forms are now used in different contexts. **Arbiter** is now restricted to the meaning 'a judge or authority', e.g. *an arbiter of taste and fashion.* For the meaning 'a person appointed to settle a dispute', the slightly older form **arbitrator** is now the correct word to use.

around / round See ROUND / AROUND in SECTION 6: USAGE.

artiste / artist Artiste means 'a professional performer, especially a singer or dancer'; it is not a feminine form of **artist**, which has the distinct meaning 'someone who works in one of the fine arts'.

ascent/assent The meaning 'climb, rise' is spelt **ascent**, the meaning 'agreement, compliance' is spelt **assent**: *After John's ascent of the Matterhorn, Mary gave her assent to his proposal.*

aside/a side Written as one word, **aside** is an adverb meaning 'to or on one side' (e.g. *She took him aside; He put it aside,* etc.) or a noun meaning 'words in a play spoken to the audience out of hearing of the other characters'. In the meaning 'on each side' it must be written as two words, e.g. *They are playing five-a-side.*

assay / essay As verbs, **assay** means 'to put to the proof' or 'to test metals chemically to determine their purity', whereas **essay** means 'to attempt'. As a noun, **assay** means 'the process of assaying', whereas **essay** is most commonly used to mean 'an extended piece of formal writing'.

assignment / assignation In law, an **assignment** is a legal transfer of a right or property, or the document that effects this. More generally, it is a task or piece of work allotted to a person. The dominant meaning of **assignation** is now 'an appointment to meet, especially between lovers'. Its original meaning of 'apportionment' is not often used now.

assurance / insurance In the context of life insurance, a technical distinction is made between **assurance** and **insurance**. **Assurance** is used of policies under whose terms a payment is guaranteed, either after a fixed term or on the death of the insured person; **insurance** is the general term, and is used in particular of policies under whose terms a payment would be made only in certain circumstances (e.g. accident or death within a limited period).

auger / augur An **auger** is a tool like a large corkscrew used for boring holes: an **augur** is a prophet or soothsayer (especially in ancient Rome). There is also a verb to **augur**, meaning either 'to predict' or 'to portend a good or bad outcome', as in *Their first date augured badly for the relationship.*

aural / oral **Aural** means 'to do with the ear' and **oral** means 'to do with the mouth'. An *oral examination* is therefore one done by speaking rather than by writing, while an *aural examination* is a medical examination of the ear. Both words are pronounced the same way, which adds to the confusion.

autarchy / autarky **Autarchy** is a rare word for autocracy or despotism; **autarky** is a policy of economic self-sufficiency.

avoid / avert / evade **Avoid** means 'to keep away or refrain from; to prevent'; **evade** can overlap with these meanings, but has a strong sense of guile or trickery in escaping from an obligation or from scrutiny, e.g. *He evaded the draft; She cleverly evaded my question.* Note also that **evasion**

has a special meaning in relation to legal obligations, where it differs from **avoidance** in denoting illegality, e.g. *Tax avoidance is canny, but tax evasion is criminal.* **Avert** means 'to turn aside' (which is its literal meaning in *averting one's gaze* etc.), and so 'to ward off (something unwelcome, such as danger)', e.g. *He kept himself busy to avert depression.*

awhile / a while **Awhile** is an adverb, whereas **a while** is a noun phrase. The distinction is illustrated by the sentence: *'Let's rest awhile', she said after a while.*

B

bail / bale One **bails out** a prisoner on remand (or, figuratively, anyone else in difficulty) but **bales out** of an aircraft. One may **bale** or **bail** the water out of a boat. Hay is bundled into **bales** and the cricketing term is spelt **bail(s)**.

bait / bate **Bait** is used to catch fish or poison rats; but one **bates** one's breath in suspense or fear.

baleful / baneful **Baleful** (from 'bale', misery) means 'threatening harm' or 'menacing', and is used in particular of people's presence or appearance, whereas **baneful** (from 'bane', poison) means 'causing harm or ruin'. Examples of correct usage are: *She gave him a baleful look; The baneful influence of her upbringing lingered.*

balmy / barmy **Balmy**, meaning 'deliciously fragrant', comes from 'balm' (an aromatic oil), whereas **barmy**, meaning 'crazy' or 'stupid', comes from 'barm' (the yeasty froth on fermenting drinks).

baluster / banister A **baluster** is a pillar supporting an ornamental rail around a gallery or terrace; the entire structure is known as a **balustrade**. A **banister** is a single post supporting a handrail at the side of a staircase; the word is generally used in the plural (**banisters**) to mean the entire structure including the rail.

bass / base Both mean 'low', but **bass** is used only in musical contexts (e.g. *the bass clef; a bass guitar*), whereas **base** is used generally to mean 'inferior' or 'ignoble'.

benzene / benzine Benzene is a hydrocarbon (C_6H_6) found in coal tar; **benzine** is a mixture derived from petroleum.

berth / birth A **berth** is for sleeping in; **birth** is being born.

beside / besides See SECTION 6: USAGE.

biannual / biennial If you are lucky you get **biannual** holidays (twice a year); if you are unlucky they are **biennial** (every two years).

blanch / blench Blanch means 'to make (something) white' (especially vegetables by dipping them in boiling water) or 'to become pale' (from fear, shock, embarrassment, etc.); a less common variant **blench** is also used in this second sense. Confusingly, there is another word **blench**, which overlaps slightly with **blanch / blench** in its meaning 'to quail, flinch', e.g. *Strong men have been known to blench at the thought of singing in public.*

bloc / block A **bloc** is a combination of parties, governments, or groups, e.g. *the former Eastern bloc countries*; use **block** for all other meanings.

boar / bore A male pig is spelt **boar**; a dull person or thing, or a tidal wave, is spelt **bore**.

bogey / bogie / bogy The golfing term (one over par) is spelt **bogey**, and the wheeled undercarriage of a railway truck **bogie**. The mischievous spirit (or other thing that causes irrational alarm) can be spelt either **bogey** or **bogy** (as can the sense 'nose picking').

born / borne Both words are past participles of the verb 'to bear'. **Born** is used only in passive constructions relating to birth, e.g. *I was born on a Friday*, and in related figurative expressions such as *an indifference born of long familiarity*. In all other meanings, the past participle of 'bear' is **borne**, e.g. *I have borne with this too long*; *The boat was borne along by the wind*. This form is also used with reference to birth when the meaning is 'brought into being' rather than 'came into being'; such constructions are usually, but not always, active, e.g. *She has borne no children*; *Of all the children borne by her only one survived*.

borrow / lend See LEND (1) in SECTION 6: USAGE.

bravery / bravado / bravura Bravery is a general word for 'courageous action or character', whereas **bravado** means 'ostentatious courage or boldness', often concealing fear or reluctance, e.g. *His defiant words were mere bravado*. **Bravura** is a brilliant or showy style of playing in music or of performance in some other field, e.g. *The speech was a bravura display*.

breach / breech Breach is a noun and verb meaning 'a break' or 'to break', e.g. *a breach of contract*; *to breach the enemy's defences*. **Breech**, a noun meaning 'the back or lower part of something', is applied principally to part of a rifle, the buttocks (now only in *breech birth*, when a baby is born bottom first), and (in the plural **breeches**) to a type of trousers.

bridle / bridal A **bridle** is used to control a horse and to **bridle** (at something) is to show indignation; **bridal** means 'relating to brides and weddings'.

bur / burr A **bur** is a clinging seed-vessel or catkin; a **burr** is a rough edge or protruberance, or a way of pronouncing 'r' in certain dialects.

business / busyness For senses relating to commercial operations or dealings, or to a person's affairs or concerns, use **business**. For 'the state of being busy', use **busyness**.

by / bye By is a preposition with a wide range of meanings; **bye** is a noun with meanings in cricket and other games or short for 'goodbye'; either spelling can be used in the expressions *by the by(e)* or *by(e)-law*.

C

cacao / cocoa / coca / coco Cacao is the South American tree from which cocoa and chocolate are made; the word **cocoa** is used only of the powdered seed pods or the drink. **Coca** is the South American shrub from which cocaine is made or its dried leaves, which are chewed for their stimulating effect. **Coco** is the coconut palm tree, its leaves (used in matting etc.), or a coconut.

cachou/cashew A **cachou** is a lozenge for sweetening the breath; **cashew** is an edible nut (and its tree).

caddie / caddy A **caddie** is an attendant who carries clubs etc. during a game of golf; a **caddy** is a container for tea.

calendar/calender/colander A **calendar** is a list of days and months, a **calender** is a type of mangle for paper or cloth, and a **colander** is a kitchen strainer.

callus/callous Callus is a noun meaning 'a hard thick area of skin or tissue'; **callous** is an adjective meaning 'unfeeling, insensitive'.

cannon/canon A **cannon** is a large gun or a stroke in billiards; a **canon** is a member of a cathedral chapter, a law, or a term in music.

canvas/canvass Canvas means either 'coarse heavy cloth' or something made from it (e.g. the sails of a boat, an oil painting). The plural is **canvases** and as a verb ('to cover or line with canvas') it has inflected forms **canvasses, canvassed, canvassing** (all with double 's'). **Canvass** is a verb meaning 'to solicit votes' and a noun meaning 'the soliciting of votes'. Its inflections retain the double 's'.

capital/Capitol Capital, the most important town or city of a country or region, is to be distinguished from **Capitol**, which is either the US legislative building in Washington DC (and other similar buildings in the US) or the Capitoline hill in Rome.

carat / caret / carrot Carat (in North America **karat**) is a measure of the purity of gold; **caret** is a mark (⁁) for showing an insertion in printing or writing; **carrot** is the vegetable.

carousal / carousel A **carousal** is a good time with drinking. A **carousel** is either a merry-go-round, or a conveyor-belt system for delivering passengers' luggage at airports.

Carver/carver These are two different words meaning types of chair. In North American English a **Carver** (with capital 'C') is a chair with arms, a rush seat, and a back having horizontal and vertical spindles. It is named after J. Carver, the 17th century governor of Plymouth Colony. In British English a **carver** (small 'c') is the principal chair of a set of dining chairs, intended for the person who carves.

caster/castor Caster is the only spelling for 'a person or machine that casts something' (e.g. a vote, glass or metal, a shadow) and **castor** is the only spelling for the oil. Both are used for the sugar, for the type of pot it is usually put in, and for the small swivelling wheel on the feet of furniture.

censer/censor/censure As nouns, **censer** is a vessel for burning incense; a **censor** is an official who controls the content of books, newspapers, and other media; and **censure** is harsh criticism. As verbs, **censor** means 'to suppress the whole or parts of a book, etc.', whereas **censure** means 'to criticize or condemn'.

cereal/serial Cereal is grain or a breakfast food made from it; a **serial** is a story in instalments: *As he ate his breakfast cereal he read the comic-strip serial in the paper.*

ceremonial/ceremonious Ceremonial, meaning 'with or concerning ritual or ceremony', is a neutral descriptive adjective, whereas **ceremonious**, meaning 'displaying special or excessive ceremony', is a more judgemental word. The difference can be seen by contrasting *The bishop made a ceremonial entry* with *She made her usual ceremonious entry to the party*: the first is an entry marked by normal or due ceremony, whereas the second is an unnecessarily elaborate or grand entry.

chop/cutlet A **chop** is a slice of pork or lamb cut from the loin, usually including a rib. A **cutlet** is a neck-chop of mutton or lamb, or a small piece of boneless veal for frying. A *nut cutlet* is a portion of meat substitute, often made from nuts and shaped like a cutlet.

choral / chorale Choral is an adjective meaning 'relating to a choir or chorus', e.g. *choral singing.* **Chorale** is a noun meaning 'a stately hymn tune' (especially one in the Lutheran tradition); in North American English it also means 'a choir or choral society'.

chord/cord A **chord** is either (in music) a group of notes sounded together to form the basis of harmony or (in mathematics and engineering) a straight line joining the ends of an arc, the wings of an aeroplane, etc. (The idiom *to strike a chord* relates, somewhat surprisingly, to the second of these meanings.) A **cord** is any kind of string, including such anatomical 'strings' as the *spinal cord* and *vocal cords*.

classic / classical See SECTION 6: USAGE.

clench / clinch Both words mean 'to grasp or close together' but they are used differently. We **clench** our teeth, fingers, and fists; but we **clinch** an argument, bargain, or deal. Lovers **clinch** when they embrace closely, and so do boxers and wrestlers when they embrace too closely. To **clinch** (not **clench**) a nail one bends the protruding point over.

climactic / climatic / climacteric **Climactic** means 'forming a climax' (e.g. *the climactic battle sequence of the film*), whereas **climatic** means 'relating to climate' (e.g. *the prevailing climatic conditions*). **Climacteric** is a noun meaning 'the period of life when fertility and sexual activity are in decline'.

coherent / cohesive **Coherent** means 'logical and consistent' and is applied to speakers and their arguments. **Cohesive** means 'tending to stick together' and is generally used either physically (as with liquid mixtures, for example) or in relation to groups, e.g. *The monarchy is a cohesive force in society.*

collude / collaborate Both words involve the idea of cooperation but **collude** implies an additional sense of fraud or dishonesty. The difference is illustrated by these sentences: *Husband and wife have collaborated on several books; Insider dealers colluded to make a profit from the company's depreciating securities.*

complacent / complaisant **Complacent** means 'smugly self-satisfied', e.g. *The British are still largely complacent about their eating habits*, whereas **complaisant**, a much rarer word, means 'acquiescent, uncomplaining', e.g. *His indiscretions grew more open but his wife remained complaisant.*

complement / compliment As a verb **complement** means 'to add to (something) in a way that enhances or improves', e.g. *A classic blazer complements a look that's smart or casual*, while **compliment** means 'to admire

and praise (someone) for something', e.g. *He complimented her on her appearance.* Both words can also be used as nouns, with corresponding meanings. The adjectival forms are also frequently confused. **Complimentary** means 'expressing a compliment' and has the additional meaning 'given free of charge', e.g. *We receive complimentary tickets.* **Complementary** means 'completing' or 'forming a complement', e.g. *My role is complementary to that of my associates*; it also has a number of special uses, e.g. in the expression *complementary medicine*.

compose / comprise See SECTION 6: USAGE.

concave / convex **Concave** means 'having an outline or surface that curves inwards like the interior of a circle or sphere', whereas **convex** means 'having an outline or surface that curves outwards like the exterior of a circle or sphere'.

condole / console **Condole** is generally followed by 'with' and means 'to express sympathy with', e.g. *Her friends came to condole with her.* **Console**, a much more common word, means 'to comfort in grief or disappointment', e.g. *They consoled themselves with the thought that they wouldn't have enjoyed the concert anyway.*

confidant / confident A **confidant** (feminine **confidante**) is someone in whom you confide; **confident** means 'sure of oneself'.

connote / denote See SECTION 6: USAGE.

contagious / contiguous A **contagious** disease is one that can be passed on by physical contact. Two things that are **contiguous** are next to each other and may actually be touching. See also CONTAGIOUS/INFECTIOUS in SECTION 6: USAGE.

contemptible / contemptuous In current use, **contemptible** means 'deserving contempt', e.g. *His contemptible attempts to blame others*, whereas **contemptuous** means 'showing contempt', e.g. *I was contemptuous of his cowardly evasions.*

continuous / continual See SECTION 6: USAGE.

co-respondent / correspondent A **co-respondent** is a person named in a divorce case; a **correspondent** is a journalist or someone who writes letters.

corps / corpse A **corps** is a body of people, especially troops; a **corpse** is a dead body.

council / counsel A **council** is an administrative body or meeting, and its members are **councillors**. **Counsel** is advice given formally and often professionally; a **counsel** is a barrister or other legal adviser. A **counsellor** is someone who gives professional advice, especially on personal and social matters; in North American English a **counselor** can also mean a courtroom lawyer. Only **counsel** can be used as a verb.

crape / crêpe **Crape** is black silk or imitation silk worn as a sign of mourning; **crêpe** is a gauze-like fabric having a wrinkled surface, a type of rubber or paper with a similar appearance, or a thin pancake.

credible/credulous **Credible** means 'believable' or 'convincing' and can be applied to a situation, statement, policy, or threat, etc. **Credulous** means 'too ready to believe, gullible' and is generally used to describe a person. Correct usage of both words is illustrated by the sentence: *Although the story was hardly credible, my friend was so credulous he believed every word of it.*

creole / pidgin A **creole** is a language formed from the contact of a European language (especially English, French, or Portuguese) with another (especially African) language. Unlike a **pidgin**, which is a very simple improvised language used mainly by traders who do not have a language in common, a **creole** is more developed and can be the mother tongue of a speech community.

crevasse/crevice A **crevasse** is a deep open crack or fissure in a glacier; in North American English the word is also used to mean a breach in a river embankment. A **crevice** is a narrow cleft or opening, usually one in the surface of anything solid such as rock or a building.

crochet / crotchet **Crochet** is a handicraft rather like knitting; a **crotchet** is a musical note.

crumby / crummy When the reference is to actual crumbs, as in *a crumby tablecloth*,

use **crumby**. When the meaning is 'dirty, squalid; inferior, worthless', use **crummy**.

cubic / cubical **Cubical** means only 'shaped like a cube', whereas **cubic** can also mean 'raised to the third power' (e.g. *a cubic metre*) as well as having various technical senses in mathematics and crystallography.

curb / kerb In British English, **curb** is a noun meaning 'a check or restraint' and a verb meaning 'to restrain', whereas **kerb** is a noun only meaning 'a stone edging to a pavement'. In North American English this last sense is also spelt **curb**.

currant / current **Current** is a noun meaning 'a moving stream of water' or an adjective meaning 'happening now'. A **currant** is a piece of dried fruit.

cygnet / signet A **cygnet** is a young swan, whereas a **signet** is a seal, often set in a ring.

Cyprus / cypress The Mediterranean island is spelt **Cyprus**, the tree **cypress**.

D

debar / disbar **Debar** means 'to exclude from admission or a right', e.g. *They were debarred from entering*, whereas **disbar** has the more specific meaning 'to deprive (a barrister) from the right to practise'.

deca-/deci- In the metric system, **deca-** means 'multiplied by 10', so that a *decalitre* is 10 litres, and **deci-** means 'divided by 10', so that a *decilitre* is a tenth of a litre or 100 ml.

decided/decisive When used of people, **decided** means 'having clear opinions' and **decisive** means 'able to decide quickly'; when used of circumstances, **decided** means 'definite, unquestionable' and **decisive** means 'deciding an issue, conclusive'. There are contexts in which both words can be used, but the implications are different: for example, *a decided victory* is one that is overwhelming, whereas *a decisive victory* is one that (whether overwhelming or not) has a definite effect on the course of a war. Similarly, *The manager is decided* means that he or she has a definite opinion on a subject, whereas *The manager is decisive* means that he or she makes decisions promptly and effectively. The corresponding adverbs are

decidedly, meaning 'unquestionably, undeniably', and **decisively**, meaning 'with conclusive effect'.

decry / descry Decry means 'to belittle or disparage', e.g. *He takes every opportunity to decry contemporary morality*; **descry** is a somewhat literary word meaning 'to catch sight of', e.g. *She descried two figures on the horizon.*

deducible / deductible Deducible means 'able to be deduced or inferred', e.g. *Her feelings were deducible from the shocked expression on her face*; **deductible** means 'that may be deducted from or taken off a total', e.g. *Such donations may be deductible for tax purposes.*

deduction / induction Among their other meanings, **deduction** is the inferring of particular instances from known or observed evidence, while **induction** is the inferring of a general rule from particular instances.

defective / deficient Defective means 'having a defect or fault', whereas **deficient** means 'having a deficiency or lack'. So *defective eyesight* or *defective goods*, etc., are not working properly; and *deficient funds* or *deficient diet*, etc., are either inadequate in quantity or lacking something essential.

definite / definitive Definite means 'clear and distinct', whereas **definitive** means 'decisive, unconditional, final' and normally refers to an answer, verdict, treaty, etc. A *definitive text* or *book*, etc., is one that is regarded as the best authority on its subject and likely to remain so. Only **definitive** has connotations of authority and conclusiveness: *a definite no* is a firm refusal, whereas *a definitive no* is an authoritative judgement that something is not the case.

defuse / diffuse Defuse means literally 'to remove the triggering device from (a bomb)' and figuratively 'to remove tension or potential danger from (a crisis, etc.)'. **Diffuse**, which correctly means 'to disperse or spread around', is often used incorrectly for **defuse** in this figurative sense, e.g. *A cut in base rates would diffuse the dispute between the Chancellor and the Prime Minister.*

dependence / dependency Dependence means 'a state of depending'; **dependency** can also mean this but is more usually 'a country or province that is dependent on another', e.g. *Gibraltar is a British dependency*. The use of **dependency** to mean **dependence** has been popularized by the recent term *dependency culture*, meaning 'a way of life determined by being dependent on state benefits'.

depositary / depository A depositary is a person or authority to whom something is entrusted, a trustee. A **depository** is either a storage place for furniture, books, etc., or a source (normally a book but occasionally a person) of wisdom or knowledge.

deprecate/depreciate See Section 6: Usage.

derisory/derisive Although the words share similar roots they have different core meanings. **Derisory** usually means 'ridiculously small or inadequate', e.g. *a derisory pay offer* or *The security arrangements were derisory*. **Derisive**, on the other hand, is used to mean 'scoffing, showing contempt', e.g. *He gave a derisive laugh.*

desert/dessert There are two unrelated words spelt **desert**: one, with stress on the first syllable, is the barren area of land, and the other, with stress on the second syllable, is what one deserves, e.g. *They got their just deserts*. The verb **desert**, meaning 'to abandon' and stressed on the second syllable, is related to the first of these words. Finally **dessert**, stressed on the second syllable, is a word for 'the sweet course of a meal'.

detract/distract To detract from something is to diminish its value or merit, e.g. *These quibbles scarcely detract from the greatness of her achievement*. To **distract** someone is to divide or draw away their attention. Although **detract** is often used in the sense of **distract**, this is still regarded as incorrect by many people.

device / devise Device is a noun meaning 'tool or contrivance', **devise** a verb meaning 'contrive or invent'.

dialectal / dialectic / dialectical Formerly all three words were used to mean 'belonging to a dialect', but only **dialectal** now serves this purpose. **Dialectic** is a form of philosophical argument by question and answer, and **dialectical** is the adjective derived from it.

dinghy / dingy A **dinghy** is a small sailing boat; **dingy** means 'drab, grimy'.

diphthong / digraph / ligature A **diphthong** is a union of two vowels pronounced in one syllable, e.g. 'i' in *find*, 'ei' in *rein*, and 'eau' in *bureau*. Two letters standing for a single sound, e.g. 'ea' in *head*, 'gh' in *cough*, are correctly referred to as a **digraph**. The typographical symbol consisting of two letters joined together, e.g. fi, fl, æ, œ, is a **ligature**.

discomfit / discomfort Discomfit means 'to thwart the plans of' or 'to embarrass or disconcert'. In this second meaning it overlaps with the unrelated verb **discomfort**, which means 'to make uneasy', and in the normal flow of speech it is not always possible to distinguish them.

discover / invent To **discover** something is to find something that was hidden or not known; to **invent** something is to devise it by human effort. The distinction can be illustrated by this sentence: *Galileo discovered the satellites of Jupiter using the telescope that he had invented.*

discreet / discrete Discreet means 'circumspect in speech or action', can be used of people or things, and is common as an adverb **discreetly**, e.g. *You can rely on me to be discreet; a discreetly lit restaurant.* **Discrete** means 'distinct, separate', e.g. *These findings must be broken down into discrete categories.*

disinterested / uninterested See SECTION 6: USAGE.

disposal / disposition In general, **disposal** is the noun corresponding to **dispose of**, meaning 'to get rid of', and **disposition** corresponds to **dispose**, meaning 'arrange'. So *the disposition of the furniture* refers to the way the furniture is laid out, whereas *the disposal of the furniture* refers to its removal. **Disposition** also has the special meaning 'temperament, natural tendency'.

dissemble/disassemble Dissemble has the meaning 'to pretend, to disguise or conceal'; it should not be used to mean 'to take apart' as if it were a shorter form of **disassemble**.

distinct / distinctive Although both words are related to the verb 'distinguish', they are used differently. **Distinct** means essentially 'separate, different', e.g. *The word has several distinct meanings,* or 'clear, unmistakable, decided', e.g. *She had a distinct impression of being watched.* **Distinctive** means 'characteristic, identifying', e.g. *The bird has distinctive black and white wing markings.* Someone with *a distinct manner of speaking* enunciates clearly; someone with *a distinctive manner of speaking* may well do the opposite.

diverse / divers Both words once shared the meaning now confined to **diverse**, i.e. 'varied, unalike', but **divers** now means 'several, sundry' without the notion of variety. The difference is illustrated by these sentences: *A polymath, she has written books on the most diverse subjects; She has written divers books on 18th-century dolls.*

dominate/domineer Dominate means primarily 'to exercise control or influence over' and is used transitively (with an object). **Domineer** is a more judgemental word meaning 'to behave in an arrogant and overbearing way' and is often used with 'over' or in the adjectival form **domineering**.

doubtful / dubious Although both words relate to doubt, **doubtful** implies uncertainty about facts, whereas **dubious** implies suspicion about value or genuineness. The following examples will clarify the differences: *He seemed doubtful of his whereabouts; The cause of the accident remains doubtful; He seemed dubious of her motives; A dubious establishment in Soho.* In many other cases the meanings overlap and either word would be appropriate.

douse / dowse To **douse** is to drench with or plunge into water, or to quench a light or flame; to **dowse** is to use a divining rod.

dowry / dower A **dowry** (the more common word) is the property or money brought by a bride to her husband, whereas a **dower** is a widow's share of her husband's estate.

draft/draught A **draft** is a preliminary sketch or version, a written order for payment by a bank, or a military detachment. A **draftsman** is someone who drafts documents. A **draught** is a current of air, a ship's displacement, a drink, or one of the pieces in the game of **draughts**. A **draughtsman** is someone who draws plans. In North American English, **draft** is sensibly used for all these meanings (except the game of **draughts**, which is called 'checkers').

E

educable / educible Educable means 'capable of being educated'; **educible** means 'capable of being educed (i.e. developed or elicited)'.

effective / efficient See EFFECTIVE/EFFECTUAL / EFFICACIOUS / EFFICIENT in SECTION 6: USAGE.

e.g / i.e. E.g. (short for Latin *exempli gratia*) means 'for example': *Many countries of Asia, e.g. India, Indonesia, and Malaysia.* I.e. (short for Latin *id est*) means 'that is': *It was natural that the largest nation (i.e. India) should take the lead.*

elegy/eulogy An **elegy** was originally a poem lamenting the dead, famous examples in English being Milton's *Lycidas* (1637) and Shelley's *Adonais* (1821). In the course of time, it came to mean any sorrowful or meditative poem or one written in the metre associated with elegies, e.g. Gray's *Elegy Written in a Country Churchyard* (1751). A **eulogy** was originally a speech honouring a dead person, but has come to mean anything formally written or spoken as a personal tribute.

elemental / elementary Elemental refers to the forces of nature and to the ancient belief in the 'four elements' of earth, water, air, and fire: it is often used in the sense 'fundamental, primal', e.g. *Heathcliff's elemental passion for Cathy.* **Elementary**, on the other hand, means 'rudimentary, introductory', e.g. *an elementary school*; *elementary mathematics.* In modern physics, **elementary** means 'not able to be decomposed', as in *elementary particle*.

elicit / illicit Confusion arises occasionally because both words are pronounced the same way. **Elicit** is a verb meaning 'to draw out or evoke (an answer, admission, etc.)', whereas **illicit** is an adjective meaning 'unlawful, forbidden'.

eligible / illegible These are more likely to be confused in casual speech than in considered writing. **Eligible** means 'fit or entitled to be chosen' (e.g. *eligible for a pension*) or 'desirable, suitable' (e.g. *an eligible bachelor*). **Illegible** means '(of writing) not clear enough to read'.

emigrant / immigrant / émigré / migrant An **emigrant** is someone who leaves his or her home country to live in another country: an **immigrant** is one who comes to live in a country from abroad. The same person is therefore an **emigrant** on going through the exit gate at a port or airport and an **immigrant** on taking up residence in the country of arrival. An **émigré** is a political emigrant (originally one from France during the French Revolution). In British English a **migrant** is either a migrating bird or animal or an itinerant worker; in Australia and New Zealand, however, the word is a synonym for **immigrant**.

eminent / immanent / imminent Things or people that are **eminent** stand out in some way, whereas something **imminent** is just about to happen (usually with connotations of threat or danger). Pantheist philosophers have argued that God is **immanent**, i.e. that He is all-pervading within the created universe.

endemic / epidemic An **endemic** disease is one that is regularly or only found among a particular people or in a particular region, whereas an **epidemic** disease is a temporary but widespread outbreak of a disease. Both words have extended meanings in relation to things other than diseases, e.g. *Skiving and malingering have reached epidemic proportions*; *Corruption is endemic in many African countries.*

enquire / inquire See SECTION 6: USAGE.

epigram / epigraph / epitaph An **epigram** is a short poem with a witty or ingenious ending, or a terse or pungent saying. An **epigraph** is a short quotation or pithy sentence put at the beginning of a book, chapter, etc., or an inscription on a tomb, building, or coin. An **epitaph** is a phrase commemorating someone who has died, especially one inscribed on a tomb or monument.

equable / equitable Equable means 'even and moderate, regular' and is typically used in such combinations as *an equable climate*, *an equable temperament*, etc. It denotes avoidance of extremes as well as avoidance of change. **Equitable** means 'just, fair' (usually with reference to several parties involved), and is typically used in such combinations as *an equitable settlement*, *an equitable solution*, etc.

erupt / irrupt Erupt has the general sense 'break out (or eject) forcibly or suddenly' and **irrupt** 'break into forcibly or suddenly'. Erupt is therefore the correct word to use of volcanoes, spots etc. on the skin, and (usually) emotions such as anger or amusement.

esoteric/exoteric/exotic Esoteric has the meaning 'intended for the initiated few, obscure', e.g. *His poetry is wilfully esoteric*; **exoteric** means the opposite, i.e. 'intended for people generally'. However, **exoteric** is sometimes confused with **exotic**, meaning 'coming from or associated with a foreign country' (often with connotations of the remarkable or bizarre, e.g. *exotic dances*).

estimable / estimatable Estimable means 'worthy of esteem, admirable'; **estimatable** means 'capable of being estimated'.

etymology / entomology Etymology is the study of the sources and development of words; **entomology** is the study of insects.

euphuism / euphemism Euphuism is an affected or high-flown style of writing or speaking, originally applied to work of the late 16th and early 17th centuries written in imitation of John Lyly's *Euphues* (1578–80). **Euphemism** is the use of an inoffensive or evasive word instead of one considered offensively direct.

evidence/evince As a verb, **evidence** means 'to attest to', e.g. *Her nervous state was evidenced by the shaking of her hands*. **Evince** means 'to show that one has (a quality)', e.g. *He evinced a sensitivity that few would have guessed*.

evoke / invoke Evoke means 'to call up (a response, a feeling, etc.)', e.g. *The scene evoked happy childhood memories*; *A generous gesture that evoked a round of applause*. **Invoke** means

'to appeal to (an agent or authority) for help, guidance, confirmation, etc.', e.g. *The congregation invoked God's mercy*; *He invoked the example of Descartes*; *The management invoked the dismissal procedure*.

exalt / exult Exalt means 'to raise, elevate' or 'to praise highly', and is often used in the participial form **exalted**, meaning 'grand, noble', e.g. *A man in his exalted position*; *The exalted style of Milton's poetry*. **Exult** means 'to feel great joy or triumph', and is common in its adjectival form **exultant**, e.g. *As the election results came in, her mood became openly exultant*.

exceedingly / excessively Exceedingly means 'very, extremely' and is used only with adjectives and adverbs, whereas **excessively**, means 'too' (with adjectives and adverbs) or 'too much' (with verbs). *An exceedingly sweet cake* may well be delicious, but *an excessively sweet cake* would be unpleasant.

exceptional / exceptionable Exceptional means 'unusual, outstanding', e.g. *A woman of exceptional charm*. **Exceptionable** means 'open to objection', e.g. *There was nothing exceptionable in her behaviour*. See also UNEXCEPTIONABLE / UNEXCEPTIONAL.

executor / executioner An executor (pronounced with the stress on the second syllable) is an official appointed to carry out the terms of a will; an **executioner** is an official who carries out a sentence of death.

exhaustive / exhausting Both words are derived from the verb 'exhaust', but relate to different meanings. **Exhaustive** relates to the meaning 'to use up the whole of' and means 'thorough or comprehensive', e.g. *an exhaustive report*. **Exhausting** relates to the meaning 'to tire out' and means 'extremely tiring' or 'draining of strength', e.g. *He leads an exhausting social life*.

exigent / exiguous Exigent means 'exacting' or 'urgent', e.g. *His need for funds was becoming exigent*; *She was an exigent critic of male vanity*. **Exiguous** means 'very small, scanty', e.g. *with exiguous regard for the truth*.

expiry / expiration The primary meaning of **expiry** is 'the end of the validity or duration of something', as in *On expiry of the lease at the end of the month*. It is also a rather formal or euphemistic word for 'death'. **Expiration** can have these meanings but much more often denotes 'the act of breathing out', which **expiry** cannot be used to mean.

explicit / express See SECTION 6: USAGE.

exposition / exposé The main meanings of **exposition** are 'an explanation or interpretation of something' and 'a public exhibition'. An **exposé** is the bringing of a hidden crime or scandal to public attention.

extant / existent Extant has a more specific sense than **existent** ('currently existing'), as it carries a strong connotation of (unexpected) survival from the past, e.g. *Belief in miracles is clearly still extant.*

F

fable / parable See ALLEGORY / FABLE / PARABLE / SYMBOLISM.

facility/faculty Facility means 'ease or ready ability to do something', e.g. *Firstborn children have greater verbal facility.* In modern usage it also has the concrete meaning 'something that provides an amenity or service', e.g. *Recreational facilities include two lighted tennis courts.* **Faculty** means 'an aptitude or ability to do something' in the sense of an inborn or inherent power rather than a proficiency developed (for example) by practice. The *faculty of language* is the natural ability of humans to speak, whereas a *facility for language* is an individual's particular skill in speaking.

factious / factitious / fractious Factious means 'characterized by faction or dissension', as in *factious quarrelling*, whereas **factitious** means 'contrived, artificial', as in *factitious reasoning.* **Fractious** is sometimes confused with **factious**; it means 'irritable, peevish', e.g. *a fractious child.* See also FICTIONAL / FICTITIOUS.

faint / feint Faint is used as an adjective meaning 'indistinct, pale' or 'feeling dizzy', as a noun meaning 'a loss of consciousness', and as a verb meaning 'to lose consciousness'. **Feint** is used as a noun meaning 'a sham attack or blow as a diversion', as a verb meaning 'to make a feint', and as an adjective denoting faint lines on ruled paper.

fatal / fateful Both words have to do with the workings of fate. In essence **fateful** means 'having far-reaching consequences', which may be good or neutral as well as bad, e.g. *The fateful day on which I first met my wife-to-be; a fateful sequence of events.* Fatal means 'causing death' (as in *fatal accident*) and by extension 'bringing ruin', e.g. *His fatal tendency to procrastination; The fatal mistake of invading Russia.* The closest synonyms to **fatal** in this meaning are 'catastrophic', 'disastrous', or 'ruinous'.

faun / fawn In Roman mythology, a **faun** was a rural deity represented as part man, part goat. A **fawn** is a young deer; to **fawn** is to flatter.

fay / fey Fay is a literary word for 'fairy'. As an adjective it has the meaning 'fairylike, elfin' and, in informal modern usage, 'precious, effeminate'. **Fey** is an unrelated word of great antiquity originally meaning 'fated to die soon' (a meaning it still has in Scottish English). In extended use it means 'strange, other-worldly, clairvoyant, whimsical'. In this last meaning it makes close contact with **fay**, but properly used **fey** still has implications of imminent death and the supernatural.

faze / phase To faze means 'to disconcert or perturb', e.g. *I was completely fazed by her behaviour*; to **phase** (something) is to arrange or execute it by stages, e.g. *A phased military withdrawal.*

fearful / fearsome Fearful means 'full of fear, frightened' and is normally followed by 'of' or by a 'that' clause specifying the cause of fear, e.g. *She remained fearful of emotional commitment.* It is also used (often in much weakened form) with reference to things and situations that may inspire fear, dread, or perplexity, e.g. *a fearful loss of life; a fearful predicament.* **Fearsome** means 'appalling or frightening, especially in appearance', e.g. *A huge Scotsman with a fearsome beard; A terrorist group with a fearsome reputation.*

ferment / foment The two verbs overlap in their figurative meanings. To **ferment** means literally 'to effervesce or cause to effervesce' and figuratively 'to excite or become excited'; and so it can be transitive (with an object) or intransitive: you can **ferment** trouble or trouble can **ferment**. **Foment** means literally 'to bathe with warm or medicated liquid' and figuratively 'to instigate or stir up'. **Foment** is only transitive: you can **foment** trouble but trouble cannot **foment**.

ferule / ferrule A **ferule** is the metal cap or ring on the end of a wooden stick etc.; a **ferrule** was a wooden implement formerly used for corporal punishment in schools.

fervent / fervid Although both words mean 'ardent, intense', **fervent** has positive connotations, whereas **fervid** can sound depreciatory; the difference is rather like that between 'warm' and 'feverish' as applied to feelings, e.g. *A fervent devotion to liberty; fervent prayers* but *A fervid interest in sex; fervid imagination*. Note also that **fervent** but not **fervid** can be applied to people as well as speech, feelings, etc., e.g. *A fervent defender of free speech*.

fictional / fictitious Fictional means 'occurring in fiction', e.g. in a novel or film, whereas **fictitious** means 'invented, unreal; not genuine'. So 'Oliver Twist' is a **fictional** name when it refers to Dickens's character, and a **fictitious** name when someone uses it as a false or assumed name instead of their own.

flaunt / flout Flaunt means 'display ostentatiously', e.g. *Tourists are advised not to flaunt their wealth*, while **flout** means 'openly disregard (a rule or convention)', e.g. *New Age Travellers flouting convention and hygiene*. The words are often confused because both suggest an element of arrogance or showing off.

flounder / founder The two words are easily confused because their form and meanings are both close. The physical meaning of **flounder** is 'to struggle in mud or while wading' and from this developed the abstract sense 'to perform a task badly; to be out of one's depth'. The corresponding meanings of **founder** are (physical, with reference to a ship), 'to fill with water and sink' and (abstract, with reference to a plan, scheme, etc.), 'to come to nothing, to fail'. In the abstract senses (where the confusion

mostly lies) it is normally people who **flounder** and plans and relationships (and suchlike) that **founder**.

forbear / forebear Forbear is a verb (pronounced with the stress on the second syllable) meaning 'to abstain from, go without', e.g. *I forebore to mention it*. **Forebear** is a noun (pronounced with the stress on the first syllable) meaning 'an ancestor or predecessor', e.g. *Her forebears were mainly Anglo-Irish; Many of Mr Blair's forebears at No. 10*.

forceful / forcible The principal use of **forceful** is in the meaning 'vigorous, powerful', e.g. *forceful personality*, whereas **forcible** means primarily 'done by or using force' (rather than by choice or persuasion), e.g. *a forcible eviction; forcible sterilization of criminals and the insane*. **Forceful** can be used of people as well as actions, whereas **forcible** is used only of actions.

foreword/forward The noun **foreword** means 'an introductory statement in a book'; **forward** is the adverb or adjective relating to frontward movement or position.

forgo / forego Forgo means 'to go without, abstain from'; **forego** means 'to go before, precede' and occurs principally in the forms **foregoing** and **foregone**.

fortuitous / fortunate See FORTUITOUS in SECTION 6: USAGE.

funerary / funereal Funerary is the standard adjective in the neutral meaning 'of or used at funerals', e.g. *funerary ashes; funerary urn*, etc. **Funereal** has the special judgemental meaning 'appropriate to a funeral', either 'deadly slow' (like a funeral procession) or 'gloomy, dreary, dismal', e.g. *moving at a funereal pace; a funereal silence*.

further / farther See SECTION 6: USAGE.

#

Gallic / Gaelic Gallic means French; Gaelic means the Celtic languages or peoples.

geezer/geyser A geezer (informal) is a man; a **geyser** is a hot spring or a bathroom water heater.

gibe / jibe / gybe To **gibe** or **jibe** is to jeer; to **gybe** (of sails) is to shift suddenly in the wind.

gild / guild To **gild** means 'to cover with gold or make golden in colour'; a **guild** is an organization or club.

glance / glimpse A **glance** is a brief look, e.g. *Catherine and Lucy exchanged glances*, whereas a **glimpse** is what is seen by taking a glance, e.g. *Catherine caught a quick glimpse of Lucy's expression*. There is a corresponding difference in the use of the verbs: *He glanced at his watch*; *The wavering moonlight allowed him to glimpse the clock*.

gourmet / gourmand A **gourmet** means 'a connoisseur of good food', but a **gourmand** means 'a person who enjoys eating and often eats too much'. **Gourmet**, unlike **gourmand**, is also used attributively, as in *gourmet food* and *a gourmet meal*.

graceful / gracious **Graceful** means 'having or showing grace or elegance' and is generally used of physical appearance and movement, e.g. *a graceful bow*. **Gracious** means 'showing grace, kindly, courteous' and refers to things that people say and do rather than their physical attributes, e.g. *a gracious apology*. It also has the meaning 'characterized by elegance and wealth', e.g. *gracious living*.

griddle / gridiron A **griddle** is a circular iron plate used for baking, toasting, etc., and a **gridiron** is a grill (i.e. a cooking utensil of metal bars for broiling or grilling).

griffin/griffon/gryphon A **griffin** (also spelt **griffon** or **gryphon**) is a fabulous creature with an eagle's head and wings and a lion's body. A **griffon** is either a small dog like a terrier or a type of large vulture.

grill / grille A **grill** is a barred utensil for cooking food or the food itself. A **grille** is a metal grid protecting the radiator of a motor vehicle or a barred opening in a wall.

grisly/grizzly **Grisly** means 'gruesome or horrible'; **grizzly** means 'streaked with grey', 'whiney', or a type of bear.

groin / groyne **Groin** is the part of the body between the belly and thigh or (in architecture) the curved edge formed by intersecting vaults; a **groyne** is a low wall or timber framework built out from a seashore to prevent beach erosion.

guarantee / guaranty Both nouns denote a formal assurance that one will fulfil an obligation. A **guarantee** usually relates to the quality of a product or service, while **guaranty** is usually an undertaking to pay a debt if the person or party primarily responsible defaults.

H

hail / hale To **hail** is to greet or summon someone; to **hale** is to drag him or her along.

hangar / hanger A **hangar** is a large shed for housing aircraft; a **hanger** is a light frame with a hook for hanging clothes.

heroin / heroine **Heroin** is the drug; the **heroine** is the principal woman in a novel, play, etc.

historic / historical **Historical** is the more usual and objective word meaning 'of or concerning history' or 'belonging to the past', whereas **historic** means 'famous or important with regard to history'. *A historical treaty* is one that took place (as opposed to one that is fictitious); *a historic treaty* is one that is of great importance in history (as opposed to one that is insignificant). **Historic** is often used with reference to famous buildings and monuments, e.g. *a historic country house*.

hoard/horde A **hoard** is a large stock or store of money or accumulated objects, especially one hidden away; a **horde** is a large collection of people or animals, especially when referred to disparagingly, e.g. *A horde of football fans*.

holey/holy The adjective meaning 'full of holes', is spelt **holey** to distinguish it in writing and print from **holy** meaning 'sacred'.

human / humane As an adjective, **human** is used predominantly in non-judgemental contexts, e.g. *the human race*; *human rights*, etc. It is also used to denote a generalized quality that distinguishes (actual or ideal) human behaviour from that of animals, gods, or machines, e.g. *His failings were all too human*. By contrast, **humane** denotes the specific quality of being civilized or compassionate in one's treatment of other people or animals, e.g. *a humane penal system; humane killing.*

hummus / hoummos / humus Hummus (or **hoummos**) is a dish made from ground chickpeas; **humus** is the organic component of soil.

hung / hanged See SECTION 6: USAGE.

hyper- / hypo- These prefixes are derived from Greek prepositions meaning 'over, above' and 'under, below' respectively. Therefore, **hyperthermia** means 'abnormally high body temperature' and **hypothermia** means 'abnormally low body temperature'; **hypertension** means 'abnormally high blood pressure' and **hypotension** means 'abnormally low blood pressure'. Both prefixes are usually pronounced in the same way, and the meaning may have to be clarified by the context in which they are used.

hyperbole / hyperbola Hyperbole is a figure of speech involving an exaggerated statement that is not meant to be taken literally, e.g. *a thousand apologies.* It should not be confused with **hyperbola**, which is a term in geometry.

hypocritical / hypercritical Hypercritical means 'excessively critical', but **hypocritical** means 'acting a pretence or according to double standards'.

hyponym / hypernym In linguistics, a **hyponym** of a given term is a more specific term in the same domain, e.g. *Spaniel is a hyponym of dog.* A **hypernym** is a more general term, e.g. *Container is the hypernym of bag, box, and cup.* Because the two words can sound the same in speech, the alternative term 'superordinate' is often used instead of **hypernym**.

hypothecate / hypothesize The correct word for 'to form or assume as a hypothesis' is **hypothesize**, e.g. *Although the evidence suggested something was going on, she was reluctant to hypothesize.* **Hypothecate**, which is sometimes wrongly used in this meaning, correctly means 'to give (money or property) as a pledge or security'. It is also used of taxation in which the money raised is used for a special purpose, e.g. *An alternative scheme*

for financing the NHS involves the introduction of a hypothecated tax.

I

illegal / illegitimate See ILLEGAL/ILLEGITIMATE/ILLICIT/UNLAWFUL in SECTION 6: USAGE.

illegible / unreadable An **illegible** text is indecipherable owing to poor handwriting or printing; an **unreadable** text can be physically deciphered but is too dull to be worth reading or too difficult to be understood.

imaginary / imaginative Imaginary means 'existing only in the imagination, not real', whereas **imaginative** means 'having or showing a high degree of imagination'. Both words can be applied to people as well as things; *an imaginary person* is one who does not really exist (e.g. is fictitious), whereas *an imaginative person* is one who is creative or inventive.

immanent / imminent See EMINENT/IMMINENT/IMMANENT.

immunity / impunity In non-medical contexts **immunity** means 'freedom or exemption from an obligation, penalty, or unfavourable circumstance', e.g. *He was offered immunity from prosecution; Suffering had given him an immunity to life's minor irritations.* **Impunity** has the more limited meaning 'exemption from punishment or from the injurious consequences of an action', e.g. *In our dreams we can do with impunity things that we cannot do in real life.*

impassable/impassible Impassable means 'incapable of being traversed' and refers to roads, stretches of countryside, etc. **Impassible** means 'incapable of feeling emotion' or 'incapable of suffering injury'.

impedance / impediment Impedance is a specialized electrical term, meaning 'the resistance of a circuit to alternating current'; **impediment** is an everyday term meaning 'a hindrance or obstruction', e.g. *He would have to write by hand but that was no impediment.*

imperial / imperious Imperial means 'relating to an empire or emperor' and hence 'characteristic of an emperor, supreme in authority'. **Imperious** is a more judgemental word and means 'overbearing, domineering'.

imply/infer Imply means 'to express indirectly, insinuate, hint at', whereas **infer** means 'to deduce or conclude from facts and reasoning'. The two words can often describe the same event, but from different angles. For instance, the sentence *The speaker implied that the General had been a traitor*, means that something in the speaker's words suggested that this man was a traitor (though nothing so explicit was actually stated), while *We inferred from his words that the General had been a traitor*, means that something in the speaker's words enabled the listeners to deduce that the man was a traitor. Mistakes occur when **infer** is used to mean **imply**, as in *Are you inferring that I'm a liar?* (instead of *Are you implying that I'm a liar?*).

impractical / impracticable Impractical means (of people) 'not having practical skills' and (of ideas, solutions, etc.) 'not realistic in practice'. **Impracticable**, meaning 'not capable of execution; infeasible' can only be applied to ideas, etc. Note also that **impractical** is mainly used in general applications, whereas **impracticable** is used of particular instances, e.g. *Her plans were always beautifully logical but utterly impractical*; *Carrying all four bags at once soon proved impracticable*. See also PRACTICAL / PRACTICABLE.

imprimatur / imprint An **imprimatur** is an official licence to print, especially one granted by the Roman Catholic Church; an **imprint** is the name of the publisher/printer, place of publication/printing, etc., on the verso of the title page or at the end of a book.

inapt / inept Inapt means 'inappropriate, unsuitable' and applies only to actions and circumstances; **inept** means 'unskilful' and can apply to people as well, e.g. *In the situation, his choice of language was inapt*; *An enthusiastic but inept dancer*.

indict / indite To **indict** is to charge someone formally with a crime or more generally to accuse; to **indite** (now rare) is to write.

inequity / iniquity Inequity is the opposite of 'equity' and means 'inequality, unfairness, injustice', e.g. *huge inequities in land*

ownership. **Iniquity** means 'gross injustice, wickedness', e.g. *the iniquity of racial prejudice*. It is fairly common for **iniquity** to be used when **inequity** is meant, but this rarely happens the other way round.

inflammable / inflammatory Inflammable means 'flammable; easily set on fire'. **Inflammatory** means 'tending to cause inflammation (of the body)' and figuratively (especially in the context of speeches, leaflets, etc.) 'tending to cause anger'. See also INFLAMMABLE in SECTION 6: USAGE.

inflict / afflict Both words are concerned with causing someone to suffer, but they have different constructions. **Inflict** has the unpleasantness as object, and **afflict** the victim, e.g. *He was determined to inflict a severe penalty on repeat offenders; Such fears afflict many otherwise rational people*. **Afflict** is often used in the passive, followed by 'with' or 'by', e.g. *He was often afflicted with convenient deafness*.

informant / informer An **informant** is a neutral term for someone who gives information. An **informer** is someone who gives information against another person to the authorities, and the word has sinister or unfavourable overtones.

ingenious / ingenuous Ingenious means 'clever, skilful, or resourceful', e.g. *an ingenious mechanic; an ingenious plot*. By contrast **ingenuous** means 'open, artless, frank', e.g. *She is both ingenuous and sophisticated by turns; an ingenuous explanation*.

inhuman / inhumane Inhuman means 'lacking the qualities proper or natural to human behaviour; cruel, brutal', e.g. *inhuman and degrading treatment; Her lack of curiosity seemed almost inhuman*. **Inhumane** is a more specific word denoting a lack of compassion in the treatment of other people (or animals), e.g. *inhumane farming methods; The triage nurse seemed inhumane but was merely overworked*. Both words can be used of people, actions, or attitudes. See also HUMAN / HUMANE.

insidious/invidious Both words involve doing or threatening harm. **Insidious** means 'proceeding inconspicuously but harmfully', e.g. *an insidious influence*, whereas **invidious** means 'likely to excite resentment or indignation', e.g. *an invidious comparison*. So **insidious** has more to do with the process and **invidious** more to do with its effect.

instantly/instantaneously Instantly means 'immediately' and refers to the point at which something happens, e.g. *He leapt instantly to his feet*, whereas **instantaneously** means 'in an instant' and refers to the (imperceptibly short) period of time that something takes, e.g. *She must have died almost instantaneously*. The result can often be the same, but the difference of emphasis is worth bearing in mind.

insure / ensure See SECTION 6: USAGE.

intense / intensive In the broad meaning 'existing in a high degree, extreme' **intense** is the word to use, e.g. *intense happiness*; *an intense shade of orange*. The word **intensive** is now reserved for the special meaning 'thorough, vigorous', e.g. *intensive care*; *an intensive inquiry*. **Intense** also tends to relate to subjective responses—emotions and how we feel—while **intensive** tends to relate to objective descriptions. Thus, *an intensive course* simply describes the type of course, i.e. one that is designed to cover a lot of ground in a short time, while *The course was very intense* describes how someone felt about it.

interment / internment Interment means 'the burial of a corpse', whereas **internment** means 'the confining of a prisoner (especially without trial)'.

irreparable / irrepairable Irreparable (pronounced with the stress on the second syllable) means 'that cannot be recovered or made good', and is used of circumstances and relationships, e.g. *irreparable consequences*; *an irreparable loss*. The word used to describe physical objects, machines, etc., that cannot be repaired is **irrepairable**, pronounced with the stress on the third syllable as in 'repair', e.g. *The lawnmower was irrepairable*. Note, however, that *irreparable damage* is the normal expression whether or not the damage is physical.

its / it's Its is the possessive form of 'it' (*The cat licked its paws*) and **it's** is a shortened form of 'it is' (*It's raining again*) or 'it has' (*I don't know if it's come*).

J

jejune / juvenile See JEJUNE in SECTION 6: USAGE.

judicial / judicious Judicial means 'relating to judges or legal processes', e.g. *a judicial inquiry*, whereas **judicious** means 'sensible, prudent; sound in judgement', e.g. *a judicious use of time*; *a judicious plan of action*. A *judicial decision* is one made by a judge in accordance with the law, whereas a *judicious decision* (whether made by a judge or some other person) is one that is wise and discerning.

junction / juncture A junction is a point at which two or more things are joined, and usually refers to physical objects. It has the special meaning of 'a point at which roads or railway lines meet or cross'. **Juncture** properly denotes 'a conjunction of events producing a critical or dramatic moment', e.g. *A crucial juncture in Irish history*, but in practice tends to mean simply 'point in time', e.g. *At this juncture he decided to have another drink*.

L

lama / llama A lama is a Tibetan or Mongolian Buddhist monk, whereas a **llama** is a South American animal.

lath / lathe A lath (plural **laths**) is a flat strip of wood. A **lathe** (plural **lathes**) is a machine for shaping wood or metal.

laudable / laudatory Laudable means 'deserving praise', whereas **laudatory** means 'expressing praise'. So an action or attitude that is **laudable** calls for a **laudatory** response.

lawman / lawyer Lawman is an informal, mainly North American, term for a law-enforcement officer, especially one in the Wild West; a **lawyer** is a professional person practising law as a solicitor or barrister.

lay / lie See SECTION 6: USAGE.

ledger / leger A ledger is an account book or a weight used in fishing; a **leger line** is a short line above or below the stave in musical notation.

legal / legitimate See LEGAL / LEGITIMATE / LAWFUL / LICIT in SECTION 6: USAGE.

lessee / lessor The **lessee** is the person who holds a property by lease, the **lessor** the person who lets a property by lease.

libel / slander Libel is a published false statement that is damaging to a person's reputation, whereas **slander** is a malicious false statement that is spoken about a person. The legal issue has become more complicated now that uncertainty exists about how far the word 'published' can be extended to cover email, Internet websites, and other forms of electronic media.

lifelong / livelong Lifelong means 'lasting or continuing for a lifetime', e.g. *his lifelong companion.* **Livelong** is a literary word used as an intensive or emotional form of 'long' in describing periods of time, e.g. *the livelong day.*

ligature / digraph See DIPHTHONG/DIGRAPH/ LIGATURE.

lightning / lightening Although lightning is historically a contracted form of lightening, the two are now distinct words. In the sense *thunder and lightning* or *lightning speed*, the spelling is always **lightning**, while in the sense 'make or become lighter' (*the lightening of the dawn sky; the lightening of my burden*), the spelling is always **lightening**.

limey / limy Limey is the adjective corresponding to the fruit, whereas **limy** relates to the caustic alkaline substance. Limey (with a capital initial letter) is a US slang term for a person from Britain.

linage / lineage Linage is a term from journalism and publishing meaning 'the number of printed or written lines in a text'; **lineage** is ancestry.

lineament / liniment Lineament (pronounced as four syllables) means 'a distinctive feature of the face', and is normally used in the plural. Liniment (three syllables) is an embrocation.

liqueur / liquor A liqueur is a strong and usually sweet alcoholic drink, such as Cointreau or Bénédictine. A **liquor** is any alcoholic drink.

liquidate / liquidize Liquidate is the word used in business contexts and in the sense 'eliminate by killing'. **Liquidize** is a more recent word meaning 'to make liquid'

(in physical senses) and is now principally used in the context of the kitchen liquidizer.

litany / liturgy A litany is a prayer consisting of a sequence of petitions, each of which is followed by an unvarying response. The word is also used in expressions such as *a litany of woes*, where it implies something long and tedious. A **liturgy** is a prescribed form of public worship, embracing many individual prayers and petitions.

Lloyd's / Lloyds The name of the London society of underwriters is spelt **Lloyd's** (also *Lloyd's list, Lloyd's Register*), whereas the name of the bank is **Lloyds TSB** (no apostrophe).

loath / loathe Loath, meaning 'averse, reluctant', as in *loath to comment*, should be distinguished from the verb **loathe** meaning 'to hate'. 'Loth' is a common misspelling of **loath**.

loose / loosen / lose Both loose and **loosen** involve removal of restraints, physical or otherwise. The difference is that **loose** releases or sets free whereas **loosen** only makes more loose (or less tight). To **loose** a prisoner from his bonds is to set him free; to **loosen** his bonds is to make them less tight although he remains a captive. The verb **lose** is sometimes mistakenly written as **loose**.

lumbar / lumber Lumbar refers to the lower back; **lumber** is either disused junk or timber.

luxuriant/luxurious Luxuriant means 'lush, profuse, or prolific', e.g. *forests of dark luxuriant foliage; luxuriant black eyelashes.* **Luxurious**, a much commoner word, means 'supplied with luxuries, extremely comfortable', e.g. *a luxurious hotel.*

lyric/lyrical Lyric is the adjective to use when referring to poetry that expresses subjective emotion in set forms such as the ode or sonnet, e.g. *a lyric poet; lyric verses.* A **lyric** is a poem of this kind or, in modern use, the words of a popular song. The main meaning of **lyrical** is 'using language of a heightened and enthusiastic kind appropriate to lyric poetry', e.g. *lyrical descriptions of the countryside; He liked to wax lyrical on the value of friendship.*

M

magnate / magnet A **magnate** is a rich and powerful person, especially in industry or business; a **magnet** attracts iron.

manikin / mannequin / manakin / mannikin Manikin, meaning 'a dwarf', 'an artist's dummy', or 'an anatomical model', is spelt this way; a dressmaker's model is a **mannequin**. A **manakin** is a tropical bird of South and Central America; a **mannikin** (sometimes also **manikin**) is a smaller bird found mainly in Africa and South Asia.

mantel / mantle A **mantle** is a cloak or something that covers entirely like a cloak, e.g. *a mantle of fresh snow*. The word is also used figuratively to mean 'responsibility or authority' especially regarded as passing from one person to another, e.g. *Eden assumed the mantle of Churchill*. **Mantel** has one meaning, usually in the longer form **mantelpiece** or **mantelshelf**, 'a shelf over a fireplace'.

marquess / marquis / marquise / marchioness A **marquess** is a British nobleman ranking between a duke and an earl, and a **marquis** is a foreign equivalent ranking between a duke and a count. A **marquise** is the wife or widow of a marquis, or a woman holding the rank of marquis in her own right. A **marchioness** is the wife or widow of a marquess, or a woman holding the rank of marquess in her own right.

marten / martin A **marten** is an animal like a weasel; a **martin** is a bird of the swallow family.

masterful / masterly See SECTION 6: USAGE.

matt/matte Matt means 'without lustre'; **matte** is a smelting product, or a masking device used in filming.

mendacity / mendicity Mendacity means 'habitual lying or deceiving', whereas **mendicity** means 'the practice or habit of begging'.

meretricious / meritorious Meretricious (derived from Latin *meretrix* 'prostitute'), means 'showily but falsely attractive', e.g. *the meretricious glamour of the fashion world*. By contrast, **meritorious** means 'showing merit, praiseworthy'.

mésalliance / misalliance Mésalliance (printed in italics because non-naturalized) normally means 'a marriage with a person of a lower social position', whereas **misalliance** is used of any unsuitable alliance.

metal / mettle Metal is iron, copper, etc.; **mettle** means 'spirit, courage', as in the expressions *show one's mettle* and *be on one's mettle*.

meter/metre A meter is a measuring instrument of some kind; a **metre** is a metric unit of distance (100 cm), or the regular pattern of strong and weak syllables in metrical poetry.

migrant / emigrant / immigrant See EMIGRANT / IMMIGRANT / ÉMIGRÉ / MIGRANT.

militate / mitigate Militate means 'to have force or effect' and is usually followed by 'against', e.g. *The rules militated against the weak, the infirm, or even the well-mannered.* **Mitigate**, on the other hand, means 'to make milder or less severe', e.g. *His disappointment was mitigated by the generous offer of a free holiday.* **Mitigate** is transitive (i.e. it takes an object), whereas **militate** is intransitive.

miner / minor A miner works underground in a mine; a **minor** is below the age of legal majority.

modus operandi/modus vivendi *Modus operandi* means 'a plan or method of working', whereas *modus vivendi* means 'a way of living or coping', most often (in law) an arrangement by which parties to a dispute can carry on pending a settlement.

moment / momentum Moment means 'importance', e.g. *an error of some moment*; **momentum** means (literally) 'the impetus gained by a moving body' or (figuratively) 'the impetus gained by a developing course of events', e.g. *The peace process is gathering momentum.*

moral / morale Moral means (adjective) 'relating to the principles of good or bad behaviour', or (noun) 'the lesson of a story or event'; **morale** means 'confidence, optimistic attitude', e.g. *The team's morale suffered from a series of defeats.*

mote/moat/motte A **mote** is a speck of dust; a **moat** is a water-filled ditch around a castle etc.; a **motte** is a castle mound.

motif / motive A **motif** is a distinctive or recurrent theme in a literary or musical work, a decorative pattern, or a single ornament on a garment. A **motive** is what induces a person to act in a particular way.

muscle / mussel Muscle is the fibrous body tissue, **mussel** the bivalve mollusc.

#

nationalize / naturalize Nationalize means 'to take (an industry etc.) into state ownership', whereas **naturalize** means 'to admit (a foreign person) into citizenship of a country' and also 'to adopt (a foreign word or custom)'. The respective nouns are **nationalization** and **naturalization**.

naturalist / naturist A naturalist is an expert in natural history; a **naturist** is a nudist.

naught / nought Naught is an archaic or literary word meaning 'nothing' that survives chiefly in phrases such as *come to naught* or *set at naught*. **Nought** is the traditional British term for the digit 0 ('zero' in North American English).

naval / navel Naval is the adjective relating to 'navy'; and **navel** is the rounded knotty depression in the centre of the belly or a kind of orange.

noisome / noisy Noisome means 'harmful, noxious'; noisy means 'making a noise'.

O

observance / observation The two words correspond to different branches in meaning of the verb 'observe'. **Observance** is the word used in connection with respecting rules, carrying out duties and obligations, and performing formal customs and rituals, e.g. *religious observance*; *observance of the usual conventions*. **Observation** is used in the more physical senses of seeing and perceiving and has the special meaning 'a remark or comment', e.g. *an army observation post*; *medical observation*; *a pointed observation*.

obsolete / obsolescent Something (either physical, or conceptual) is **obsolete** when it is outdated and no longer used. It is **obsolescent** when it is falling out of use, i.e. is becoming **obsolete** but is not yet actually so.

official / officious The main meanings of **official** are 'in the nature of an office', e.g. *official duties*, and 'authorized or confirmed by someone in authority', e.g. *The official attendance was over 10,000*. By contrast, **officious** is a judgemental word meaning 'asserting authority aggressively or intrusively', and is most commonly used of a person or the actions of a person, e.g. *officious traffic wardens*.

Olympic / Olympian / Olympiad Olympic is used principally of the games of ancient times and their modern revival, e.g. *an Olympic athlete*. The noun **Olympiad** means 'a particular celebration of the Olympic Games', or (in dating events in ancient Greece) 'the period of four years between Olympic Games'. **Olympian** refers to Mount Olympus and to the Greek gods traditionally held to make their home there; in modern use it often denotes an attitude of superiority or aloofness, e.g. *He showed an Olympian detachment from political events*.

omit / emit To **omit** something is to leave it out, e.g. *He was omitted from the team owing to injury*. To **emit** something is to send it out, e.g. *He emitted a sudden scream*.

ordinance / ordnance / ordonnance An **ordinance** is an authoritative decree or a religious rite, whereas **ordnance** is artillery or the government service dealing with military stores and materials. **Ordonnance** is a somewhat rare word meaning 'the systematic arrangement of parts in a building or an artistic composition'.

ostensible / ostensive / ostentatious Ostensible means 'apparent' or 'professed', e.g. *Although an ostensible revolutionary, he enjoyed a comfortable bourgeois lifestyle*. It is often used in the adverbial form **ostensibly**. **Ostensive**, a much rarer word, means 'directly demonstrative' and is normally used in technical contexts in linguistics or philosophy, e.g. *She gave an ostensive definition of the word 'nose' by pointing to her own*. **Ostentatious**, which is less likely to be confused with the other two, means 'pretentious and showy'.

outcast / outcaste An **outcast** is a rejected person or a homeless wanderer; an **outcaste** is a casteless Hindu or (by extension) a person who has been expelled from his or her social class.

overlay / overlie The verb **overlie** (past tense **overlay**) means 'to lie or rest on top of', e.g. *Thick clays overlie the granite*. **Overlay** (past tense **overlaid**, past participle **overlain**) means 'to put on top of, to coat or cover', e.g. *She overlaid the walls with a pale wash*; *His criticisms were overlaid with humour*. See LAY / LIE in SECTION 6: USAGE.

P

paean / paeon / peon A **paean** is a song of praise (originally to a Greek god) or an outburst of acclamation, e.g. *the paeans of the critics*; a **paeon** is a metrical foot originally associated with classical paeans. A **peon** is a poor farm labourer in Spanish America or an attendant or foot soldier in India.

palate / palette / pallet The **palate** is the roof of the mouth; a **palette** is the range of colours used by an artist or the small tray they are placed on; a **pallet** is a wooden platform on which goods are stacked or a straw bed or mattress.

parable / fable See ALLEGORY / FABLE / PARABLE / SYMBOLISM.

parricide / patricide In current use **parricide** is the killing of a parent or other near relative, whereas **patricide** is more specifically the killing of one's father. Both are used to denote either the crime or the person who commits it.

passed / past **Passed** is the past tense and past participle of the verb 'to pass', e.g. *The time passed quickly*; *We passed a church*; *I have passed my exam*. **Past** is an adjective, preposition, or adverb, e.g. *The time for worrying is past*; *We drove past a church*; *He hurried past*.

pastel / pastille A **pastel** is an artist's crayon or a light shade of a colour, whereas a **pastille** is a small sweet or lozenge.

peaceable / peaceful In general, **peaceable** means 'disposed to peace, not quarrelsome' and refers primarily to people or activities, e.g. *European explorers found the indigenous peoples mainly peaceable*. The adverb **peaceably** occurs almost as often as the adjective, e.g. *On the whole they lived peaceably together*. The more common word **peaceful** means 'characterized by peace, tranquil', e.g. *a peaceful spot in the countryside*; *a peaceful interlude*.

pedal / peddle To **pedal** is to operate the pedals on a bicycle etc.; to **peddle** is to sell small articles from door to door, to supply illegal drugs, or to spread anything else considered undesirable, e.g. *peddling racial hatred*.

peer / pier A **peer** is a noble, or one's contemporary; a **pier** is a structure built out into the sea, or a pillar that supports a heavy load.

pendant / pendent / pennant The noun **pendant** means 'a hanging jewel or ornament', or in nautical use 'a short rope hanging from the head of a mast'; the adjective **pendent** means 'hanging or overhanging'. A **pennant** is a tapering flag, especially one flown at the masthead of a ship.

perquisite / prerequisite **Perquisite** usually means 'an extra benefit or privilege', e.g. *Free gym membership was one of the perquisites of the job*. The word is often shortened to 'perk'. **Prerequisite** means 'something required as a precondition', e.g. *A general education in the sciences is a prerequisite of professional medical training*.

perspicacious / perspicuous **Perspicacious** means 'having mental penetration or discernment' and its corresponding noun is **perspicacity**. **Perspicuous**, on the other hand, means 'clear to understand' (with reference to people and statements), and its noun is **perspicuity**. The following examples show the correct use of the nouns, which are more often confused than the adjectives: *It didn't take much perspicacity to tell that she was infatuated with Robert*; *His later writings gained in subtlety what they lost in perspicuity*.

perverse / perverted **Perverse** means 'stubbornly unreasonable' (of people) or 'contrary, paradoxical' (of circumstances), e.g. *His perverse refusal to acknowledge the obvious truth*; *Her kindness had the perverse effect* *of increasing his animosity.* **Perverted** means 'departing from right opinion or conduct' and is commonly used with reference to abnormal or deviant sexual behaviour, e.g. *a perverted use of his talents*; *perverted desires*.

petrel / petrol A **petrel** is a sea bird; **petrol** is a fuel obtained from crude oil (**petroleum**).

phantasm/phantom In current usage **phantom** primarily means 'a ghost', 'a figment of the imagination', e.g. *a phantom illness*, or 'something obscure and clandestine', e.g. *payments into phantom bank accounts*; **phantasm** means 'a visual illusion or apparition', e.g. *drug-induced phantasms*, or 'an illusory likeness of something', e.g. *phantasms of hope*.

physiognomy / physiology **Physiognomy** means 'the cast or form of a person's features', whereas **physiology** means 'the science of the functions of living organisms and their parts'.

pidgin / creole See CREOLE / PIDGIN.

piebald / skewbald A **piebald** horse or other animal is one having irregular patches of two colours, especially black and white. A **skewbald** animal has irregular patches of white and another colour (other than black).

plaid/tartan A **plaid** is a length of fabric worn over the shoulder as part of the ceremonial dress of members of the pipe bands of Scottish regiments. It should be distinguished from **tartan**, which is a woollen cloth with a pattern of different coloured stripes crossing at right angles, each pattern being associated with a particular clan. A **plaid** can be made from **tartan** cloth.

plain / plane As nouns, a **plain** is flat land, while a **plane** is a level surface, an aircraft, a tree, or a tool used in carpentry.

plaintiff / plaintive A **plaintiff** brings a case in a law court; **plaintive** means 'mournful'.

pore / pour The verb **pore** means 'to be absorbed in the study of', e.g. *She sat poring over law reports.* It is sometimes mistakenly written as **pour**, perhaps by false analogy with 'pouring attention' over something.

practical / practicable **Practical** usually has a general application, denoting what is possible in practice as distinct from theory, or what is suitable for its purpose, e.g. *You must take a practical approach to finding work; The new uniform was practical as well as smart.* **Practicable** means 'able to be carried out, feasible' and is more usually applied to a particular instance under consideration, e.g. *Getting there by public transport is not really practicable.* **Practical** (but not **practicable**) can also be applied to a person, meaning 'sensible and realistic, good at manual tasks'. See also IMPRACTICAL / IMPRACTICABLE.

precede / proceed To **precede** is to go before or ahead of something; to **proceed** is to begin or continue a course of action.

precipitate / precipitous **Precipitous** has the physical meaning 'sheer like a precipice', e.g. *a precipitous staircase.* In its abstract sense it is concerned with the over-rapid progress of an action and retains the notion of steep descent, e.g. *a precipitous decline.* **Precipitate** is concerned rather with the inception of an action and means 'hasty, rash, inconsiderate' or 'headlong, violently hurried', e.g. *His precipitate decision to resign.* It is here that the two words come closest, since any action that is **precipitate** in its inception is likely to be **precipitous** in its performance or consequences.

premier / premiere **Premier** is a noun meaning 'prime minister' or an adjective meaning 'first in order or importance', e.g. *New Zealand's premier rock band;* **premiere** is a noun meaning 'the first performance or showing of a play or film' and a verb meaning 'to give a premiere of', e.g. *The film will be premiered next week.*

prescribe/proscribe **Prescribe** (a much commoner word) means either 'issue a medical prescription' or 'recommend with authority', e.g. *The doctor prescribed antibiotics.* **Proscribe**, on the other hand, is a formal word meaning 'condemn or forbid', e.g. *Gambling was strictly proscribed by the authorities.* A **prescribed** book is therefore one that is chosen for a course of study, whereas a **proscribed** book is one that is forbidden or banned.

prevaricate / procrastinate **Prevaricate** means 'act or speak in an evasive way', e.g.

He prevaricated at the mention of money. **Procrastinate**, on the other hand, means 'put off doing something', e.g. *The politicians will procrastinate until it is too late.* The meanings are closely related—if someone prevaricates they often also procrastinate—but the senses should be carefully distinguished.

principal/principle Principal is both adjective and noun and essentially means 'chief', e.g. *my principal objection; Meet the principal of my college.* **Principle** is a noun only and means 'a fundamental basis of a system of thought or belief', e.g. *The principles of democracy; Is there a principle at stake here?* In the plural it can also mean 'rules of conduct', e.g. *They seem to have no moral principles.* The usual mistake is to use **principle** for the adjective **principal**.

prone/supine Prone means 'lying face down'; **supine** means 'lying face up' and has the figurative meaning 'spineless, cowardly'.

propellant / propellent The noun **propellant**, meaning 'a thing that propels' (especially a rocket fuel or the agent in aerosol sprays), is the more familiar word. **Propellent** is an adjective meaning 'capable of driving or pushing forward'.

prostate / prostrate The **prostate** is a gland surrounding the neck of the bladder in male animals. **Prostrate** is an adjective and verb: the adjective (pronounced with the stress on the first syllable) means 'lying horizontally', especially in the figurative sense of being overcome by grief or some other strong feeling, and the verb (pronounced with the stress on the second syllable) means 'to throw (oneself) on the ground in submission'.

prudent / prudential / prudish Prudent is a judgemental word meaning 'circumspect, judicious', whereas **prudential** is merely descriptive in identifying actions and attitudes that have to do with prudence, e.g. *prudential motives.* **Prudish** is an entirely distinct word meaning 'affecting extreme modesty or propriety in sexual matters'.

puny / puisne Puny means 'weak, small', e.g. *ill-fed puny children; a puny response to his critics.* **Puisne** (derived from French *puis né*

'born afterwards') means 'inferior'. A **puisne judge** is a judge of a superior court inferior in rank to chief justices.

purposely / purposefully / purposively Purposely means 'on purpose, intentionally', e.g. *She purposely avoided his gaze.* **Purposefully** corresponds to the adjective 'purposeful' and means 'with a strong purpose, resolutely', e.g. *She set off purposefully down the road.* The more formal and technical word **purposively** means 'for a particular purpose, with a particular intention', e.g. *A new society will have to be built by human beings working purposively and creatively.*

put / putt Put (pronounced like the ordinary verb) is used in athletics to mean 'throw, cast', e.g. *to put the shot;* a **putt** (pronounced like 'gut') is a stroke in golf.

R

rabbet / rabbit A **rabbet** is a groove in woodwork; **rabbit** is the animal.

rack / wrack See SECTION 6: USAGE.

radical / radicle Radical is the general word and a technical term in mathematics, chemistry, and linguistics; **radicle**, meaning 'a very small root or root-like structure' is used only in botany and anatomy.

rebound / redound The image with the verb **rebound** is of something bouncing back; with **redound** it is of a tide or wave flooding back. When circumstances **rebound on** someone they have a harmful effect on the person or people responsible for them, e.g. *The allegation will rebound on the party making it.* By contrast, when a circumstance **redounds to** someone's advantage or credit, it contributes to it, e.g. *His steadfastness will surely redound to his credit.* Although contrary examples of **redound** can be found, they are fairly rare.

recoup / recuperate Recoup can be used transitively to mean 'reimburse', e.g. *He had little time to recoup his losses,* or intransitively to mean 'to make good one's loss', e.g. *Her debts were so extensive that she returned to the parental home to recoup.* **Recuperate** is used intransitively to mean 'to recover from illhealth, a loss, etc.', e.g. *The half-time whistle* *gave him a chance to recuperate*. The transitive use of **recuperate** in such sentences as *He recuperated his health* or *She recuperated her expenditure* is considered poor style (in the first case use 'recover', in the second **recoup**).

regretful/regrettable Regretful means 'feeling or showing regret', e.g. *She shook her head with a regretful smile*, while **regrettable** means 'giving rise to regret; undesirable', as in *The loss of jobs is regrettable*. See also RE-GRETFULLY in SECTION 6: USAGE.

resister / resistor A resister is someone who resists, especially a member of a wartime Resistance group; a **resistor** is an electronic device that reduces the flow of an electric current.

resource / recourse / resort Resource (often used in the plural) means 'a thing, expedient, or capability to which one can turn in need', e.g. *mineral resources*; *a woman of great inner resources*. **Recourse** means 'the action of turning to a possible source of help', e.g. *She took recourse to the law*. As a noun, **resort** means 'a thing to which one can turn in difficulty', e.g. *the last resort*: as a verb, it means 'to take recourse in', e.g. *He resorted to abuse*.

reverend / reverent Reverend is deserving reverence, **reverent** is showing it, e.g. *reverend antiquity*; *an over-reverent attitude*. For the use of **Reverend** as a title see SECTION 6: USAGE.

reversal / reversion Reversal is the noun corresponding to the verb 'reverse', and means primarily 'the changing (of a decision)', e.g. *the reversal of his earlier policies*: **reversion** corresponds to the verb 'revert', and means primarily 'a return to', e.g. *The style represents a reversion to classical Japanese tradition*.

review / revue A review is a general survey or assessment of something, particularly in the form of a published criticism of a book, play, etc. A **revue** is a theatrical entertainment consisting of a series of short acts or sketches.

rhyme / rime Rhyme is the matching of terminal sounds in lines of poetry, or a short piece of rhyming verse; **rime** is frost.

risky / risqué Risky is the general word meaning 'involving risk', whereas the French loanword **risqué** means 'slightly indecent' (espe- cially with reference to humour) and therefore risking shock.

rout / route / root To rout is to vanquish or put to flight, e.g. *I saw her rout her accusers*; to **route** is to send by a particular route, e.g. *I will route my complaint via the chairman*. To **rout out** is to find something by searching, e.g. *I managed to rout out the truth*, but to **root about** is to search unsystematically, e.g. *I rooted about in my desk for her letter*.

S

saccharin/saccharine Saccharin is a noun denoting a sugar-substitute; **saccharine** is an adjective meaning (literally) 'sugary' or (figuratively) 'unpleasantly over-polite or sentimental'.

salubrious/salutary Salubrious means 'giving health' and hence also 'pleasant, agreeable', e.g. *a salubrious breeze*; *a far from salubrious prospect*. **Salutary** means 'producing healthy effects' and hence 'beneficial', usually in an admonitory context, e.g. *a salutary reminder of the dangers we face*.

sanguine / sanguinary Sanguine originally meant 'blood-coloured' but now primarily means 'optimistic, confident' from an earlier association of blood with this type of temperament, e.g. *a sanguine view of the prospects for peace*. By contrast, **sanguinary** has retained its more physical meanings 'accompanied by blood' and 'bloodthirsty', e.g. *the sanguinary history of the Balkans*.

satire / satyr Satire is the use of ridicule to expose folly or evil; a **satyr** is a goatlike woodland deity, or a lustful man.

sceptic / septic A sceptic is a habitual doubter; **septic** means 'relating to disease or putrefaction caused by bacteria', e.g. *a septic wound*; *septic tank*.

scrimmage / scrummage Scrimmage is the more general word for 'a rough struggle or brawl' and is a technical term in American football, whereas **scrummage** (usually shortened to **scrum**) is the term used in rugby football.

scull / skull A **scull** is a small oar or a rowing boat for a single oarsman; the bone of the head is the **skull**.

seasonable / seasonal Seasonable means 'usual or suitable for the season' or 'opportune', e.g. *Although seasonable, the weather was not suitable for picnics*; *She waited for a seasonable moment to press her request*. **Seasonal** means 'of, depending on, or varying with the season', e.g. *Seasonal changes posed problems for mills situated on larger rivers*.

sensual / sensuous See SECTION 6: USAGE.

sestet / sextet A **sestet** is the second part of a sonnet, consisting of six lines; a **sextet** is a musical work for six parts or a group of six musicians.

sew / sow Sew means 'to form stitches with a needle and thread' and has the past form **sewed** and the past participle **sewn** or **sewed**. **Sow** means 'to plant (seed)' and has the past form **sowed** and the past participle **sown** or **sowed**.

sewage / sewerage Sewage is waste matter carried by sewers; **sewerage** is a system of sewers.

sheer / shear Sheer, the less common verb, means 'swerve or change course quickly', e.g. *The boat sheers off the bank*. **Shear**, on the other hand, usually means 'cut the wool off (a sheep)' but can also mean 'break off (usually as a result of structural strain)', e.g. *The pins broke and the wing part sheared off*. There is also an adjective **sheer** meaning 'very steep', 'transparent', or 'unmitigated', e.g. *a sheer drop*; *a sheer nightdress*; *sheer nonsense*.

site / cite To **site** something is to locate or install it in a particular place; to **cite** someone or something is to refer to or quote him, her, or it.

slander / libel See LIBEL / SLANDER.

slush / sludge / slosh Sludge is usually applied to something relatively thick and less liquid, e.g. to wet clinging mud or slimy deposits, whereas **slush** more typically describes thawing snow or melting ice. **Slosh** is a verb meaning 'to move with a splashing sound'.

sole / soul A **sole** is a fish, or the underneath of one's foot or shoe; the **soul** is one's spiritual part.

sometime / some time Sometime generally means 'at some unspecified point of time', e.g. *You must come for dinner sometime*; when used before a noun it can also mean 'former' or 'occasional', e.g. *my sometime boss*; *a sometime petty criminal*. When written as two words **some time** means 'an unspecified amount of time' or 'a considerable amount of time', e.g. *After some time had passed*; *This may take some time*.

specious / spurious Specious began its life meaning 'having a fine outward appearance', but later acquired the unfavourable meaning 'plausible but in fact wrong', e.g. *a specious argument*. **Spurious** means 'not genuine, not being what it purports to be'. A **specious** claim is one that is attractive but insubstantial whereas a **spurious** claim is one based on a false premise.

spiritual / spirituous Spiritual is now the general word relating to the spirit or soul, and **spirituous** that referring to distilled alcoholic drinks. In older writing **spirituous** is sometimes found as a synonym of **spiritual**.

stalactite / stalagmite A **stalactite** hangs down from the roof of a cave, and is formed from dripping water containing rich minerals. A **stalagmite** rises up from the floor and is formed from deposits also caused by dripping.

stationary / stationery Stationary is an adjective and means 'not moving' whereas **stationery** is a noun and denotes paper and writing materials.

stile / style A **stile** is a set of steps in a wall or fence; **style** is appearance, manner, or fashion.

storey / story A **storey** is one level of a building; a **story** is a narrative.

straight / strait Straight has many meanings in modern English, primarily 'extending uniformly in the same direction without a curve or bend'. **Strait** has the basic meaning 'tight, narrow' and is used as a noun meaning 'a narrow passage of water connecting two seas'. Note the common combinations *straight-faced* and *straightforward* but *strait-laced*, *straitjacket*, and *dire straits*.

strategy / tactics In war, as in politics and business, **strategy** is used of an overall plan of action embodying certain principles and objectives, and **tactics** is used of the detailed means adopted to achieve them.

substantial/substantive Both words mean 'having substance', but **substantial** is the more general word used to mean 'having importance, value, or reality; considerable', whereas **substantive** is a more specialized word used to mean 'relating to the essential elements of a thing'. **Substantial** discussions are therefore lengthy and wide-ranging ones, whereas **substantive** discussions deal with the most important topics. Similarly, **substantial** agreement means 'agreement on much', whereas **substantive** agreement means 'agreement on what is essential'. **Substantive** often occurs in technical contexts such as law and parliamentary procedure; for example, *a substantive motion* is one that deals specifically with a subject in due form. See also SUBSTANTIAL in SECTION 6: USAGE.

summon/summons Summon is a verb only, whereas **summons** is a noun and verb. A **summons** (plural **summonses**) is an order to appear before a judge or magistrate, and to **summons** someone is to issue them with such an order. **Summon** is the ordinary word meaning 'to call formally', as in *The chairman summoned the members to a meeting*.

suppositious / supposititious **Suppositious** means 'based on assumption rather than fact; hypothetical', e.g. *The evidence is purely suppositious*: **supposititious** means 'fraudulently substituted', e.g. *The supposititious heir to the Romanov fortune*.

supine / prone See PRONE / SUPINE.

swat / swot Swat is the spelling for the verb meaning 'to hit sharply' and the corresponding noun. **Swot** is a British colloquialism meaning 'to study hard' and 'someone who studies hard'.

symbolism / allegory See ALLEGORY / FABLE / PARABLE / SYMBOLISM.

systematic / systemic The word in general use in the meaning 'done according to a plan or system' is **systematic**, e.g. *systematic learning*; *a systematic search*. The much less common word **systemic** is mostly confined to technical uses in medicine and linguistics, and has the meaning 'relating to a system as a whole rather than to a part of it', e.g. *a systemic disease*; *systemic grammar*.

T

tactics / strategy See STRATEGY / TACTICS.

tartan / plaid See PLAID / TARTAN.

tasty / tasteful Tasty is now restricted to the contexts of food and (informally) of sex appeal, e.g. *a tasty young thing*. It is not used in the context of 'good taste' (i.e. aesthetic judgement), for which **tasteful** is the appropriate adjective. The opposite word **tasteless**, however, is used in all meanings, physical and abstract, e.g. *a tasteless sandwich*; *a tasteless remark*.

taught / taut The past tense of 'teach' is **taught**; **taut** is the opposite of loose or slack.

tetchy / touchy / testy Tetchy means 'irritable, peevish', as does **testy**; **touchy** means 'over-sensitive, likely to take offence'.

thrash / thresh To thrash is to beat (physically or metaphorically), e.g. *We thrashed the other team 6–0*, whereas to **thresh** is to separate grain.

throes / throws Throes, meaning 'violent pangs or convulsions' (e.g. *death throes*; *the throes of revolution*), is spelt in this way, and should be distinguished from **throws** as a part of the verb 'throw'.

titillate / titivate Titillate means 'to excite or stimulate', e.g. *Her news certainly titillated his interest*, and often has sexual overtones (especially in the noun derivative **titillation**). **Titivate** means 'to adorn or smarten', e.g. *She titivated herself up for the party*. **Titivate** is often mistakenly used for **titillate**, though the reverse mistake is much more rare.

ton / tonne / tun A ton is 2240 pounds (UK) or 2000 pounds (US); a **tonne** is a metric ton, equivalent to 1000 kilograms. A **tun** is a cask or measure of wine.

tortuous / torturous Tortuous means 'full of twists and turns', e.g. *a tortuous route*; *a tortuous explanation*. **Torturous** means 'involving or causing torture', e.g. *a torturous five days of fitness training*. In extended senses, however, **tortuous** is used to mean 'excessively lengthy and complex' and hence may become hard to distinguish from **torturous**. A *tortuous judgement* is one that has many complicating features, and a *torturous judgement* is one that is painfully difficult to make; these are two aspects of a similar outcome. **Tortuous** is more common in this range of meanings and is usually the better choice.

transcendent / transcendental Transcendent is used in general contexts to mean 'surpassing others', e.g. *of transcendent importance*, and in theological discussion to mean (of God) 'above and distinct from the universe'. **Transcendental** means 'visionary, beyond experience' and has several technical senses in philosophy (especially that of Kant). It is also used in the term *transcendental meditation*.

triumphal / triumphant Triumphal is a classifying word denoting things connected with victory, e.g. *a magnificent triumphal arch*; *a triumphal procession*. **Triumphant** is more descriptive and means 'exulting in a victory or success' with a wide range of applications, e.g. *The triumphant British team*; *He gave a triumphant laugh*; *She chaired the meeting to a triumphant conclusion*.

troop / troupe A **troop** is an armoured unit of soldiers or a group of Scouts, whereas a **troupe** is a company of actors or performers. Correspondingly, a **trooper** is a soldier in an armoured unit (and, in the USA and Australia, a mounted police officer) and a **trouper** is a member of a group of actors or performers and (figuratively) 'a staunch colleague', e.g. *She proved an absolute trouper*.

turbid / turgid In their literal meanings, **turbid** means 'opaque and cloudy', e.g. *The river was slow and turbid*, and **turgid** means 'swollen and overflowing', e.g. *The river was turgid after the heavy rains*. In their figurative meanings, both refer to styles of writing.

Turgid, meaning 'inflated, bombastic', is the more commonly used, e.g. *turgid and unreadable prose*, whereas **turbid** means 'confused, muddled', e.g. *wild and turbid imagery*.

U

underlay / underlie The verb **underlay** (past **underlaid**) means 'to lay something under', e.g. *He underlaid the tiles with felt*. The verb **underlie** (past tense **underlay**, past participle **underlain**) means 'to lie under', 'to be the basis of', or 'to exist beneath the surface of', e.g. *The arrogance that underlay his good manners*. See LAY/LIE in SECTION 6: USAGE.

unexceptionable / unexceptional Unexceptionable means 'not open to objection', e.g. *This view is unexceptionable in itself*, while **unexceptional** means 'not out of the ordinary; usual', e.g. *The hotel was adequate but unexceptional*. In practice the meaning of **unexceptionable** is often somewhat indeterminate between 'not open to objection' and 'ordinary', as in *The food was bland and unexceptionable* or *The candidates were pretty unexceptionable*. See also EXCEPTIONAL/EXCEPTIONABLE.

urban / urbane Urban means 'relating to a city or cities in general'; **urbane** means 'cultured and smooth-mannered'.

V

valance / valence / valency A valance is a short curtain round the edge of a canopy or bed. **Valence** and **valency** are terms in chemistry relating to the combining power of atoms.

venal/venial These two unrelated words both have to do with forms of transgression. **Venal** means 'able to be bribed, corrupt' and is used of people and their actions; **venial** means 'pardonable' and refers in Roman Catholic teaching to minor or pardonable sins (as distinct from mortal sins which bring eternal damnation).

vicious / viscous Vicious means 'nasty, aggressive, or cruel', whereas a **viscous** liquid is one that is thick and slow-flowing.

villain/villein A villain is an evil-doer; a **villein** was a medieval serf.

W

waive / wave Waive means 'to refrain from insisting on, to dispense with', e.g. *She waived her usual fee*; *Let's waive the formalities*. Confusion with **wave** mainly arises in the constructions 'wave aside' and 'wave away', which can have a similar meaning to **waive**, e.g. *When offered a fee, she simply waved the subject away with her hand*. A **waiver** is the act of foregoing a right or claim, or a formal written statement to this effect, e.g. *He signed a waiver renouncing any future claims on the estate*. To **waver** is to fluctuate or be unsteady, e.g. *a wavering light*; *She never wavered in her purpose*.

who's / whose The form **who's** represents a contraction of 'who is' or 'who has', while **whose** is a possessive pronoun or determiner used in questions, as in *Whose is this?* or *Whose turn is it?*

wreath / wreathe Wreath is the noun, e.g. *His widow laid a wreath*; **wreathe** is the related verb meaning 'to decorate with or as with a wreath' or 'to move in a twisting way, writhe', e.g. *She was wreathed in smiles*; *Smoke wreathed up in the air*.

write off / right off To **write off** something is to acknowledge its complete loss, e.g. *He wrote off the money she owed him*, or (informally) to damage it irreparably, e.g. *He wrote off the car*; **right off** means 'immediately, right away'.

Y

yoke / yolk A **yoke** is a wooden crosspiece fixed over the necks of work animals, or (metaphorically) a burden or oppressive force, e.g. *The yoke of foreign domination*. A **yolk** is the yellow part of an egg.

Section 6: Usage

This Section provides an alphabetical list of words that, for one reason or another, require special care. The problems associated with each word are clearly set out, usually with the help of illustrative quotations, and the reader is offered pragmatic advice on the best policy to adopt in each case. The main aim is to recommend the meaning or construction most appropriate for formal writing or speaking, but some attention is paid to informal and American usage.

Problems of usage can be divided into several different categories. Some words are easy to misuse because they are commonly misunderstood; examples include **egregious**, **feasible**, **forensic**, *and* **jejune**, *none of which means exactly what you might think. Others have developed extended or weakened meanings that are not fully accepted in formal contexts, despite their wide use elsewhere; these include* **chronic**, **refute**, *and* **unique**. *In several cases of this kind, special care is needed because the word has become a symbolic battleground for linguistic conservatives and those with a more liberal approach; famous examples are* **hopefully** *(as sentence adverb) and* **disinterested** *(in the sense 'not interested').*

Alternatively, advice may be needed on the appropriate constructions to be used with certain words: is it **averse from** *or* **averse to**, **different from**, **different to**, *or* **different than***?*

Apart from questions of clarity and correctness, there are also subtler issues of register, nuance, and tone that can prove every bit as problematic. Why do some readers grit their teeth at the phrases **as and when** *or* **as per usual**, *while others wince at* **advices**, **parameter**, **interface** *(verb), or* **toilet***? How is it that using the word* **coloured** *to mean 'non-white' risks a charge of racial insensitivity (or worse), whereas using the term* **person of colour** *carries no such risk and may even enhance one's credibility?*

These problems and many others like them are addressed in the list below. The pitfalls of solecism, cliché, and circumlocution are pointed out, and the Section offers a safe guide through the dangerous territory of political correctness. Cross-references are indicated by the use of SMALL CAPITALS.

A

a / an There is still some disagreement over the form of the indefinite article to use preceding certain words beginning with 'h': *a historical document* or *an historical document*; *a hotel* or *an hotel*. The form depends on whether the initial 'h' is sounded or not: **an** was common in the 18th and 19th centuries, because the initial 'h' was commonly not pronounced for these words. In standard modern English the norm is for the 'h' to be pronounced in words like 'hotel' and 'historical', and therefore the indefinite article **a** is used; however, the older form, with the silent 'h' and the indefinite article **an**, is still encountered, especially among older speakers.

aboriginal / aborigine When referring to indigenous peoples in general, **aboriginal** should be used as the singular and **aboriginals** or **aborigines** as the plural. However, when referring to the aboriginal inhabitants of Australia, **Aborigine** and **Aborigines** (with capitals) are now preferred.

access In more recent years, **access** has taken on a verbal meaning 'to gain access to (data held in a computer)', e.g. *Employees can now access these files directly from their home computers*. By extension, a new meaning has arisen in popular psychology and self-help writing, 'to get in touch with (one's deeper feelings)', e.g. *Men must learn to access their rage*. This sense is not so universally accepted as the computing one. Use of the verb in still more general contexts, such as *The kitchen may be accessed from the dining room*, should be avoided (use 'reach', 'approach', 'enter', etc.)

account In the sense of 'to reckon, consider', **account** is not followed by 'as', e.g. *I did not account him wise.*

activate / actuate Both verbs mean 'to make active' but they are used differently. **Activate** is the normal word in physical or mechanical contexts such as burglar alarms, traffic lights, or flight plans, whereas **actuate** is normally used in the context of human behaviour, where it has the sense 'motivate or incite', e.g. *He was actuated by no unworthy motives*. Note also that actuate is generally restricted to less appealing abstract qualities such as anger, greed, jealousy, malice, etc. However, some older texts use **actuate** in a mechanical sense and there is a growing (mainly American) tendency to use **activate** in the sense 'motivate', e.g. *Are they really activated by concern for public morality?*

actress The term **actor** is now increasingly preferred for performers of both sexes, and the feminine form may even be considered insulting. See -ESS.

AD This is normally printed in small capitals and should be placed before the numerals, as in AD 375 (not 375 AD). The reason for this is that AD is an abbreviation of *anno domini*, which means 'in the year of our Lord'. However, it is normal to write *the*

3rd century AD (not AD *the 3rd century*). The culturally neutral CE (for 'Common Era') is sometimes used in preference to AD. See also BC.

address The verb **address** is often used in business or official writing as a vague synonym for 'consider' or 'tackle', e.g. *We are addressing the problem and will let you have a reply soon*. Although occasional ambiguity may arise from this usage (e.g. *The minister has been addressing the letter in question*), a more general objection is the way in which the verb is often used as a cover for inaction. More precise verbs are usually available and should be used if possible.

advices In the sense of 'instructions' or 'comments', this is still a favourite pomposity among lawyers, e.g. *I await your advices in respect of this matter*. It is better to be precise and use one of the alternatives given above.

advise The verb **advise** has become near-universal in business English for 'inform', 'tell' or 'let me know'; however, to avoid ambiguity it is better to use one of these and keep **advise** for 'give advice to'. This prevents such officialese as *Please be advised that your cheque is in the post* (which, apart from usually being untrue, begins with four redundant words).

affinity This word should always be followed by 'between' or 'with', not 'to' or 'for', e.g. *Ann felt an affinity with them* (Iris Murdoch); *Points of affinity between Stephen and Bloom* (Anthony Burgess).

African American This is the currently accepted term in the US for Americans of African origin, having first become prominent in the late 1980s. The term **Afro-American**, first recorded in the 19th century and popular in the 1960s and 1970s, now has a somewhat dated ring. In Britain, BLACK is the standard term.

aftermath Although this word derives from an agricultural term meaning 'second mowing or crop', it is now used of any after-effects, especially unpleasant ones, e.g. *The aftermath of war*. It is pedantic to object to the sense 'unpleasant consequences' on the ground of derivation.

agenda Although the term **agenda** comes from a Latin plural noun meaning 'things to be done', in modern English it is normally used as a singular noun, e.g. *It's a short agenda this morning*. As such it takes the standard plural form **agendas**. See also DATA/DATUM; MEDIA.

aggravate This word is commonly used in informal contexts to mean 'to annoy or exasperate', rather than 'to make worse or more serious'; this is considered incorrect by traditionalists, on the grounds that it is too radical a departure from the etymological meaning 'to make heavy'. An example of correct formal usage is *The psychological stress aggravates the horse's physical stress*. However, both **aggravate** and the adjective **aggravating** have been used in the looser sense of 'irritate'/'irritating' by many respected writers, e.g. *He had pronounced and aggravating views* (Graham Greene).

ago When **ago** is followed by a clause, the clause should be introduced by 'that' rather than 'since', e.g. *It was sixty years ago that I left this place* (not *It was sixty years ago since I left this place*).

ain't The use of **ain't** was widespread in the 18th century, typically as a contraction for 'am not'. It is still perfectly normal in many dialects and informal speech in both Britain and North America. Today, however, it does not form part of standard English and should never be used in formal or written contexts, except in representations of dialect speech or humorously. See also AREN'T.

alibi The word **alibi**, which in Latin means 'elsewhere', has been used since the 18th century to mean 'the assertion by an accused person that he or she was elsewhere at the time'. In the 20th century a new sense arose (originally in the US) with the meaning 'an excuse or justification', e.g. *Pregnancy is no alibi*. This use may seem a fairly common and natural extension of the core meaning, but is still regarded as incorrect by some traditionalists.

all / all of In British English it is normal to use **all**, rather than **all of**, before nouns to signify 'the whole or every one of something', e.g. *All the king's men*. However, **all of** is usual before pronouns, e.g. *And so say all of us*, and in constructions in which it parallels 'none of', e.g. *Marshall Stone has all of the problems but none of the attributes of a star* (Frederic Raphael). The general use of **all of** before nouns is American only.

all right / alright The merging of **all** and **right** to form the one-word spelling **alright** is not recorded until the end of the 19th century (unlike other similar merged spellings such as 'already', which date from much earlier). There is no logical reason for insisting on **all right** as two words, when other single-word forms such as altogether have long been accepted. Nevertheless, it is still considered by many people to be unacceptable in formal writing. Therefore, **alright** should generally be avoided in writing, even where standard spelling is somewhat cumbersome, e.g. *I wanted to make sure it was all all right*.

allude The words **allude** and **allusion** are not mere synonyms for 'refer' and 'reference'. **Allude** means 'refer indirectly' and an **allusion** is an indirect reference, e.g. *He would allude to her...but never mention her by name* (E. M. Forster).

although / though The form **although** can always be replaced by **though**, the only difference being that **although** tends to be more formal. Some uses of **though** are not interchangeable with **although**, however: e.g. adverbial uses (*It was nice of him to phone, though*) and uses in phrases with 'as' or 'even' (*She doesn't look as though she's listening*).

alumnus / alumna The term **alumnus**, meaning a former student of a particular school or college, is nearly always reserved for males: the term **alumna** specifies a female former student. In the plural **alumni** can be used to refer to students of either sex or both, while **alumnae** refers to females.

America To English speakers outside North America, the term **America** means first and foremost the US, while **North America** is used to denote a larger geographical area including also Canada and Mexico. The terms **American** and **North American** are used correspondingly as adjectives and nouns. **Central America**

refers to the countries in the narrow strip of land to the south of Mexico (including Guatemala, Nicaragua, and Panama), and **South America** to the region to the south of the Panama Canal, including Argentina, Brazil, Chile, etc. **Central America** is often considered part of North America in geographical contexts and part of South America in political or cultural contexts.

American Indian The term **American Indian** has been steadily replaced in the US, especially in official contexts, by the more recent term **Native American** (first recorded in the 1950s and becoming prominent in the 1970s). The latter is preferred by some as being a more accurate and respectful description (the word 'Indian' recalling Columbus' assumption that, on reaching America, he had reached the east coast of India), as well as avoiding the stereotype of cowboys and Indians in the stories of the Wild West. However, while the terms **Indian** and **Red Indian** are now regarded as old-fashioned and inappropriate, **American Indian** is still widespread in general use even in the US and is not normally regarded as offensive by American Indians themselves. Nevertheless, since the category **American Indian** is very broad, it is preferable, where possible, to name the specific people, as Apache, Comanche, or Sioux, etc.

an See A/AN.

analogous This word, which means 'similar in certain respects', should not be used as a mere synonym for 'similar'.

and **1** It is still widely taught and believed that conjunctions such as **and**, **but**, and **because** should not be used to start a sentence, the argument being that such a sentence expresses an incomplete thought and is therefore incorrect. However, writers down the centuries from Shakespeare to David Lodge have readily ignored this advice, usually for rhetorical effect, e.g. *What are the government's chances of winning in court? And what are the consequences?*; *I would do so readily if I was a millionaire. But I am not a millionaire.*

2 A small number of verbs, notably **try**, **come**, and **go** can be followed by **and** with another verb, e.g. *We're going to try and ex-*plain *it to them* or *Why don't you come and see the film?* The structures in these verbs correspond to the use of the 'to'-infinitive, as in *We're going to try to explain it to them* or *Why don't you come to see the film?* This use is normally only idiomatic with the infinitive of the verb and not with other forms (i.e. it is not possible to say *I tried and explained it to them*) and is regarded as wrong by some traditionalists. However, these uses are extremely common in just about every context and can certainly be regarded as part of standard English.

animal companion See COMPANION ANIMAL.

anticipate Anticipate in the sense 'to expect, foresee' is well-established in informal use (e.g. *He anticipated a restless night*), but is regarded as incorrect by some people. For this reason it is better to use **expect** in formal contexts. In any case, **anticipate** cannot be followed, as **expect** can, by the infinitive (*I expect to see him* or *him to come*) or a personal object (*I expect him today*) and cannot mean 'expect as one's due' (*I expect good behaviour from pupils*). The formal sense of **anticipate**, 'to take some action to forestall, or benefit from, a future event' is illustrated in such sentences as *She had anticipated execution by suicide* (Robert Graves).

antithetical This word means 'contrasted, opposite', not merely 'different' or 'opposed'. *His behaviour is antithetical to all his declared principles* is correct formal usage: *We are strongly antithetical to such behaviour* is not.

any When used as a pronoun **any** can be used with either a singular or a plural verb, depending on the context: e.g. *We needed more sugar but there wasn't any left* (singular verb) or *Are any of the new videos available?* (plural verb).

anyone / any one See ONE (3).

approve When followed by a direct object **approve** has the sense 'authorize', e.g. *The naval plan was approved by the war council* (A. J. P. Taylor). However, when followed by 'of' it has the sense 'consider good', e.g. *All the books approved of by young persons of cultivated taste* (C. P. Snow). These two senses should be kept distinct. In particular,

approve should not be used in the second sense with a direct object, as in *Laziness, rudeness, and untidiness are not approved in this establishment* (correctly *approved of*).

apropos Although this word appears frequently in business and official English, it is clearer and less pompous to write 'about', 'concerning' or 'with reference to'.

apt See LIABLE/APT.

Arab / Arabian **Arab** is now the usual term for a native of Arabia or an Arabic-speaking country. **Arabian** is generally used as an adjective, especially in geographical contexts (e.g. *Arabian peninsula*; *Arabian camel*). The language is **Arabic** (as are the numerals and the gum).

aren't As well as being the standard contraction of 'are not', **aren't** is a recognized colloquialism for 'am not' in e.g. *Aren't I clever?* The strictly 'correct' form *Am I not clever?* can sound stilted, even in formal contexts. See also AIN'T.

Argentine / Argentinian Both words can be used either as a noun (i.e. a native of Argentina) or as an adjective (i.e. belonging to Argentina). However, only the former is used in the phrase *the Argentine Republic*.

around See ROUND/AROUND.

as In the sense 'that, which, or who' **as** is now non-standard and should be avoided in writing except when representing regional speech, e.g. *I know somebody who knows this kid as went blind* (Alan Sillitoe).

as and when This never seems to mean anything more than 'when' or 'if' and often serves to blur the distinction between the two, e.g. *As and when the go-ahead is given, the project will involve the construction of a new underground station.* Use 'when' or 'if' as appropriate. See also UNLESS AND UNTIL.

as at / as from / as of These phrases are frequently used in business and official writing to introduce dates. **As at** means simply 'on', e.g. *The value of your shares as at 5 April was £924.* Normally it is clearer and simpler to write 'on'. **As from** is used in formal dating to mean 'on and after (a date)', e.g. *as from 15 October.* **As of**, originally American only but now quite widespread in Britain, has the same meaning and use. The phrases *as of now*, *as of tomorrow*, and the like, are informal only.

Asian / Asiatic In Britain, **Asian** is used to refer to people who come from (or whose forebears came from) the Indian subcontinent, while in North America it is used to refer to people from the Far East. In either case, when referring to individual people **Asian** should be used rather than **Asiatic**, which is now widely considered offensive. However, **Asiatic** remains standard in scientific and technical use, for example in biological and anthropological classifications. See also EURASIAN.

aside from In American usage **aside from** means 'apart from, except for'. It remains non-standard in British English.

as if, as though Both phrases should be followed by a verb in the past tense when the sentence refers to an unreal possibility, e.g. *It's not as though he lived like a Milord* (Evelyn Waugh). They should be followed by the present tense when the statement is true, or might be true, e.g. *I suppose you get on pretty well with your parents. You look as though you do* (Kingsley Amis).

as per This is often used in official or business writing to mean 'in accordance with', e.g. *I enclose the form as per our conversation.* It is better to avoid mixing English and Latin in the same phrase, so prefer *I enclose the form as discussed* or some other construction. The phrase *as per usual* is strictly informal only. See also PER.

attention Although commonly used, the phrase *Someone called it to my attention* represents an illogical reversal of the idiom; *Someone called* (or *drew*) *my attention to it* or *Someone brought it to my attention* would be better in formal contexts.

at the end of the day This is a waffling way of saying 'ultimately', 'eventually' or 'in the end', any of which should be preferred. The only thing that can truly be said to occur at the end of the day is nightfall.

Australoid The word **Australoid** belongs to a set of terms introduced by 19th-century anthropologists attempting to categorize human races. Such terms are associated with outdated notions of racial types, and so are now potentially offensive and best avoided. See also CAUCASIAN; MONGOLOID.

author Some traditionalists dislike the use of **author** as a verb to mean 'be the author of', arguing that it is simpler and clearer to say 'write'. However, this usage is now well established, especially in North America, and has been around since the end of the 16th century. **Co-author** is widely accepted as a verb in both British and American English.

avail yourself This archaic-sounding expression is common in official writing, e.g. *If you fail to avail yourself of the facilities above, your electricity supply could be disconnected.* Prefer *If you do not use* (or *take up* or *make use of*) *one of the repayment methods shown above…*

avenge / revenge In most contexts these verbs are interchangeable. One may **avenge** (or **revenge**) oneself 'on' an offender and **avenge** (or **revenge**) a wrong 'on' the perpetrator. Note, however, that one may **avenge** (but not **revenge**) an injured person other than oneself. **Avenge** also carries a stronger sense of justifiable retribution, as distinct from mere retaliation.

averse Traditionally, and according to Dr Johnson, **averse from** is preferred to **averse to**. The latter is condemned on etymological grounds (the Latin root translates as 'turn from'). However, **averse to** is entirely consistent with ordinary usage in modern English (on the analogy of 'hostile to', 'disinclined to', etc.) and is part of normal standard English.

aware **Aware** is normally followed by a phrase beginning with 'of' or 'that', e.g. *She was acutely aware of technical questions.* However, it can also be linked with an adverb in the sense 'aware of, appreciative of (the subject indicated)', e.g. *She was very technically aware.* This usage is chiefly American but is increasingly common in British English. In popular usage **aware** is sometimes used alone in the sense 'well-informed', e.g. *a very aware person.* This use should be avoided in formal contexts.

B

bacillus Bacteria belonging to the genus *Bacillus* are called **bacilli** (singular **bacillus**). However, the terms **bacillus** and **bacilli** are also correctly applied to certain rod-shaped bacteria that do not belong to the genus *Bacillus*.

backward / backwards In most adverbial uses **backward** and **backwards** are interchangeable: *The car rolled slowly backward* and *The car rolled slowly backwards* are both equally acceptable. In American English **backward** tends to be preferred to **backwards**, while in British English it is the other way round. As an adjective, on the other hand, the standard form is **backward** rather than **backwards**: uses such as *a backwards glance* (as opposed to *a backward glance*) are unusual, though not incorrect. The same remarks apply to **forward/forwards**, **inward/inwards**, **outward/outwards**, etc.

bacteria / bacterium **Bacteria** is the plural form (derived from Latin) of **bacterium**, and not a singular noun. Like any other plural it should be used with the plural form of the verb: *The bacteria causing salmonella are killed by thorough cooking,* not *The bacteria…is killed by thorough cooking.* However, the unfamiliarity of the form means that **bacteria** is sometimes mistakenly treated as a singular form.

Bantu The word **Bantu** became a strongly offensive term under the old apartheid regime in South Africa, especially when used to refer to a single individual of African descent. In standard current use in South Africa the words BLACK or 'African' are used as collective or non-specific terms for African peoples. Outside South Africa, **Bantu** continues to be accepted as a neutral 'scientific' term for the group of languages and their speakers collectively. See also KAFFIR.

bastard In the past, the word **bastard** was the standard term in both legal and non-legal use for 'an illegitimate child'. However, it now has little importance as a legal term and features in general usage only as a term of abuse.

bc This is normally printed in small capitals and should be placed after the numerals, as in 55 BC. When a range of dates is given, the second date should be put in full, as in 55–53 BC (since 55–3 BC has another meaning). The culturally neutral BCE ('before Common

Era') is sometimes used in preference. See also AD.

because **1** For advice about beginning a sentence with **because** and other conjunctions, see AND (1).

2 For advice on the construction **the reason…is because**, see REASON (2).

beg the question The original meaning of this phrase belongs to the field of logic. Beg the question is a translation of Latin *petitio principii*, literally 'laying claim to a principle', i.e. assuming the truth of something that ought to be proved first. The phrase is used in this original sense in the following sentence: *By devoting such a large part of the budget for the fight against drug addiction to education, we are begging the question of its significance in the battle against drugs.* To some traditionalists this is still the only correct meaning. However, over the last 100 years or so another, more general use has arisen: 'to invite an obvious question', as in *Some definitions of mental illness beg the question of what constitutes normal behaviour.* This is by far the commonest use today and is widely accepted in modern standard English. More loosely still, the phrase is sometimes used to mean 'to avoid giving a straight answer'; this is incorrect and should be avoided.

behalf / part *On behalf of Smith*, meaning 'in Smith's interest', or 'as Smith's representative' should not be confused with *on the part of Smith*, meaning 'done by Smith'; **behalf** cannot replace **part** in *His death was due to panic on his part.*

beside / besides It is sometimes said that **beside** should not be used to mean 'apart from, in addition to' and that **besides** should be used instead, e.g. one should write *He commissioned work from other artists besides Minton*, rather than *from other artists beside Minton.* According to this view, **beside** should be used only of spatial relationships, or in figurative adaptations of these, e.g. *beside oneself with joy; quite beside the point.* Although there is little logical basis for such a view, it is worth being aware of the potential ambiguity in the use of **beside**: *Beside the cold meat, there are platters of trout and salmon* could mean either 'the cold meat is next to the trout and salmon' or 'apart from

the cold meat, there are also trout and salmon'.

better In the construction '(one) had better do (something)' the word 'had' acts like an auxiliary verb and in informal spoken contexts it is often dropped, as in *You better not come tonight.* In writing, the 'had' may be contracted (*You'd better not come*) but it should not be dropped altogether.

between **1** There is no objection to the use of **between** to express relations, actions, etc. involving more than two parties; 'among' should not be substituted in, e.g., *Cordial relations between Britain, Greece, and Turkey.*

2 See also CHOOSE BETWEEN, CHOICE BETWEEN.

billion In traditional British usage a **billion** is a million million (1,000,000,000,000 = 10^{12}), a **trillion** is a million³ (10^{18}), and a **quadrillion** is a million⁴ (10^{24}). However, American usage makes each step up from 'million' a power of 1,000; i.e. million = 1000^2, **billion** = 1000^3, **trillion** = 1000^4, **quadrillion** = 1000^5. For the quantity 'thousand million' ($1000^3 = 10^9$), many British people now use the American **billion** and most British national newspapers have officially adopted it too. To avoid any possible confusion it is probably safest to use 'thousand million' or 'million million' (or numerals); however, where the sense is vague, e.g. *a billion miles away, billions of stars,* the exact value is immaterial.

bimonthly The word **bimonthly** (and other similar words such as **biweekly** and **biyearly**) is ambiguous, as it can mean both 'every two months' and 'twice a month'. The only way to avoid this ambiguity is to use alternative expressions such as 'fortnightly', 'every six months', etc. In the publishing world, the meaning of **bimonthly** is more fixed and is invariably used to mean 'every two months'.

black Evidence for the use of **black** to refer to African peoples (and their descendants) dates back at least to the late 14th century. Although the word has been in continuous use ever since, other terms have enjoyed prominence too: in the US COLOURED was the term adopted in preference by emancipated slaves following the American Civil War, and this was itself superseded in the

US in the early 20th century by NEGRO as the term preferred by prominent black American campaigners such as Booker T. Washington. With the civil rights and Black Power movements of the 1960s, **black** was adopted by Americans of African origin to signify a sense of racial pride; it has now (since the 1980s) been largely superseded by AFRICAN AMERICAN. **Black** remains the most widely used and generally accepted term in Britain today.

blonde / blond The alternative spellings **blonde** and **blond** correspond to the feminine and masculine forms in French, but in English the distinction is not always made, as English does not have such distinctions of grammatical gender. Thus, *a blond woman* or *a blonde woman*; *a blond man* or *a blonde man* are all used. The word is undoubtedly more commonly used of women, though, and in the noun the spelling is invariably **blonde**.

bored The normal constructions for **bored** are 'bored by' or 'bored with'. More recently, 'bored of' has emerged (probably by analogy with 'tired of'), but this construction is not yet considered acceptable in standard English.

borrow See LEND (1).

Britain / Great Britain / British Isles / England Use of these terms often causes confusion. Geographically, **Great Britain** refers to the large island consisting of mainland England, Scotland, and Wales. Politically, it means these three countries (since the Act of Union of 1707); it therefore includes small islands governed from the mainland but excludes Northern Ireland, the Isle of Man, and the Channel Islands. **Britain** is an informal term with no official status; it often means the same as **Great Britain** but can also include Northern Ireland. The **British Isles** is a geographical term for the group of islands comprising Great Britain, Ireland, and the smaller islands around them, whatever their political status. The term is disliked by some Irish people but there is no accepted alternative. The **United Kingdom** is a political term, in full 'the United Kingdom of Great Britain and Northern Ireland', and includes these

territories but not the Isle of Man or the Channel Islands.

England strictly refers to a single political division of Great Britain, but is commonly substituted for **Britain**, especially in American English. This causes much offence in Scotland and Wales, and should be avoided in British English. The same is true of the corresponding ethnic designation **English** used instead of **British**.

broker The term **broker** was officially replaced on the London Stock Exchange by **broker-dealer** in 1986, **broker-dealers** being entitled to act both as agents and principals in share dealings.

but For advice about beginning a sentence with **but** and other conjunctions, see AND (1).

C

can / may Careful writers take particular care with **can** and **may**. The first means 'is able to' as in *Helen can take solid food now that her jaw is mended*. The second means 'is permitted to', as in *Helen may take solid food because the doctor says it's safe to do so*. In spoken or informal English this distinction is often ignored and **can** is used for expressions denoting permission: *Can I ask you a few questions?* Although this use of **can** is not regarded as incorrect, **may** is a more polite way of asking for something and is the better choice in more formal contexts. See also MAY/MIGHT.

candelabra / candelabrum Going by the original Latin forms, the correct singular is **candelabrum** and the correct plural is **candelabra**. However, these forms are often not observed in practice: the singular form is assumed to be **candelabra** and hence its plural is interpreted as **candelabras**.

cannot Both the one-word form **cannot** and the two-word form **can not** are acceptable, but **cannot** is far more common in all contexts.

Caucasian In the racial classification developed by Blumenbach and others in the 19th century, the category **Caucasian** or **Caucasoid** included peoples whose skin colour ranged from light (in northern

Europe) to dark (in parts of North Africa and India). Although the classification is outdated and the categories are not now accepted as scientific, the term **Caucasian** has acquired a more restricted meaning. It is now used, especially in the US, as a synonym for 'white or of European origin', e.g. *The police are looking for a Caucasian male in his forties.* See also AUSTRALOID; MONGOLOID.

Celsius / centigrade Celsius rather than centigrade is the standard accepted term when giving temperatures: use *25° Celsius* rather than *25° centigrade*.

centre about, centre around The construction **centre about** or **around**, meaning (figuratively) 'to revolve around, have as its main centre', has been denounced as incorrect since it first appeared in the mid 19th century. The argument is that it is illogical, since 'centre' designates a fixed point and the prepositions 'about' and 'around' are not used to refer to fixed points. The use is very well established, however, and, given the extension of the sense away from geometrical exactitude, it is difficult to sustain the argument that it is incorrect. It can be avoided by using **centre in** or **on**.

century **1** Strictly speaking, centuries run from the year 01 to the year 100 inclusive, meaning that the new century begins on the first day of the year 01 (i.e. 1 January 2001). In practice and in popular perception, however, the new century (and the new **millennium**) began when the significant digits in the date changed, i.e. on 1 January 2000, when 1999 became 2000. Beware of ambiguity here.

2 Since the 1st century ran from the year 1 to the year 100, the number (i.e. second, third, fourth, etc.) used to denote the century will always be one digit higher than the corresponding cardinal digit(s). Thus, 1066 is a date in the 11th century, 1542 is a date in the 16th century, and so on.

chairman / chairperson / chair See -MAN.

challenged The use of **challenged** with a preceding adverb (e.g. *physically challenged*), originally intended to give a more positive tone than terms such as DISABLED or HANDICAPPED, arose in the US in the 1980s and

quickly spread to Britain and elsewhere. Despite the originally serious intention, the term was rapidly subverted by uses designed to make fun of the attempts at euphemism and whose tone was usually clearly ironic: examples include *cerebrally challenged*, *conversationally challenged*, and *follicularly challenged* (i.e. bald). The term should therefore be used with caution.

character To avoid verbosity, it is better to use an abstract noun rather than a construction using **character** with an adjective, e.g. write *the antiquity of the fabric*, not *the ancient character of the fabric*. See also NATURE.

charisma This was originally a theological term (plural **charismata**) designating any of the gifts of the Holy Spirit. In general use, it now means the capacity to inspire followers with devotion and enthusiasm.

Chinese / Chinaman Chinese is the standard word, both as a noun (with plural the same) and an adjective, for people and things relating to China. **Chinaman** has developed unfavourable overtones and is no longer in ordinary use.

choose between, choice between These constructions are normally followed by 'and' in written English but sometimes by 'or'. The following sentence uses both conjunctions: *The poorest girl alive may not be able to choose between being Queen of England or Principal of Newnham; but she can choose between ragpicking and flowerselling* (G. B. Shaw).

Christian name In recognition of the fact that modern English-speaking societies have many religions and cultures, not just Christian ones, the term **Christian name** has largely given way, at least in official contexts, to alternative terms such as **given name**, **first name**, or **forename**.

chronic The correct meaning of this word is 'persisting for a long time': it is used most specifically of medical conditions that are long-lasting, though perhaps intermittent (the opposite is 'acute'), and by extension of other similar conditions, e.g. *The commodities of which there is a chronic shortage* (George Orwell). However, the word is now sometimes used to mean 'habitual, inveterate', e.g. *a chronic liar*, or 'very bad', e.g. *The film was chronic*. The former use is considered to be incorrect by some people and the latter is, at best, extremely informal.

classic / classical Classical is the customary word when reference is to the arts and literature of ancient Greece and Rome, e.g. *a classical scholar*; *classical civilization*. In general use, it also denotes serious 'art' music in the Western tradition, i.e. that of Bach, Mozart, Beethoven, Wagner, Mahler, etc., although musical historians use the word more strictly to refer to the music of the 18th century after the Baroque period and before the onset of Romanticism. More recently **classical** has come to be widely used in marketing circles to denote anything of traditional design, e.g. *a classical desk lamp*.

In correct use **classic** means either 'of acknowledged excellence' (e.g. *the classic textbook on the subject*) or 'remarkably typical' (e.g. *a classic case of cerebral palsy*). In much general use, however, it has come to mean little more than 'significant, noteworthy', e.g. *classic stupidity*; *a classic 1970s porn movie*.

cleft lip Cleft lip is the standard accepted term and should be used instead of **harelip**, which can cause offence.

co-author See AUTHOR.

cohort The earliest sense of **cohort** was 'a unit of men within the Roman army (one tenth of a legion)'. Over the centuries the sense of the word was naturally extended to mean 'a band of warriors' or 'any group of persons banded together in common cause'. However, in the mid 20th century a further sense developed in the US, meaning 'a companion or colleague', as in *Young Jack arrived with three of his cohorts*. Although this use is well established, there are still many people who object to it on the grounds that **cohort** should only be used for groups of people, never for individuals. For this reason it is best avoided.

coloured In South Africa, Coloured (with a capital 'C') denotes a person of mixed descent, and in the plural denotes a racial group as officially defined under the former apartheid laws. The use of **coloured** (no capital) by white people in Britain to mean 'non-white' is now considered old-fashioned and rather offensive, but is still heard among older speakers: use BLACK or ASIAN or more precise terms such as Afro-Caribbean, Bengali, etc.. The term PERSON OF COLOUR is, however, considered entirely politically correct.

come and See AND (2).

companion animal Companion animal is a somewhat more formal term for 'pet' and is generally restricted to larger animals such as dogs and cats. In the US the term **animal companion** has gained some currency as a politically correct alternative to 'pet', which is disliked by supporters of animal rights.

compare with / compare to Is there any difference between **compare with** and **compare to**, and is one more correct than the other? There is a slight difference, in that it is usual to use 'to' rather than 'with' when asserting the resemblance of two different things, as in *To call a bishop a mitred fool and compare him to a mouse* (G. B. Shaw). Similarly, in the sense 'estimate the similarity or dissimilarity between', it is traditionally held that 'with' is more correct than 'to', as in *You've got to compare method with method, and ideal with ideal* (John le Carré). However, in practice the distinction is not clear-cut and both **compare with** and **compare to** can be used in either context without error.

The same general rule (and the same looseness in practice) applies to the use of **comparable to/with** and **in comparison with/to**. Note that in each case the first alternative is the more common: *Coleridge's productivity is certainly not comparable to Wordsworth's*, but *In comparison with Wordsworth, Coleridge was by no means prolific*.

complete For advice on the use of **complete** with words such as 'very' and 'more', see UNIQUE.

compose / comprise In the active voice, **compose** means 'constitute, make up' with the constituents as subject and the whole as object, e.g. *The tribes which composed the German nation*. In the passive, the whole is subject and the constituents object, e.g. *The German nation was composed of tribes*. The proper constructions with **comprise** are the converse of those used with **compose**. In the active, **comprise** means 'consist of', with the whole as subject and the constituents as object, e.g. *The faculty comprises* *the following six departments.* In the passive, **comprise** means 'be embraced in', with the constituents as subject and the whole as object, e.g. *Fifty American dollars comprised in a single note* (Graham Greene).

Confusion has arisen because when **comprise** is used in the active voice (as in *The country comprises twenty states*) it is more or less synonymous with the passive use of **compose** (as in *The country is composed of twenty states*). As a result, such constructions as *The six departments that comprise the faculty* or *The faculty is comprised of six departments* have become extremely common, although they are not correct according to traditional usage. One simple rule to remember is that **comprise** is never followed by 'of'; particular care should be taken to avoid the active form of this error, e.g. *The property comprises of bedroom, bathroom, and kitchen*, in which the mistake is particularly glaring. See also INCLUDE.

compound The use of the verb **compound** to mean 'make (something bad) worse', as in *This compounds their problems*, has an interesting history. It arose through a misinterpretation of the legal phrase *compound a felony*, which, strictly speaking, means 'forbear from prosecuting a felony in exchange for money or other consideration'. The 'incorrect' sense has become the usual one in legal contexts and, by extension, in general senses too, and is now accepted as part of standard English.

condole Condole, meaning 'to express sympathy', is always followed by 'with', e.g. *Many...had come...to condole with them about their brother* (Revised English Bible).

conduce Conduce, meaning 'to lead or contribute (to a result)', is always followed by 'to', as is the adjective **conducive**: e.g. *The enterprise... conduced to cut-price jobs* (J. I. M. Stewart).

conform Conform may be followed by 'to' or 'with', e.g. *The United Nations...conformed to Anglo-American plans* (A. J. P. Taylor); *Having himself no...tastes he relied upon whatever conformed with those of his companion* (John le Carré).

connote / denote Connote does not mean the same as **denote**. Whereas **denote** refers to the literal, primary meaning of

something, **connote** refers to other characteristics suggested or implied by that thing. Thus, one might say that the word 'mother' **denotes** 'a woman who is a parent' but **connotes** qualities such as protection and affection. Although the two terms are kept rigidly distinct in logic, in popular usage **connote** frequently verges on the sense of **denote**. Denote, however, should never be used in the senses of **connote**.

consensus Because **consensus** means 'general agreement', the phrase *consensus of opinion* is tautologous and *general consensus of opinion* is doubly so. **Consensus** covers it, in a word.

consist There is a distinction in usage between **consist of**, meaning 'be made up of', and **consist in**, meaning 'have as its essence'. An example of the latter sense is *All enjoyment consists in undetected sinning* (G. B. Shaw).

contagious / infectious In practice, there is little or no difference in meaning between **contagious** and **infectious** when applied to disease: both mean, roughly, 'communicable'. There is, however, a difference in emphasis or focus between the two words. **Contagious** tends to be focused on the person or animal affected by the disease (e.g. *Precautions are taken with anyone who seems contagious*), while **infectious** emphasizes the agent or organism which carries the disease (e.g. *The infectious agent thought to be responsible for BSE in cattle*).

continuance / continuation There is a subtle distinction in usage here based on two senses of the verb 'to continue'. While **continuance** relates mainly to the sense 'to be still in existence', **continuation** relates mainly to the sense 'to resume', e.g. *The great question of our continuance after death* (J. S. Huxley); *As if contemplating a continuation of her assault* (William Trevor).

continuous / continual There is some overlap in meaning between **continuous** and **continual**, but the two words are not wholly synonymous. Both can mean roughly 'without interruption' (*a long and continual war; five years of continuous warfare*), but **continuous** is much more prominent in this sense and, unlike **continual**, can be used to refer to space as well as time, as in *There is continuous development along the coast*. **Continual**, on the other hand, typically means 'happening frequently, with intervals between', as in *The bus service has been disrupted by continual breakdowns*. Overall, **continuous** occurs much more frequently than **continual** and is found in many technical and specialist uses ranging from grammar and education to mathematics.

convince / persuade Convince used (with an infinitive) as a synonym for **persuade** first became common in the 1950s in the US, as in *She convinced my father to branch out on his own*. Some traditionalists deplore the blurring of distinction between **convince** and **persuade**, maintaining that **convince** should be reserved for situations in which someone's belief is changed but no action is taken as a result (*He convinced me that he was right*) while **persuade** should be used for situations in which action results (*He persuaded me to seek more advice*). In practice the newer use is well established and used by well-respected writers.

cousin The children of brothers or sisters are **first cousins** to each other; the children of first cousins are **second cousins** to each other; and so on. The child of one's first cousin, or the first cousin of one's parent, is one's **first cousin once removed**; the grandchild of one's first cousin, or the first cousin of one's grandparent, is one's **first cousin twice removed**; and so on.

crescendo In music, a **crescendo** is a gradual increase in loudness; hence, used figuratively, the word means 'a progressive increase in force or effect'. Do not use it for 'climax', e.g. in *The storm reached a crescendo* (correctly *a climax*) *at midnight*.

cripple The word **cripple** has long been in use to refer to 'a person unable to walk through illness or disability' and is recorded (in the *Lindisfarne Gospels*) as early as AD 950. In the 20th century the term has acquired offensive connotations and has now been largely replaced by broader terms such as 'DISABLED person'.

criteria / criterion Strictly speaking, the singular form (following the original Greek) is **criterion** and the plural form is **criteria**. It is a common mistake, however, to use **criteria** as if it were a singular, as in *A further criteria needs to be considered*.

crucial Crucial is used in formal contexts to mean 'decisive, critical', e.g. *The first five years of a child's life are crucial*. Its use to mean 'very important', as in *It is crucial not to forget your passport*, should be restricted to informal contexts.

D

data / datum In general, the singular form is **datum**, not **data**, as shown by the following examples: *The object under scrutiny is compared with an observed or preconceived datum* (singular); *The data support a trend that has so far been supported only by anecdotal evidence* (plural). However, in computing and related fields, **data** is now often used as if it were a singular collective noun (like 'information'), e.g. *You can guarantee that the data is accurate*. This use is acceptable. In other contexts, **data** should be used (like 'facts') with a plural verb, e.g. *These data do lend some support to the prevailing public opinion*. **Data** cannot be preceded by 'a', 'every', 'each', 'either', or 'neither', and cannot be given a plural form 'datas'. See also AGENDA; MEDIA.

day and age, this The phrase slid into the language in the 1940s and is now a much ridiculed cliché. It should be avoided in favour of more straightforward terms such as 'nowadays' or 'at the present time'.

de- See RE-.

deaf mute In modern use **deaf mute** has acquired offensive connotations (implying, wrongly, that such people are without the capacity for communication). It should be avoided in favour of other terms such as 'profoundly deaf'.

deceptively Deceptively belongs to a very small set of words whose meaning is genuinely ambiguous in that it can be used in similar contexts to mean both one thing and also its complete opposite. A *deceptively smooth surface* is one which appears smooth but in fact is not smooth at all, while a *deceptively spacious room* is one that does not look spacious but is in fact more spacious than it appears. But what is a *deceptively steep* *gradient*? Or a person who is described as *deceptively strong*? To avoid confusion, it is probably best to reword and not to use **deceptively** in such contexts at all.

decimate The usual sense of this word is now 'to destroy a large proportion of'. This use is considered inappropriate by some people because the original and literal sense is 'to kill or remove one in ten of' (as practised by victorious Roman armies). In any case, this word should not be used to mean 'to defeat utterly'.

delusion / illusion A general distinction can be drawn between these two words, although it is not absolute. **Delusion** denotes a false belief held tenaciously, arising mainly from the internal workings of the mind; e.g. *He's been sent here for delusions. His most serious delusion is that he's a murderer* (Robert Graves). **Illusion** denotes a false impression derived either from the external world, e.g. *an optical illusion*, or from faulty thinking, e.g. *I still imagine I could live in Rome, but it may be an illusion* (Iris Murdoch). It is in this second sense that **illusion** is almost equivalent to **delusion**. Note, however, that **delusion** carries the sense of 'being deluded (by oneself or another)', whereas no verb is implied in **illusion**; on the other hand, one can be said to be 'disillusioned', whereas **delusion** forms no such derivative.

demean When used with an adverbial expression, the verb **demean** has the sense 'to behave (in a certain manner)', e.g. *He demeaned himself well*. Occasionally this sense of **demean**, which relates to the noun 'demeanour', is used without an adverb, as in *She had no idea how to demean herself*. However, to **demean** someone or something can also mean 'to degrade it, lower it in status', e.g. *Nor must you think that you demean yourself by treading the boards* (W. Somerset Maugham). Both constructions are particularly common with 'oneself'.

denote See CONNOTE/DENOTE.

depend In the sense of 'to be controlled or determined by (a condition or cause)' **depend** is followed by 'on' or 'upon', e.g. *It all depends on how you look at it*. In spoken English and informal use it is quite common for the 'on' to be dropped in sentences, e.g. *It all depends how you look at it*; nevertheless, in well-formed written English the 'on' should always be retained.

deprecate / depreciate Deprecate means 'to express disapproval of, to deplore', e.g. *Many older people deprecated the film's attitude to drugs and sex*. **Depreciate** means either (without an object) 'to become lower in value or price', e.g. *Older cars can depreciate very rapidly*, or (with an object) 'to disparage or belittle', e.g. *Virginia was always too ready to depreciate her achievements*. In this second sense, **deprecate** is often used in place of **depreciate**, despite being regarded as incorrect by traditionalists. This occurs especially with the adjectives **self-deprecating** and **self-deprecatory** and the noun **self-deprecation**, where the meanings are closer to **depreciate** than **deprecate**, e.g. *His air of humorous self-deprecation masked a deeper arrogance*. These forms and uses are now fully established. As a result **depreciate** is being more and more confined to its financial meaning in relation to currencies, share values, etc.

dice / die Historically, **dice** is the plural of **die**, but in modern standard English **dice** is both the singular and the plural: *throw the dice* could mean a reference to either one or more than one dice. In general usage the old singular, **die**, is found only in such idioms as *the die is cast*, and *straight* (or *true*) *as a die*. However, it also has several specialist uses: a **die** can mean 'a device for stamping, cutting, or moulding', in which case the correct plural is **dies**, or (in architecture) 'the cubical part of a pedestal between the base and the cornice', in which case the plural is **dice**.

dichotomy In non-technical use, **dichotomy** means 'differentiation into two contrasting categories' and is frequently followed by 'between', e.g. *An absolute dichotomy between science on the one hand and faith on the other*. It is not a synonym for 'difference', 'ambivalence', or DILEMMA.

different Different from, different than, and different to: are there any distinctions between these three collocations, and is one more correct than the others? Despite the preference for **different from** among traditionalists, it is difficult to sustain the view that one is more correct than the others in modern standard English. There is little difference in sense between the three, and all of them are used by respected writers.

Different from is the most favoured by good writers, and is acceptable in all contexts, e.g. *It is also an 'important' book, in a sense different from the sense in which that word is generally used* (George Orwell). **Different to** is common informally. It sometimes sounds more natural than **different from**, e.g. when yoked with a phrase involving 'similar to': *His looks are neither especially similar nor markedly different to those of his twin brother.* **Different than** is established in American English, but is not uncommon in British use, e.g. *Both came from a different world than the housing estate outside London* (Doris Lessing). Although sometimes considered incorrect by conservative British critics, **different than** usefully avoids the repetition and the relative construction required after **different from** in sentences like *I was a very different man in 1935 from what I was in 1916* (Joyce Cary). This could be recast as *I was a very different man in 1935 than I was in 1916* or simply...*than in 1916*. Similarly, *The American theatre, which is suffering from a different malaise than ours*, is greatly preferable to...*suffering from a different malaise from that which ours is suffering from.*

Different to and **different than** are especially common when **different** is part of an adverbial clause or when the adverb 'differently' is used, e.g. *Puts one in a different position to your own father* (John Osborne); *Things were constructed very differently now than in former times* (Trollope).

differential This is a technical term in mathematics, an abbreviation for 'differential gear', or a difference in wage between groups of workers. It is not a synonym for 'difference'.

differently abled Differently abled was first proposed (in the 1980s) as an alternative to DISABLED, HANDICAPPED, etc. on the grounds that it gave a more positive message and so avoided discrimination towards people with disabilities. Despite this, the term has gained little currency and has been criticized as both over-euphemistic and condescending. The accepted term in

general use is still **disabled**. See also CHALLENGED.

dilemma Strictly speaking, a **dilemma** is a choice between two (or more) undesirable alternatives, e.g. *The dilemma of cutting public services or increasing taxes* (The Times). However, the looser use of the term to mean any perplexing situation involving choice, e.g. *The dilemma of the 1960s about whether nice girls should sleep with men* (Alan Watkins), is now standard. The use of **dilemma** as a mere synonym for 'problem' is still generally regarded as incorrect and should be avoided in written English.

direct / directly The adverb **directly** is used in most of the main senses of the adjective **direct**, e.g. *She spoke to me very directly*; *The wind is blowing directly on shore*; *He lived directly opposite*, etc. However, **directly** is not generally used to mean 'straight', since it can also mean 'without delay', e.g. *Just a night in London – I'll be back directly* (Iris Murdoch). In such cases **direct** is normally used as the adverb: *I travelled direct to London.* Note also that in the sense 'without intermediaries' either **direct** or **directly** can be used correctly, e.g. *Why don't you deal directly with the wholesalers?* (G. B. Shaw); *I appeal now, over your head...direct to the august oracle* (G. B. Shaw).

disabled The word **disabled** came to be used as the standard term in referring to people with physical or mental disabilities in the second half of the 20th century, and it remains the most generally accepted term in both British and American English today. It superseded outmoded, now sometimes offensive, terms such as CRIPPLED, and HANDICAPPED and has not been overtaken itself by newer coinages such as DIFFERENTLY ABLED or CHALLENGED.

disinterested / uninterested Nowhere are the battle lines more deeply drawn in usage questions than over the difference between **disinterested** and **uninterested**. According to traditional guidelines, **disinterested** should never be used to mean 'not interested' (for which the proper word is **uninterested**) but only to mean 'impartial', as in *The judgements of disinterested outsiders are likely to be more useful*. However, this distinction has been gradually eroded and is ignored in much current usage. Those who rage against this development should perhaps be aware that both words have changed their principal meaning several times over the centuries. In the present state of the language, the recommendation must be to restrict **disinterested** to the meaning 'impartial' and to use alternative words when necessary to avoid possible misunderstanding.

The use of the noun **disinterest** to mean 'a lack of interest, indifference' is often objected to on the same grounds as the use of **disinterested** to mean 'not interested'. However, **disinterest** is rarely used in any other sense and the alternative 'uninterest' is rare. The noun from **disinterested** meaning 'impartial, unbiased' is **disinterestedness**.

documentation In business and official writing this is often used as a pompous synonym for 'documents', e.g. *We will let you have the documentation in the next ten days.* In nearly every case 'documents' will do.

Down's syndrome Of relatively recent coinage, **Down's syndrome** is the accepted term in modern use for this condition; former terms such as MONGOLISM, which are likely to cause offence, should be avoided.

drunk / drunken In older and literary usage, **drunken** is the form used before a noun (*a drunken sailor*) and **drunk** the form used in predicates (*that sailor is very drunk*). However, in modern English there is a different distinction: **drunk** and **drunken** now usually mean respectively 'intoxicated' and 'fond of drinking', e.g. *They were lazy, irresponsible, and drunken; but today they were not drunk.* **Drunken** also means 'exhibiting drunkenness', e.g. *a drunken brawl.*

due to The use of **due to** in the sense 'owing to, because of' (e.g. *He had to retire due to an injury*) is frequently condemned as incorrect on the grounds that **due** is an adjective, not a preposition, and that as such it must be attached to a noun. An example of traditional usage (in which the adjective **due** is correctly attached to the noun 'diseases') is *Half the diseases of modern civilization are due to starvation of the affections in the young* (G. B. Shaw). However, the prepositional use of **due to**, first recorded at the end of the

19th century, is now common in all types of writing and can be regarded as part of standard English. Writers who wish to avoid it should substitute 'owing to' or 'because of'.

duly If this favourite of business and official writers means anything, it means 'in the correct manner'. For example: *I am pleased to tell you that as a qualifying shareholder, an application for shares duly made by you will receive special treatment. This means that, if you duly apply in the offer...* and so on. Here the company could have avoided repetition by saying on the application form that only correctly completed forms would qualify for the offer. In many other cases, the word could be deleted with no loss of meaning at all.

dumb Although **dumb** meaning 'not able to speak' is the older sense, it has been overwhelmed by the newer sense (meaning 'stupid') to such an extent that the use of the first sense is now almost certain to cause offence. Alternatives such as **speech-impaired** should be used instead. See also MUTE.

dwarf In the sense 'an abnormally small person', **dwarf** (like **midget**) is normally considered offensive. However, there are no accepted alternatives in the general language, since terms such as **person of restricted growth** have gained little currency.

E

east/eastern/easterly As an adjective **east** means 'situated in, near, or facing the east', e.g. *on the east side of town; the castle's east wing.* It is spelt with a capital initial when forming part of a recognized name, e.g. *New York's East Side; East Africa.* The adjective **eastern** can be used with much the same meaning (e.g. *the eastern part of the country*) and in these cases the choice between **east** and **eastern** is chiefly a matter of idiom. However, **eastern** has the further sense 'coming from or typical of the east (of a country, the world, etc.)' In this sense it denotes regional and cultural association rather than physical position and is often spelt with a capital initial (e.g. *Eastern forms of art; Eastern mysticism*). **Easterly** is used chiefly of a wind blowing from the east (e.g.

a bleak easterly wind) and also of movement towards the east or a position achieved by this movement (e.g. *We took an easterly course; the most easterly part of the constellation*).

What is said here applies equally to **north**, **south**, and **west**, and their corresponding forms.

effective / effectual / efficacious / efficient All these words mean 'having an effect', but with different applications and shades of meaning. **Effective** means 'having a definite or desired effect' that is actual rather than theoretical, e.g. *Her attempts to please him were rarely effective; She was an effective speaker*. **Effectual** means 'capable of producing the required result or effect' and is often more theoretical than actual, e.g. *These reforms may or may not be effectual*. A person can be described as **effective** but not as **effectual** (although he or she can be described as **ineffectual**, i.e. 'incapable of producing results'). **Efficacious** likewise applies only to things, and means 'producing or sure to produce the required effect', e.g. *an efficacious remedy*. **Efficient** refers to a person's or thing's capacity to do work and produce results with minimum effort and cost, e.g. *His attempts to do the ironing were enthusiastic but rarely efficient*. In recent use, **efficient** is sometimes preceded by a noun that defines the scope of the efficiency, e.g. *energy efficient; cost efficient*.

egoism / egotism These words have slightly different senses. **Egoism** (adjective **egoistic**) denotes self-interest, e.g. *Egoistic instincts concerned with self-preservation or the good of the Ego* (Gilbert Murray). The word is often contrasted with 'altruism'. The more frequently used **egotism** (adjective **egotistic**) denotes the practice of talking or thinking excessively about oneself, self-centredness, e.g. *He is petty, selfish, vain, egotistical; he is spoilt; he is a tyrant* (Virginia Woolf). The same distinction applies to the use of the nouns **egoist** and **egotist**. In practice, however, the senses tend to overlap, e.g. *Human loves don't last…they are far too egoistic* (Iris Murdoch); *A complete egotist in all his dealings with women* (Joyce Cary).

egregious This word originally had the sense 'outstanding' but is now only used to mean 'outstandingly bad'. However, in formal usage it should still be coupled with a word implying badness, such as 'ass', 'folly', 'waste', etc., e.g. *Wark tenderly forgives her most egregious clerical errors* (Martin Amis). **Egregious** does not mean simply 'offending, errant', as in *a particularly egregious driver*. Nor is the increasingly common use of **egregious** to mean 'notorious' or 'tediously overexposed' (*the egregious Lord Archer*) yet accepted as standard.

either Either can mean 'one or other of the two', e.g. *Simple explanations are for simple minds. I've no use for either* (Joe Orton), or 'each of the two', e.g. *Every few kilometres on either side of the road, there were…guardposts* (Graham Greene). The second sense is always used with reference to a thing that comes naturally in a pair, e.g. 'end', 'hand', 'side'. This use is sometimes ignorantly condemned by people who insist that 'each' should be used in all such cases; however, it is commonly found in good writers of all periods.

elder / eldest The adjective **elder** is used of the earlier-born of two related or indicated persons, e.g. *The first and elder wife…returned…to Jericho* (Muriel Spark); *He is my elder by ten years*. **Eldest** is used of the first-born or oldest surviving member of a family group but is rarely used in other contexts, e.g. *my eldest son* but *the oldest of those present*.

elide The standard meaning of the verb **elide** is 'omit', most frequently used as a term to describe the way that some sounds or syllables are dropped in speech, as for example in contractions such as 'I'll' or 'he's'. The result of such elision is that the two surrounding syllables are merged; this fact has given rise to a new sense of **elide**, with the meaning 'join together; merge', e.g. *The two things elided in his mind*. This new sense is now common in general use.

elusive, illusory Elusive (rather than 'elusory') is the usual adjective to the verb 'elude'; however, **illusory** (rather than 'illusive') is that related to 'illusion'.

emotive / emotional Although the senses of these two words overlap, they are not simply interchangeable. **Emotive** is used to mean 'arousing intense feeling', while **emotional** tends to mean 'characterized by intense feeling'. Thus an *emotive issue* is one that is likely to arouse people's passions, while an *emotional response* is one that is itself full of passion. Note also that **emotive** is not used at all to describe a person as being liable to excessive emotion.

England See BRITAIN/GREAT BRITAIN/BRITISH ISLES/ENGLAND.

enjoin Note that the usual constructions with this verb are 'to enjoin (an action, etc.) on someone', but 'to enjoin (someone) to (do something)', e.g. *To...enjoin celibacy on its...clergy*; *That enables and enjoins the citizen to earn his own living* (G. B. Shaw). In legal writing the construction 'to enjoin (a person) from (doing something)' is also found.

enormity This word is now commonly used to mean 'great size', e.g. *wilting under the enormity of the work*, but this is regarded as incorrect by some people. The original and preferred meaning is 'extreme wickedness (of something)', as in *the enormity of the crime*. The use of **enormity** as itself a synonym for 'monstrous crime' is common in such phrases as *the enormities of the Nazi regime*; however, this too is disapproved of by some traditionalists.

enquire / inquire Usage guides have traditionally drawn a distinction between **enquire** and **inquire**, implying that, in British English at least, **enquire** is used for general senses of 'ask', while **inquire** is reserved for uses meaning 'make a formal investigation'. In practice, however, **enquire** (and **enquiry**) is more common in British English while **inquire** (and **inquiry**) is more common in American English, but otherwise there is no readily discernible distinction in the way the two words are used.

ensure See INSURE/ENSURE.

enthuse The verb **enthuse** is formed as a back-formation from the noun 'enthusiasm' and, like many verbs formed from nouns in this way (especially those originating from the US), it is regarded by traditionalists as unacceptable. It is difficult to see why: this is a perfectly respectable means for creating new words in the language (verbs like 'classify', 'commentate', and 'edit' were also formed as back-formations from nouns, for example) and

enthuse itself has now been in English over 150 years. In very formal contexts, however, it may still be safer to write *show enthusiasm* or *inspire with enthusiasm*.

eponymous The adjective **eponymous** means 'giving one's name to (a book, place, etc.)', e.g. *Beowulf, the eponymous hero of the Old English poem of that name*; *The eponymous founder of Constantinople*. The reverse construction, e.g. *Emma, heroine of the eponymous novel by Jane Austen*, is incorrect.

equal For advice on the use of **equal** with such words as 'more' and 'very', see UNIQUE.

equally as This construction is frequently used when the writer means simply 'equally' or 'as'; for example, in the sentence *How to apply it was equally as important* the word 'as' can simply be dropped, while in *The Government are equally as guilty as the Opposition* the word 'equally' is redundant.

Eskimo In recent years, the word **Eskimo** has come to be regarded as offensive (partly through the associations of the now discredited folk etymology 'one who eats raw flesh'). The peoples of northwest Canada and Greenland prefer to call themselves INUIT. **Eskimo**, however, continues to be the only term that can be properly applied to the Arctic peoples as a whole and is still widely used in anthropological and archaeological contexts.

especially / specially In the broadest terms, both words mean 'particularly' and the preference for one word over the other is linked with certain conventions of use rather than with any deep difference in meaning. For example, there is little to choose between *written especially for Jonathan* and *written specially for Jonathan* and neither is more correct than the other. On the other hand, in sentences such as *He despised them all, especially Sylvester*, substitution of **specially** is too informal for written English, while in *The car was specially made for the occasion*, substitution of **especially** is somewhat unusual. Overall, **especially** is by far the commoner of the two.

Esq. This abbreviation is a 16th century shortening, as a written form of address, of **esquire**, which originally denoted 'a young aspirant to knighthood who attended and served a knight', and was later extended to refer to other classes of men including peers, lawyers, and so on. By the mid 20th century **Esq.** had become a courtesy designation, principally in correspondence, with no significance as to rank. When **Esq.** is used, it follows the name and replaces any prefixed title ('Mr', 'Dr', 'Capt.', etc.) that would otherwise be used. With one exception (American lawyers addressing each other), its use is restricted to Britain, and even here it is dying out as other conventions come into use.

-ess The suffix **-ess** has been used since the Middle Ages to form nouns denoting female persons, using a neutral or a male form as the base (as **hostess** and ACTRESS from 'host' and 'actor', for example). Despite the apparent equivalence between the male and female pairs of forms, they are rarely equivalent in terms of actual use and connotation (consider the differences in meaning and use between 'manager' and **manageress** or PRIEST and **priestess**). In more recent decades, as the role of women in society has changed, many of these feminine forms have become problematic and are now regarded as old-fashioned, sexist, and patronizing (e.g. **poetess**, **authoress**). The 'male' form is increasingly being used as the 'neutral' form, so that the gender of the person concerned is simply unspecified. Note also that in some cases (e.g. **mayoress**, **ambassadress**) the **-ess** form denotes the wife of a male office-holder; particular care should be taken not to refer in this way to a woman who holds the office in her own right.

etc. Etc., from Latin *et cetera*, meaning 'the rest', is perhaps the best understood and most frequently employed Latin abbreviation. Although **etc.** is sometimes said to stand for 'extreme thought collapse' because of the vague thinking that its overuse can encourage, it is harmless if used in moderation and if precision is not required. Note also that if a list is introduced by a word like 'such as' or 'includes', **etc.** is unnecessary because the reader knows the list is incomplete, e.g. *The burglar stole televisions, videos, etc.* but *The stolen goods included televisions, videos and stereos*.

-ette The use of **-ette** as a feminine suffix for forming new words is relatively recent: it was first recorded in the word **suffragette** at the beginning of the 20th century and has since been used to form only a handful of well-established words, including **usherette** and **drum majorette**, for example. In the modern context, where the tendency is to use words which are neutral in gender, the suffix **-ette** is not very productive and new words formed using it tend to be restricted to the deliberately flippant or humorous, as, for example, **bimbette** and **punkette**.

Eurasian In the 19th century the word **Eurasian** was normally used to refer to a person of mixed British and Indian parentage. In its modern uses, however, the term is more often used to refer to a person of mixed white American and South East Asian parentage. See also ASIAN.

event The phrase **in the event of**, meaning 'in case of', is followed by a noun or gerund ('-ing' form), e.g. *In the event of the earl's death, the title will lapse*. The construction **in the event that**, used for 'if', is condemned by many traditionalists; it is even less acceptable with 'that' omitted, e.g. *In the event the car overturns*.

ever When placed after a 'wh'-question word, **ever** should be written separately, e.g. *Where ever have you been?*; *When ever is he coming?*; *Who ever would have thought it?*; *Why ever did you do it?*; *How ever shall I escape?* When used with a relative pronoun or adverb to give it force, **ever** is written as one word with it, e.g. *Wherever you go I'll follow*; *Whenever he washes up he breaks something*; *There's a reward for whoever* (not *whomever*) *finds it*; *Whatever else you do, don't get lost*; *However it's done, it's difficult*.

excepting The preposition **excepting** is only used after 'not' and 'always', e.g. *The finest of all modern songwriters, not excepting Cole Porter*. In all other constructions the correct preposition is **except**.

excess The phrase **in excess of** is common in business and official English, e.g. *The Data Centre, which processes in excess of 1200 jobs per week*. It is clearer and simpler to write 'more than'.

expect **1** The use of **expect** to mean 'suppose, think' (e.g. *I expect you'd like a drink?*) is informal only.

2 See also ANTICIPATE.

explicit / express Although both these adjectives mean 'clearly and openly expressed', there is a slight shade of difference in usage. **Explicit** has the sense 'leaving nothing implied', e.g. *I had been too tactful… too vague…But I now saw that I ought to have been more explicit* (Iris Murdoch). **Express**, on the other hand, has the sense 'definite, unmistakable in import', e.g. *Idolatry fulsome enough to irritate Jonson into an express disavowal of it* (G. B. Shaw). Unlike **explicit**, **express** can only be used before a noun (as in the example above) and can only be applied to a statement, denial, etc., not to the person making it.

exposure to This phrase should not be used for 'experience of', e.g. as in *Candidates who have had exposure to North American markets*.

F

farther See FURTHER/FARTHER.

fatwa A **fatwa** is a legal ruling given by an Islamic religious leader. It came dramatically to Western attention in 1989 when by such a ruling Iran's Ayatollah Khomeini called for the death of the writer Salman Rushdie for publishing *The Satanic Verses* (1988), which many Muslims considered blasphemous. **Fatwa** is already undergoing extensions of meaning, and is erroneously used to mean 'sentence of death' (which, in the case of Rushdie, it meant only in effect). The plural in English contexts is **fatwas**.

feasible According to traditionalists, the correct meaning of this word is 'capable of being done, possible', e.g. *Walking all night was not feasible without the aid of moon or torch.* The use of **feasible** to mean 'likely' or 'probable', as in *the most feasible explanation*, has been in the language for centuries but is objected to on etymological grounds. For this reason it is advisable to avoid this sense in formal writing.

fewer / less Strictly speaking, the rule is that **fewer**, the comparative form of 'few', is used with words denoting people or countable things (*fewer members; fewer books; fewer than ten contestants*). **Less**, on the other hand, is used with mass nouns, denoting things that cannot be counted (*less money; less music*). In addition, **less** is normally used with numbers (*less than 10,000*) and with expressions of measurement or time (*less than two weeks; less than four miles away*). But to use **less** with count nouns, as in *less people* or *less words*, is incorrect in standard English. This is one of the most frequent errors made by native speakers of English, although in written sources the error is found less frequently.

finalize See -IZE (1).

fireman / firefighter See -MAN.

fish The normal plural is **fish**, e.g. *a shoal of fish; he caught two huge fish.* The older form **fishes** is still used, when referring to different kinds of fish, e.g. *freshwater fishes of the British Isles.*

flammable See INFLAMMABLE.

following Traditionalists point out that **following** is properly an adjective (meaning 'consequent upon') and should not be used as a quasi-preposition, independent of any noun, in such sentences as *The prologue was written by the company following an incident witnessed by them.* An example of correct formal usage would be: *The incident occurred during demonstrations following the hanging of two militants.* Although the prepositional use is now well established, it can give rise to ambiguity, e.g. *Police arrested a man following the hunt.* In any case, **following** should not be used merely for 'after' (e.g. *Following supper they went to bed*).

for In clauses constructed with the 'to'-infinitive, the subject of the clause is normally preceded by **for**, e.g. *For him to stay elsewhere is unthinkable.* But if the clause is a direct object, **for** is omitted: hence the construction in *I could not bear for him to stay elsewhere* is non-standard in British English (although common in North America).

forbid When the verb **forbid** is followed by a personal object, two constructions are possible: one uses the 'to'-infinitive, e.g. *My means forbade me to indulge in such delightful fantasies* (Lawrence Durrell), and one uses the gerund ('-ing' form), e.g. *Politeness...forbade my doubting them* (Dickens). In formal style, the object takes the possessive case in this second construction (*my doubting them* not *me doubting them*). The construction **forbid** plus gerund should not be used with 'from' in formal contexts, as in *She has an injunction forbidding him from calling her on the telephone.* See also PREVENT.

forensic Strictly speaking, this means 'of or used in courts of law', e.g. *forensic science.* However, a second sense has now developed 'of or involving forensic science', so that e.g. *forensic examination* is used to refer to scientific rather than courtroom procedures. This second sense is often deplored, but is widespread.

former, latter Traditionally, **former** and **latter** are used in relation to pairs of items: either the first of two items (**former**) or the second of two items (**latter**). The reason for this is that **former** and **latter** were formed as comparatives, and comparatives are correctly used with reference to just two things, while a superlative is used where there are more than two things. So, for example, strictly speaking one should say *the longest of the three books* but *the longer of the two books.* In practice, **former** and **latter** are now sometimes used just as synonyms for 'first' and 'last' and are routinely used to refer to a contrast involving more than two items. Such uses, however, are not acceptable in good English style.

fortuitous The traditional, etymological meaning of **fortuitous** is 'happening by chance': a *fortuitous meeting* is a chance meeting, which might turn out to be either a good thing or a bad thing. In modern English, however, **fortuitous** is often used to refer only to fortunate outcomes and the word has become more or less a synonym for 'lucky' or 'fortunate'. This use is frowned upon as being not etymologically correct and is best avoided.

forward / forwards See BACKWARD/BACKWARDS.

fruition When used in the sense of 'fulfilment', especially in such phrases as *Her plans were finally brought to fruition, etc.*, **fruition** was once stigmatized but is now standard.

fuck Historically, **fuck** is one of the most taboo words in English, whether used in its literal sexual meaning or as an expletive. Until quite recently it rarely appeared in print and was never heard on television; even today, there are a number of euphemistic ways of referring to it in speech and writing, e.g. 'the F-word', or 'f***'. Today, sensitivity to the word (and to the issue of 'bad language' in general) varies considerably. Among the younger and more metropolitan sections of society the words **fuck**, **fucking**, etc., tend to be used quite casually by both sexes and all classes; however, many older and more conservative people are still deeply and sincerely offended by their use, and this should be borne in mind.

-fuls / -s full The combining form **-ful** is used to form nouns meaning 'the amount needed to fill', e.g. *a cupful of water.* The plural of such words is formed with '-s', e.g. *three spoonfuls of sugar.* By contrast *three cups full* would denote the individual cups rather than a quantity regarded in terms of a cup used as a measure, and would be used in contexts such as *They brought us three cups full of water.*

fulsome Although this word is still sometimes used in its original sense of 'copious, abundant', **fulsome** is now a pejorative term meaning 'excessive, cloying, or insincere', e.g. *They listened to fulsome speeches* (Beryl Bainbridge). This can give rise to ambiguity; for one person *fulsome praise* may mean no more than 'generous praise' while for another it may mean 'nauseating sycophancy'. For this reason alone, it is best to avoid the word altogether if the context is likely to be sensitive.

fun The use of **fun** as an adjective meaning 'enjoyable', as in *We had a fun evening* is not fully accepted in standard English and should only be used in informal contexts. There are signs that this situation is changing, though, given the recent appearance in American English of comparative and superlative forms 'funner' and 'funnest', formed as if **fun** were a normal adjective.

further / farther Is there any difference between **further** and **farther** in *She moved further down the train* and *She moved farther* *down the train*? Both words share the same roots: in the sentences given above, where the sense is 'at, to, or by a greater distance', there is no difference in meaning, and both are equally correct. **Further** is a much commoner word, though, and is in addition used in various abstract and metaphorical contexts, (for example referring to time) in which it would be unusual to substitute **farther**, e.g. *Have you anything further to say?*; *We intend to stay a further two weeks*. The same distinction is made between **farthest** and **furthest**: *The farthest point from the sun* versus *This research team has gone furthest in its analysis*.

G

gay Gay meaning 'homosexual' became established in the 1960s as the term preferred by homosexual men to describe themselves. It is now the standard accepted term throughout the English-speaking world. As a result, the centuries-old other senses of **gay** meaning either 'carefree' or 'bright and showy' have more or less dropped out of natural use. The word **gay** cannot be readily used unselfconsciously today in these older senses without arousing a sense of double entendre, despite concerted attempts by some to keep them alive. **Gay** in its modern sense typically refers to men (**lesbian** being the standard term for homosexual women) but in some contexts it can be used of both men and women. See also QUEER.

gender / sex The word **gender** has been used since the 14th century as a grammatical term, referring to the classes of noun in Latin, Greek, and other languages designated as masculine, feminine, or neuter. It has also long been used in the sense 'the state of being male or female', but this did not become a common standard use until the mid 20th century. Although the words **gender** and **sex** both have the sense 'the state of being male or female', they are typically used in slightly different ways: **sex** tends to refer to biological differences, while **gender** tends to refer to cultural or social ones.

geriatric The adjective **geriatric** means 'pertaining to the health and welfare of the

elderly'; it is very informal (and may be offensive) to use it for 'old' or 'outdated', or as a noun meaning 'old, outdated, or senile person'.

get, got Primary-school teachers' exasperation at the overuse of these words has left many people afraid to use them at all in formal writing. The alternatives 'receive' and 'obtain' are plain enough but there is no harm in **get** and **got** (words with a thousand years of common use behind them) when you feel that their simplicity and informality are helpful. *I got your letter yesterday* and *I will get someone to deal with the problem* are both perfectly good written English (although some may find them excessively informal).

girl Girl is falling out of use as a term applied to adult women, partly under pressure from the feminist movement and partly because some of the institutions with which the word is associated (e.g. the employment of female domestics) have become obsolete. However, the use remains active in several contexts: in referring to a regular female companion as e.g. *Richard's girl* or *girlfriend*; in titles of books and films and the lyrics of popular songs; in the expressions *glamour girl*, *cover girl*, *page three girl*, etc., and in the plural use of *the girls* to refer to a group of young women friends. In general use, however, 'woman' or 'young woman' are to be preferred. See also LADY.

go and See AND (2).

gotten As past participles of 'get', **got** and **gotten** both date back to Middle English. The form **gotten** is not used in British English but is very common in American English, though even there it is often regarded as non-standard. In American English, **got** and **gotten** are not identical in use. **Gotten** usually implies the process of obtaining something, as in *He had gotten us tickets for the show*, while **got** implies the state of possession or ownership, as in *I haven't got any money*.

graffiti In Italian the word **graffiti** is a plural noun and its singular form is **graffito**. Traditionally, the same distinction has been maintained in English, so that **graffiti**, being plural, would require a plural verb: *The graffiti were all over the walls*. By the same token, the singular would require a singular verb: *There was a graffito on the wall.* Today, these distinctions survive in some specialist fields such as archaeology but sound odd to most native speakers. The most common modern use is to treat **graffiti** as if it were a mass noun, similar to a word like 'writing', and not to use **graffito** at all. In this case, **graffiti** takes a singular verb, as in *The graffiti was all over the wall.* Such uses are now widely accepted as standard, and may be regarded as part of the natural development of the language. See also AGENDA; DATA; MEDIA.

Great Britain See BRITAIN/GREAT BRITAIN/ BRITISH ISLES/ENGLAND.

H

half The use of **half** to mean 'half-past (the hour)' is indigenous to Britain and has been remarked on since the 1930s, e.g. *We'd easily get the half-five bus* (William Trevor); it remains non-standard.

handicapped In the sense referring to a person's mental or physical disabilities, the word **handicapped** is first recorded in the early 20th century. It was the standard term in British English until relatively recently but, like many terms in this sensitive field, its prominence has been short-lived. In reference to physical disability, it is now rather dated and may even be found offensive. It has been superseded by more recent terms such as DISABLED. See also CHALLENGED; DIFFERENTLY ABLED.

hang In modern English **hang** has two past tense and past participle forms: **hanged** and **hung**. **Hung** is the normal form in most general uses, e.g. *They hung out the washing*; *She hung around for a few minutes*, but **hanged** is the form normally used in reference to execution by hanging, e.g. *The prisoner was hanged*. The reason for this distinction is a complex historical one: **hanged**, the earlier form, was superseded by **hung** sometime after the 16th century; it is likely that the retention of **hanged** for the execution sense may have to do with the tendency of archaic forms to remain in the legal language of the courts.

hardly, scarcely, rarely 1 Words like **hardly**, **scarcely**, and **rarely** should not be used with negative constructions. Thus, it is correct to say *I can hardly wait* but nonstandard to say *I can't hardly wait*. This is because adverbs like **hardly** and **rarely** have a negative force and it is a well-known grammatical rule of standard English that double negatives are not acceptable. Words like **hardly** behave as negatives in other respects as well, as for example in combining with words like 'any' or 'at all', which normally only occur where a negative is present (thus, standard usage is *I've got hardly any money* but not *I've got any money*).

2 When used in the sense 'only just (after)', **hardly**, **scarcely**, and **rarely** are followed by 'when' or 'before', not 'than', e.g. *Hardly had Grimes left the house when a tall young man… presented himself at the front door* (Evelyn Waugh).

harelip See CLEFT LIP.

have 1 There has been a great deal of debate on the difference between the two forms **have** and **have got** in such sentences as e.g. *We have fifty pounds between us* or *We have got fifty pounds between us*. A traditional view is that **have got** is chiefly British, while **have** is chiefly American. Actual usage is more complicated: **have got** is in fact also widely used in American English, while in both Britain and North America **have** is more formal than **have got**. The same remarks apply to the forms used in questions and negatives, i.e. *Do you have a room?*; *We don't have any rooms* on the one hand, and *Have you got…?*; *We haven't got…* on the other. The **do…have** form is generally more American than the **have got** construction; it is also considered more appropriate in writing to use **don't have** rather than **haven't got**. See HAVE (1) in PART II of SECTION 1: GRAMMAR.

2 Another controversial issue is the insertion of a superfluous **have** in statements that present a hypothetical situation, e.g. *I might have missed it if you hadn't have pointed it out* (rather than the standard … *if you hadn't pointed it out*). This construction has been around since at least the 15th and 16th centuries. More recently, there has been speculation among grammarians and linguists that this insertion of **have** may represent a kind of subjunctive and is actually making a useful distinction in the language.

However, it is still regarded as an error in standard English.

3 A common mistake is to write the word **of** instead of **have** (or **'ve**), e.g. *I could of told you that* instead of *I could've told you that*. The reason for the mistake is that the pronunciation of **have** in unstressed contexts is the same as that of **of**, and the two words are confused when it comes to writing them down. Although common, the error is unacceptable in standard English.

having said that This is a waffling way of writing 'but', 'however', or 'even so', and is generally better avoided. (Addicts can withdraw slowly with 'that said'.)

he Until recently, **he** was used uncontroversially to refer to a person of unspecified sex, as in *Every child needs to know that he is loved*. In recent decades, this use has become problematic owing to concern about sexism in language. Even those who considered it a useful and inoffensive convention must concede that the use of **he** in such cases now looks old-fashioned and risks alienating some readers. Use of THEY as an alternative to **he** in this sense (*Everyone needs to feel that they matter*) has been common since the 18th century and is becoming more and more accepted both in speech and in writing. Another alternative is **he or she**, though this can become tiresomely long-winded when used frequently.

heir apparent The phrase denotes one whose right of inheritance cannot be superseded by the birth of another heir (as opposed to an **heir presumptive**, whose right can be so superseded); it does not mean 'seeming or obvious heir'. However, the phrase is now used very loosely to mean someone considered likely to succeed to a position, job, etc., e.g. *The prime minister has no heir apparent*.

help The phrases *more than one can help*, or *as little as one can help* are illogical but established idioms, e.g. *They will not respect more than they can help treaties extracted from them under duress* (Winston Churchill).

hence A useful but regrettably uncommon word. It can mean 'as a result' (*hence the election will take place next week*) or 'from now' (*The election will take place two weeks hence*).

here- Most of the adverbs constructed from **here-** (e.g. **herewith, hereby, hereof, heretofore, hereinbefore, hereto, herein**) smell of old law books. Moreover, they rarely add much to the meaning of the sentences they appear in. *I hereby declare* just means 'I declare'. *The document attached hereto* just means 'the document attached' or 'the document attached to this'. Happily, these words are slowly disappearing from business and legal use. See also THERE-.

Hindustani Hindustani was the usual term in the 18th and 19th centuries for the native language of northwest India. The usual modern term is **Hindi** (or **Urdu** in Muslim contexts), although **Hindustani** is still used to refer to the dialect of Hindi spoken around Delhi, which is widely used throughout India as a lingua franca.

Hispanic In North America, **Hispanic** is the standard accepted term when referring to Spanish-speaking people living in the US. Other, more specific, terms such as **Latino** (person of Latin American origin) and **Chicano** (person of Mexican origin) are also used where occasion demands.

HIV Since the abbreviation stands for 'human immunodeficiency virus', the word 'virus' is strictly redundant in the phrase **HIV virus**, although this is now established usage.

Hmong The term **Hmong** is now usually preferred for this mountain people of South East Asia. The Chinese name **Miao** (or **Meo**) was until recently more common in English contexts and is still seen.

hoi polloi **1** Some traditionalists argue that this phrase, which is Greek for 'the many, the masses', should not be preceded by 'the', as in e.g. *The screen with which working archaeologists baffle the* hoi polloi (Frederic Raphael). The reason given is that *hoi* is itself the Greek word for the definite article (nominative masculine plural), so a further 'the' is redundant. Such arguments miss the point: once established in English, expressions such as **hoi polloi** are treated as a fixed unit and are subject to the rules and conventions of English. Evidence shows that use with 'the' has now become an accepted part of standard English usage.

2 Hoi polloi is sometimes used incorrectly to mean 'upper class', i.e. the exact opposite of its normal meaning. It seems likely that the confusion arose by association with the similar-sounding but otherwise unrelated word 'hoity-toity' (meaning 'arrogant, haughty').

hopefully The traditional sense of **hopefully**, 'in a hopeful manner', has been used since the 17th century. In the second half of the 20th century a new use as a sentence adverb arose, meaning 'it is to be hoped that', as in *Hopefully, we'll see you tomorrow*. This second use is now much commoner than the first but is widely believed to be incorrect.

Why should this be? People do not criticize other sentence adverbs, e.g. 'sadly' (as in *Sadly, her father died last year*) or 'fortunately' (as in *Fortunately, he recovered*). Part of the reason is that **hopefully** is a rather odd sentence adverb: while many others, such as 'sadly', 'regrettably', and 'clearly', may be paraphrased as 'it is sad/regrettable/clear that …', this is not possible with **hopefully**. A further objection is that ambiguity can arise from the interplay of the different senses of the word, e.g. as in *Any decision to trust Egypt…and move forward hopefully toward peace…in the Middle East* (*Guardian Weekly*). Altogether, it is clear that use of **hopefully** has become a shibboleth of 'correctness' in modern English usage, and it is wise to be aware of this in formal or written contexts.

Hottentot The Afrikaans word **Hottentot** (first recorded in the late 17th century) was applied by white Europeans to the Khoikhoi peoples of southern Africa, in particular the Nama. It is now regarded as offensive with reference to people and should always be avoided in favour of **Khoikhoi** or **Nama**. The only standard use for **Hottentot** in modern English is in the names of animals and plants.

however **1** When used as a more leisurely alternative to 'but', **however** normally needs to be preceded and followed by a comma, e.g. *It seems clear that your opponent lied in court: we do not believe, however, that she is likely to be convicted of perjury*. The following sentence shows a common mistake with **however**: *You have told us that the ring was stolen while the back door was left open, however, the policy only covers theft from your home if force is used to enter or leave*. In this case, the force of **however** relates to the second half of the sentence (*the policy only covers*) rather than the first; therefore, the comma that precedes **however** is not enough and a semicolon or full stop is necessary.

2 For advice on **however** versus **how ever**, see EVER.

humanitarian Sentences such as *This is the worst humanitarian disaster the country has seen* involve a loose use of the adjective **humanitarian** ('having the interests of mankind at heart') to mean 'human'. This use is quite common, especially in journalism, but is not generally considered good style.

I

if **1 If** and **whether** are more or less interchangeable in such sentences as *I'll see if he left an address* and *I'll see whether he left an address*, although **whether** is generally regarded as more formal and suitable for written use.

2 In certain constructions (usually linking two adjectives or adverbs) **if** can be ambiguous, e.g. *A great play, if not the greatest, by this author*. It is best to paraphrase such sentences as, e.g., either *A great play, though not the greatest by this author* or *A great play, perhaps* (or *very nearly*) *the greatest by this author*.

ignorant **Ignorant** is better followed by 'of' than by 'about', e.g. *The residents are…ignorant of their rights* (*Independent*).

ilk **Of that ilk** is an old Scots term, meaning 'of the place of the same name', e.g. *Wemyss of that ilk* means 'Wemyss the laird or proprietor of Wemyss'. By a misunderstanding **ilk** has acquired the modern meaning 'sort, lot' (usually pejorative), e.g. *Joan Baez and other vocalists of that ilk* (David Lodge). Although some traditionalists regard the modern use as incorrect, it is the only common current use and is now part of standard English.

illegal / illicit / illegitimate / unlawful Something is **illegal** when it is against the law in all circumstances, e.g. *illegal drug use*, **illicit** when it is against the law in some circumstances or otherwise prohibited, e.g. *il-*

licit drinking, and **illegitimate** when it is contrary to custom, common justice, or the laws of logic, e.g. *an illegitimate child; an illegitimate assumption*. **Unlawful** is a somewhat old-fashioned word that can refer to divine as well as human law. See also LEGAL/LEGITIMATE/LAWFUL/LICIT.

illusion See DELUSION/ILLUSION.

illusory See ELUSIVE, ILLUSORY.

impact When used figuratively, **impact** is best confined to contexts of someone or something striking another, e.g. *The most dynamic colour combination if used too often loses its impact*. It is weakened if used as a mere synonym for 'effect' or 'influence'. A related development is the use of **impact on** as a phrasal verb, e.g. in *When produce is lost, it always impacts on the bottom line*. This is now quite common in business writing but disliked by many people, who regard it as unacceptable jargon. It is better to use 'make an impact on', 'have an effect on' or some equivalent phrase.

inchoate This word means 'just begun or rudimentary, underdeveloped', e.g. *Trying to give his work a finished look – and all the time… the stuff's fatally inchoate* (John Wain). It does not mean 'chaotic' or 'incoherent', although it is often used incorrectly in these senses.

include **Include** has a broader meaning than 'comprise' or 'consist of'. In the sentence *The accommodation comprises two bedrooms, bathroom, kitchen, and living room*, the word 'comprise' implies that there is no accommodation other than that listed. **Include** can be used in this way too, but it is also used in a non-restrictive way, implying that there may be other things not specifically mentioned that are part of the same category, as in *The price includes a special welcome pack*. See also COMPOSE/COMPRISE.

Indian See AMERICAN INDIAN.

infectious See CONTAGIOUS/INFECTIOUS.

inflammable / flammable The words **inflammable** and **flammable** both have the same meaning, i.e. 'easily set on fire or excited'. This might seem surprising, given that the prefix 'in-' normally has the function of negation, as in words like 'indirect' and 'in-

sufficient'. It might be expected, therefore, that **inflammable** would mean 'not easily set on fire'. In fact, **inflammable** is formed using a different Latin prefix 'in-', which has the meaning 'into'. The opposite of **inflammable** and **flammable** is either **non-inflammable** or **non-flammable**. Where there is any danger of **inflammable** being understood to mean the opposite, i.e. 'not easily set on fire', **flammable** should be used to avoid confusion.

inquire See ENQUIRE/INQUIRE.

insignia **Insignia** is, in origin, a plural noun, e.g. *Fourteen different airline insignia* (David Lodge); its singular, rarely encountered, is **insigne**. Use of 'insignias' as a plural form is non-standard. See also REGALIA.

insure / ensure There is considerable overlap between the meaning and use of **insure** and **ensure**. In both British and American English the primary meaning of **insure** is the commercial sense of providing financial compensation in the event of damage to property; **ensure** is not used at all in this sense. For the more general sense of 'make sure', **ensure** is more likely to be used, but the two words are often interchangeable, particularly in American English, e.g. *Bail is posted to insure that the defendant appears for trial*.

interface The word **interface** is relatively new, having been in the language (as a noun) only since the 1880s. The noun has two specialized technical meanings: a surface forming a common boundary, e.g. *The interfaces between solid and solid, solid and liquid*, or a piece of equipment in which interaction occurs between two systems, processes, etc., e.g. *Modular interfaces to adapt the general-purpose computer to the equipment*.

This second sense, popularized by frequent use in the language of computing, has given rise to a more general meaning. **Interface** is now commonly used to mean 'a point, place, or means of interaction', e.g. *Experts looked at the crucial interface between broadcasters and independents*, or, as a verb, 'to interact', e.g. *The ideal candidate will have the ability to interface effectively with other departments*. Traditionalists object to this usage on the grounds that the word has become no more than a pretentious synonym for (nouns) 'meeting-point, liaison, link', etc., or (verb) 'interact (with)'.

interpersonal Once the preserve of psychologists, **interpersonal** has crept into the language of the curriculum vitae, in which no applicant's credentials are adequate without an endorsement of his or her *interpersonal skills*, i.e. the ability to deal effectively with other people. It is also widely used by sociologists to refer to the ways in which people treat each other in everyday life, e.g. *The relevance of interpersonal and family problems.*

Inuit The peoples inhabiting the regions from northwest Canada to western Greenland prefer to be called **Inuit** rather than ESKIMO, and this term now has official status in Canada. By analogy, the term **Inuit** is also used, generally in an attempt to be politically correct, as a synonym for **Eskimo** in general. However, this latter use, in including people from Siberia who are not Inupiaq-speakers, is, strictly speaking, not accurate.

invite The use of **invite** as a noun meaning 'invitation' remains informal only.

inward / inwards See BACKWARD/BACKWARDS.

ironic, ironically The noun **irony** can mean either a use of language in which the intended meaning is very different from the literal sense of the words used (*Chaucer's use of multiple irony*) or an ill-timed or perverse outcome (*the ironies of history*). The adjectives **ironic** or **ironical** and the adverb **ironically** are commonly used in both senses of **irony**, e.g. *Ironical silent apology for the absence of naked women and tanks of gin from the amenities* (Kingsley Amis); *The fact that after all she had been faithful to me was ironic* (Graham Greene). Some people object to this second use, especially when **ironic** or **ironically** introduces a trivial oddity, e.g. *It was ironic that he thought himself locked out when the key was in his pocket all the time.*

-ize Adding **-ize** to a noun or adjective has been a standard way of forming new verbs for centuries, and verbs such as 'characterize', 'terrorize', and 'sterilize' were all formed in this way hundreds of years ago. For some reason, people object to recent

formations of this type: during the last century, there were objections raised against **prioritize, finalize, privatize,** and **hospitalize,** among others. There seems to be no coherent reason for this, other than an assertion (often unfounded) that perfectly good alternatives already exist, and a feeling that those who overuse such new coinages are vulgar and pretentious. Here, as elsewhere, it may be suggested that those coinages that fill a genuine gap in the language are likely to survive, while those that are merely voguish will disappear.

J

jejune Jejune properly means 'meagre, scanty; dull or uninteresting' and is used primarily of ideas or arguments. It is derived from the Latin word *jejunus* meaning 'fasting', and originally meant 'without food' in English. In more recent decades, this traditional meaning of **jejune** has lost ground to a newer meaning 'puerile, childish, naïve', which has arisen by a somewhat bizarre association with 'juvenile', e.g. *Her political enthusiasms were embarrassingly jejune.* Although this use is quite common, it should be avoided in favour of the many readily available alternatives.

jobber On the London Stock Exchange the term **jobber** was officially replaced by **broker-dealer** in 1986, broker-dealers being entitled to act as both agents and principals in share dealings.

K

Kaffir The word **Kaffir**, first recorded in the 16th century, was originally simply a descriptive term for certain black peoples of southern Africa (mainly the Xhosa and Zulu). Now it is always a racially abusive and offensive term when used of people, and in South Africa its use is actionable. See also BANTU.

Khoikhoi See HOTTENTOT.

kind of, sort of 1 Kind of and sort of should not be followed by 'a' before the noun, e.g. write *a kind of shock* not *a kind of a shock.*

2 Kind of and sort of may be used in either singular or plural constructions, e.g. *These* *kinds of questions are not relevant* or *This kind of question is not relevant*. Although the mixture of plural and singular in e.g. *They would be on those sort of terms* (Anthony Powell) is quite common, it is regarded as incorrect except in informal use.

3 The adverbial use of **kind of** or **sort of** in e.g. *I kind of expected it*, is informal only.

koala In general use, **koala bear** (as opposed to **koala**) is widespread. Zoologists, however, regard this form as incorrect on the grounds that, despite appearances, koalas are completely unrelated to bears.

kudos Kudos comes from Greek and means 'praise'. Despite appearances, it is not a plural form but a mass noun like 'glory' or 'fame'. This means that there is no singular form 'kudo' and that use as a plural is incorrect: such sentences as *He received many kudos for his work* are therefore nonstandard and should be rephrased e.g. *He received a great deal of kudos....*

L

lady / woman The division of usage between these two words is complex and is caught up in issues of social class. Traditionally, **lady** denotes social standing and refinement and is the female equivalent of 'gentleman', whereas **woman** is the normal word that is generally neutral in tone but in some contexts can sound overdirect or discourteous, e.g. *Which of you women is Mrs Jones?* As well as its use as a title, **lady** is used in certain fixed expressions, such as *lady of the house*, *the Ladies* (i.e. a women's public lavatory), *a lady's man*, and others, and in the form of address *ladies and gentlemen*. In America, though less so in Britain, **lady** has developed an informal meaning rather like 'dame', both as a form of address (*Where are you going, lady?*) and in third-person reference (*She's some lady!*) It should finally be mentioned that the feminist movement generally disfavours **lady** as being socially and historically loaded, and prefers the more neutral **woman** despite its occasional bluntness of tone. This preference is likely to influence the future of the words' usage considerably.

Lapp Although the term **Lapp** is still widely used and is the most familiar term to many people, the people themselves prefer to be called **Sami**.

Latino See HISPANIC.

latter See FORMER, LATTER.

lavatory See TOILET.

lay / lie The verb **lay** means, broadly, 'put something down', as in *They are going to lay the carpet*. The past tense and the past participle of this verb is **laid**, as in *They laid the groundwork* or *She had laid careful plans*. The verb **lie**, on the other hand, means 'be in a horizontal position to rest', as in *Why don't you lie on the floor?* The past tense of this verb is **lay** (*He lay on the floor*) and the past participle is **lain** (*She had lain on the bed for hours*). Note also that in standard English **lay** is a transitive verb and **lie** intransitive.

In practice many speakers make the mistake of using **lay**, **laying**, and **laid** as if they meant **lie**, **lying**, **lay**, and **lain**, e.g. *Why don't you lay on the bed* (correctly **lie**); *She was laying on the bed* (correctly **lying**); *He had laid on the floor for hours* (correctly **lain**). The transitive use of **lie**, as in *Lie it on the table*, is also nonstandard. Curiously, the past **lay** and the participle **lain** are quite often wrongly used for **laid** out of a false sense that these forms are more formal and correct, e.g. *He had lain this peer's honour in the dust*. The noun meaning 'a prolonged stay in bed in the morning' is **lie-in** not 'lay-in'.

leading question This was originally a legal phrase meaning 'a question that prompts the desired answer', e.g. *The solicitor...at once asked me some leading questions... I had to try to be both forthcoming and discreet* (C. P. Snow). In weakened use a **leading question** tends to mean 'an awkward, pointed, or loaded question', or even 'principal question', but these usages are considered incorrect by some people.

learn / teach In modern standard English, it is incorrect to use **learn** to mean **teach**, as in *That'll learn you* (correctly *That'll teach you*). This use has been recorded since the 13th century and for a long time was not considered incorrect, being used over the centuries by such writers as Spenser, Bunyan, and Samuel Johnson. It is now only found in non-standard and dialect use.

learning difficulties The phrase **learning difficulties** became prominent in the 1980s. It is broad in scope, covering general conditions such as DOWN'S SYNDROME as well as more specific cognitive or neurological conditions such as dyslexia and attention deficit disorder. In emphasizing the difficulty experienced rather than any perceived 'deficiency', it is considered more positive than other terms such as **mentally handicapped** (see MENTAL) and is now the standard accepted term in official contexts, especially in Britain.

legal / legitimate / lawful / licit All four words share the basic meaning 'conforming to the law'. Something is **legal** when it is authorized by the law of the land, **legitimate** when it conforms to custom or common justice, and **lawful** (a more old-fashioned word) when it conforms to moral or divine law. **Legal** is the only choice in the neutral descriptive meaning 'relating to the law' (e.g. *legal language*), and **legitimate** alone has the meaning 'born of married parents'. **Licit**, which means 'not forbidden', is the least used of all these words. See also ILLEGAL/ILLICIT/ILLEGITIMATE/UNLAWFUL.

lend **1** Like other reciprocal pairs of words, **lend** and **borrow** are often confused. Common uses in a number of British dialects include *Can I lend your pen?* (correct standard use is *Can I borrow your pen?*).

2 There is no noun **lend** in standard English, where **loan** is the correct word to use. However, it is used informally in a number of dialects and varieties, including Scottish, Northern Irish, and northern English, as in e.g. *Can I have a lend of your pen?* The use of **loan** as a verb is best restricted to financial contexts, e.g. *The gas industry is…loaning money to Government* (*Observer*). It should not be used merely as a variant for **lend**.

lesbian See GAY.

less See FEWER/LESS.

lesser **Lesser** means 'not so important or impressive as the other or others' e.g. *The lesser celandine; Of the two, Jonson is the lesser artist*. It should not be used as a synonym for 'smaller' or 'lower', as in the incorrect sentence *A lesser fee should now be charged*.

lest **Lest**, meaning 'for fear that' or 'in case' is very formal; it is followed by 'should' or (in exalted style) the subjunctive, e.g. *Lest the eye wander aimlessly, a Doric temple stood by the water's edge* (Evelyn Waugh); *Lest some too sudden gesture or burst of emotion should turn the petals brown* (Patrick White). Such constructions as *She was worrying lest he was attacked* (correctly *be attacked*) or *She is using headphones lest she disturbs anyone* (correctly *disturb anyone*) are non-standard.

liable / apt When used with an infinitive to express the idea of the probability of something, **liable to** and **apt to** are virtually interchangeable: *In weather like this he is apt to bowl at the batsman's head* (Robert Graves); *The kind of point that one is always liable to miss* (George Orwell). However, as these quotations illustrate, **apt to** has a strong sense of habitual tendency, while **liable to** can indicate mere possibility. A further point is that **liable to** generally implies that the action or state described is undesirable (from the point of view of the grammatical subject); *Receiving in the bedroom is liable to get a woman talked about* (Tom Stoppard). **Apt to** carries no such implication.

Note also that **liable to** or **liable for** can be followed by a direct object to give the sense 'subject to, responsible for': *You could be liable to a heavy fine; He is liable for any damage caused.* There are no parallel constructions for **apt**. According to some traditionalists, this is the only correct sense of **liable**; others object only to the use of **liable** as an all-purpose synonym for 'likely' (with no sense of an undesirable outcome). See also PRONE.

like **1** **Like** can be used as a preposition to mean 'such as', e.g. *Good writers like Dickens.* However, in formal contexts some people prefer 'such as' to be used, especially if more than one example is mentioned, e.g. *He dealt in types, such as the rich bitch, the honest whore, the socializing snob* (*London Magazine*).

2 **Like** is often used as a conjunction to mean 'as', 'as if', or 'in the same way that', e.g. *You wake like someone hit you on the head* (T. S. Eliot); *Everything went wrong…like it does in dreams* (Iris Murdoch). Although this use of **like** is not uncommon in formal writing, and has been used by many respected authors, it is best avoided, except informally.

likely In the sense 'probably', **likely** must be preceded by 'more', 'most', 'quite', or 'very' in British English, e.g. *Its inhabitants... very likely do make that claim for it* (George Orwell). The use of **likely** without the qualifying adverb is standard only in American English, e.g. *They'll likely turn ugly* (Eugene O'Neill).

linguist The word means both 'one whose subject is linguistics' and 'one skilled in the use of languages'; there is no other suitable term in either case.

literally In its standard use **literally** means 'in a literal sense, as opposed to a non-literal or exaggerated sense', e.g. *I told him I never wanted to see him again, but I didn't expect him to take it literally*. In recent years an extended use of **literally** (and also **literal**) has become very common, where the word is used deliberately in non-literal contexts for added effect, e.g. *They bought the car and literally ran it into the ground*. This use should be avoided in writing or formal speech, since it almost invariably involves absurdity, e.g. *The dwarfs mentioned here are literally within a stone's throw of the Milky Way* (New Scientist); *King George VI, who had literally been catapulted onto the throne* (Prince Edward).

loan See LEND (2).

locate In standard English it is not strictly correct to use **locate** as a mere synonym for 'to find', e.g. *It drives him out of his mind when he can't locate something*. **Locate** should be used more precisely to mean 'to discover the exact place or position of', e.g. *One club member was proposing to use an echo sounder to help locate fish in the lake*.

lot 1 The expressions **a lot of** and **lots of** are used before nouns to mean 'a large number or amount of'. In common with other words denoting quantities, **lot** itself does not normally function as a head noun, meaning that it does not itself determine whether the following verb is singular or plural. Thus, although **lot** is singular in *a lot of people were assembled*, the verb which follows is not singular. In this case the word 'people' acts as the head noun and, being

plural, ensures that the following verb is also plural. See also NUMBER.

2 A lot of and **lots of** are very common in speech and writing but they still have a distinctly informal feel. **A lot of** is just about acceptable, whereas **lots of** is not. The more obvious alternatives include 'many' or 'a large number of'.

lunch / luncheon In modern English **lunch** should normally be used, except in fixed expressions like *luncheon voucher* or in very formal invitations.

M

madam / madame Madam is a now somewhat formal or affectedly courteous form of address to a woman; it tends to be used only when there is no alternative because the woman's name, job title, etc. is not known. When addressing royalty, the shorter form **ma'am** is used. **Madame**, pronounced with the stress on the second syllable, is the right form of address to a woman from any foreign nation (not necessarily French), and is also a term (should one be needed) for a woman brothelkeeper.

majority Strictly speaking, **majority** should be used with countable nouns to mean 'the greater number', as in *the majority of cases*. Use with uncountable nouns to mean 'the greatest part', as in *I spent the majority of the day reading* or *She ate the majority of her dinner* is not considered good standard English, although it is common in informal contexts. It follows from this that the noun and verb used with **majority** should both be plural, e.g. *The majority of the plays produced were failures* (G. B. Shaw). Note also that while 'great' (or 'huge', 'vast', etc.) can precede **majority**, the use of 'greater', 'greatest' is redundant, as this is already implied by the word **majority**. See also MINORITY.

man Traditionally the word **man** has been used to refer not only to adult males but also to human beings in general, regardless of sex. There is a historical explanation for this: in Old English the principal sense of **man** was 'a human being', and the words 'wer' and 'wif' were used to refer specifically to 'a male person' and 'a female person' respectively. Subsequently, **man**

replaced 'wer' as the normal term for 'a male person', but at the same time the older sense 'a human being' remained in use.

In the later 20th century the generic use of **man** to refer to 'human beings in general' (as in *Reptiles were here long before man appeared on the earth*) became problematic; the use is now often regarded as sexist or at best old-fashioned. In some contexts, alternative terms such as 'the human race' or 'humankind' may be used, and most sentences using 'all men' or 'no man' can be rephrased using 'all people' or 'nobody', etc. However, in other cases, particularly in compound forms, alternatives have not yet become established: there are no standard accepted alternatives for 'manpower' or the verb 'to man', for example.

-man Traditionally, the form **-man** was combined with other words to create a term denoting an occupation or role, as in **fireman**, **layman**, **chairman**, and **freshman**. As the role of women in society has changed, many of these terms have been challenged as sexist and out of date. As a result, there has been a gradual shift away from **-man** compounds except where referring to a specific male person.Alternative gender-neutral terms are used, e.g. **firefighter** and **fresher**, and new ones which only a few decades ago seemed odd or awkward today seem unexceptional e.g. **chairperson** (or **chair**), **layperson**.

masterful / masterly Some writers maintain a distinction between **masterful** and **masterly**, using **masterful** to mean 'powerful and able to control others' (*a masterful tone of voice*) and **masterly** to mean 'with the skill of a master' (*a masterly performance*). In practice the two words overlap considerably in the second meaning. Note, however, that when **masterful** is used in the sense 'very skilful' it is generally to describe a person, e.g. *He's just got a marginal talent he's masterful at exploiting*, while **masterly** usually describes an achievement or action, e.g. *This was a masterly realization of the score*.

maximize Correctly used, this word means 'to make as great as possible'. It should not be used for 'to make as good, easy, etc. as possible' or 'to make the most

of' as in *To maximize customer service*; *To maximize this situation*. See also MINIMIZE.

may / might May can be used to indicate either permission or theoretical possibility, e.g. *You may have another cake*; *The rope may not take his weight*. The word **might** is used in both these senses (but more commonly the second) as the past tense or subjunctive of **may**, e.g. *The rope might have broken if he hadn't let go*; *If I might say so*. **May** is informal in both these cases. In past-tense constructions referring to possibility, **may** is only correct when the possibility referred to remains open – either because the situation is unresolved or because its outcome is unknown. Hence, *He may have killed himself* means that suicide is suspected but not certain, whereas *He might have killed himself* means that the person concerned is lucky to be alive.

In other constructions expressing possibility, **may** and **might** are virtually interchangeable, the only difference being one of emphasis: *She may come tomorrow*, for example, implies rather more certainty than *She might come tomorrow*. See also CAN/MAY.

meaningful Meaningful is essentially the opposite of 'meaningless', i.e. 'having meaning', as in *a meaningful utterance*. However, 'meaning' has other senses, which are reflected in the more recent use of **meaningful** to signify 'valid, worthwhile, noteworthy', e.g. *meaningful dialogue*; *a meaningful relationship*; *meaningful results*. In this sense, **meaningful** has been a somewhat overused vogue word since the late 1970s and is now often mocked. There is no problem with using the word when the notion of something having meaning is present, e.g. *They exchanged meaningful looks*, but alternatives such as 'important', 'significant', or 'effective' should be considered when it is importance rather than meaning that is the issue.

means In the sense 'that by which a result is brought about' the noun **means** may be used either as a singular or as a plural, e.g. (singular) *The press was, at this time, the only means…of influencing opinion* (A. J. P. Taylor); (plural) *All the time-honoured means of meeting the opposite sex* (Frederic Raphael). However, beware of mixing singular and plural, as in *The right to resist by every* (singular) *means that* *are* (plural) *consonant with the law of God*. In the sense 'money resources' **means** is always a plural noun, e.g. *You might find out from Larry…what his means are* (G. B. Shaw).

media The word **media** comes from the Latin plural of **medium**. The traditional view is that it should therefore be treated as a plural noun in all its senses in English and be used with a plural rather than a singular verb, e.g. *The communication media inflate language because they dare not be honest* (Anthony Burgess). An example of the correct use of the singular would be: *Television is the most important medium for getting known by the general public*. In practice, in the sense 'television, radio, and the press collectively', **media** now behaves as a collective noun (like 'staff' or 'clergy', for example), which means that it is now becoming acceptable in standard English for it to take either a singular or a plural verb. Nevertheless, this use is still regarded as wrong by some people, and the incorrect plural form 'medias' should certainly be avoided. See also AGENDA; CRITERIA/CRITERION; DATA/DATUM.

mental **1** The use of **mental** in compounds such as **mental hospital** and **mental patient** is first recorded at the end of the 19th century and was the normal accepted term in the first half of the 20th century. It is now, however, regarded as old-fashioned, sometimes even offensive, and has been largely replaced by the term **psychiatric** in both general and official use.

2 The terms **mental handicap** and **mentally handicapped**, though widely used a few decades ago, have fallen out of favour in recent years and have been largely replaced in official contexts by newer terms such as LEARNING DIFFICULTIES.

methodology This means a body of methods or the study of method and its application in a particular field. It is often misused as a posh word for 'method'.

Miao See HMONG.

mickle / muckle The original proverb *Many a little makes a mickle* is now better known in the corrupted (and nonsensical) form *Many a mickle makes a muckle*. **Mickle** and **muckle** are, by origin, merely variants of the same (now dialect) word meaning 'a

large amount'. However, the common use of the proverb in its corrupted form has spawned a widespread misunderstanding: that **mickle** means 'a small amount', and **muckle** means the opposite, 'a large amount'.

might See MAY/MIGHT.

millennium See CENTURY (1).

minimize Correctly used, this word means 'to reduce to, or estimate at, the minimum', e.g. *Each side was inclined to minimize its own losses in battle*. It is not a mere synonym for 'lessen' or 'reduce' and cannot be qualified by adverbs like 'greatly'. See also MAXIMIZE.

minister In its ecclesiastical sense, **minister** is the term to use for a member of the clergy in the Presbyterian, Lutheran, and Nonconformist Churches; it is also the term preferred by low-church Anglicans. Care should be taken before using the term as a synonym for PRIEST, as it implies an essentially Protestant view of church organization and the role of the clergy.

minority The phrase *a large* (or *vast*, etc.) *minority* can mean either 'almost half', or 'a number who are very much the minority': although it usually means the former, it is best to avoid the ambiguity. See also MAJORITY.

Mongolism The term **mongol** was adopted in the late 19th century to refer to a person suffering from DOWN'S SYNDROME, owing to the similarity of some of the physical symptoms of the disorder with the normal facial characteristics of East Asian people. This use is now unacceptable and considered offensive.

Mongoloid The terms **Mongoloid**, NEGROID, AUSTRALOID, and so on, were introduced by 19th-century anthropologists attempting to classify human racial types, but today they are recognized as having very limited validity as scientific categories. Although occasionally used when making broad generalizations about the world's populations, in most modern contexts they are potentially offensive, especially when used of individuals. The names of specific peoples or nationalities should be used instead wherever possible.

more than one This phrase is followed by a singular verb and is referred back to by singular pronouns, e.g. *More than one popular dancing man inquired anxiously at his bank* (Evelyn Waugh).

Ms This, pronounced 'miz', is now the courtesy title of choice for many women who do not wish their marital status to be disclosed by **Miss** or **Mrs**. Use it unless the woman has asked to be addressed by a different title. If a woman signs her letters 'Susan Hopkins' without indicating a preferred title, there is no harm in writing to her as *Dear Susan Hopkins* or *Dear Ms Hopkins*.

Muhammad, Muslim The name of the founder of Islam is now spelt **Muhammad** in English, not 'Mohammed'. The word for a follower of Islam (and the corresponding adjective) is **Muslim**, not 'Moslem' or other older forms. 'Muhammadan' (a term often used in the past) is now considered offensive by Muslims themselves in suggesting that Muhammad and not Allah is the object of worship.

muckle See MICKLE/MUCKLE.

mute To describe a person without the power of speech as **mute** (especially as in DEAF MUTE) is today likely to cause offence. Nevertheless, there are no accepted alternative terms in general use (see DUMB).

mutual Traditionally, it has long been held that the only correct use of **mutual** is in describing a reciprocal relationship: *mutual respect*, for example, means that the parties involved feel respect for each other. The use of **mutual** to mean simply 'held in common', as in *They had a mutual friend*, is held to be incorrect. This latter use has a long and respectable history, however. It was first recorded in Shakespeare, and has since appeared, most famously, as the title of Dickens's novel *Our Mutual Friend*. It also has the advantage of avoiding the ambiguity of e.g. *their common friend*.

N

Nama See HOTTENTOT.

native In contexts such as *a native of Boston* the use of the noun **native** is quite acceptable. However, when used as a noun without qualification, as in *This dance is a favourite with the natives*, the word is more problematic. In modern use it is often used semi-humorously to refer to the local inhabitants of a particular place (*New York in the summer was too hot even for the natives*). In other contexts it has an old-fashioned feel and, because of being closely associated with a colonial European outlook on non-white peoples living in remote places, it may cause offence.

Native American *See* AMERICAN INDIAN.

nature To avoid verbosity, it is better to use an abstract noun rather than a construction using **nature** with an adjective, e.g. write *the dangerousness of the spot*, not *the dangerous nature of the spot*. See also CHARACTER.

need, want **1** The two legitimate constructions exemplified by *Your hair needs* (or *wants*) *cutting* and *We want* (or *need*) *this changed* are not correctly to be combined into *We need* (or *want*) *this changing*.

2 The two constructions in *That shirt needs* (or *wants*) *washing* and *That shirt needs* (or *wants*) *to be washed* have more or less the same meaning. Both are acceptable in standard English, but a third construction, *That shirt needs washed*, is restricted to certain dialects of Scotland and North America and is not considered standard.

Negro The word **Negro** was adopted from Spanish and Portuguese and first recorded from the mid 16th century. It remained the standard term throughout the 17th–19th centuries and was used by prominent black American campaigners in the early 20th century. Since the 1960s, however, when BLACK was favoured as the term to express racial pride, **Negro** (together with related words such as **Negress**) has dropped out of favour and now seems out of date or even offensive.

neighbourhood When used with numbers or sums of money *in the neighbourhood of* is an unnecessarily cumbersome periphrasis for 'round about', 'approximately', etc.

neither The use of **neither** with another negative, as in *I don't like him neither* or *I'm not much good at reading neither* is recorded from the 16th century onwards, but is not thought to be good English. This is because it is an example of a double negative, which, though standard in some other languages and found in many dialects of English, is not acceptable in standard English. In the sentences above, 'either' should be used instead.

nigger The word **nigger** was first used as an adjective denoting a black person in the 17th century and has had strong offensive connotations ever since. Today it remains one of the most racially offensive words in the language. Ironically, it has acquired a new strand of use in recent years, being used by black people as a mildly disparaging way of referring to other black people.

non- See UN-/NON-.

non-flammable See INFLAMMABLE.

nonplussed In standard use **nonplussed** means 'surprised and confused', as in *She was nonplussed at his eagerness to help out.* In American English a new use has developed in recent years, meaning 'unperturbed'— more or less the opposite of its traditional meaning—as in *He was clearly trying to appear nonplussed.* This new use probably arose on the assumption that 'non-' was the normal negative prefix and must therefore have a negative meaning. Although the use is common, it is not yet considered standard.

normalcy The use of **normalcy** to mean 'the state or quality of being normal' is chiefly American. Prefer **normality.**

north / northern / northerly See EAST/ EASTERN/EASTERLY.

not only While the most natural position for the word ONLY in a sentence is very often just before the verb, placing **not only** here is generally poor style and runs the risk of ambiguity. For example, in the sentence *Katherine's marriage not only kept her away, but at least two of Mr. March's cousins* (C. P. Snow), the phrasing *kept not only her* would be better. If placing **not only** before the verb is inevitable, the verb should be repeated after 'but (also)', e.g. *It not only brings the coal out but brings the roof down as well* (George Orwell).

no way The use of this phrase to mean 'not at all, by no means', e.g. *No way will you stop house prices going up again,* or 'certainly not', e.g. *'Did you go up in the elevator?' 'No way!'* is chiefly American and informal only.

null and void Null means **void** ('of no effect'), so there is no need for both words in a phrase like *The agreement is null and void.* Prefer simply **void** or some other term, such as 'worthless' or 'invalid'.

number The construction **the number of** plus plural noun is used with a singular verb, e.g. *The number of people affected remains small.* Here it is the noun **number** rather than the noun 'people' which is taken to agree with the verb. By contrast, the apparently similar construction **a number of** plus plural noun is used with a plural verb, e.g. *A number of people remain to be contacted.* In this case it is the noun 'people' which acts as the head noun and with which the verb agrees. **A number of** here works as if it were a single word, such as 'some' or 'several'. See also LOT (1).

obligate In Britain, this verb is only used in legal contexts (meaning 'to constrain by law'). There seems no gain in using it (as often in American usage) as a synonym for 'oblige'.

oblivious In the sense 'unaware of', **oblivious** may be followed either by 'of' or 'to', e.g. *'When the summer comes,' said Lord Marchmain, oblivious of the deep corn…outside his windows* (Evelyn Waugh); *Rose seemed oblivious to individuals* (Angus Wilson). This second sense is now fully established in the language.

obscene It is better to restrict this word to the sense 'offensive to prevailing standards of (sexual) decency' and to avoid using it as a general term of disapproval, e.g. *obscene pay rises in the board room.*

octopus The standard plural in English is **octopuses**. However, the word **octopus** comes from Greek and the Greek plural form **octopodes** is occasionally used. The plural form 'octopi', formed according to rules for Latin plurals, is incorrect.

of For the mistake of using **of** for **have**, see HAVE (3).

off of The use of **off of** to mean **off**, e.g. *He took the cup off of the table*, is non-standard and to be avoided. Although this use is recorded from the 16th century and is logically parallel to the standard 'out of', it is now restricted to dialect and informal contexts, particularly in North America.

on See UPON.

one **1** One is used as a pronoun to mean 'anyone' or 'me and people in general', as in *One must try one's best*. In modern English it is generally only used in formal and written contexts, outside which it is likely to be regarded as pompous or over-formal. In informal and spoken contexts the normal alternative is 'you', as in *You have to do what you can, don't you?*

2 Until quite recently, sentences in which **one** is followed by 'his' or 'him' were considered perfectly correct; e.g. *One must try his best*. These uses are now held to be ungrammatical: **one's** should be used instead.

3 Any one, every one, and some one are written as two words only to emphasize the numerical sense of a single person or thing, e.g. *Any one of us can do it*; *Every one of these is broken*. Otherwise they are written as one word, e.g. *Anyone who wants to can come*; *Everyone makes mistakes*.

ongoing Ongoing has a valid use meaning 'that is happening and will continue', e.g. *The refugee problem in our time is an ongoing problem* (Robert Kee). The vague or tautologous use of **ongoing** should be avoided, particularly in the cliché *ongoing situation* (see SITUATION).

only The traditional view is that the adverb **only** should be placed next to the word or words whose meaning it restricts, e.g. *I have seen him only once* rather than *I have only seen him once*. The argument for this, a topic which has occupied grammarians for more than 200 years, is that if **only** is not placed correctly the scope or emphasis is wrong, and could even result in ambiguity.

However, in normal, everyday English, the impulse is to state **only** as early as possible in the sentence, generally just before the verb, e.g. *I only want some water* is the natural

way of saying *I want only some water*. The result is, in fact, hardly ever ambiguous: few native speakers would be confused by the sentence *I have only seen him once* (and the supposed 'logical' sense often emerges only with further clarification, as in *I've only seen him once, but I've heard him many times*). If confusion seems genuinely possible, then place **only** before the item which it limits, e.g. *The coalminer is second in importance only to the man who ploughs the soil* (George Orwell). See also NOT ONLY.

on to / onto The preposition **onto** written as one word (instead of **on to**) is recorded from the early 18th century and has been widely used ever since, but is still not wholly accepted as part of standard English (unlike 'into', for example). However, in American English **onto** is more or less the standard form and this is likely to become the case in British English before long. Note also that when used in the specialized mathematics sense, the form is invariably **onto**.

Nevertheless, it is important to maintain a distinction between the preposition **onto** or **on to** and the use of the adverb 'on' followed by the preposition 'to': *She climbed on to* (or *onto*) *the roof* but *Let's go on to* (not *onto*) *the next point*.

opine This unusual verb smells of pomposity in British English, e.g. *The barrister opined that the case would fail in court*. This is a pity as avoiding it can lead to wordiness (e.g. *It is the opinion of the barrister that...*) Alternative verbs include 'believe', 'consider', or 'say'. In Indian English *opine* is standard and not pompous.

orient / orientate The two verbs are virtually synonymous. In general use, **orientate** seems to predominate, but either is acceptable.

oriental The word **oriental** has an out-of-date feel as a term denoting people from the Far East; it tends to be associated with a rather offensive stereotype of the people and their customs as inscrutable and exotic. In American English, ASIAN is the standard accepted term in modern use; in British English, where **Asian** tends to denote people from the Indian subcontinent, specific terms such as 'Chinese' or 'Japanese' should be used.

other than In the correct use of this phrase, **other** should be either an adjective or a pronoun, e.g. *He was no other than the rightful lord*; *The acts of any person other than myself*. The use of **other** as an adverb in e.g. *We cannot react other than angrily* is strictly speaking incorrect: **otherwise than** should here be used instead..

ourself The standard reflexive form corresponding to 'we' and 'us' is **ourselves**, as in *We can only blame ourselves*. The singular form **ourself**, first recorded in the 15th century, is sometimes used in modern English, typically where 'we' refers to people in general. This use, though logical, is uncommon and not widely accepted in standard English. See also THEMSELF.

out The use of **out** as a preposition meaning **out of**, as in *He threw it out the window*, is common in informal contexts but is not widely accepted in standard English.

outside / outside of **1** Is there any difference between *The books have been distributed outside Europe* and *The books have been distributed outside of Europe*? Broadly speaking, both have the same meaning and either is acceptable in standard English. However, the use of **outside of** is much commoner and better established in American than in British English.

2 The use of **outside of** to mean 'apart from' is informal only, e.g. *The need of some big belief outside of art* (Roger Fry, in a letter).

outstanding Do not use **outstanding** in the sense 'remaining undetermined, unpaid, etc.' where ambiguity with the sense 'eminent, striking' can arise, e.g. *In a moment we'll give you the other outstanding results* (in a sports commentary).

outward / outwards See BACKWARD/ BACKWARDS.

overly The use of **overly** to mean 'excessively, too' in such phrases as *overly cautious* is still regarded by some people as an Americanism. For this reason it may be better to use 'excessively', 'too', or 'over-' instead; for **not overly**, 'not very' or 'none too' make satisfactory replacements.

overseas / oversea **Overseas** is now more usual than **oversea** as both adjective and adverb.

owing to Unlike DUE TO, **owing to** has for long been established as a compound preposition meaning 'because of', e.g. *My rooms became uninhabitable, owing to a burst gas-pipe* (C. P. Snow). However, the clumsy phrase *owing to the fact that* is better avoided: use a conjunction like 'because'.

pace *Pace*, from the Latin word *pax* 'peace', means 'by the leave of' and is used to express polite disagreement with the person cited, e.g. *Our civilization, pace Chesterton, is founded on coal* (George Orwell). It does not mean 'according to (someone)' or 'notwithstanding (something)'.

pants In British English **pants** (plural noun) means 'underpants', whereas in American English it means 'trousers or slacks'. The distinction can cause problems.

parameter Until recently, use of the word **parameter** was confined to mathematics, statistics, and related fields, in which it has several highly specialized meanings. Since around the mid 20th century, however, it has been used in the general language as a technical-sounding word for 'a limit or boundary', as in *They set the parameters of the debate*. This use, probably influenced by the word 'perimeter', has been criticized as a weakening of the technical sense. However, it is now generally accepted as part of standard English.

part See BEHALF/PART.

partially / partly Apart from the (rare) use of **partially** to mean 'in a partial or biased way', these two words are largely interchangeable. However, there is a general tendency to use **partially** to mean 'not completely; to a limited degree only' and **partly** to mean 'not as a whole; only in a part or parts', e.g. *partially sighted*; *only partially awake*; *partly clothed*; *partly made of wood*. In particular, **partly** is used in the construction 'partly (this) and...partly (that)', e.g. *partly in verse and partly in prose*.

peer In such phrases as *She had no peer in her field*, **peer** means 'equal', not (as is sometimes thought) 'superior'.

pence / pennies Both **pence** and **pennies** have existed as plural forms of 'penny' since at least the 16th century. The two forms now tend to be used for different purposes: **pence** refers to sums of money (*five pounds and sixty-nine pence*) while **pennies** refers to the coins themselves (*I left two pennies on the table*).

In recent years, **pence** has sometimes been used in the singular to refer to sums of money amounting to one penny, e.g. *The chancellor will put one pence on income tax*. However, this singular use is not widely accepted in standard English.

people See PERSONS/PEOPLE.

per It is a sound general rule not to use this Latin word when an English equivalent exists and is idiomatic: it is better, for example, to say *The salary is £25,000 a year* rather than *The salary is £25,000 per year*, and *We will send the goods by parcel post* rather than *We will send the goods per parcel post*. **Per** is best reserved for use in official contexts, in Latin phrases such as *per annum*, and in formulaic expressions such as *miles per hour* and *kilometres per gallon*. See also AS PER.

peremptory Peremptory means 'admitting no denial or refusal' and not (perhaps by confusion with 'perfunctory') 'abrupt, sudden'. A *peremptory decision* is not one that has been hastily reached but one that is definitive.

perfect See UNIQUE.

persistency / persistence Persistency means 'perseverance', e.g. *They made repeated requests for compensation, but an official apology was the only reward for their persistency*. Persistence is sometimes used in this sense, e.g. *England's winning try was just reward for their persistence*, but more often for 'continued existence', e.g. *The persistence of this primitive custom*. **Persistency** cannot be used in this second sense.

person of colour The term **person of colour** is first recorded at the end of the 18th century. It was revived in the 1990s as the recommended term to use in some official contexts (especially in the US), to refer to a person who is not white. The term is not common in general use, however, and terms such as **non-white** are still used. See also COLOURED.

persons / people The words **people** and **persons** can both be used as the plural of 'person' but they are not used in exactly the same way. **People** is by far the commoner of the two words and is used in most ordinary contexts, e.g. *A group of people*; *Several thousand people have been rehoused*. **Persons**, on the other hand, tends now to be restricted to official or formal contexts, as in *This vehicle is authorized to carry twenty persons*; *No persons admitted without a pass*.

persuade See CONVINCE/PERSUADE.

peruse The verb **peruse** means 'read thoroughly and carefully'. It is sometimes mistakenly taken to mean 'read through quickly, glance over', as in *Later documents will be perused rather than studied in depth*.

petit bourgeois, petty bourgeois The meaning is the same. If the former is used, the correct French inflections should be added: *petite bourgeoise* (feminine), *petit(e)s bourgeois(es)* (plural); also *petite bourgeoisie*.

phenomenon The word **phenomenon** comes from Greek, and its plural form is **phenomena**. Correct usage is illustrated by the following examples: *This phenomenon can best be observed in Santander, that most elegant of ferry ports*; *Men began to regard these phenomena with more composure*. It is a mistake to treat **phenomena** as if it were a singular form, as in *This is a strange phenomena*, or to create a plural form 'phenomenas'.

picaresque Picaresque refers to a style of fiction dealing with the episodic adventures of rogues. It does not mean 'transitory' or 'roaming'.

pivotal This word means 'crucial, decisive', e.g. *The tax issue was pivotal to the result of the election*. It should not be used merely to mean 'vital'.

plead In a law court a person can **plead guilty** or **plead not guilty**. The phrase 'plead innocent' is not a technical legal term, although it is commonly found in general use.

plus The use of **plus** as a conjunction meaning 'and furthermore', e.g. *plus we will be pleased to give you personal financial advice*, is considered incorrect by many people.

polity This word means either 'a form of civil government', (e.g. *a republican polity*) or 'a state'. It does not mean 'policy' or 'politics'.

polytechnic In Britain the term **polytechnic** has largely dropped out of use. This is because the Higher and Further Education Act (1992) gave British polytechnics the right to award their own degrees and style themselves universities.

portentous In traditional usage, **portentous** means either 'like a portent, ominous', e.g. *Fiery-eyed with a sense of portentous utterance* (Muriel Spark), or 'prodigious, awe-inspiring', e.g. *A truly portentous achievement*. More recently a third sense has developed, in which **portentous** is used to mean 'solemn, pompous', e.g. *A portentous commentary on Holy Scripture* (Lord Hailsham). This sense is sometimes criticized, but is an established, slightly jocular use. The form 'portentious' (due to the influence of 'pretentious') is erroneous.

post-, pre- The use of these prefixes as full words should be avoided, e.g. in *Post the death of Diana*. Similarly, the use of such compounds as 'pre-war', 'post-Internet', etc., as adverbs in e.g *Some time pre-war there was a large contract out for tender* (*Daily Telegraph*) is generally considered poor style.

pp In formal correspondence, **pp** (or **per pro**) is often used when one person signs a letter on behalf of another. Traditionally, it should be placed before the name of the person doing the signing rather than before the name of the other person. This is because the original Latin phrase *per procurationem* means 'through the agency of'. However, **pp** is now often taken to mean 'on behalf of' and is placed before the name of the person who has not signed, and this has become standard practice in many offices.

pre- **1** See POST-, PRE-.

2 See RE-.

predicate When followed by 'of', the verb **predicate** means 'to assert as a property of', e.g. *That easy Bohemianism – conventionally predicated of the 'artistic' temperament* (J. I. M. Stewart). When followed by 'on', it means 'to found or base (a statement etc.) on', e.g. *Their conclusions are predicated on sound research*. However, this second sense tends to sound pretentious and it is better to use 'found' or 'base'.

pre-empt **Pre-empt** can mean either 'to acquire in advance', e.g. *Contributions pre-empt a slice of incomes which would otherwise be available for saving* (Enoch Powell), or 'to preclude', e.g. *The Nazi régime by its own grotesque vileness pre-empted fictional effort* (*Listener*). The second sense is generally better expressed by 'preclude' or 'forestall'. In any case, **pre-empt** is not a synonym for 'prevent'.

prefer **1** In constructions using **prefer**, the rejected alternative is normally introduced by 'to', e.g. *People preferred darkness to light* (Revised English Bible). However, when the rejected alternative is an infinitive, it is preceded by 'rather than' (not 'than' alone), e.g. *I'd prefer to be stung to death rather than to wake up…with half of me shot away* (John Osborne). The construction 'prefer…over' is chiefly American.

2 In constructions using **preference**, the alternatives are usually introduced by 'for' and 'over', e.g. *The preference for a single word over a phrase or clause* (Anthony Burgess). However, **in preference** is always followed by 'to'.

3 Because **preferable to** means 'more desirable than' it should be intensified by 'far', 'greatly', or 'much', not 'more'.

prejudice In its most commonly used sense of 'bias', **prejudice** is followed by 'against' or 'in favour of'. However, in the sense of 'detriment', it is followed by 'to' (*without prejudice to his own interests*) and in the sense of 'injury', it is followed by 'of' (*to the prejudice of his own interests*).

prepared The use of **prepared** with an infinitive, to mean 'willing and able (to do something)' has been criticized, but is now established usage, e.g. *One should kill oneself, which, of course, I was not prepared to do* (Cyril Connolly).

presently Presently can mean either 'soon', e.g. *Presently we left the table and sat in the garden-room* (Evelyn Waugh), or 'now', e.g. *The praise presently being heaped upon him* (*Economist*). The second sense (long current in American English) is regarded as incorrect by some people but is widely used and often sounds more natural than 'at present'.

prestigious The main sense of this adjective is now 'having prestige', e.g. *A career in pure science is still more socially prestigious... than one in engineering* (*The Times*). The older meaning 'characterized by magic, deceptive', e.g. *The prestigious balancing act which he was constantly obliged to perform* (*Times Literary Supplement*), is now rare and liable to be misunderstood.

prevent When used with a personal object, **prevent** is followed by either 'from' plus the gerund ('-ing' form), or by the possessive case with the gerund, e.g. *He tried to prevent me from going* or *...prevent my going*. The construction *prevent me going* is widespread but somewhat informal. See also FORBID.

priest In its Christian context a **priest** is an ordained minister of the Roman Catholic, Orthodox, or Anglican Church (above a deacon and below a bishop), authorized to perform certain rites and administer the sacraments. The term MINISTER is preferred by more Protestant denominations. Owing to its strong pagan overtones, the term **priestess** is offensive when applied to a woman priest or minister of any Christian church. See -ESS.

prioritize See -IZE.

prior to This somewhat pompous way of saying 'before' tends to produce clumsy, verbless constructions, e.g. *Prior to the abandonment of the mine by the company...* instead of *Before the company abandoned the mine...* It is better to keep **prior** as an adjective (*prior approval; prior discussion*) or as a noun for people in charge of monasteries.

pristine Traditionally, **pristine** means either 'ancient, original' or 'unspoilt', e.g. *the pristine simplicity of our Saxon-English* (Benjamin Disraeli); *Pristine snow reflects about 90 per cent of incident sunlight* (Fred Hoyle). The more recent use of **pristine** to

mean 'spotless', 'pure', or 'fresh' is criticized by some people.

prone Like **liable to** and **apt to**, **prone to** can be used with an infinitive to indicate probability, e.g. *He is prone to ask leading questions*; like **liable** it can also be used with a direct object to mean 'subject to', e.g. *My literary temperament rendering me especially prone to 'all that kind of poisonous nonsense'* (Cyril Connolly). The main distinction is that **prone** is nearly always used with personal subjects. See also LIABLE/APT.

proportion In careful writing **proportion** is used to mean 'a comparative part', rather than a mere 'part'.

protagonist The correct meaning of this word is 'chief or leading person in a story or incident'. In Greek drama, from which the term originates, there was only one protagonist, but this is no reason to debar the use of the word in the plural, e.g. *We...sometimes mistook a mere supernumerary in a fine dress for one of the protagonists* (C. S. Lewis). More controversial is the modern use of **protagonist** to mean 'an advocate or champion of a cause, etc.', e.g. *The flawed economics of the nuclear protagonists' case*. This new sense probably arose from confusion with 'proponent' and by analogy with 'antagonist', the 'pro-' in **protagonist** being interpreted as meaning 'in favour of'. In fact, the 'prot-' in **protagonist** derives from the Greek root meaning 'first'. For this reason some traditionalists regard the newer use as incorrect, although it is now widespread.

protest When used transitively **protest** means 'to affirm solemnly', e.g. *He protested his innocence*. The sense 'object to', in e.g. *The residents have protested the sale*, is American only.

proved / proven For complex historical reasons, **prove** developed two past participles: **proved** and **proven**. Both are correct and can be used more or less interchangeably, e.g. *This hasn't been proved yet*; *This hasn't been proven yet*. In British English **proved** is more common, with the exception that **proven** is always used when the word is an adjective coming before the noun, e.g. *a proven talent*, not *a proved talent*. The use of **proven** as a past participle is, however, standard in Scots and American English.

Q

quadrillion See BILLION.

queer The word **queer** was first used to mean 'homosexual' in the early 20th century: it was originally, and usually still is, a deliberately offensive and aggressive term when used by heterosexual people. In recent years, however, some homosexual people have taken the word **queer** and deliberately used it in place of GAY or 'homosexual', in an attempt to deprive it of its negative power. This use of **queer** is now well established among homosexuals (especially as an adjective or noun modifier, as in *queer rights*; *queer bashing*) and at present exists alongside the other, deliberately offensive use.

question The construction **no question that** (or **but**) means 'no doubt that', e.g. *There can be no question that the burning of Joan of Arc must have been a most instructive and interesting experiment* (G. B. Shaw). However, **no question of** means 'no possibility of', e.g. *There can be no question of tabulating successes and failures* (C. S. Lewis). See also BEG THE QUESTION; LEADING QUESTION.

quite When used to qualify adjectives, adverbs, nouns, and verbs, **quite** sometimes causes difficulty because it has two branches of meaning which are not always distinguishable (especially in print which lacks the support of voice intonation). The older 'stronger' meaning of **quite** is 'completely, entirely', e.g. *You are a humourist… Quite a humourist* (Jane Austen); this remains the dominant sense in American English but tends to be restricted to set expressions in British English, e.g. *I quite agree*. The 'weaker' meaning of **quite** is 'rather, fairly', e.g. *The music was at times quite loud*; *We quite like what you have done*. This emerged in the 19th century and is now the dominant meaning in British English.

When **quite** qualifies adjectives and adverbs, the weaker meaning normally occurs with so-called 'gradable' adjectives (those that can be qualified by 'more', 'very', 'somewhat', etc.) such as *good, bad, large, small*, whereas the stronger meaning occurs with 'non-gradable' adjectives such as *different, enough, excellent, impossible*. So *quite good* will normally mean 'fairly good'

whereas *quite different* will normally mean 'entirely different'. However, examples can readily be found (especially with adverbs) which either leave the choice of meaning unclear or suggest a meaning somewhere between the two extremes, e.g. *I can get by quite happily without you*; *His writing style has changed quite noticeably*.

quote The use of **quote** as a noun meaning 'quotation' is informal only, except in finance (meaning a statement of current market price) and in commerce (meaning a tender or estimate of costs).

R

race In recent years, the association of **race** with the discredited theories of 19th-century anthropologists and the dangerous ideologies they gave rise to, has led to the word itself becoming problematic. Although still used in general contexts, it is now often replaced by other words that are less emotionally and ideologically charged, such as 'people(s)' or 'community'.

rack / wrack The relationship between the forms **rack** and **wrack** is complicated. The most common noun sense, 'a framework for holding and storing things', is always spelt **rack**, never **wrack**. The figurative senses of the verb, deriving from the type of torture in which someone is stretched on a rack, can, however, be spelt either **rack** or **wrack**: thus *racked with guilt* or *wracked with guilt*; *rack your brains* or *wrack your brains*; *the bank was racked by internal division* or *wracked by internal division*. In addition, the phrase **rack and ruin** can also be spelt **wrack and ruin**. In all the contexts mentioned here, **rack** is always the commoner spelling.

rarely See HARDLY, SCARCELY, RARELY.

re It is often said that **re**, meaning 'the matter of', should be used in headings and references, as in *Re: Ainsworth versus Chambers*, but not as a normal word meaning 'about, concerning', as in *Thanks for your note re the meeting on Tuesday*. However, the evidence suggests that **re** is now widely used and accepted in this second sense in business and official writing. In more general contexts it is preferable to write 'in reference to', 'about', or 'concerning'.

re- In modern English, the tendency is for words formed with prefixes such as **re-** to be unhyphenated. One general exception to this is when the word to which **re-** attaches begins with 'e': in this case a hyphen is often inserted for clarity, e.g. **re-examine**, **re-enter**, **re-enact**. A hyphen is sometimes also used where the word formed with the prefix would be identical to an already existing word, e.g. write **re-cover** (meaning 'cover again', as in *We decided to re-cover the dining-room chairs*) to avoid confusion with **recover** (meaning 'get better in health'). Similar guidelines apply to other prefixes such as **de-** and **pre-**.

reason 1 The construction **the reason why...is** has been objected to on the grounds that the subordinate clause should express a statement, using a 'that'-clause, not imply a question with a 'why'-clause, e.g. *The reason (that) I decided not to phone* rather than *The reason why I decided not to phone*.
2 An objection is also made to the construction **the reason...is because** as in *The reason I didn't phone is because my mother has been ill*. The objection is made on the grounds that either 'because' or 'the reason' is redundant; it is better to use the word 'that' instead (*The reason I didn't phone is that...*) or rephrase altogether (*I didn't phone because...*). Nevertheless, both the above usages are well established and, though more elegant phrasing can no doubt be found, they are generally accepted in standard English.

Red Indian See AMERICAN INDIAN.

referendum The plural **referendums** is preferable to **referenda**.

refute The core meaning of **refute** is 'prove (a statement or theory or person) to be wrong', as in *attempts to refute Einstein's theory*. In the second half of the 20th century, a weakened sense developed from the core one, meaning simply 'deny', as in *I absolutely refute the charges made against me*. Traditionalists object to the second use on the grounds that it is an unacceptable degradation of the language, but it is now widely found.

regalia This plural noun, meaning 'emblems of royalty or of an order', has no singular in ordinary English. However, in current English usage it behaves as a collective noun, similar to words like 'staff' or 'government'. This means that it can be used with either a singular or plural verb, e.g. *The regalia of Russian tsardom is now displayed in the Kremlin* or *The regalia of Russian tsardom are now displayed...* See also INSIGNIA.

region The use of **in the region of** as an unwieldly periphrasis for 'round about' or 'approximately' is better avoided.

register office Although **register office** is the correct official term, the form **registry office** dominates in informal and non-official use.

regretfully **Regretfully** is used as a normal adverb to mean 'in a regretful manner', as in *He sighed regretfully*, but it is also used as a sentence adverb meaning 'it is regrettable that', as in *Regretfully, the trustees must turn down your request*. In this latter use it is synonymous with **regrettably**. Despite objections from traditionalists, this use is now well established and is included in most modern dictionaries without comment. See also HOPEFULLY; THANKFULLY.

rein The idiomatic phrase **a free rein**, which derives from the literal meaning of using reins to control a horse, is sometimes misinterpreted and written as 'a free reign'. This is incorrect.

renege The verb **renege**, meaning 'to fail to fulfil an undertaking', is usually constructed with 'on', e.g. *The government has reneged on its commitment to the Health Service*.

responsible for This can mean 'liable to be called to account for', e.g. *I'm not responsible for what uncle Percy does* (E. M. Forster), 'obliged to take care of', e.g. *The Prime Minister was directly responsible for the security service* (Harold Wilson), or 'the cause of', e.g. *A war-criminal responsible for so many unidentified deaths* (Graham Greene). Beware of using **responsible** in the first or second of these senses where sense three can be understood, e.g. *As Minister of State for the Environment he is directly responsible for pollution.*

restive This word can mean either 'unmanageable, rejecting control, obstinate', e.g. *The I.L.P....had been increasingly restive during the second Labour government* (A. J. P. Taylor), or 'restless, fidgety', e.g. *The audiences were...apt to be restive and noisy at the back* (J. B. Priestley). This second sense is objected to by some, but is quite commonly used by good writers.

revenge See AVENGE/REVENGE.

Reverend As a title **Reverend** is used for members of the clergy; the traditionally correct form of address is the *Reverend James Smith* or *the Reverend J. Smith*, rather than *Reverend Smith* or simply *Reverend*. Other words are prefixed in titles of more senior clergy: bishops are **Right Reverend**, archbishops are **Most Reverend**, and deans are **Very Reverend**. The abbreviation **Revd** (plural **Revds**) should be used in preference to 'Rev'.

round / around Are **round** and **around** interchangeable in all contexts? In many contexts in British English they are, as in *She put her arm round him*; *She put her arm around him*. There is, however, a general preference for **round** to be used for definite, specific movement (*She turned round*; *A bus came round the corner*), while **around** tends to be used in contexts that are less definite (*wandering around for ages*; *costing around £3,000*) or for abstract uses (*a rumour circulating around the cocktail bars*). In American English, the situation is different. The normal form in most contexts is **around**; **round** is generally regarded as informal and is only standard in certain fixed expressions, as in *All year round* and *They went round and round in circles*.

S

sad Sad has developed a new meaning 'pathetically inadequate or unfashionable', which can be applied to people or their actions or accoutrements, e.g. *A sad attempt to establish his intellectual credentials*; *Trainspotters with sad haircuts*. It is easy to see how this arose from the traditional meanings of the word, but it remains informal only.

same It is non-standard to use **same as** for 'in the same way as', e.g. *But I shouldn't be able to serve them personally, same as I do now* (L. P. Hartley).

Sami See LAPP.

sanction As a verb, **sanction** means 'to give approval to, to authorize'. It does not mean 'impose sanctions on'.

sank / sunk Historically, the past tense of **sink** has been both **sank** and **sunk** (*the boat sank*; *the boat sunk*), and the past participle has been both **sunk** and **sunken** (*the boat had already sunk*; *the boat had already sunken*). In modern English, however, the past is generally **sank** and the past participle is always **sunk**. The form **sunken** now only survives as an adjective, as in *sunken garden* or *sunken cheeks*.

sat, stood The use of the past participles **sat** and **stood** with the verb 'to be', meaning 'sitting' or 'standing', is common in British English but non-standard, e.g. *I'd be sat there falling asleep* (Kingsley Amis).

sc. This abbreviation for Latin *scilicet* 'to wit' sometimes appears in legal, academic, or other formal contexts. It is used to indicate that a word has been supplied or substituted to render an expression intelligible, e.g. *He asserted that he had met him* (sc. *the defendant*); *'I wouldn't of* (sc. *have*) *done'* was her answer.

scabrous This means (literally) 'rough, scaly' or (figuratively) 'risqué, indecent', e.g. *Silly and scabrous titters about Greek pederasty* (C. S. Lewis). It does not mean 'scathing, scurrilous'.

scarcely See HARDLY, SCARCELY, RARELY.

scarify In standard use, this means 'to loosen or scratch the surface of'. The use of **scarify** to mean 'scare, terrify' is informal only.

scenario In the entertainment industries, a **scenario** means 'an outline of the plot of a film, play, etc.', or (in older use) 'a completed film script'. The word can also be used to mean 'a postulated (usually future) sequence of events', e.g. *Several of the computer scenarios include a catastrophic rise in global temperatures*. This further sense is valid when a detailed narrative of events that might happen is denoted. In formal English the word should not be used loosely to mean 'scene', 'situation', 'circumstance', etc., e.g. *a nightmare scenario*.

Scottish / Scot / Scots / Scotch These terms are all variants of the same word but in modern English they have developed different uses and connotations. The normal everyday word used to mean 'of or relating to Scotland or its people' is **Scottish**, as in *Scottish people; Scottish Gaelic; She's English, not Scottish*. The normal, neutral word for 'a person from Scotland' is **Scot**, along with **Scotsman**, **Scotswoman**, and the plural form **the Scots** (or, less commonly, **the Scottish**). The word **Scotch**, meaning either 'of or relating to Scotland' or 'a person/the people from Scotland', was widely used in the past by Scottish writers such as Robert Burns and Sir Walter Scott. However, it has come to be disliked by many Scottish people and is now regarded as old-fashioned in most contexts. It survives in certain fixed phrases, as for example *Scotch egg* and *Scotch whisky*. **Scots** is now used chiefly as a noun and adjective referring to the form of English spoken and used in Scotland, as in *a Scots accent* or *'Nicht' is the Scots word for 'night'*.

senior, superior Both words are followed by 'to'. As they already contain the idea of 'more' they cannot be construed with 'more…than', e.g. *There are several officers senior (or superior) in rank to him*, not *…more senior (or more superior) in rank than him*.

sensibility **Sensibility** means 'sensitiveness of feeling', e.g. *The man's moving fingers…showed no sign of acute sensibility* (Graham Greene). It does not mean 'possession of good sense'.

sensual / sensuous The words **sensual** and **sensuous** are frequently used interchangeably to mean 'gratifying the senses', especially in a sexual sense. This goes against a traditional distinction, by which **sensuous** is a more neutral term, meaning 'appealing to the senses (rather than the intellect or the emotions)', as in *The interior is a sensuous baroque mix of gilt and candle wax*, while **sensual** relates to indulgence or gratification of the senses, as in *a sensual massage*. As these examples show, **sensuous** tends to be used with regard to the aesthetic aspects of sense experience, while **sensual** has a strong sexual implication. In fact the word **sensuous** is thought to have been invented by Milton (1641) in a deliberate attempt to avoid the sexual overtones of **sensual**. In practice, the connotations are such that it is difficult to use **sensuous** in this sense. While traditionalists struggle to maintain a distinction, the evidence suggests that the 'neutral' use of **sensuous** is rare in modern English. If a neutral use is intended it is advisable to use alternative wording.

serendipitous This adjective is formed from **serendipity**, meaning 'the faculty of making pleasant discoveries by accident'. It does not mean merely 'fortunate'.

sex See GENDER/SEX.

shall / will The traditional rule is that when writing of future events **shall** is used with first person pronouns, while **will** is used with second and third persons, but that when writing of promises, obligations or commands, the **wills** and **shalls** change places. In practice, however, **shall** and **will** are today used more or less interchangeably in statements (though not in questions). One result of this blurring is that confusion can now arise when legal documents use **shall** in an effort to impose an obligation, e.g. *The tenant shall pay the rent on time*. 'Must' is clearer for this purpose and should be preferred if there is any risk of confusion. For more information, see SHALL/WILL in PART II of SECTION 1: GRAMMAR.

she The use of the pronoun HE to refer to a person of unspecified sex, once quite acceptable, has become problematic in recent years and is now usually regarded as old-fashioned or sexist. One of the responses to this has been to use **she** in the way that **he** has been used, as in *Only include your child if you know she won't distract you*. In some types of writing, for example books on childcare or feminist theory, this use of **she** has become quite common. In most contexts, however, it is likely to be distracting in the same way that **he** now is, and alternatives such as **he or she** or THEY are preferable.

sic (Latin 'thus') *Sic* is placed in brackets after a quoted word or phrase to show that this is given exactly as in the original, e.g. *Daisy Ashford's novel* The Young Visiters (sic). The reader is thus reassured that certain errors or oddities belong to the quoted text and have not been introduced by the quoter. Unless literal transcription is important, it is generally better to correct any simple errors in quoted material silently, and not to use *sic*. In particular, it should not be used to gloat over the slips of others or as a supercilious comment on someone else's prose style. See also SC.

sick In standard British English, **sick** means 'about to vomit, in the act of vomiting' when used as part of a predicate, e.g. *I felt sick*; *I was violently sick*, and 'unwell' or 'relating to illness' when used before a noun, e.g. *a sick man*; *sick pay*. The use of **sick** for 'unwell' in such sentences as *I was very sick with the flu* is still generally regarded as an Americanism, except in the phrase *off sick* ('away on sick leave').

similar The standard construction for **similar** is with 'to', as in *I've had problems similar to yours*. However, in British English, the construction 'similar as' is sometimes used instead, as in *I've had similar problems as yourself*. This is not accepted as correct in standard English.

situation **Situation** is a useful noun for 'state of affairs' which may validly be preceded by a defining adjective, e.g. *the financial situation*; *the military situation*. However, the substitution of a noun for an adjective before **situation** is often tautologous, as in *a crisis situation*; *people in work situations* ('crises' and 'work' are themselves 'situations'). The use of longer phrases to modify **situation** should be avoided, e.g. *the deep space situation*; *a balance-of-terror situation*, as should the cliché *on-going situation*.

slow / slowly The word **slow** is normally used as an adjective, e.g. *a slow learner*; *the journey was slow*. It is also used as an adverb in certain specific contexts, including compounds such as *slow-acting* and *slow-moving* and the expression *a go-slow*. Other adverbial use is informal and usually regarded as non-standard, e.g. *He drives too slow*; *Go as slow as you can*. In such contexts standard English uses **slowly** instead. In this respect the use of **slow** and **slowly** contrasts with the use of 'fast', which is completely standard in use as both an adjective and an adverb; there is no word 'fastly'.

sneaked / snuck The traditional standard past form of **sneak** is **sneaked**, e.g. *She sneaked round the corner*. An alternative past form, **snuck** (*She snuck past me*), arose in North America in the 19th century. Until very recently **snuck** was confined to American dialect use and was regarded as non-standard. However, in the last few decades its use has spread, particularly in North America, where it is now generally regarded as a standard alternative to **sneaked**.

so When used to mean 'therefore', **so** may be preceded by 'and' but need not be, e.g. *I had received no word from Martha all day, so I was drawn back to the casino* (Graham Greene).

so-called **So-called** has long been used in the sense 'called by this term, but not entitled to it'; however, it is now often used without implication of incorrectness, especially in scientific writing.

sooner In standard English, the phrase **no sooner** is followed by 'than', as in *We had no sooner arrived than we had to leave*. This is because **sooner** is a comparative, and comparatives are followed by 'than' (*earlier than*; *better than*; etc.). It is incorrect to follow **no sooner** with 'when', as in *We had no sooner arrived when we had to leave*.

sort of See KIND OF, SORT OF.

south / southern / southerly See EAST/EASTERN/EASTERLY.

spastic The word **spastic** has been used in medical senses since the 18th century. In the 1970s and 1980s it became a term of abuse, used mainly by schoolchildren, directed towards any person regarded as incompetent or physically uncoordinated. Nowadays, the use of the word **spastic**, whether as a noun or as an adjective, is likely to cause offence, and it is preferable to use phrasing such as *people suffering from cerebral palsy* instead.

specially See ESPECIALLY/SPECIALLY.

specialty In British English, this is a legal term for a type of deed. The use of **specialty** as an equivalent of **speciality** is restricted to North America.

spectate The use of **spectate** as a verb meaning 'to be a spectator' is informal only. 'Watch' is usually an adequate substitute.

spinster The development of the word **spinster** is a good example of the way in which a word acquires strong connotations to the extent that it can no longer be used in a neutral sense. From the 17th century the word was appended to names as the official legal description of an unmarried woman: *Elizabeth Harris of London, Spinster*; this type of use survives today in some legal and religious contexts. In modern everyday English, however, **spinster** cannot be used to mean simply 'unmarried woman'; it is now always a derogatory term, referring or alluding to a stereotype of an older woman who is unmarried, childless, prissy, and repressed.

sprang / sprung In British English, the standard past tense of **spring** is **sprang** (*She sprang forward*), while in American English the past can be either **sprang** or **sprung** (*I sprung out of bed*).

squaw Until relatively recently, the word **squaw** was used neutrally in anthropological and other contexts to mean 'an American Indian woman or wife'. With changes in the political climate, however, the word can no longer be used in American English without being offensive. In British English, the word has not acquired offensive connotations to the same extent, but it is nevertheless now regarded as old-fashioned.

stood See SAT, STOOD.

stratum In Latin, the word **stratum** is singular and its plural form is **strata**. In English, this distinction is maintained. It is therefore incorrect to use **strata** as a singular or the form 'stratas' as the plural: write *a new stratum was uncovered* but *a series of overlying strata*.

-style The use of an adjective plus **-style** to qualify a noun (e.g. *European-style clothing*) is acceptable. However, use of an adjective or noun plus **-style** to form an adverb is somewhat informal, e.g. *A revolution, British-style* (A. J. P. Taylor).

substantial Substantial can mean 'of real value', 'of solid material', 'having much property', or 'in essentials', e.g. *substantial damages*; *a substantial door*; *a substantial landowner*; *substantial agreement*. It is not merely a synonym for 'large'. See also SUBSTANTIAL/SUBSTANTIVE in SECTION 5: COMMON CONFUSABLES.

substitute Traditionally, the verb **substitute** is followed by 'for' and means 'put (someone or something) in place of another', as in *She substituted the fake vase for the real one*. From the late 17th century, however, **substitute** has also been used with 'with' or 'by' to mean 'replace (something) with something else', as in *She substituted the real vase with the fake one*. This can be confusing, since the two sentences shown above mean the same thing, yet the object of the verb and the object of the preposition have swapped positions. Despite the disapproval of traditionalists, the second use is now well established, especially in some scientific contexts.

such as See LIKE (1).

sunk See SANK/SUNK.

superior See SENIOR.

suspender In British English a **suspender** is usually a clip device holding up the top of a woman's stocking, whereas in American English **suspenders** are what the British call 'braces', i.e. straps holding up (men's) trousers. Failure to use the appropriate term may cause hilarity.

swam / swum In standard English, the past tense of **swim** is **swam** (*She swam to the shore*) and the past participle is **swum** (*She had never swum there before*). In the 17th and 18th centuries **swam** and **swum** were used interchangeably for the past participle, but this is not acceptable in standard modern English.

synchronize When used as a transitive verb, **synchronize** means 'to make simultaneous', e.g. *We synchronized our watches*; *The soundtrack had been poorly synchronized with the pictures*. It is not a synonym for 'combine' or 'coordinate'.

T

teach See LEARN/TEACH.

thankfully Thankfully has been used for centuries to mean 'in a thankful manner', as in *She accepted the offer thankfully*. Since the 1960s it has also been used as a sentence adverb to mean 'fortunately', as in *Thankfully, we didn't have to wait*. Although this has not attracted as much attention as the use of HOPEFULLY to mean 'it is to be hoped that', it has been criticized for the same reasons. It is, however, far commoner now than the traditional use.

the When used with a comparative **the** has the sense 'thereby', e.g. *What student is the better for mastering these distinctions?* This combination cannot be used with 'than', as in the incorrect sentence *He is the better student than his sister*. One should also avoid writing 'any the more' or 'none the less' where a simple 'any more' or 'no less' is wanted, in e.g. *The intellectual release had been no less* (not *none the less*) *marked than the physical*.

themself The standard reflexive form corresponding to 'they' and 'them' is **themselves**, as in *They can do it themselves*. The singular form **themself**, first recorded in the 14th century, has re-emerged in recent years in connection with the singular gender-neutral use of **they**, as in *This is the first step in helping someone to help themself*. The form is not widely accepted in standard English, however. See THEY.

then Then may precede a noun as a neat alternative to 'at that time', e.g. *the then Prime Minister*. It should not be placed before the noun if it would sound equally well in its usual position, e.g. *John Major was the then Prime Minister* could equally well be…*was then the Prime Minister*. Rather than *the then existing constitution* write *the constitution then existing*.

thence See WHENCE.

there- Most of the adverbs constructed from **there**, e.g. **therein**, **thereon**, **thereof**, etc., are very formal and should be avoided in ordinary writing (this does not include certain idiomatic adverbs, e.g. 'thereabouts', 'thereby', 'thereupon'). In many cases a simple 'there' can be substituted, e.g. *We did not question this reasoning, and there lay our mistake* (Evelyn Waugh): a lesser writer might have written **therein**. See also HERE-.

they The word **they** (with its counterparts **them**, **their**, and THEMSELF) has been used as a singular pronoun to refer to a person of unspecified sex since at least the 16th century. In the late 20th century, as the traditional use of HE to refer to a person of either sex came under scrutiny on the grounds of sexism, this use of **they** became more common. It is now generally accepted where it follows an indefinite pronoun such as 'anyone', 'no one', 'someone', or 'a person', as in *Anyone can join if they are a resident* and *each to their own*. The use of **they** after singular nouns is now increasingly common, though less widely accepted, especially in formal contexts. Sentences such as *Ask a friend if they could help* still run the risk of being criticized as ungrammatical.

though See ALTHOUGH/THOUGH.

through Though convenient, the use of **through** to mean 'up to and including', e.g. *Friday through Tuesday*, is American only.

till / until In most contexts, **till** and **until** have the same meaning and are interchangeable. The main difference is that **till** is generally considered to be more informal than **until** and occurs less frequently in writing. In addition, **until** tends to be the natural choice at the beginning of a sentence: *Until very recently, there was still a chance of rescuing the situation*. Interestingly, while it is commonly assumed that **till** is an abbreviated form of **until** (the erroneous spellings "till' and "til' reflect this), **till** is in fact the earlier form.

toilet This is now the commonest word in British English for what used to be called the **water closet** or **WC**. The word was formerly regarded with distaste by upper- and middle-class speakers, who preferred to go to the **lavatory**. Although some older speakers still feel this distaste quite strongly, **toilet** is the word now used on signs and notices when more specific reference to 'ladies' or 'gents' is not given. In middle-class British conversation **loo** (of uncertain origin) has become a regularly used alternative. In American English, the regular terms are **restroom**, **bathroom**, and **washroom**, with **john** as a more informal alternative. Many slang terms and euphemisms exist in both varieties.

too The use of **too** followed by an adjective before a noun should be confined to special effects, e.g. *A small too-pretty house* (Graham Greene). In normal prose it is a clumsy construction, e.g. *The crash came during a too-tight loop.*

toothcomb The forms **toothcomb** and **fine toothcomb** arose from a misreading of the compound noun 'fine-tooth comb'. They are now established expressions whose illogicality it is pedantic to object to.

tragedy Tragedy originally meant a kind of drama in which the principal character or characters suffer death or other misfortune, generally through a combination of fate and their own folly. This sense has been extended to refer to major misfortunes in real life, including purely accidental ones, and then further to more trivial and ephemeral setbacks, such as defeat in a sports event. The word is best reserved for uses in which serious misfortune is involved.

transpire The standard general sense of **transpire** is 'come to be known', e.g. *It transpired that Mark had been baptized a Catholic.* From this, a looser sense has developed, meaning 'happen or occur', e.g. *I'm going to find out exactly what transpired.* This looser sense, first recorded in American English towards the end of the 18th century and listed in US dictionaries from the 19th century, is often criticized for being jargon, a pretentious word used where 'occur' and 'happen' would do just as well. In practice, the two senses are indistinguishable in many contexts.

tribe In historical contexts, the word **tribe** is broadly accepted, e.g. *The area was inhabited by Slavic tribes.* However, when used to refer to a community living within a traditional society today, the word is problematic. It is strongly associated with past attitudes of white colonialists towards so-called primitive or uncivilized peoples and for this reason, it is generally preferable to use alternative terms such as 'community' or 'people'.

trillion See BILLION.

try and See AND (2).

U

un- / non- The prefixes **un-** and **non-** both mean 'not', but there is often a distinction in terms of emphasis. **Un-** tends to be stronger and less neutral than **non-**: consider, for example, the differences between **unacademic** and **non-academic** in the sentences *His language was refreshingly unacademic* and *A non-academic life suits him.*

unequivocal This means 'not ambiguous, unmistakable', e.g. *His refusal…was unequivocal. 'Not in a million years' was the expression he used* (P. G. Wodehouse). The adverb is **unequivocally**. The forms 'unequivocable' and 'unequivocably' are erroneous.

unique **1** The core meaning of **unique** is 'the only one of its kind', e.g. *This vase is considered unique.* However, the word has also developed a secondary, less precise sense of 'unusual, remarkable, singular', e.g. *The most unique man I ever met.* This second sense is regarded by many people as incorrect, so it is better to use a suitable synonym.
2 There is a set of adjectives—including **unique, complete, equal, infinite,** and **perfect**—whose core meaning embraces a mathematically absolute concept and which therefore, according to a traditional argument, cannot be modified by adverbs such as 'really', 'quite', or 'very'. According to this argument, something either is **unique** (or **complete** or **infinite**) or it is not, and there are no in-between stages. In practice, the situation is more complex than this, since some of these words (notably **unique** and **perfect**) have developed weakened senses in which they no longer relate to an absolute concept; in such cases the use of 'fairly', 'rather', 'somewhat', etc., is no longer illogical.

unless and until Such sentences as *Unless and until the conditions are met, the deal is off* smell of officialdom. Either 'unless' or 'until' will do. See also AS AND WHEN.

unlike The adverb **unlike** may govern a noun, noun phrase, or pronoun, just as 'like' may, e.g. *A sarcasm unlike ordinary sarcasm* (V. S. Pritchett). Its use to govern a clause or adverbial phrase, e.g. *She was behaving unlike she'd ever behaved before; Unlike in countries of lesser economic importance,* is not considered standard English. It can often be avoided by using 'as' with a negative instead, e.g. the first example above may be rewritten *She was behaving as she'd never behaved before.*

until See TILL/UNTIL.

untouchable In senses relating to the traditional Hindu caste system, the term **untouchable** and the social restrictions accompanying it were declared illegal in the constitution of India in 1949 and that of Pakistan in 1953. The official term today is **scheduled caste**.

upon The preposition **upon** has the same core meaning as the preposition **on**. However, in modern English **upon** tends to be restricted to more formal contexts or to established phrases and idioms, as in *Once upon a time* and *Row upon row of seats.*

V

various In standard English the word **various** is normally used as an adjective and determiner. It is sometimes also used as a pronoun followed by 'of', as in *various of her friends had called.* Although this pronoun use is similar to that of words such as 'several' and 'many' (e.g. *several of her friends had called*), it is sometimes regarded as incorrect.

verbal / oral It is sometimes said that the true sense of the adjective **verbal** is 'of or concerned with words', whether spoken or written (as in *verbal abuse*), and that it should not be used to mean 'spoken rather than written' (as in *a verbal warning*). For this latter sense, it is said, the adjective **oral** should be used instead. In practice, however, **verbal** is well established in this sense and, in certain idiomatic phrases (such as *a verbal agreement*), cannot be simply replaced by **oral**.

vermin This collective noun is usually treated as plural, e.g. *A lot of parasites, vermin who feed on God's love and charity* (Joyce Cary).

vest In British English, a **vest** is an undergarment for the top part of the body and also a garment worn by athletes. In American English the first of these is called an **undershirt**, and **vest** is a term for what the British call a **waistcoat** or for a short sleeveless jacket worn by women.

via The traditional meaning of **via** is 'by way of (a place)', e.g. *to London via Reading.* Its use to mean 'through the agency of', e.g. *They had sent a photo of Tina as a baby to the ... mother via a social worker* (*Independent*) is somewhat informal.

W

want See NEED, WANT.

well The adverb **well** is often used in combination with past participles to form adjectival compounds, e.g. *well adjusted, well intentioned, well known.* As far as hyphenation is concerned, the general principle is that if the adjectival compound is placed attributively (i.e. it comes before the noun), it should be hyphenated (*a well-intentioned remark*) but that if it is placed predicatively (i.e. standing alone after the verb), it should not be hyphenated (*her remarks were well intentioned*). Exceptions to the second part of this rule occur where the combination is to be distinguished in meaning from the two words written separately, e.g. *He is well-spoken* but *The words were well spoken.*

west / western / westerly See EAST/EASTERN/EASTERLY.

what ever, when ever, where ever See EVER.

whence Strictly speaking, **whence** means 'from what place', as in *Whence did you come?* Thus, the preposition 'from' in *From whence did you come?* is redundant and its use is considered incorrect by some. The same remarks apply to **hence**, which means 'from the place or source previously mentioned'. However, the use of both these words with 'from' is very common and can be found in examples by reputable writers from the 14th century onwards. It is now broadly accepted in standard English.

whether See IF (1).

while **1** The primary sense of **while** is temporal, meaning 'during the time that', e.g. *They had begun drinking while he prepared to cook*, or 'at the same time as', e.g. *She enjoyed drawing while she was being read to.* However, **while** is also frequently used with concessive or contrastive rather than temporal force, e.g. *While I enjoy his company, I couldn't live with him*; *I live in London, while my sister lives in New York*. In the first of these examples **while** is equivalent to 'although', and in the second it is equivalent to 'whereas'. Although sometimes frowned on by traditionalists, these uses are very well established in the language. Instances of possible ambiguity between the different types of meaning are sometimes adduced, but they are usually contrived and unlikely to arise in practice (such as the old chestnut *The curate read the first lesson while the rector read the second*).

2 The forms **while** and **whilst** are interchangeable in standard English (assertions that one should be reserved for the temporal sense and the other for the sense 'although, whereas' are not supported by usage). However, **whilst** is becoming unusual (especially in American English) and now has a slightly old-fashioned and formal feel.

3 In some dialects of Northern England, **while** is used to mean 'until', as in *I waited while six o'clock*. This use is not standard English.

white The term **white** has been used to refer to the skin colour of Europeans or people of European extraction since the early 17th century. Unlike other labels for skin colour such as 'red' or 'yellow', **white** has not been generally used in a derogatory way. In modern contexts there is a growing tendency to prefer terms that relate to geographical origin rather than skin colour: hence the current preference in the US for AFRICAN AMERICAN rather than BLACK and **European** rather than **white**.

whoever **1** In the sense 'any one who, no matter who', it is best to use **whoever** for the objective case as well as the subjective, rather than the somewhat stilted **whomever**, e.g. *Whoever he painted now was transfigured into that image on the canvas* (Kathleen Jones). Beware of introducing the objective **whomever** incorrectly, as in *A black mark for whomever it was that ordered the verges to be shorn* (*Daily Telegraph*). See WHO/WHOM in PART II of SECTION 1: GRAMMAR.

2 For advice on **whoever** versus **who ever**, see EVER.

-wise In modern English the suffix **-wise** is often attached to nouns to form 'viewpoint' adverbs meaning 'concerning or with respect to', as in *confidence-wise*, *tax-wise*, *price-wise*, *time-wise*, *news-wise*, and *culture-wise*. The suffix is very productive and widely used in modern English, but most of the words so formed are considered inelegant or not good English style. The use of the same suffix to form adverbs of manner in certain fixed expressions like *clockwise* is, however, totally accepted.

without The use of **without** to mean 'unless' is non-standard, e.g. *Do not leave without you tell me.*

woman See LADY/WOMAN.

worthwhile When the adjective **worthwhile** is used attributively (i.e. before the noun) it is always written as one word, e.g. *a worthwhile cause*. However, when it is used predicatively (i.e. it stands alone and comes after the verb), it may be written as either one or two words, e.g. *We didn't think it was worthwhile* or *worth while*.

wrack See RACK/WRACK.

wreak In the phrase **wrought havoc**, as in *They wrought havoc on the countryside*, **wrought** is an archaic past tense of 'work' and is not, as is sometimes assumed, a past tense of **wreak**. The use of the phrase **wreak havoc** in the present or future tense is therefore, strictly speaking, incorrect.

write **1** People are often told not to begin letters or reports with **I write** or **I am writing** because it is obvious that they are writing. But *I write to explain the department's policy on...* is quite harmless—you could not launch in with *I explain...* On the other hand, *I write to inform you that...* might as well be deleted, as nothing useful has been said.

2 The use of **write** with a personal object, e.g. *I will write you about it*, is not acceptable British English (but is good American English).

Section 7: Style and Format

This Section brings together two aspects of writing that are more often treated separately—style (manner of writing) and format (type of writing). This is by design. As well as being clear, succinct, and readable, a good style must be appropriate to the format (friendly note, formal report, legal documents, etc.): it also has to be tailored to the wider situation—the who?*,* when?*,* where?*, and* why? *of communication.*

PART I: EFFECTIVE STYLE deals with the nuts and bolts of writing prose: eight simple guidelines, illustrated with over 70 examples, show you how to clarify, simplify, and tighten up your writing. We cannot all be novelists, or even journalists, but anyone who works at it can acquire a plain functional style that gets the point across without muddle or palaver. The guidelines offered here are tried and tested. Professional editors use them on a daily basis, and testing with focus groups has shown a clear preference for writing that observes them.

Successful communication involves more than plain words and a clear sentence structure, however. Writing does not take place in a vacuum; there are always wider factors to consider, notably those of audience, occasion, and purpose—whom are we addressing, under what circumstances, and to what end? More particularly, there is the format we are using, and the rules and conventions that go with it. PART II: EFFECTIVE USE OF FORMATS begins with a general look at these issues and goes on to consider specific formats—the letter, the email, the college dissertation, and the press release, among others. In each case, understanding the format and the implications it has for style, structure, and content is the key to success.

PART I: EFFECTIVE STYLE

The following pages have one aim: to help you to master a plain and effective English prose style. This is prose with a purpose—an unpretentious medium designed to convey content as quickly and clearly as possible. It is the kind of English that ought to characterize business and official writing of every kind, but too rarely does.

Advice is presented in eight guidelines covering such basic matters as sentence length, vocabulary, and the use of active vigorous verbs. It is important to grasp that these are guidelines, not rules. There is a guideline to aim for an average sentence length of 15–20 words in a document, but there is no ban on longer sentences. There is a guideline to use words your readers are likely to understand, but there is no rule prohibiting technical terms. Nor do the guidelines offer a set of quick fixes. Writing will still be hard work, but it should get easier and more rewarding as you start to see results. Following the style points suggested here will not earn you any major literary prizes, but it should mean that what you write can be understood at first reading by a reasonably literate and well-intentioned person. In the worlds of industry, commerce, and administration, this is clearly a significant advantage.

The examples of poor style used in the following pages are all sadly authentic, and most have been taken from business letters or official documents—words have only been changed to protect the authors' anonymity or to provide enough context for the examples to make sense.

Guideline 1: Control Sentence Length

Busy people tend to recoil when they see a long involved sentence snaking its way across the page. Here is one from an accountant's letter to his self-employed client:

> *Our annual bill for services (which unfortunately from your viewpoint has to increase to some degree in line with the rapid expansion of your business activities) in preparing the accounts and dealing with tax (please note there will be higher-rate tax assessments for us to deal with on this level of profit, which is the most advantageous time to invest in your personal pension fund, unless of course changes are made in the Chancellor's Budget statement) and general matters arising, is enclosed herewith for your kind attention.*

At one level, the sentence is easy to read—all the words are clear enough for a literate client. What makes it hard work is its length and muddle, with asides and additions tagged on as they sprang into the writer's mind.

Muddle is more likely in a long sentence unless the construction is simple and well organized. Instead of making one main point—and perhaps one related subsidiary point—a long sentence force-feeds the reader with point after point after point. This demands more concentration and short-term memory, leading to overload if the topic is complicated.

But what length of sentence is too long? Ignore advice that prescribes an upper limit, though if you regularly exceed 40 words you will certainly weary your readers. It is better to aim for an average of 15 to 20 words throughout. The key word is 'average', so not all sentences need to be in this range; indeed, there should be plenty of variety. While an occasional short sentence will punch home an important point effectively, too many will make your writing dull and staccato. There is no lower limit: a sentence could be just one word, such as *Why?*, or two words, such as *I disagree*.

There are five main ways of dealing with overlong sentences:

- Split and disconnect
- Split and connect
- Use a list
- Cut verbiage
- Discard the sentence and start again

Split and disconnect

Full stops enable readers to digest your latest point and prepare for the next. A sentence can make good grammatical sense and still be too long for most people to grasp at first reading. If a sentence seems long, look for the main break in the sense and ask yourself if a full stop inserted here could make things easier for your reader. In many cases, it is possible simply to split and disconnect—that is, to strike out a conjunction such as *and* or *but*, and to insert a full stop with no further rewriting.

Split and connect

This means putting in a full stop and restarting the sentence with a connecting word like *however*, *but*, *so*, *also*, *yet* or *further*. The technique is particularly useful with sentences that start with a clause beginning *while*, *although*, or *despite*. This example comes from a lawyer's letter:

> Whilst *it is expected by the donor's family that the present arrangement for caring for the donor will continue for the rest of her life*, should it at any stage become necessary to transfer the donor once more into a nursing institution, *the donor's family envisages that the second-floor flat*

> *will be sold and the donor's share in the proceeds used to provide any additional income necessary to ensure her continued well-being.*

The obvious break point is after *life* in the second line. Striking out the initial *Whilst* creates a complete first sentence and the next can begin with *but*:

> *It is expected by the donor's family that the present arrangement for caring for the donor will continue for the rest of her life.* But *should it at any stage become necessary to transfer the donor once more into a nursing institution...* (and so on)

The letter could still be greatly improved, but one simple change has already made a big difference.

Use a list

Vertical lists break up long sentences into manageable chunks. They are particularly useful when describing a procedure, as in this safety message to hospital staff about a machine for keeping babies warm:

> *The attachment of the warmer support-bearing assembly system must be checked to ensure that it is adequately lubricated, its securing screws are tight and that the warmer head can be easily repositioned without the support bearing sticking.*

Not a hard sentence for people in the trade —and only 38 words long—but easier to follow in a vertical list:

> *The attachment of the warmer support-bearing assembly system must be checked to ensure that:*
>
> *(a) it is adequately lubricated;*
>
> *(b) its securing screws are tight;*
>
> *(c) the warmer head can be easily repositioned without the support bearing sticking.*

For more on lists, see GUIDELINE 6 below.

Cut verbiage

Sometimes the key ideas in a long sentence are buried under verbiage:

> *The organizers of the event should try to achieve greater safety both from the point of view of ensuring that the bonfire itself*

does not contain any unacceptably dangerous materials such as aerosol cans or discarded foam furniture and from the point of view of ensuring the letting-off of fireworks in the designated area, with easily identifiable wardens to be available during the event to prevent people indiscriminately letting off fireworks, to the possible danger of people attending the event.

The redundant words include *from the point of view of* (twice), *itself*, *unacceptably* (what are 'acceptably' dangerous materials?), *discarded* (they would hardly be on the bonfire otherwise), *during the event* and *to the possible danger of people attending the event* (redundant because crowd safety is what the whole sentence is about). With verbiage removed, a few minor modifications, and an extra full stop, the sentence becomes:

The organizers of the event should try to achieve greater safety by ensuring that the bonfire does not contain any dangerous materials such as aerosol cans or foam furniture, and that fireworks are let off only in the designated area. Easily identifiable wardens should be present to prevent people letting off fireworks indiscriminately.

The first sentence could also be converted into a list, using the first *that* as a pivot and deleting the second *that*:

The organizers of the event should try to achieve greater safety by ensuring that:

- *the bonfire does not contain any dangerous materials such as aerosol cans or foam furniture;*
- *fireworks are let off only in the designated area.*

For more on identifying and eliminating verbiage, see GUIDELINE 3 below.

Discard the sentence and start again

When there is no hope of untangling a sentence by other means, all you can do is discard it and rewrite. Here is that accountant's sentence from a few pages back:

Our annual bill for services (which unfortunately from your viewpoint has to increase to some degree in line with the

rapid expansion of your business activities) in preparing the accounts and dealing with tax (please note there will be higher-rate tax assessments for us to deal with on this level of profit, which is the most advantageous time to invest in your personal pension fund, unless of course changes are made in the Chancellor's Budget statement) and general matters arising, is enclosed herewith for your kind attention.

It is no good just putting in full stops because the new sentences won't make any sense, and using a vertical list doesn't seem feasible. Nor does it help to make fewer points—it is all useful detail, though verbiage like *from your viewpoint, general matters arising, herewith*, and *kind* could all be cut. So we need to start again and plan out the main points, which are:

(a) Here is our annual bill for services.

(b) We're charging more than last year for two reasons: your business has grown rapidly, and we'll have to work out a higher-rate tax assessment as you've made a lot more profit.

(c) Now is a good time to pay into your pension fund as you'll get higher-rate tax relief on your contributions, unless the rules alter in the Chancellor's Budget.

With the points reordered so that the good news comes first, this becomes:

Now is a good time for you to pay into your pension fund as you will get higher-rate tax relief on your contributions – unless the Chancellor's Budget changes the rules.

I have enclosed our annual bill for services. Unfortunately it is higher than last year. This is because your business has grown rapidly and, since your profits are much greater, I will need to calculate a higher-rate tax assessment.

Four sentences – and readily understood at first reading. The last paragraph could also be written as a vertical list:

I have enclosed our annual bill for services. Unfortunately it is higher than last year. This is because:

- *your business has grown rapidly; and*
- *I will have to work out a higher-rate tax assessment as your profits are much greater.*

Guideline 2: Use Words Your Readers Will Understand

Here is a secretary of state refusing an assistant's request for a pay rise:

Because of the fluctuational predisposition of your position's productive capacity as juxtaposed to government standards, it would be momentarily injudicious to advocate an increment.

And here is a local government official being obstructive to citizens who wish to display posters in a public library:

Your request raises a question as to the provenance and veraciousness of the material, and I must consider individually all posters of a polemic or disputatious nature.

Both sentences overdress simple ideas, clothing them in phrases designed to impress not inform. In more deferential times, people might have been impressed. Now, they smell pomposity and dislike being put to the trouble of translating.

For business writers this may have costly consequences. An accountancy firm wrote this in a business proposal:

At present the recessionary cycle is aggravating volumes through your modern manufacturing and order processing environments which provide restricted opportunities for cost reduction through labour adjustments and will remain a key issue.

What they probably meant was:

Output and orders have fallen because of the recession but there is little scope for reducing the workforce.

Whatever they meant, they didn't win the business. If a selling point is obscured by gobbledygook it ceases to be a selling point. An aeronautics firm wrote to a prospective customer:

We would anticipate being able to optimize the engine design from an emissions point of view.

In such a haystack of verbiage, the needle of meaning could easily have been missed:

We expect to be able to redesign the engine to reduce emissions.

There are two main ways of removing jargon, officialese, and pompous language from what you write:

- Use simpler alternatives
- Where necessary, reconstruct your sentences

Use simpler alternatives

The scope for using plain words—and the opposite—is rich in English because we have so many words with the same or similar meanings. For example, the cauldron which bubbled for centuries with bits of Latin, French, Old Norse, and Old English threw up several synonyms for *start*—including *begin, commence, initiate, institute* and *originate*. There is room for all these words, but *start* and *begin* are the natural first choices in everyday writing. Similarly, there is no loss of meaning in writing *so* rather than *accordingly*, *if* rather than *in the event of*, and *paid work* rather than *remunerative employment*.

Rewriting with this in mind is not usually difficult, once we break the habit of using certain hand-me-down words and phrases. A local government department is here writing to a tenant who has fallen behind with her rent. In law, the authority doesn't have to rehouse tenants it regards as deliberately homeless:

In the event of your being evicted from your dwelling as a result of wilfully failing to pay your rent, the council may take the view that you have rendered yourself intentionally homeless and as such it would not be obliged to offer you alternative permanent housing.

Using plain words and splitting the sentence, this could become:

If you are evicted from your home because you deliberately fail to pay your rent, the council may decide that you have made yourself intentionally homeless. If this happens, the council does not need to offer you alternative permanent housing.

Similarly, a hospital wants to resolve the chaos in its car parks by charging parking fees:

> If my proposals are accepted, the income from fees would ensure that car parking control could be effected without utilising monies that should be expended on health care.

This becomes:

> If my proposals are accepted, the income from fees would ensure that car parking could be controlled without using money that should be spent on health care.

A firm's conditions of service say:

> Holidays will be taken by mutual agreement after the exigencies of the service have been considered.

This becomes:

> Holidays will be taken by mutual agreement after the needs of the service have been considered.

Reconstruct the sentences

The technique here is to spot the unusual word or phrase and to use its plain meaning as an aid in revising the sentence.

A trade union writes to its members:

> It behoves management to give details of the planned redundancies, and it is incumbent on all members to participate fully in this dispute.

Sending the obsolete words back to their vaults, this becomes:

> Management should [or has a duty to] give details of the planned redundancies, and all members should [or must] participate fully in this dispute.

A treasurer's report explains how many errors are being made when handling payments:

> An approximate frequency for the mistakes was given by Mrs Jones as ten a month.

This becomes:

> Mrs Jones said that about ten mistakes a month were being made.

A company training officer is explaining a trend towards computer-based training:

> The ready availability of computer-based tutorials associated with applications software has become prevalent since the development of Microsoft Windows.

To a fellow professional, none of these words would be hard to understand. But look more closely at what is being said:

> The ready availability...has become prevalent

Since ready availability and prevalence are so similar in meaning, the writer was probably trying to say:

> Computer-based tutorials associated with applications software have become readily available since the development of Microsoft Windows.

Here plain words make the meaning clearer and the sentence crisper.

Using unusual words

The chief reason for writing at work is to give information in a way that is readily understood—to bridge the gap between what you know and what the reader knows. Generally, plain words do this best.

Sometimes, however, an unusual word is exactly right for the job, expressing just what you need to say. Then you should use it and either give an explanation or trust the context to explain; you should not always hope that busy readers will be willing to consult a dictionary. In a technical document, there is a place for technical words, which will be plain enough to technical people. But while doctors might readily understand cardiac atheroma and pulmonary oedema, a mass audience would get a clearer sense of the ailments from furring-up of the heart's arteries and fluid in the lungs. There is just no point saying that a person is exhibiting xanthochromia and diaphoresis if you can equally well say he is yellow and sweating.

The same applies to the specialized language used by lawyers—their notwithstanding, in pursuance of, heretofore, and so on; usually, alternatives are readily available and (despite well-rehearsed arguments to the contrary) there is no good reason for avoiding them. Legal language is only an extreme example of the tendency of every trade, profession, and field of activity to develop its own characteristic jargon. Sometimes this can be necessary to avoid ambiguity, imprecision, or long-windedness. However, such private dialects tend to become habitual and self-perpetuating. Try to stand back from what you have written and read it with an outsider's eye.

Sometimes educated writers are surprised to learn that words they think ordinary are unknown to the person sitting next to them on the train. It is never wise to assume that others know all the words you do. Writers who want to be readily understood need to develop a keen sense of who their readers are and the words they are likely to understand. Generally speaking, the place for unusual words is in literature and journalism, where readers are prepared to travel further with a writer's flight of fancy.

Conquering fear

The main cause of bloated, show-off writing is fear. First there is fear that being clear means being definite and that being definite leaves no room for wriggling. Yet if writers want to hedge, a plain English style lets them. They can evoke a full range of doubt and uncertainty—and even the possibility of being just plain wrong—with such words as *may*, *might*, *could*, *should*, *perhaps*, *normally*, and *generally*.

Then there is the fear that if you write simply you will not be thought sufficiently eminent, scientific, or literary. This fear was examined in a research study in 1978. Over 1,500 scientists from industry and the academic world were asked their opinion of two short pieces of scientific writing. Both pieces gave exactly the same facts in the same sequence of points, and used the same five technical terms. The only difference was in the style of the non-technical language. The first version used everyday words and short, simply constructed sentences. The second did the opposite, though without going to extremes. Nearly 70 per cent of the scientists preferred the plain version; they also found it 'more stimulating' and 'more interesting'. Three-quarters judged the writer to be more competent as a scientist and to have a better organized mind.

So don't be afraid of plain English. Carefully used, it will reveal your competence far better than the wooden style of so many academic and technical journals.

Guideline 3: Use Only as Many Words as You Really Need

Part of writing well is writing tight, ruthlessly cutting dross. Most readers are busy people who want to find out the main points of your message, fast. Making them read excess words is an unfriendly act, especially in business where a deluge of unwanted paper falls on everyone at every level.

Not that shorter is always better; sometimes you need more words to make a point clear. Moreover, your writing should not be so plain or tight that you come across as blunt and rude. Being ruthless with words needn't mean being graceless with people. The key is to let the first draft stand as long as possible, then return and revise it with all this in mind. Then revise it again. And probably again. In business, of course, time is against you: that letter or report must go out tonight. And unnecessary words are not always so obvious – they have to be sniffed out. There are three main techniques for tightening up your prose:

- Striking out useless words

- Pruning the dead wood and grafting on the vigorous

- Rewriting completely

Striking out useless words

The most obviously useless words are straight repetition:

> *The cheque that was received from Classic Assurance was received on 13 January.*

Was received occurs twice, so the sentence could say:

> *The cheque from Classic Assurance was received on 13 January*

or better still:

The cheque from Classic Assurance arrived on 13 January.

Spotting this kind of problem becomes harder as the distance between repetitions increases:

The standard of traffic management on the A57, A59, and A623 is of a lower standard than on other major roads in the region.

It doesn't make sense to say that a *standard...is of a lower standard*, so the rewrite would be:

The standard of traffic management on the A57, A59, and A623 is lower than on other major roads in the region.

Wordiness often comes from trying to make a simple procedure sound impressive:

A new bank account is in the process of being set up for you.

Delete four words and this becomes:

A new bank account is being set up *for you.*

The verb *carry out* (like undertake and *perform*) always merits suspicion. Often, it can simply be deleted:

Work is required to be carried out on the flue and funnels

becomes

Work is required on the flue and funnels.

Or *carry out* can be cut by strengthening the verb it supports:

The firm does not intend to remove the lime trees but it is necessary to carry out pruning to the trees to keep them healthy.

This becomes:

The firm does not intend to remove the lime trees but they need to be pruned *to keep them healthy.*

It is not always this easy to see redundancy. Take this sentence:

For the benefit of new members, the secretary described the rules of the committee and the remit that had been given to it.

Since *remit* means the committee's terms of reference and a remit must, by its nature, be *given*, the last six words are redundant:

For the benefit of new members, the secretary described the rules of the committee and its remit.

Cut out useless phrases like *it should be pointed out that, it must be noted that, I should mention that, I would inform you that* and *I would stress that.* Better just to point it out, note it, mention it, or stress it.

Pruning the dead wood, grafting on the vigorous

Dead wood often makes a fine pretence of being alive, so a keen eye is needed here. In this example, ten unnecessary words could be replaced by one:

May I draw your attention to the final account dated 28 June from which I note that six payments of £18 were credited to your account from 28 March to 25 August, totalling £108.

The first six words are courteous but they delay the main message unduly and could go. Then, *from which I note* is pompous – what matters is not what the writer notes but what the final account shows. Using the vigorous verb *shows*, the sentence becomes:

The final account dated 28 June shows *that six payments of £18 were credited to your account from 28 March to 25 August, totalling £108.*

Certain words are prime suspects for pruning. They include the abstract nouns *situation, aspect, facility, issue, element, factor, matter* and *concept*. All are occasionally useful but they tend to be overworked at the expense of more concrete words.

Another phrase often accompanied by verbiage is *the fact*. There is *given the fact that* and *in the light of the fact that* (which just mean 'as' or 'since'); *despite the fact that* (which means 'although'); and *the fact of the matter is* (which, if it means anything, means 'the fact is'). Here, the first six words could simply be replaced by *as*:

In view of the fact that the central heating was fitted by Union Gas, they have cancelled the bill in the interests of good customer relations.

Rewriting completely

When there are far too many words for the message but neither of the first two methods will work, a total rewrite is the only alternative. Various signals may alert you to this need:

- The meaning isn't clear.

- The sentence is long and the verbs are few.

- The verbs are feeble—for example, they are smothered by nouns (see GUIDELINE 5 below), they are in the passive voice (see GUIDELINE 4), or they are parts of *to be* or *to have*.

For example, an engineer is writing about the cost of materials for a road scheme:

> *Overestimating on one type of material could have a detrimental cost effect for the clients, depending on the prices in the Bill of Quantities.*

Alarm bells should ring at *have a detrimental cost effect*. First because *have* seems feeble as the solitary verb in the sentence, and second because *detrimental cost effect* is a pompous way of expressing the simple idea that the clients might have to pay more. So the whole sentence could say:

> *Overestimating on one type of material could* cost the clients more, *depending on the prices in the Bill of Quantities.*

While this saves only four words, there is now a strong verb, *cost*, and the message is immediately apparent.

An insurance firm is thinking of publishing a guidance booklet for managers of company car fleets. Its internal report on the idea begins:

> AIM OF PROPOSED CAR FLEET MANAGEMENT GUIDE
>
> *This guide would have the objective of highlighting to car fleet managers the best way to achieve, and the benefits of adopting, a professional approach vis-à-vis managing a car fleet.*
>
> *There are only a few publications at present covering the subject of car fleet management and with no current insurance company involvement there*

> *would appear to be a definite market niche for us to explore.*

This makes sense but is far too flabby:

- *Would have the objective of* is a wordy way of saying 'aims' or 'seeks to'.

- In plain words, *vis-à-vis* means 'towards' or 'to'.

- Sentences beginning *there are, there is* and *there were* are often wordy and reduce the strength of any remaining verbs. Two *there* verbs are present here.

- In *the subject of car fleet management*, the first three words are redundant because readers know that 'car fleet management' is a subject.

- *No current insurance company involvement* smothers the verb *involve*. In any case, a more expressive verb would be *publish* or *produce*.

- *Insurance company* could be cut to *insurer*.

So a first redraft might say:

> AIM OF PROPOSED CAR FLEET MANAGEMENT GUIDE
>
> *This guide would* show *car fleet managers how they could best achieve a professional approach to managing a car fleet and the benefits of doing so.*
>
> *At present, only a few publications cover car fleet management. None of them is produced by insurers so there is a definite market niche for us to explore.*

A second redraft would go a little further:

> *This guide would show car fleet managers how to do their work more professionally and why this would benefit them.*
>
> *Few publications cover car fleet management, none of them produced by insurers. So there is a definite market niche for us to explore.*

The original had 72 words, this has 50. What remains is tight and doesn't waste the reader's time.

Guideline 4: Prefer the Active Voice

This sentence has an active voice verb:

Fred is demolishing the building

while this has a passive voice verb:

The building is being demolished by Fred.

For a more technical account, see the entries ACTIVE and PASSIVE in GRAMMAR: PART III. The following paragraphs explain:

- How to recognize both types of verb
- How to convert one to the other
- Why the active should be your first choice
- How using *I* and *we* can make formal reports more readable
- When the passive can be useful

Many writers have damned the passive voice unreservedly. Some 50 years ago George Orwell wrote *Never use the passive where you can use the active*, but this is going much too far. Certainly the active tends to make the writing tighter, more personal, and introduces action earlier in sentences. The passive tends to do the reverse yet is still a valuable tool, as we will see.

Recognizing active voice verbs

Putting the 'doer' – the person or thing doing the action in the sentence – in front of its verb will usually ensure that the verb is in the active. The following sentences all have active verbs:

The President wants *an improved health service.*

I walked *up the stairs.*

Armies are *on the march.*

She hates *going to work.*

Icecream tastes *revolting.*

Most of us favour active verbs when we speak. People would think you were odd if you continually said things like *The house is being bought by me* instead of *I am buying the house*, though the meaning is the same if they are spoken with the same stresses.

Occasionally a verb can be followed by a doer yet remain active:

She used to hate going to work, said *her sister.*

Here *her sister* follows *said* but the verb is still active because *said her sister* is grammatically identical to *her sister said*.

Recognizing passive voice verbs

In most sentences with a passive verb, the doer follows the verb or is not stated, as here:

(i) *Three mistakes* were admitted *by the director.*

(ii) *Coastal towns* are damaged *by storms.*

(iii) *Verdicts* will *soon* be delivered *in the Smith case.*

In (i) and (ii), the doers (*director* and *storms*) follow the verbs through which they act. In (iii) the doer is not stated; no one can tell who or what will give the verdicts.

To put (i) and (ii) into the active, bring the doer to the start of the sentence:

The director *admitted three mistakes.*

Storms *damage* [or *are damaging*] *coastal towns.*

To convert (iii) into the active, you would need to know the doer:

The judge *will soon deliver verdicts in the Smith case.*

An almost infallible test for passives is to check whether the verb consists of part of the verb *to be* and a past participle (the *-ed* form of a verb). The verbs in the three examples given all conform to this pattern.

Computerized grammar checkers search for passives by applying the same test. Unfortunately this will occasionally throw up phantom passives. For example, *is tired* would be flagged as a passive in the sentence:

A man who is tired of London is tired of life

as it appears to fulfil the criteria of having part of *to be* and the past participle of *to tire*. But it cannot be a passive because no doer can be attached to *is tired* and none is implied. *Tired* in each case is a description of the man, not part of the verb. The verb *is* is in the active voice.

Converting passives to actives

Though using the active in the examples that follow will produce only small gains in clarity and economy, a general preference for active over passive will significantly improve the readability of most documents.

A financial adviser writes to his client:

> We have been asked by your home insurers to obtain your written confirmation that all their requirements have been completed by yourself.

By applying the test, *have been asked* and *have been completed* are revealed as passives. Use of the active, putting the doers in front of the verbs, would give:

> *Your home insurers* have asked *us to obtain your written confirmation that you* have completed *all their requirements.*

A safety official writes:

> A recommendation was made by inspectors that consideration be given by the company to the fitting of an interlock trip between the ventilation systems to prevent cell pressurisation.

Converting passive to active, the sentence becomes:

> *Inspectors* made *a recommendation that the company* give *consideration to the fitting of an interlock trip between the ventilation systems to prevent cell pressurisation.*

If we bring out the strong verbs hidden beneath *recommendation* and *consideration*, the sentence becomes even crisper – and ten words shorter than the original:

> *Inspectors* recommended *that the company* consider *fitting an interlock trip between the ventilation systems to prevent cell pressurisation.*

Verbs provide so much useful information that readers prefer to get them early in sentences; this tends not to happen when the verbs are passive. Placing an important verb late forces readers to store large chunks of text in their short term memory while they wait to discover the doer and what the action will be. The problem is worsened if there are other hurdles, like brackets containing exceptions and qualifications:

> If you decide to cancel your application, a cheque for the amount of your investment (subject to a deduction of the amount (if any) by which the value of your investment has fallen at the date at which your cancellation form is received by us) will be sent to you.

You decide and *has fallen* are active, while *is received* and *will be sent* are passive. *Will be sent* needs converting into the active because it is too far (36 words) from the noun it refers to, which is *cheque*. Making this single change would produce:

> If you decide to cancel your application, we will send you *a cheque for the amount of your investment (subject to a deduction of the amount (if any) by which the value of your investment has fallen at the date at which your cancellation form is received by us).*

This would be the first stage in a comprehensive kill of brackets and other debris that would produce:

> If you decide to cancel your application, we will send you a cheque for the amount of your investment less any fall in its value at the date we receive your cancellation form.

This is a third shorter than the original. Using the active voice has enabled other healthy writing habits to come into play.

Using *I* or *we* in formal reports

The myth that *I* and *we* should be avoided in formal reports has crippled many writers, causing them to adopt clumsy and confusing constructions like referring to themselves as *the writer* or using impersonal passives like *it is thought*, *it is felt*, *it is understood* and so on. With a sentence like:

> It is considered that fluoridation of drinking water is beneficial to health

readers have to guess who is expressing the view—the writer, wider scientific opinion, public opinion, or all three. In reports, readers should not have to guess. Attempts to prohibit *I* and *we* are particularly strange in that any other person, creature, or thing may be mentioned in a report.

If you are writing on your own behalf, use *I* and *my* judiciously, but don't overdo it for fear of seeming arrogant and self-important. If you are writing on behalf of two or more people, let *we* and *our* do the same job. (If there is some overriding reason why these tactics are impossible, you should still make sure that most of your sentences have clear doers – perhaps the name of your section or organization.)

Writers of scientific and technical material will especially benefit from using *I* and *we*, which are becoming commonplace in many journals including the *British Medical Journal*. Unless a journal specifically prohibits these words—and most do not—you should feel free to use them. Almost everyone who writes about scientific and technical writing now recommends this. Don't be seduced by the idea that impersonal writing makes you sound more scientific: no one ever became a scientist by wearing a white laboratory coat.

Warning: passives can be useful

Passive verbs have their uses and it would be silly—as well as futile—to outlaw them. There are five main reasons for using them:

- To defuse hostility – actives can sometimes be too direct and blunt.

- To avoid having to say who did the action, perhaps because the doer is irrelevant or obvious from the context.

- To focus attention on the receiver of the action by putting it first, e.g.

  An 18-year-old girl has been arrested by police in connection with the Blankshire murders.

- To spread or evade responsibility by omitting the doer, e.g.

  Regrettably, your file has been lost.

- To help in positioning old or known information at the start of a sentence or clause, and new information at the end.

The last point relates to an important benefit of the passive. Read these two sentences about a nuclear reactor:

Concern has been raised about arrangements for gaining immediate access to the chimney. Winch failure or the presence of debris between the platform edge and the chimney internal wall may necessitate access.

The second sentence, written in the active voice, doesn't seem to follow from the first, whose primary focus—placed late in the sentence—is about *gaining access*. Now try it with the second sentence in the passive voice:

Concern has been raised about arrangements for gaining immediate access to the chimney. Access may be needed if the winch fails or there is debris between the platform edge and the chimney internal wall.

The topic of the second sentence, *access*, is now introduced early in that sentence and developed. There is a clear link between the focus of the first sentence and the topic of the second—a common device that helps the writing to flow by taking the reader from the known to the unknown.

Guideline 5: Use Strong Lively Verbs

Good verbs give your writing its power and passion and delicacy. It is a simple truth that in most sentences you should express action through verbs, just as you do when you speak. Yet in so many sentences the verbs are smothered, all their vitality trapped beneath heavy noun phrases based on the verbs themselves. This Guideline is about releasing the power in these smothered verbs.

Business and official writers are particularly given to smothering their verbs:

- People don't *apply* for a travel pass, they *make application*.

- Speakers don't *inform* the public, they *give information*.

- Officials don't *urgently consider* a request, they *give it urgent consideration*.

- Staff don't *evaluate* a project, they *perform an evaluation*.

- Scientists don't *analyse* data, they *conduct an analysis*.

- Citizens don't *renew their library books*, they *carry out a process of library book renewal*.

In each case the simple verb is being converted into a noun that needs support from another verb. The technical term for a noun that masks a verb in this way is **nominalization**. There is nothing wrong with nominalization as such—it is a useful part of the language. But overusing it tends to make sentences longer and freeze-frame the action.

The following examples show how vigorous verbs can improve sentences containing nominalizations, making them more powerful and concise. Three types of construction are considered:

- Nominalization linked to parts of *to be* or *to have*

- Nominalization linked to active verbs or infinitives

- Nominalization linked to passive verbs

Nominalization linked to parts of *to be* or *to have*

If you come across *have*, *is*, *was*, etc. linked to a nominalization, you have good reason for suspecting that improvement is possible – as in this example from an official letter:

> *I have now had sight of your letter to Mr Jones.*

The main verb is *had* while the nominalization is *sight*, which smothers *see*. So it would be simpler to say:

> *I have now seen your letter to Mr Jones.*

This example is from a business letter:

> *Funding and waste management have a direct effect on progress towards the decommissioning of plant and equipment.*

The main verb is *have* while the nominalization is *effect*, which smothers *affect*. It is crisper to write:

> *Funding and waste management directly*

affect *progress towards the decommissioning of plant and equipment.*

A combination of part of *to be* and a nominalization is easy to see in this example:

> *The original intention of the researchers was to discover the state of the equipment.*

The nominalization is *intention*, smothering *intend*, while *was* acts as a prop. A revision would say:

> *Originally the researchers* intended *to discover the state of the equipment.*

Nominalization linked to active verbs or infinitives

This construction is easy to rewrite, as the presence of active verbs usually means that the word order can be preserved.

A group of conservationists is writing to a local government department:

> *The group considers that the director of community services should proceed with the introduction of as many mini-recycling centres as the budget allows.*

The nominalization is *introduction*, propped up by *proceed*. The rewrite would use the active voice to revive the smothered verb *introduce*:

> *The group considers that the director of community services should* introduce *as many mini-recycling centres as the budget allows.*

A company report explains what some of the staff do:

> *The team's role is to perform problem definition and resolution.*

Two nominalizations, *definition* and *resolution* are propped up by *to perform*. Using the smothered verbs *define* and *resolve*, this becomes:

> *The team's role is* to define and resolve *problems.*

A government department writes:

> *The policy branch has carried out a review of our arrangements in order to effect improvements in the reporting of accidents.*

Here there are two nominalizations, *review* and *improvements*, supported by *carried out* and *effect* respectively. Using vigorous verbs would produce:

> The policy branch has reviewed *our arrangements in order* to improve *the reporting of accidents.*

Nominalizations linked to passive verbs

This construction is harder to revise because changing from passive to active disrupts the original word order. To compensate, however, the satisfaction is usually greater.

A housing association writes:

> *Notification has been received from the insurers that they wish to reissue the Tenants Scheme Policy.*

The nominalization is *notification* and the passive is *has been received.* Using the smothered verb *notify* produces:

> The insurers have notified *us that they* wish to reissue the Tenants Scheme Policy.

A safety officer writes:

> *An examination of the maintenance records for the plant was carried out by Mr Patel.*

This becomes, by the same technique:

> Mr Patel examined *the maintenance records for the plant.*

More complex rewriting

Sometimes the difficulties are harder to spot. But remember the common signals – nominalizations (often ending in *-ion*), passive voice, the verbs *make* and *carry out*, and verbs derived from *to be* or *to have.*

A local government department writes:

> *The committee made a resolution that a study be carried out by officials into the feasibility of the provision of bottle banks in the area.*

The rewriting task can be split into three operations:

(i) The nominalization *resolution* becomes a strong verb: *the committee resolved that.*

(ii) The nominalization *study* becomes the active verb *study*: *officials should study.*

(iii) The nominalization *provision* becomes a present participle (*-ing* form of the verb): *the feasibility of providing bottle banks in the area.*

So the complete result reads:

> The committee resolved that officials should study the feasibility of providing bottle banks in the area

or better still:

> The committee resolved that officials should investigate whether providing bottle banks is feasible in the area.

An accountant writes:

> The incidence of serious monetary losses in several transactions entered into by the firm during the year is causing us great concern.

Incidence, meaning 'rate of occurrence', is not derived directly from a verb. Here it is probably used as a way of saying *occurrence.* The real verb should be *occur*, so a rewrite could say:

> The serious monetary losses that have occurred in several transactions entered into by the firm during the year are causing us great concern.

Then, putting the verb at the start of the sentence and tidying up the rest, the result would be:

> We are greatly concerned about the serious monetary losses that have occurred in several of the firm's transactions during the year.

This is only one word shorter than the original—too small a gain to justify the effort, if brevity was the only criterion. Much more important is that the sentence can now be read without stumbling.

Guideline 6: Use Vertical Lists

Vertical lists have become a common feature of many documents since the 1970s, helping to break up complicated text and present information in manageable chunks. For example, instead of writing this:

> Our inspections will be targeted on food factories. Inspectors will investigate food factory performance, establish each

occupier's performance, establish the occupier's knowledge of health and safety risks in the industry and identify which other parts of our organization could provide us with support for law enforcement

we could write this:

Our inspections will be targeted on food factories. Inspectors will:

- *investigate food factory performance;*
- *establish each occupier's performance;*
- *establish the occupier's knowledge of health and safety risks in the industry; and*
- *identify which other parts of our organization could provide us with support for law enforcement.*

Though this takes up more space it is very easy to grasp.

Vertical lists can cause problems in three areas:

- Keeping the listed items in parallel
- Punctuating the listed items
- Numbering the listed items

Keeping the listed items in parallel

A dietitian is explaining how a patient should cut her salt consumption:

To restrict your salt intake, you should:

- *not add salt at the table;*
- *use only a little salt in cooking;*
- *do not use bicarbonate of soda or baking powder in cooking;*
- *avoid salty food like tinned fish, roasted peanuts, olives.*

All the listed items are understandable individually and they are all commands, so to that extent they are in parallel. But the third point doesn't fit with the lead-in or 'platform' statement. Together they are saying:

you should do not use bicarbonate of soda or baking powder in cooking

which is nonsense. Obviously, *do* should be struck out to create a true parallel struc-

ture. It might then be a good idea to group the positive and negative commands:

To restrict your salt intake, you should:

- *not add salt at the table;*
- *not use bicarbonate of soda or baking powder in cooking;*
- *use only a little salt in cooking;*
- *avoid salty food like tinned fish, roasted peanuts, olives.*

Unfortunately the job isn't complete, as there is now an odd mixture of positive and negative. The best solution might be to shift the remaining positive statement into the platform:

To restrict your salt intake, you should only use a little salt in cooking and you should not:

- *add salt at the table;*
- *use bicarbonate of soda or baking powder in cooking;*
- *eat salty food like tinned fish, roasted peanuts, olives.*

Sometimes a platform needs to be created to maintain the parallel structure. Here, a clerk is being told how to do a task:

- *You should check that the details of the self-certificate or medical certificate match those on the person's information card.*
- *You should check that the certificate has been completed correctly and conforms to the rules on validity.*
- *That the certificate covers the period of absence.*

By the third item the writer must have become tired of writing *You should check that*. Rather than omit it, he or she should have converted it into a platform, producing:

You should check that:

- *the details of the self-certificate or medical certificate match those on the person's information card;*
- *the certificate has been completed correctly and conforms to the rules on validity;*
- *the certificate covers the period of absence.*

Often a vertical list is easier to read if each listed item has a similar grammatical structure. For example, they could all be statements that begin with infinitives or active verbs or passive verbs or present participles. In this list, all the listed items are passive verb statements:

The inspector should check that:

- *the vehicle is properly marked with hazard plates;*

- *the engine and cab heater are switched off during loading and unloading of explosives;*

- *any tobacco or cigarettes are kept in a suitable container and matches or cigarette lighters are not being kept in the cab;*

- *the explosives are securely stowed;*

There would be no harm in adding some active-voice statements as long as they made sense when linked to the platform:

- *there are no unsecured metal objects in the vehicle's load-carrying compartments;*

- *the vehicle is carrying one or more efficient fire extinguishers.*

When statements with different grammatical structure are mixed haphazardly, the reader has to stop and backtrack. In this example, the listed items have infinitives, actives, passives or no verbs at all:

When the committee's work began, it established the following aims:

- *make the regulations simple to understand and up to date in structure and layout;*

- *to update forms and leaflets where necessary with details of current fees;*

- *the effects of competition will be considered;*

- *the creation of a document summarising details of the regulations which will enable people to focus on key issues and requirements;*

- *recent changes in legislation should be taken into account.*

As these points are supposed to be aims, they could all be put into the infinitive:

When the committee's work began, it established the following aims:

- *to make the regulations simple to understand and up to date in structure and layout;*

- *to update forms and leaflets where necessary with details of current fees;*

- *to consider the effects of competition;*

- *to create a document summarising details of the regulations which will enable people to focus on key issues and requirements;*

- *to take account of recent changes in legislation.*

Readers get used to the pattern here; they can then concentrate better on the meaning.

Punctuating the listed items

Vertical lists need punctuating as consistently as possible so that readers get used to a pattern and are not distracted by deviations. Here is a typical example of inconsistency:

The new job-holder will:

- *develop a set of guidelines for clean wastepaper recycling*

- *Introduce green bins for clean wastepaper at appropriate places;*

- *monitor compliance with departmental targets.*

Two of the listed items begin with a lower-case letter and one with a capital. One of them ends with a semicolon, another with a full stop, and the first with nothing at all.

Many organizations use a two-part standard in their publications.

The **first part of the standard** is that when a listed item is a sentence or sentence fragment that relies on the platform statement to give it meaning, it should begin with a lower-case letter and end with a semicolon —except for the final item, which should normally end with a full stop. This produces the following result:

The new job-holder will:

- *develop a set of guidelines for clean wastepaper recycling;*

- introduce green bins for clean
  wastepaper at appropriate places;
- monitor compliance with departmental
  targets.

If you wish, you could add *and* after each of
the first two semicolons or, more conventionally, after the final semicolon only. If
you wanted to show that only one of the
jobs had to be done, you would put *or* after
the first two semicolons or, more conventionally, after the final semicolon only:

The new job-holder will:

- develop a set of guidelines for clean
  wastepaper recycling;
- introduce green bins for clean
  wastepaper at appropriate places; or
- monitor compliance with departmental
  targets.

Alternatively you could use this kind of set-
up, which stresses the *or*:

The new job-holder will:

- develop a set of guidelines for clean
  wastepaper recycling;

or • introduce green bins for clean
  wastepaper at appropriate places;

or • monitor compliance with
  departmental targets.

Rarely will you want to continue a sentence
beyond a list as this could overburden the
reader's short-term memory. If you do, a
good solution is to end your last listed item
with a semicolon and continue the sentence with a lower-case letter:

The new job-holder will:

- develop a set of guidelines for clean
  wastepaper recycling;
- introduce green bins for clean
  wastepaper at appropriate places; and
- monitor compliance with departmental
  targets;

but the work must always take place
within existing budgetary restrictions.

The **second part of the standard** applies to
listed items that are complete sentences
and don't depend on the platform statement to give them meaning. These can
begin with a capital and end with a full stop.
For example:

The speaker made three points:

- Aboriginal people across the world have
  been persecuted in the name of
  civilisation and religion.

- Even so-called enlightened governments
  have broken treaties made in good faith
  by aboriginals.

- Despair among aboriginals will lead
  either to their cultural disintegration or
  uprisings against authority.

This treatment is particularly useful when
a listed item is long and detailed, perhaps
with several separate sentences; in such
cases it would seem odd if the listed item
began with a lower-case letter, went on
with a new sentence, and ended in a semicolon.

Normally it is not a good idea to end listed
items with a comma because the signal is
not strong enough—a semicolon or full
stop gives more warning of a major break.
An alternative is to use no punctuation at
all: this is favoured by many contemporary
designers because of its clean uncluttered
look – but you must be sure that there are
no problems in following the sense.

Numbering the listed items

There is no need to number the listed items
if you or the reader will not need to refer to
them again, or if you wish to avoid suggesting that the items are in order of priority. Instead, just use a dash followed by a
space, or a bullet.

Other options are arabic numbers (1, 2, 3),
bracketed letters (a), (b), (c), or bracketed
roman numerals (i), (ii), (iii). Roman numerals can be used if you need to put a list
within a list—but this is more common in
text books or legal documents than in
everyday writing:

The court may in an order made by it in
relation to a regulated agreement include
provisions:

(a) making the operation of any term of the
order conditional on the doing of specified
acts by any party;

(b) suspending the operation of any term of
the order:

(i) until the court subsequently directs; or

(ii) until the occurrence of a specified act or omission.

Guideline 7: Put Your Points Positively When You Can

In writing, negatives include *un-* words like *unnecessary* and *unless*; verbs with negative associations like *avoid* and *cease*; and all the obvious words like *not, no, except, less than, not less than* and *not more than*. When readers are faced with a negative, they must first imagine the positive alternative then mentally cancel it out. So when a newspaper declares:

It is surely less painful to be unemployed if one is not sober, drug-free and filled with a desire to work

readers have to work very hard to assemble the meaning.

A single negative is unlikely to cause problems, though many a voter has paused, pen poised, when confronted with the polling booth challenge:

Vote for not more than one candidate

instead of the plainer and positive:

Vote for one candidate only

But when two, three, or more negatives are gathered together in the same sentence, meaning may become obscure, as in this note from a lawyer to his client, an underwriter:

Underwriters are, we consider, free to form the view that James Brothers have not yet proved to their satisfaction that the short-landed bags were not discharged from the ship, and were not lost in transit between Antwerp and Dieppe, when they were not covered by this insurance policy

—a labyrinth that perhaps only the lawyer who created it could negotiate successfully. The going is a little easier here in a pension contract:

'Dependent relative' includes a member's child or adopted child who has not attained the age of 18 or has not ceased to receive full-time education or training.

Put positively this would say:

'Dependent relative' includes a member's child or adopted child who is aged 17 or

under or is in full-time education or training.

Just as *at least* is an ever-present help in a document full of *not-less-thans*, the word *only* —which is positive but restrictive—is a useful converter of negative to positive:

The government will not consent to an application if those with a legal interest in the common land object to the application, except in exceptional circumstances.

In this rewrite *not* and *unless* both vanish under the influence of *only*:

Only in exceptional circumstances will the government consent to an application if those with a legal interest in the common land object to the application.

Arguably, this rewriting has produced a slight change of emphasis. The original emphasis is restored somewhat if we write:

If those with a legal interest in the common land object to an application, the government will consent to it only in exceptional circumstances.

Negatives are, of course, useful. Many commands are more powerful in the negative, which is why they have a place in procedures and instruction manuals. Even a double negative like:

Do not switch on the power unless you have made all the necessary checks

is more forceful and urgent than:

Only switch on the power when you have made the necessary checks.

But avoid overusing negatives, and make sure that those you do use are necessary.

Guideline 8: Try to Avoid Sexist Usage

Although sexist usage is not strictly a matter of clarity, any writing habit that builds a barrier between you and half your readers must reduce the impact of your message. So even if you disagree with the view that sexist writing reinforces prejudice and discrimination, it is still wiser to use inclusive language. Occasional silliness apart (*the art of one-upping* doesn't have quite the same ring as *one-upmanship*), inclusive writing usually makes more sense and is more accurate. There are several strategies that can be adopted here.

Using sex-neutral terms

This means avoiding words which suggest that maleness is the norm or superior or positive, and that femaleness is non-standard, subordinate, or negative. Sex-specific terms like *businessmen*, *firemen*, *poetess*, *headmaster*, and *sculptress* can be replaced by less restrictive words: *business people* (or *executives*), *firefighters*, *poet*, *headteacher*, and *sculptor*. Some sex-specific terms may survive this trend, because they reflect a genuine distinction or a continuing reality. *Fishers* and *fisherfolk* seem unlikely to gain popular acceptance as alternatives to *fishermen* on the open sea, yet *anglers* is a convenient sex-neutral term for those who fish for sport. There seem not to be any palatable alternatives for such terms as *manned space flight* and *craftsmanship*, although *working hours* is a good substitute for *man hours* and *manufactured* will stand in for *man-made*.

For further detailed guidance see the entries HE, -ESS, MAN, and -MAN in SECTION 6: USAGE.

Using titles

It is better to avoid *he*, *his*, or *him* when you intend to include both men and women. Instead of:

> *Solvent abuse is not a crime but if a police officer finds a young person under 17 sniffing solvents,* he *should take* him *to a secure place such as the police station, home, or hospital*

you could repeat the short titles of both people:

> *Solvent abuse is not a crime but if a police officer finds a young person under 17 sniffing solvents,* the officer *should take* the person *to a secure place such as the police station, home, or hospital*.

Using *he or she*

Using *he or she* and *him or her* is also feasible in many cases. To avoid confusion, however, it would probably be better to use it for just one of the people in the example given above:

> *Solvent abuse is not a crime but if a police officer finds a young person under 17 sniffing solvents,* he or she *should take the person* to a secure place…

Repeated use of *he or she* and similar terms becomes clumsy and obtrusive. The alternatives, *s/he* or *he/she*, look ugly and cannot be spoken easily.

In guidance to police officers, it would also be feasible to use *you*.

> *Solvent abuse is not a crime but if* you *find a young person under 17 sniffing solvents,* you *should take* him or her *to a secure place*…

Using the plural

A further alternative, and often the best, is to use the plural:

> *Solvent abuse is not a crime but if police officers find a young person under 17 sniffing solvents,* they *should take the person to a secure place*…

It is also becoming more acceptable to flout the grammatical conventions set in the 18th century and to do what Shakespeare did when he wrote:

> *God send everyone their heart's desire*

In other words, to revive the old use of *they*, *them*, and *their* as singulars:

> *Give details of your partner's income. If* they *have been unemployed for more than 12 months*…

> *You may find that an individual has levels of competence in several skills beyond those required in their current role. This will occur when someone has developed their skills and potential in readiness for other opportunities.*

These read smoothly enough, although the second may be better in the plural:

> *You may find that individuals have levels of competence in several skills beyond those required in their current roles. This will occur when they have developed their skills and potential in readiness for other opportunities.*

For more on this, see THEY in SECTION 6: USAGE.

Postscript: the alternatives are worse

To reject all these ideas as bad compromises or examples of 'political correctness gone mad' means accepting the kind of writing found in this advert from the 1920s, in which all typists are assumed to be women and all managers men:

> By dictating…you enable your typist to be typing all day, not wasting half the morning taking notes…She writes more letters and does her work more easily and accurately. Also the Dictaphone saves the time of the chief. We hardly like to talk about the 'afterhours' work, but it is acknowledged that closing time is the time when men who bear the real burdens oftentimes get down to their serious work. Then is the time when a man can concentrate, when there are no interruptions, no clicking of typewriters, no buzz of conversation to disturb his train of thought…Here it is that the Dictaphone comes into its own; it records the accumulated letters for the typist first thing in the morning, the chief's desk is clear – his mind relieved, and he arrives next day with only the 'current' matter to receive his attention.

PART II: EFFECTIVE USE OF FORMATS

AN APPROACH TO FORMAT

Writing as Conversation

There is a sense in which all communication —written or spoken, formal or informal—is a kind of conversation. Thinking about writing in this way can have several benefits. For one thing, it dispels fear: after all, most of us use speech quite naturally and without obvious problems every day of our lives. Secondly, seeing our writing as part of a conversation can help us to step back from the details of grammar and phrasing and focus on certain features of the wider situation:

- the **people** involved
- the **subject matter** and the language required to discuss it
- **where** and **when** the communication is taking place
- our **purpose** in communicating

This is always salutary, and leads on to a third benefit; thinking in this way provides a fresh approach to the whole question of **format**.

All communication has a format, whether it is a telephone conversation, a letter, or an annual report, and each format has its own conventions and rules. But here it is easy to get the wrong idea in one way or the other. Learning a list of rules will not by itself make you a great, or even a good, communicator. Nor were the rules devised to make problems —to cramp your style or to trip up the uninitiated. Formats and the rules that govern them have grown up to meet the different needs of people engaged in different kinds of 'conversation'. Properly understood and applied, with sensitivity to the wider situation, they will help you to communicate more easily, more confidently, and more effectively.

Types of conversation

Consider the following postcard:

Tuesday

We're just about settled in – amidst the chaos. Hope you'll come and see us when

Christmas is out of the way. Dave, Pip and Gemma send their love –

Pete

Here the writer, Pete, is presenting one side of a continuing 'conversation' with a close friend or relative. The two obviously know each other quite well—there are no real preliminaries and the dialogue gets going straight away. Although there is some kind of communication going on, not a lot of hard information is being exchanged; clearly, transmitting facts from one person to another is not the main aim. It is what some writers on language call 'phatic communion'—verbal communication used to establish social relationships rather than to impart information. A lot of background information is taken for granted; for example, Pete assumes that his reader knows who *we* are and understands the situation which involves them *settling in*.

Such situations are common in everyday life, and not only in spoken conversation. Postcards, greetings cards, and notes we leave at home for other members of the household—all are occasions for this kind of easy-going, personal communication, where there appear to be few rules provided that those involved understand each other.

A little further along the scale of formality comes this email:

Martin,

Sorry I missed you when you were over in Slough last week. I've had a chat with Maria and we think you should do your presentation during the first session of the conference. The reps will still all be bright-eyed and bushy-tailed then – by the time we get to the afternoon of the second day they're all decidedly jaded.

We thought about forty minutes would probably be enough – what do you think?

The people involved here know each other quite well and can take a lot for granted: they don't have to stand on ceremony; the situation they are discussing is understood by both, so they don't have to do a lot of explaining and they have some shared technical terms (e.g. *presentation*, *reps*). As a result they can cover a lot of ground in a brief space. The email is friendly and informal but no less businesslike because of that.

Sometimes, however, we have to communicate with people we don't know very well—if at all—in situations that are more complex. Consider the following telephone conversation:

A: *Good afternoon, Celtic Water, Pat speaking.*

B: *Good afternoon. The name is Williams; we live at Mordegrave, and for about five weeks now we've been promised a filter on our water supply, because the quality is not up to standard.*

A: *Right. Can I have your postcode, please, Mrs Williams?*

B: *JR1 4ZQ.*

A: *And the house number or name?*

B: *The Larches.*

A: *Right.*

B: *Now can I just fill you in?*

A: *Yes.*

B: *Four weeks after this was promised—a week ago last Friday—I rang your office—*

A: *Right.*

B: *I rang on Friday morning. I was told that someone would either ring me on Friday afternoon or Monday morning. Now when that didn't happen, I rang last Tuesday afternoon—exactly a week ago—*

A: *Yes.*

B: *—and I was told that the people in Bangor would by then have had the message and that I would hear by the end of the week. Now once again there's been a deafening silence and I'm beginning to lose patience, I'm afraid.*

A: *Yes, I can appreciate that. I'll get on to the depot myself. Now I'm looking to see if we've got a date for you. There is a job on this—*

B: *Yes, a date would help.*

A: *I'm just going to have a look on the job now to see if they have got anything on this.*

B: *Right. Thank you very much.*

And so the conversation continues, with both participants making sure that they have understood clearly what is going on and behaving to each other with polite formality. A has gone through the opening routine of all such calls: establishing the caller's name, postcode, and address. B has identified herself and set out the reasons for her call with clarity and brevity. They have then moved on to try to work out what ought to be done. Although B is probably in fact annoyed that the company have not done anything, she uses a formal tone and approach calculated to achieve her ends, keeping A on her side, rather than starting in a confrontational way.

Although this is a piece of spoken communication, it is quite easy to imagine an exchange of letters that would cover the same ground in a similar way. Compare, however, this letter from a solicitor:

Dear Mr & Mrs Grayson,

Re: The Larches, Dunscombe Road, Poole

Further to our recent inspection of your property I write to confirm that if placed on the open market I would recommend an asking figure in the region of £120,000–£130,000 (max.).

Whilst writing I confirm that our sale fee, for Sole Agency, is 1.50% plus VAT.

In the event of our being instructed and the property subsequently being withdrawn from the market an administration charge of £120 plus VAT would be made.

Should you require additional coverage in Bournemouth we are able to provide this as although we do not directly have a Bournemouth Office, we have a link up with Mandel Price whereby we are able to offer a Joint Agency at a special rate of 1.75%. You may not feel that this is necessary but it is an option worth considering.

Should you have any further queries please do not hesitate to contact me.

Yours sincerely,

Peter March

This is clearly a different kind of communication. For one thing, little new information is being given here. Peter March and the Graysons have already met and discussed the subject. Now Peter March is writing to confirm what was said and to put it on the record. The letter forms part of any future business relationship between them. This recording function is a very important feature of written communications.

Understanding the situation

So all our uses of speech and writing can be placed on a spectrum from informal chat through to legal documents. A lot of the time we are perfectly comfortable with the way in which we express ourselves, and it is only in a number of specialized or unusual situations that we have to think carefully about how to communicate. This is not, usually, because we are incapable of expressing ourselves in those situations, but rather that we are unsure of where to place them on the scale of situations we have experienced and feel confident about.

When you feel that a particular piece of communication is likely to cause problems, try to work out where it fits into your own range of experience. Find situations in the past that are similar and recall how you tackled them. Focus on those in which you felt that you communicated effectively: try to remember the 'tone of voice' you used—even if it was a written communication. If you find that you are remembering a number of situations in which you did *not* communicate effectively, analyse where things went wrong.

In all forms of communication there are a number of constants: features that we have to pay attention to if we are to get our message across effectively. We considered these briefly at the beginning of this discussion and have now seen them in action in a series of examples:

• people

Here we have to think about how well we know our audience and so how informal we can afford to be, as well as how much we can take for granted about their knowledge and language skills.

• subject matter

We have to choose the right language to deal with the subject matter we are discussing. The solicitor's letter quoted had to use the correct terminology for dealing with property sales, for example. At the same time, the language chosen has to be appropriate for the audience. If the listener or reader doesn't understand the terminology—even if it is correct—then communication will fail.

• time and place

The actual setting in which we are communicating can affect the way in which we do so. Imagine two young colleagues in an office setting, taking part in a meeting with an older person who is their section manager. Now imagine the same two discussing the meeting together in a cafe as they take their lunch break. Very probably the way in which they address each other and the language they use will be different on the two occasions. The same factors come into play in written communications. Some businesses require their employees to use language in special ways when preparing reports or making presentations.

• purpose

Every communication has a purpose, and many have more than one. It is important to keep your purpose in mind if you wish to communicate effectively. Caller B in the telephone conversation about the water filter had her purpose clearly in mind right from the start of that conversation. As a result, although A was being given a number of things to do (possibly time-consuming and tiresome), her task was made much easier.

Understanding the format

As we have seen, we also have a great range of different forms of communication available to us. The illustrations given so far cover:

- postcard
- email
- telephone conversation
- letter

And, of course, there are many others. We have said that each format has its own 'rules' and seen something of what this means in practice. An email, for example, does not work in quite the same way as a letter. You *can*, it is true, write a conventional letter and send it by email, but many people would probably find it a little over-formal to do this. Similarly, if you were to send a letter couched in the more informal style of many email messages, it would probably raise a few eyebrows.

It is not just a question of etiquette, of course. Apart from helping you to find an appropriate style and tone of voice, understanding the format will help you to choose the most suitable structure for your work. It may even help you to originate and organize the content. In the pages that follow we look first at the formats used most frequently at work and in the home – the letter, the fax, the email. Then comes a discussion of the two kinds of extended writing that are most likely to be required from those who are not professional writers – the work-related report and the college essay or dissertation. Finally there is a quick look at several more specialized formats.

Although the main focus is on these formats and how to use them successfully, a lot of attention will still be paid to the wider situation – the *who, what, where, when,* and *why* of communication.

EVERYDAY FORMATS

Business Letters

Here letters are placed before faxes and email messages. This ordering probably does not reflect the frequency with which we use these different media, but although most of us use letters less than we did, especially for social and personal communication, they still have a key role to play in many areas of life.

Letters have an importance and permanence that are comforting and reassuring. Even when we transact business by phone, we like to 'have something in writing' to confirm what we have agreed, and employers often lay great stress on the letters written by those applying for jobs—even

to the extent of demanding that these be handwritten rather than word-processed.

The result of this special status of letters is that they can prove quite difficult to write. Some writers, faced with having to write a job application, freeze up and cannot even think of a first sentence. So much seems to hang on what we write—our whole personality, career, life so far, will be judged when the letter is opened and read.

Yet there is nothing inherently 'special' about letters. They are just another technology of communication – one that might be considered outdated, expensive, and rather time-consuming. The general rules we apply when using any other form of communication still hold. We have to consider:

- our **purpose** in writing
- our **audience**
- the **conventions** which govern the ways in which letters are usually set out (and which our audience will expect)

The conventions of letter-writing are placed last in this list because they are often given undue importance; it would be mistaken to believe that once you have mastered them, you know how to write a good letter. Knowing how to structure the body of the letter and being sure that you have adopted the right tone are far more important.

The following paragraphs focus on what are often called 'business' letters—letters we write to people we do not know, or to those whom we know but with whom we have a business relationship rather than a personal one. They are usually letters written 'to get something done'.

Structuring the letter

If you find a particular letter difficult to write, it may well be because you have not worked out clearly in your mind what its purpose is. Begin by asking yourself these questions:

- Why am I writing this letter—what has led up to it?
- What do I hope to get out of it (my maximum aims)?

- What do I expect to get out of it (my realistic aims)?
- What is the best way to achieve this? What information do I need to provide? What arguments do I need to use?

Leaving aside for a moment the precise way in which the letter should begin, most business letters have a clear three-part structure:

(i) An **introduction** which sets out briefly the subject matter and purpose of the letter.

(ii) The **body** of the letter in which you develop and explain your purpose step by step.

(iii) A **conclusion** in which you set out what you want to achieve.

Introduction. The introduction to a letter must state clearly **what** the letter is about.

This enables the recipient to make an initial decision about what to do with it. (Deal with it quickly, put it in a heap of mail to be dealt with at an appointed time, pass it on to someone else…) One way of doing this is to give the letter a heading immediately after the salutation:

Dear Mr and Mrs Green,

Personal Overdraft. Account No: 12345678

The heading is usually underlined or in bold type.

More importantly, it should be clear, concise, and written in modern English. Shun such archaic usages as *instant* and *ultimo*, which are still sometimes used to mean *this month* and *last month* respectively (*Thank you for your letter of the 10th ultimo…*) Even the conventional *re* ('in the matter of') is far from universally understood and should be avoided in letters addressed to the general public.

Lastly, whether the heading is short or long, don't keep referring to it in the rest of the letter with such phrases as *with reference to the above-mentioned matter* or *in connection with the aforementioned.*

The introduction should also indicate **why** the writer is writing it.

A heading such as the one quoted only gives a general idea of the subject matter. The introduction should go on to spell out the writer's purpose:

I am pleased to confirm the renewal of your Personal Overdraft of £1000.

These two functions can be expressed in a simple sentence or two. In fact, in the example given, the heading is not strictly necessary because the following sentence repeats most of the information it contains. It could be rephrased to read:

I am pleased to confirm the renewal of your Personal Overdraft of £1000 on account number 12345678.

And that, essentially, is all the introduction has to do. When you have read it, you should have a clear idea of what the letter is going to be about and enough information to be able to decide how to tackle the rest of it.

Body. The letter now has to move steadily and convincingly towards the conclusion (in which you will explain what you want done, or reinforce the significance of the information you have set out). The more clearly information is expressed, and the more tellingly different items are linked, the better the letter. To see how this can work, we will look at a sequence of letters about the same subject. First, here is the body of the letter we have already quoted:

You can overdraw up to your limit whenever you want, but you should not be permanently overdrawn by the whole amount. Please remember that personal overdrafts are repayable on demand. Details of interest and charges that apply to this overdraft are enclosed.

Personal Overdraft Protection has been arranged for Mr Green, and a monthly insurance premium of £8.00 will be collected from your account on the first working day of each month. Your protection certificate, which includes details of cover, is also enclosed.

Each of these paragraphs has a clear topic. The first is about using the overdraft facility and the second concerns overdraft protection, an insurance protecting the user against being unable to repay the overdraft in the event of illness or unemployment.

Unfortunately Mr and Mrs Green had not requested this insurance and didn't want it. Their letter of reply followed a similar pattern:

> Dear Mrs White,
>
> Personal Overdraft on account number
>
> 12345678
>
> Thank you for your letter of 1st October, in which you say that Personal Overdraft Protection has been arranged at a rate of £8 per month.
>
> We don't recall asking for this protection. If we did, it was by an oversight and we do not wish to have it. We shall be grateful if you will arrange to stop it and make sure that no deductions are made for it.
>
> If this protection is a condition of the overdraft facility, then we do not wish to have the overdraft facility. It certainly isn't worth £96 p.a. before use. We only ever use it by accident when we forget to transfer money from our Deposit Account. It would be much more satisfactory if you offered the service of automatically topping up one account from another when it gets below a certain level.

Here the heading and first paragraph introduce the subject matter and link it to Mrs White's previous letter. The second paragraph deals with the subject of the unrequested insurance. The third moves the discussion on to a related but different topic. It introduces what is clearly the writer's main complaint.

Of course, such letters can have considerably more material in the body than is the case here. But the approach should be similar. Each paragraph is about a separate topic, or aspect of the main topic, and leads logically on to the next.

Clear, logical paragraphing can be a great help in getting your point across. The type of layout now often seen, in which each sentence appears as a separate paragraph, works against this, and can make letters unnecessarily difficult to read.

Conclusion. The main point of the conclusion is to underline the purpose of the let-ter and, sometimes, to spell out the action the writer would like taken. In the bank's letter, the final paragraph read:

> If you require further information regarding your Personal Overdraft, please contact me and I will be happy to answer any queries you may have.

This isn't necessarily asking for any further action, but it is intended to leave the reader feeling positive towards the writer, which is always a useful aim. The Greens, however, had other uses for the conclusion to their letter:

> We look forward to receiving your confirmation that the Overdraft Protection has been cancelled.

This is positive and unambiguous, leaving the reader in no doubt about what the writer would like to see happen.

It is always best to keep the finish simple, warm, and sincere. In a sales letter you could reiterate an important action point:

> I look forward to receiving your application soon.

When replying to enquiries or requests from members of the public, a good all-purpose sign-off is I hope this is helpful (much better than the negative and servile I am sorry I cannot be more helpful). Alternatively, if you are trying to close a correspondence with a difficult customer, you could try:

> I hope you will understand our position and I regret that we cannot help any further.

Getting the tone right

So far the writing of letters has been treated as if business letters were directed to, and received by, anonymous recipients. Of course they are not; they are received and read by individual human beings with thoughts and feelings. What makes such letters difficult to write at times is that although one is aware of this obvious fact, one has no idea of who will actually read the letter.

This is one reason why business letters sometimes fall back on jargon, over-formality, and even pomposity. Some time later in the negotiations between Mr and

Mrs Green and the bank, an assistant manager wrote them a letter apologizing for what had happened:

Dear Mr & Mrs Green,

Your letter of 13th October has been referred to me.

I take this opportunity to apologize, unreservedly, for our error in this connection. Upon examination it would appear that our letter of the 1st October, referring to insurance cover on your overdraft, was sent in error. I can assure you that at no time have insurance premia been debited to your account. I believe a colleague has now sent an amended renewal letter to you, confirming your facility has been marked forward at its existing level.

You mention that you would like to explore the possibility of our setting up an automatic transfer between your Current Account and your Deposit Account. I can confirm that such a facility is, occasionally, extended to our customers. This facility would need to be agreed by a member of the Bank's management and should you wish to pursue this option I would suggest that you contact a member of our Customer Facing Staff.

I again apologize for any inconvenience caused to you following the issue of our letter of the 1st October and look forward to hearing from you if I may be of any further assistance in this or any other matter.

Yours sincerely,

It would be difficult to argue that this letter is a success: not only is it rather long-winded, but it is expressed in an awkward, pompous, and jargon-ridden way.

Here are some of the expressions it uses, with 'translations' alongside:

Expression	**'Translation'**
our error in this connection	the mistake we made
your facility has been marked forward at its existing level	your overdraft arrangement has been renewed
This facility would need to be agreed by a member of the management and should you wish to pursue this option I would suggest that you contact a member of our Customer Facing Staff.	You would need to arrange this with one of our Bank's Managers. If you would like to do this, please ask one of our staff.

The writer would benefit from studying PART I of this Section—particularly GUIDELINE 2: Use Words Your Readers Will Understand.

Some writers are afraid of becoming too informal and offending the reader. But this should not be a real risk. The gap between writing and speaking is not so large. Imagine that instead of writing the letter, you are communicating the same subject matter face to face, speaking to a complete stranger. It is unlikely that you would offend by being too informal. You would adopt a neutral tone, and take care to explain clearly and simply what you had to say. A letter should do exactly the same thing. If you wouldn't normally say to a customer, *Should you wish to pursue this option I would suggest that you contact a member of our Customer Facing Staff*, then don't write it either.

To avoid excessive formality and pomposity:

- **Avoid using the passive.** As we saw in PART I, passive constructions (e.g. *Our letter was sent in error*) avoid the need for personal pronouns such as *I* or *we*. As a result they are favoured by less-than-confident writers who wish to sound more impersonal and 'authoritative' and by those eager to hide or spread the responsibility for something. The usual effect is one of pomposity mixed with evasiveness. Unless there are very good reasons for not doing so, use a personal pronoun and the active form instead (e.g. *We sent you that letter by mistake.*)

- **Avoid jargon** whenever possible. Terms like *Customer Facing Staff* and *your facility has been marked forward at its existing level* may mean something to the writer, but they are likely to alienate the general public.

- **Use shorter sentences** rather than longer ones.

To avoid unsuitable informality:

- **Don't give in to your own feelings.** When you are making a complaint and feel that you are in the right it is easy to cause offence. You may even wish to do so, but if you do, you are less likely to get satisfaction.

- **Don't try to be clever.** Some writers get carried away with their own eloquence and don't know when to stop. They risk causing unintended offence simply because they like to hear the sound of their own voice. For example, they start discoursing on how the recipient's organization ought to be managed. Such gratuitous advice is very unlikely to further your cause.

- Be clear and to the point, but **don't be too blunt**.

Greeting and ending

In British English there is a fairly simple choice of greeting and ending for business letters. Presented in descending order of formality it is:

Greeting	Ending
Dear Sir,	*Yours faithfully,*
Dear Madam,	*A. B. Capstick*
Dear Sir or Madam,	
Dear Mr Green,	*Yours sincerely,*
Dear Mrs Green,	*Alan Capstick*
Dear Miss Green,	(or *Alan*)
Dear Ms Green,	
Dear Alan,	*Yours sincerely, Moira* (or, commonly, *With best wishes, Yours sincerely, Moira*)

Increasingly the *Dear Sir...Yours faithfully* formula is being abandoned in favour of the less formal *Yours sincerely* versions. *Dear Sir...Yours faithfully* is retained for very formal occasions: threatening letters from government departments, banks, and lawyers, for example. In the past it was acceptable to address an unknown correspondent as *Dear Sir*, regardless of gender, but not today. So unless you know the gender of the person you are addressing (in which case you probably know them well enough to use their name and *Yours sincerely*) you are forced to use the rather awkward *Dear Sir or Madam*.

The drawback of the *Yours sincerely* formula is that you have to have a name to address it to. Here three problems can arise:

(i) You do not know the recipient's name. In this case, you are forced back on to using a job description, real or invented: *Dear Personnel Manager*, *Dear Fellow Sufferer*, or whatever. If you are not happy with that, stick to *Dear Sir or Madam...Yours faithfully*.

(ii) You have a surname but no first name, so you do not know whether you are addressing a man or a woman. Unless you are happy with *Dear A. B. Capstick...* you have to use a job description, or use *Dear Sir or Madam...*, as above.

(iii) You know that the recipient is a woman but do not know how she likes to be addressed. (Not, incidentally, the same as knowing her marital status—some married women prefer to be addressed as *Ms*.) Here it is best to play safe and use *Ms*.

The other awkwardness that can arise is whether to address the recipient as *Dear Mrs Green*, or as *Dear Lynda*. If you have met or spoken to them, then generally there is no problem: use a first name. For many people, however, this is not acceptable if they have never met or spoken to the person concerned (although for others, especially younger writers, this is not a problem). If, when addressing a person you do not know at all, you feel that a first name is too informal and a title plus surname is too formal, you can try the intermediate position of *Dear Lynda Green*, although for some that is a rather artificial compromise.

Letter layout

There is a considerable choice of how to set out a formal letter. Different organizations have different styles governing:

- the positioning of the recipient's address
- the punctuation of the address
- the spacing and alignment of paragraphs

- the spacing and alignment of the ending (*Yours sincerely* or *Yours faithfully* and signature)

The modern trend favours a simple uncluttered presentation; the address block, for example, often appears with no punctuation or very little. The main point is to adopt a layout that is clear and consistent.

Fax

The fax (short for 'facsimile') was the first of the 'written' electronic media to become widely available. Its advantages are that:

- it is quick
- it can contain pictures as well as words
- the recipient does not have to be there to receive it
- it is generally cheaper than a telephone call

Like a letter, a fax is a technology, a way of passing a message from one person to another. It is different from the letter because it is relatively new. Letters have been used for centuries, so traditions and conventions of letter-writing have developed. It is true that you can ignore these conventions, if you wish, but they are still there, and they affect people's attitudes towards what you write. Because the fax is new, there are fewer fixed rules or conventions about how it should be written.

But there are some. At the very least, a message that is going to be transmitted by fax must carry certain information if it is to reach the person for whom it is intended. The following points are usually essential:

- The company or organization to which the fax is addressed

- The person within that organization for whom the fax is intended

- Their fax number (because often the writer of the fax is not the person who is going to transmit it)

- The number of pages (so that the recipients can check that they have received the whole fax)

- The sender's name

- The sender's company or organization

- Their fax number (and possibly their phone number and email address in case there have been problems about transmitting or receiving the fax)

- The date

At its simplest this information can be carried by a stick-on fax label. Most companies now supply preprinted forms for the first page of a fax, with a series of prompts to show the information required.

Although there are few formal conventions, message faxes tend to fall into three main categories:

The handwritten fax

For transacting everyday business, quickly, with someone you know well, a simple handwritten note with a fax label attached may be all that is needed. More often, however, you will want something that is word-processed, more formal, or both.

The letter fax

For many informal or semi-formal situations, it is useful to send a fax that is really a letter in disguise. In this case, once you have included the essential information listed above, it is a letter like any other and the normal conventions apply. Remember, however, that a fax—even more than any other communication to an organization—can be read by anyone in an office, so it is not the best way to send information that is confidential or sensitive.

The memo fax

For more formal situations, or where it is a matter of company policy, it is common practice to model the fax on a memo. In this case it will probably be expected to serve as a note or record for future reference: it should therefore be clear, self-explanatory, and relatively formal in tone. It will usually be organized into a series of numbered points under a subject heading.

Email

Email (short for 'electronic mail') is increasingly used instead of letters or faxes.

Within any organization that has computers linked to a network, internal email is a simple way of passing information and ideas around the office. Moreover, if your computer is connected to the Internet, then you can communicate in a similar way with computers many miles away. Most Internet provision now costs the same as a local call, so sending email to anywhere in the world is very cheap.

Typically, you compose and key in any messages you want to send before connecting to the network, dial up the Internet service provider (which is normally done automatically via the software), and, once you are online, send your messages and download (i.e. collect and save) any that have been sent to you. You then disconnect and read your mail. The whole operation takes a few minutes and costs a matter of pence. Writing the messages is done at your computer keyboard; there is no need for paper and no need to get up, dictate a letter, pick up the phone. It is as near instant as it is possible to get.

Other advantages

Apart from being quick and cheap, email has a number of other advantages which don't take long to discover:

- The messages you send are in the form of text. This means that your correspondents can include them in computer programs of their own (e.g. a word-processed text).

- Because they are just text, you don't have to spend a lot of time worrying about layout, typefaces, paper quality, or print quality, so you can focus on the words.

- A by-product of this is that email is uncluttered and unstuffy. A typical email message is short and informal.

- Email is in many ways even more convenient than the telephone. But it is a written message, so the technology is leading to the re-birth of the personal letter.

- As well as sending simple messages you can attach computer files—for example, desk-top publishing (DTP) pages, graphics, or spreadsheets—which others can then use in their own work.

- The software allows you to send the same message to a number of recipients, for the cost of one message, which is particularly useful when you are a member of a work group or interest group.

- When you receive an email and wish to reply to it, you can attach your reply to the message. This keeps the correspondence together, which is useful when checking back what has already been said.

When you use this facility, you will probably find that the on-screen 'form' you are offered to use for your reply begins with the text of the message you are replying to. Since your correspondent doesn't need to re-read this, it is best either to delete the whole message except for its heading, or to delete selectively, just leaving relevant headings or extracts of text to provide a context for your own message.

Technicalities

When you use an email program you have to provide a certain amount of information in order to send a message. The screen provides prompts showing what is required. It is similar to filling in a fax form.

Popular email programs also offer a number of other facilities, including:

- the automatic addition of a 'signature', which can be anything you like, but might, for example, include your name, postal address and telephone number

- the option of keeping a copy of emails you send out

- various options about the electronic format in which messages are sent

- an address book for keeping email addresses of regular correspondents

- a filing system for sorting and storing messages

Using email

As already noted, email is quick, easy, and cheap to use. Replying to messages takes but a moment—so it is all the more important to do so promptly (and, preferably, briefly).

The medium invites informality, but this can be abused or mistaken and it is important to remember that an email message, like any other message, may well be read by someone other than the person to whom it was originally addressed. Verbal or other indiscretions may let you down when you least expect it. On the other hand, email is a great opportunity to correspond easily, clearly, and without stuffiness.

MORE EXTENDED FORMATS

Reports

Modern life depends on the flow of information. For managers this can seem a mixed blessing, as their in-trays overflow with reports on this and proposals about that, all clamouring for a response.

Yet management, along with many other aspects of life, is impossible without information. Before you can make a decision you need to have at your disposal all the relevant facts, and these often come in the form of a report. It is important, therefore, that such documents are prepared and constructed in the most useful possible way.

Types of report

Most documents designed to provide information leading to action can be placed on a spectrum. At one end is what might be called the **report proper**, intended to provide accurate and unbiased information about a situation. If it deals with possible courses of action, it presents all the possibilities and their likely outcomes without favouring one above another.

At the other extreme is the **proposal**, which is, from the outset, openly and unashamedly biased. Its purpose is to promote a particular course of action. Like the report it provides information and judgements about that information, but it uses these to further its own ends. If other possibilities are considered, it is only to show why they are wrong and the favoured one is right. An example is the proposals that authors prepare to convince publishers that they should publish their books. These often contain considerable detail, spelling out not only what the book contains but also where in the market it is placed and how it compares (favourably, of course) with the competition.

Most reports and proposals fall somewhere between these two extremes. They are designed to be read by decision makers. They survey a range of information, make judgements about it, and come to conclusions, often in the form of recommendations. Some of these documents will tend towards the objective end of the spectrum, while others will take a more committed stance, but all tend to follow similar patterns and to be prepared in similar ways.

Preparing a report

Objective. It is impossible to write a clear and cogent report without a clear objective, or set of objectives. So it is important to formulate this as precisely—and briefly— as possible at the outset. For example:

> To survey the present practice of the teaching of mental arithmetic in the authority's secondary schools, to assess present standards, and to make recommendations about what can be done to improve them.

Audience. It is also very important to have a clear idea of the audience for the report. The example above could be aimed at a number of different audiences:

- local authority inspectors
- head teachers
- subject teachers
- parents of children at local schools
- governors of local schools

Each of these audiences has a different understanding of the subject and different concerns. So while it is relatively easy to work out what to say and how to say it to one of these audiences, addressing your report to all five is much more difficult.

Planning your research. Doing the necessary research for a report is much easier if you begin by making two lists:

- questions you need to ask
- people and places where you hope to find the answers

The second list may well not be as complete as the first. It may be necessary to do preliminary research in order to complete it. In the example we are following, you might ask this question:

> What is the current classroom practice?

and then, on reflection you might decide to break it into two:

> (i) What do teachers say they do in the classroom?
>
> (ii) What do they actually do?

Clearly, question (i) is fairly easy to get answered, but question (ii) is much more tricky. If time does not allow a personal inspection of a representative sample of lessons, you must look for secondary sources of information, research data and other publications. But where? In this situation the local authority schools inspectorate would clearly be a logical starting point. The person who can answer questions directly is an important resource, but so is the person who can direct you to where you can find out answers to the questions that are left.

Sources of information. Given the very diverse nature of all the reports that people are asked to write, it is impossible to provide a useful detailed list of sources of information. The following list is intended to cover the general areas that need to be considered:

- Direct observation

  Possibly the most dependable, but also the most time-consuming, source of information.

- People

  Using personal contacts (via email, telephone, fax), questionnaires, meetings, focus groups.

- Publications

  Books, journals, government publications including legislation.

- Research findings

  A wide range of commercial, government, academic, and other independent organizations sponsor and carry out research and publish their findings.

- Documents and data within your own organization

Scheduling research. Your list of questions and sources of information can be used to generate a list of things to do. Some of these may be easy and informal, like asking a colleague for an opinion or a piece of information. Others will be more complex and time-consuming, such as contacting a provider of commercial information, acquiring a list of publications, discovering which are relevant, acquiring and reading them, finding relevant information, and making notes on it.

So it is important to make a research plan:

- Group similar activities together, especially those which involve contacting the same people.

- Identify those topics which are going to take a long time and so need to be started as early as possible.

- Work out whether any aspects are interdependent and decide the order in which they must be tackled.

- Calculate approximately how long each part of the research is likely to take.

- Order the actions logically, using all this information.

Structuring the report

The structure of a report is determined by its content and the needs of its readers. While the following structure is not the only one, it is a popular one and contains all the features that would be expected in a fairly lengthy report. Those in italics should appear in all reports, regardless of length.

1. Contents list
2. *Executive summary*
3. *Introduction*
4. *Body of the report*
5. *Conclusions*
6. Recommendations
7. Appendices
8. Bibliography

Contents list. If the report is any more than a few pages long it needs a contents list detailing the main sections and the pages on which they appear.

Executive summary. The readers of a report are usually busy people. They do not have time to wade through page after page of text just to find out which parts of a report may be of value to them—if any. The purpose of the executive summary is to set out the substance of the report briefly and in such a way that busy readers can see at a glance whether the report is relevant to them and, if so, which aspects of it are of most interest. Ideally it should not exceed one side of A4. Executive summaries that run to several pages can be self-defeating.

You may also wish to include your principal recommendations here.

Introduction. This should contain the following information:

- The origins of the report

  The background and events leading to the need for the report.

- Its terms of reference

  The scope (and limitations) of the report and its purpose.

- How it was conducted and by whom

  This can also include acknowledgements of help received.

- Other introductory information

  It is important to think of the readers of the report and to include at this point any other background information they will need in order to understand the material in the body of the report.

Body of the report. The main part of the report contains:

- a detailed account of what your research discovered

- the conclusions that you draw from it

- references to sources that you have quoted. The sources should be listed in the bibliography, and the references should follow a standard pattern (see below).

A report of any length will be divided into a number of main **sections**, each on a separate topic or theme. These in turn will probably be subdivided into subsections. All sections and subsections will need headings and, to avoid confusion, it is very desirable to use a **numbering system**. A commonly used one is decimal: the first main section is numbered 1; subsections are then numbered 1.1, 1.2, etc., and their subsections become 1.1.1, 1.1.2, and so on.

The body of the report will consist of the **details** of the research—often in the form of tables, charts, and figures, with relevant quotations. The argument may be presented in continuous prose, as a series of bullet points, or as a mixture of the two.

If the material you are handling is detailed, there is a danger that the main thrust of your argument will become obscured by details. In such situations it is better to place highly detailed material in appendices and to refer to it in the body of the report in numbered **notes**. While the reference number appears at the relevant point in the text, the note giving chapter and verse can be placed either at the foot of the page or at the end of the section or chapter. If there are not too many notes, it is better to put them at the bottom of the page, since it is irritating for the reader to have to keep turning pages to find the relevant note. If there are a lot of notes, however, they are better placed at the end of the chapter, since to place them at the foot of the page will make the pages look messy and unbalanced.

It is essential that when published or unpublished textual **sources** are referred to, they are clearly identified and readers are enabled—should they so wish—to check the original. In the case of books, the following information should be given:

- the name(s) of the author(s)

- the full title

- the name of the publisher and place of publication

- the year of first publication or, if it is a subsequent edition, the number of the edition and the date of its publication

A common style for doing this is:

Seely, J. (1998):*The Oxford Guide to Writing and Speaking*—Oxford: Oxford University Press

This information should appear in the **bibliography** at the end of the report. References to the book in the text should simply use the author's name and date followed by the page(s) referred to:

Seely (1998), pp. 34–5

References to periodicals and journals should appear in the bibliography in this style:

Haywood, K. T. (1997): 'Teaching mental arithmetic to 11-year-olds'— *Modern Maths Quarterly* 15, pp. 34–37

Conclusions. Each section of the report should lead to a number of conclusions. At the end of the section these are spelt out and the reasoning behind them explained. If there is a separate 'Conclusions' section these conclusions are pulled out and repeated as an ordered sequence, with reference back to the body of the report as necessary.

Recommendations. Not all reports present recommendations; some are merely required to present a set of information based on research. Where there are recommendations, these may be presented as part of the report's conclusions, or in a separate section which may be placed towards the end of the report, after the conclusions, or immediately after the executive summary. Indeed, some writers prefer to make their recommendations part of the executive summary, since they are an important part of what the busy reader wants to know first.

Appendices. The value of placing certain lengthy detailed information in a series of appendices (sometimes called **annexes**) has already been mentioned. The type of information that may go in appendices includes:

• a detailed description of the research method, including the questionnaire(s) used and how the sample was selected

• the research brief and the members of the team producing the report

• detailed research data

• case studies

Addressing your readership

The importance of thinking carefully about your readers has already been mentioned when considering the content and structure of the report. It is equally important to remember your readers when drafting the report itself.

Normally a report should be written in a fairly impersonal and formal style. Reports are formal documents and, even if you have a very good idea of who will read what you write and know them all quite well, you cannot know for certain who will read it at some point in the future. Reports are usually stored for later reference and may be passed to anyone with a legitimate interest in the subject, so it is unwise to write them in too relaxed or informal a style.

On the other hand this is not to suggest that you should imagine that you are a 19th-century civil servant. In particular, try to avoid writing sentences that are too long or involved—always a danger when the material itself is far from simple. The following sentence, for example, is difficult to follow because it sets up a fairly complicated hypothesis and then follows through its implications all in one sentence:

If the managerial group constitutes an internal labour market and the non-managerial group does not because it is peripheral, we should expect to see differences in the following characteristics: entry points, attachment to the organization, and career development of the two groups.

It would be better to recast it as two sentences:

It could be argued that the managerial group constitutes an internal labour market whereas the non-managerial group does not because it is peripheral. If so, we should expect to see differences between the two groups in the following characteristics: entry points, attachment to the organization, and career development.

This says the same thing but, because it forms two sentences, the logic of the argument is easier to follow.

For advice on the use of personal pronouns (*I* and *we*) in formal reports, see PART I, GUIDELINE 4.

Essays, Papers, and Dissertations

What the report is to the business world, the essay, paper, and dissertation are to the academic community. From the sixth-form essay to the Ph.D. thesis, the writing of an extended piece of prose is used to demonstrate and measure the writer's grasp of a given subject.

There is, however, a major difference between these two types of writing. A manager normally reads a report in order to learn new information about a topic—the writer knows more about the subject than the reader. A university lecturer reads a paper or dissertation in order to judge how well the writer has understood the subject; here the reader probably knows more about the subject than the writer.

This is one of the reasons why some students have writing problems. It seems artificial to be telling the reader something that he or she already knows. In addition, the dissertation is almost certainly by far the longest piece of writing the student has ever undertaken; the task seems daunting. It seems impossible to prepare, initiate, and then control such an extended piece of prose, even leaving aside the additional difficulties caused by one's uncertainty about the purpose and audience of such a text.

Such a view is not uncommon and can be crippling, but there is a positive side to each of the negatives it contains. The fact that the reader already has a good knowledge of the subject means that there is no need to provide a lot of low-level explanation at the outset. The academic context means that there are well-established conventions for structuring and composing this type of writing—and readily available research material. The situation in which it is written means that plenty of time is allowed for writing it. Most important of all, extended writing of this type allows the writer really to get to grips with a substantial subject and come to understand it fully.

This chapter goes through the process of writing an essay, paper, or dissertation step by step. For convenience it refers to an 'essay' throughout, but this should be taken to refer to the whole range of writing of this type. The main differences between an essay on the one hand and a dissertation on the other are that the dissertation is much longer and has a more elaborate formal structure. This is dealt with at the end.

Preparation

It is difficult to write at any length without some form of preparation. Nevertheless it is surprising how many writers do just launch themselves into writing straightaway, only to find that after a page or two they come to a halt, uncertain as to how to proceed. Planning may be a lengthy process, but it need not be. How much you do depends on the subject, how well you know it, and how much research you need to do.

Defining the subject. Some of the problems a writer may face arise because the subject of the essay has not been clearly defined or understood. Sometimes teachers set topics that are imprecise or vaguely worded. But if students just go along with this and write the essay without trying to define the subject more precisely, then they only have themselves to blame. It is better either to tackle the person who set the subject and ask them to clarify it, or, failing that, to redefine it yourself. (If you do this, you should, of course, make it clear that you have done so.)

'Not answering the question' *may* be the fault of the questioner. More often, however, it is the fault of the writer, who has not thought carefully enough about what the question means. A good starting point is to ask yourself, 'What is the question asking me to *do*?' Essay questions often provide helpful clues to what is expected. For example:

1 *What is the likely impact of the Internet on British business?*

2 *What is meant by 'factoring'?*

3 *In King Lear,* Gloucester *and Lear both
learn through suffering. In what other
ways are they similar and how might
their circumstances be said to be
different?*

4 *'In 1997 Britain was in danger of
becoming a one-party state.' Discuss.*

5 *What were the main events leading up
to the Hundred Years' War?*

Each of these questions asks the writer to
perform a different task:

• analyse

Question 1 asks the writer to examine a
particular phenomenon and analyse its
likely effects. Analytical questions ask the
writer to tease out the significant features
of a situation, to describe them, and to explain why they are significant.

• define

Question 2 asks for a definition of an economic term. The writer is required to list its
defining features and to support this definition by reference to good examples from
the real world.

• compare and contrast

Question 3 refers to two characters from a
play who have similarities and differences
and asks the writer to set these out. The
question does not ask the writer to describe
one character, describe the other, and then
compare them. Instead the writer has to
find key features of similarity and difference and build the essay up around these.

• argue a case

Question 4 puts a challenging interpretation of a piece of recent history and asks
the writer to examine the two sides of the
argument and evaluate them.

• narrate

Here the writer is being asked to tell a story.
The danger of narrative is that writing it
seems easy: anyone can tell a story and
many people enjoy doing so. As a result
writers often fall back on narrative, when
they should be analysing, defining, or arguing.

Each of these types of question has its own
distinctive structures and approaches.
Sometimes questions are 'pure' examples
of one type, as in the examples quoted.
Often they are hybrids, combining two or
more types in one question.

Generating ideas. Once you have analysed
the wording of the question and decided
what kind of question it is, you can begin
to develop your ideas. It is a good idea to
'think on paper'. In its simplest form this
just involves jotting down a list of ideas as
they occur to you. However, some other
ways of arranging your ideas can be helpful
in generating the structure and sequence,
as well as the content, of your work. For instance, questions of the 'compare and contrast' type lend themselves to putting ideas
into two or more columns, with obvious
implications for the structure of an essay.
With more open questions of the 'analyse'
type a useful alternative is the 'web' or
'spider' diagram. This involves jotting down
a few main ideas at random on the page,
and then drawing lines or arrows to indicate the logical connections between them.
As your main ideas suggest subsidiary
points or arguments, the diagram will become more complex and the best way of
organizing your material should become
clearer.

Research. Three key points to remember
about effective research are:

• Make effective notes. Although taking
notes is more laborious than making
photocopies, notes are often more useful
because they force you to focus on the
text and determine its key points.

• Keep a careful record of the source of all
material, including full bibliographical
details.

• Distinguish carefully between information and ideas that you have abstracted
from a source and direct quotations.
Otherwise you risk using someone else's
words as if they were your own (plagia-
rising).

Ordering your material. Once your ideas
and material have been developed, you can

begin to order them into a logical sequence. How you do this will be determined by the demands of the question and how you have decided to respond to it.

(i) You need to decide first how many main sections there should be, apart from an introduction and a conclusion. There should be enough to encompass all the ideas you have generated, but few enough for the pattern of the essay to be clear to the reader.

(ii) You should decide how best to order these sections so that your material can be presented in a logical and interesting way.

(iii) You can then arrange your material, fitting all your ideas into the relevant sections.

(iv) Now decide how you will introduce your essay and conclude it. The introduction needs to indicate the approach you propose to take, but should avoid giving the game away right at the start. If you tell the reader everything that you are going to say in the course of the first paragraph, there is little incentive to read on. Similarly the conclusion should refer to the main points you have made without being repetitive; but if possible you should save up a telling, interesting, or amusing point for the conclusion, so that the reader's interest is held until the very last sentence.

Writing

People approach the process of writing (and rewriting) in such different ways that it seems futile to lay down any too general rules about working method. Some prefer to revise their work sentence by sentence as they go along; others are unwilling to alter anything until they have completed a first draft. Approaches to the routines and mechanics of writing also vary wildly. The main thing is to find out what suits you (writing on screen, on paper, or in your head while pacing the room?) and to refine the various techniques and procedures involved as you gain experience. Here two key points are worth stressing.

- It is important to achieve the right tone of voice in your writing. The convention is that essays, papers, and dissertations are written in a fairly impersonal and formal style. This convention is worth

respecting unless there are good reasons for doing otherwise. Among other things it usually means that you should write in normally paragraphed prose rather than using bullet points or other similar devices.

- If your essay is going to be cogent and coherent, it needs to be built up of carefully constructed paragraphs. In particular you need to look carefully at the way in which paragraphs are linked. The reader should be led naturally and easily from one key point to the next without sudden leaps or unexplained changes of topic.

Quotations and references. Make sure that it is clear when you are quoting directly from another person. Short quotations can go into the body of your text, marked off by quotation marks. Longer quotations should be separated and indented.

All quotations should be properly attributed. In an essay of any length it is better to list all works referred to separately at the end. They can then be referred to briefly, as previously described.

Dissertations

In essence, a dissertation is an extended essay, but saying this can be misleading. Once a piece of writing reaches a certain length a number of new problems arise—mainly because the reader finds it increasingly difficult to keep a grasp of what is going on. The writer, therefore, needs to keep checking that the reader is still following the argument. This is partly a question of structure and partly one of writing approach.

Structure. Readers need as many structural devices as possible to help them keep track of the argument. These can include:

- A table of **contents.**

- An **introduction** explaining the nature of the subject, the treatment, and the reasons for choosing this approach.

- Division of the text into **sections** or **chapters.** Each should be treated as an essay in its own right with:

– an introduction which introduces the subject matter and explains its link to what has gone before

– a conclusion which sums up the main points and leads on to the next section.

- A **conclusion** which sums up the entire argument, referring back, where necessary, to specific sections of the main text.

- A **bibliography** and list of other sources used.

It is worth pointing out, however, that different universities and other institutions have their own rules about how a text should be structured. Some, for example, say that subheadings are unacceptable, while to others bullet points are not to be used.

Writing approach. A dissertation can be anything up to 20,000 words long. Inevitably you will need to write more than one draft. Some sections will probably go through several drafts before you are satisfied with them, while a few troublesome sentences or paragraphs may need more attention still. Many colleges that require a dissertation as part of a final assessment require students to submit a full first draft for comment by a supervising tutor before the final draft is begun.

As you write, you should try to carry in your mind the structure of the whole dissertation, being aware of how what you are writing at this particular moment relates to what has gone before and what is yet to come. When you are working on a first draft this is difficult to achieve, but it is certainly something you should remember when you come to redraft a section. As you read the first draft through, keep checking how the parts relate to each other and asking yourself whether you are providing sufficient signposts for your readers as they travel with you from the beginning to the end.

Above all, make use of whatever help other people can give you. All writers, however skilful and experienced, depend on constructive criticism from people whose judgement they trust.

Other considerations. As was noted above, many institutions provide detailed guidelines on how to prepare a dissertation, which must, of course, be followed. These will almost certainly include the question of presentation. Any set of dissertations submitted for assessment will almost certainly divide into three categories:

- those which fail to observe the presentation guidelines given to students

- those which do the minimum required

- those whose writers have used the guidelines and have done everything in their power to make their work as clear and reader-friendly as possible

Given the pressures of time and workload under which the assessors have to work, there are no prizes for guessing which dissertations will receive the most favourable treatment.

MORE SPECIALIZED FORMATS

Press Releases

If you have something you wish to publicize, then you should aim to have it reported in local, regional, or national press, radio, or TV. It is always possible, of course, to buy advertising space and put your message across in that way. But getting a report in the press or on the air has the distinct advantage of being free. Reports also tend to be given more attention and credence.

You might wonder why a newspaper or local radio station should be interested in the news you wish to promote. They may well not be particularly interested, but they almost certainly need it. The media have a voracious appetite for material; the radio or television station has so many hours of airtime to fill, and the newspaper so many column inches to occupy. Their resources for collecting material are limited, so ready-made news is a godsend—provided that it is interesting to their audience (or can be made so) and is in a form that is easy to use.

The commonest way of contacting the media with a story that you would like them to publish is to issue a **press release**. This can be distributed to the newsdesks of the outlets you wish to contact (preferably preceded by a personal contact to make sure that the right person gets the release and knows what it is about), or it can be issued at a press conference to which reporters are invited.

Before constructing a press release, it is worth studying how news reports are put together. If you can pattern your text on actual report style you will make the journalist's job a lot easier and so increase the chances of getting the story published. The report that follows is taken from a regional newspaper and could well have originated in a press release. Note how the story is structured in a particular way:

LEE'S A HIGH FLIER

His career is taking off and now at 20 he's teaching others to be pilots

PILOT Lee Bayliss is reaching new heights of expertise in his soaraway career.

He has become Britain's youngest flying instructor at the age of 20. Lee had his first flying lesson for his 13th birthday, earned his pilot's licence at 17 and got a commercial licence a year later.

Now Lee, from Twyning, near Tewkesbury, whose ambition is to become an airline pilot, has become an instructor at the South Warwickshire flying school at Stratford upon Avon.

'I decided I wanted to fly when I was four,' he said. 'My mother worries about me. She stopped my father flying because she thought it was too dangerous, but I wouldn't stop.'

Lee worked in a flour factory and took other temporary jobs to raise the £18,000 needed to finance his high-flying career.

He caught the flying bug while jetting off with his parents Tony and Heather on family holidays.

Mr Bayliss, aged 47, works as a civil engineer while Lee's brother, also called Tony, 22, runs the family's smallholding.

'My husband never took his pilot's licence because I was unhappy about him flying,' said Mrs Bayliss.

'I went up with him in a light-aircraft once and didn't like it one bit.

'I tried to talk Lee out of it but he was

determined that it was something he wanted to do.

'I still worry about him and I make sure that he always rings me after going up to put my mind at rest.'

Flying-school principal Rodney Galiffe said Lee flew through his exams and got first-time passes in all of them.

'We've checked it out and he definitely is the youngest instructor,' he said.

'He did everything as quickly as possible and qualified as an instructor in the shortest possible time.'

At first sight the ordering of information in a news story like this seems rather wayward. It appears to jump around in time so that a lot of events that happened at the beginning of the real story (like Lee working to earn money for his lessons) come nowhere near the beginning of the news report. There is a good reason for this, however. Most people do not read a newspaper like a novel, beginning on page 1 and working steadily through until they reach the end. They dot around, scanning a page until something interesting catches their eye. Then they may read just part of the report before moving on again.

The structure of the story about Lee Bayliss is based on this habit of reading. It begins with a **heading** and **subheading** designed to catch the eye. The **lead paragraph** (the one beginning *Pilot Lee Bayliss…*) continues this approach before the succeeding two or three paragraphs tell the **main story** briefly and clearly. At this point some readers will opt out, but others will be more interested and will have the patience to read on. So the remainder of the report offers more **interesting details** (the flour factory, the family holidays) about the main story, **background information** (Lee's family) and, if available, **comments** by people involved (Mrs Bayliss, the flying instructor). This has the added advantage of extending the human interest of the story.

Constructing a press release

When you construct a press release, you should bear all this in mind:

- Give it a **heading** designed to inform readers what the story is about but which also catches their interest.

- If appropriate add a **subheading** and a **lead paragraph** which develops interest and leads into the main story.

- Tell the **main story** in two or three *short* paragraphs.

- Follow this with one or two paragraphs containing **interesting details** and another two or three which provide **background information**.

- If you have any useful **quotations or comments**, use these to round the story off.

Whenever possible, give the story a human-interest angle. For example your press release may be about the company's success in doubling its overseas sales of portable crop sprayers; but if your sales director has just returned from an interesting and unusual trip to remote parts of East Africa, use this as a key feature of the story to attract interest.

Two other key features should always appear in a press release. At the beginning the reader should be told when the story can be used. If it is for **immediate use**, then this should be stated. Otherwise it should be made clear that the story is **embargoed until...** followed by the time and date when it can be used.

At the end of the story should be stated the name of the person who can be contacted for further information and their contact details.

Instructions

Everyone has favourite examples of ambiguous instructions:

- On a tin of chocolate pudding: *Before opening, stand in boiling water for ten minutes.*

- In an aircraft maintenance manual: *Check undercarriage locking pin. If bent, replace.* (The operator examined the pin. It was indeed bent, so he put it back. The aircraft crashed.)

- On the door of a health centre: *Family Planning – please use rear entrance.*

In practice, however, poorly written instructions are rarely so funny. Apart from the vexation and waste of time they cause, bad instructions are bad for business. Customers think twice about buying from a company whose instructions have proved useless before. In some countries consumer protection regulations require that instructions and safety information accompanying a product are taken into account when deciding whether it is faulty. Manufacturers can be held liable for injury or damage caused by poor safety information. The selling of unsafe consumer goods can lead to criminal prosecution.

So, what goes wrong in the writing of instructions, and how can problems be put right? Usually one or more of the following six rules has been broken.

1 Know your readers

Most readers will not have used the product before – that's why they're reading the instructions. But what else can you find out about them? Will they be technically knowledgeable or complete novices? Will they be children or adults? Under what conditions will they be using the instructions?

Learning about these things and making the right assumptions will affect the words you use. An experienced carpenter might readily understand the instruction

> *Screw pendant bolts into door plates using cheese-head screws*

but most do-it-yourselfers would need an illustration of pendant bolts, door plates, and cheese-head screws.

2 Use imperatives

By using the imperative (the 'command' form of a verb) you are putting the action early and helping to keep the message simple.

Imagine you are instructing office staff how to fill in this box on a computer screen:

| New Cost Centre Code |
| New Cost Centre Name |
| Parent Cost Centre Code |

Using the passive voice you could write:

> The code of the new cost centre should be entered into the New Cost Centre Code field.
>
> The name of the new cost centre (maximum 40 characters) should then be entered into the New Cost Centre Name field.
>
> The code of the parent cost centre should then be entered into the Parent Cost Centre Code field.
>
> When satisfied, the 'Do' key should be pressed to commit the new cost centre to the database.

Or you could write it much more crisply in the imperative:

> Enter the code of the new cost centre into the New Cost Centre Code field.
>
> Enter the name of the new cost centre (maximum 40 characters) into the New Cost Centre Name field.
>
> Enter the code of the parent cost centre into the Parent Cost Centre Code field.
>
> When satisfied, press the 'Do' key to commit the new cost centre to the database.

This is simpler because the readers know from the start of each sentence what action is required of them. Even simpler would be to assign numbers to the three fields and then write:

> Enter the correct code in field 1.
>
> Enter the correct name (maximum 40 characters) in field 2.

and so on.

3 Use short paragraphs

Readers waste time and make mistakes if the information they need is buried in long paragraphs. In this example a local authority inspector is trying to persuade a restaurant owner, whose dirty kitchens she has been visiting, to do his washing-up hygienically. Notice that there are no numbered steps or short paragraphs. The information looks boring and complicated, and you probably feel little inclination to read it:

> After the preliminary sorting of the utensils and scraping off of food residues into the refuse containers, the utensils should be washed in the first sink, piece by piece, in clean hot water at a temperature of about 60°C with a detergent added. This temperature is too hot for the hands and the operative should wear rubber gloves and use a dish mop. The water should be changed as often as it becomes dirty or greasy. After this, the utensils should be suitably arranged in the wire baskets available for immersion in the sterilizing sink. The utensils should be placed so that no two pieces touch each other and that all the surfaces of every piece are exposed to the rinse water. The rinse will be ineffective if plates or saucers are piled on top of one another or if cutlery is merely heaped in the basket. The sterilizing rinse in the second sink should be of clean hot water without added detergent or chemical and at a temperature of not less than 77°C and the utensils should remain in the water for a full two minutes. At this temperature care should of course be taken not to immerse the hands. The purpose is to raise the temperature of the utensils to that of the water so that they will air-dry almost instantly on removal. The temperature of the water should be maintained at about 77°C throughout and accordingly this sink should be fitted with a device to record the temperature of the water. When the two minutes are up, the basket should be removed from the sink and stood temporarily on a draining board and as soon as the utensils are dry and cool enough to be handled, they should be put in a clean place awaiting re-use.

The words are reasonably plain, the punctuation is sound, and none of the sentences is impossibly long. But the whole thing needs splitting into short paragraphs and transforming into the imperative. First we need an introductory sentence, perhaps this:

> You should make sure that your staff follow these instructions.

Then the points need redrafting in the imperative:

> (1) Sort the utensils and scrape off waste food into the bins.

(2) Wash the utensils in the first sink, piece by piece, in clean hot water at a temperature of about 60°C with a detergent added. This temperature is too hot for your hands, so wear rubber gloves and use a dish mop.

(3) Change the water as often as it becomes dirty or greasy.

(4) Put the utensils in the wire baskets available for immersion in the sterilizing sink. Arrange the utensils so that no two pieces touch each other and that all the surfaces of every piece are exposed to the rinse water. The rinse will not do its job if plates or saucers are piled on top of one another or if cutlery is merely heaped in the basket. The sterilizing rinse should be of clean hot water without added detergent or chemical and at a temperature of at least 77°C.

(5) Put the wire baskets containing the utensils in the water for a full two minutes. At this temperature, take care not to immerse your hands. The purpose is to raise the temperature of the utensils to that of the water, so that they will air-dry almost instantly on removal. Maintain the water temperature at about 77°C throughout. To check this, make sure the sink is fitted with a suitable thermometer.

(6) When the two minutes are up, remove the basket from the sink and stand it temporarily on a draining board.

(7) As soon as the utensils are dry and cool enough to be handled, put them in a clean place awaiting re-use.

These improvements have arisen not from a total rewrite but from two simple structural tactics (paragraphing and numbering), and one simple style tactic (the use of imperatives).

4 Use separate headed sections

Normally it is wise to split the instructions into separate sections whose headings identify the purpose of each action.

A common sequence of sections is:

● **Introductory explanation, overview, or summary**

This tells readers the purpose of the activity, what it will achieve and how long it should take. Sometimes users with experience of similar tools or equipment will benefit from a quick-start procedure. In long instructions, a contents list will help.

● **Tools or materials required**

Giving this information saves readers from having to stop the job whenever a new tool is needed.

● **Definitions**

These explain any terms the readers may not understand. Definitions may also be needed of everyday words carrying special or limited meanings in the instructions.

● **Warnings**

If these come after the instructions, they are useless and could be dangerous. Warnings should be given twice: once in the introduction and again just before the instruction to which they relate. Make clear that the warnings must be followed and are not just recommended practice. Could the product be modified to eliminate the hazard?

● **Main text**

Split into headed sections.

Headings should be 'predictive'—that is, they should tell the reader what is coming up in the paragraph—and, if possible, stimulating. Label headings, like *Spillages* or *Storage* are weaker than *What to do about spillages* or *How much should be stored?*

5 Use appropriate illustrations

If a message can be simply conveyed in words, there is no need for illustrations (and vice versa). Words are particularly good for getting abstract ideas across, dealing with fine differences in meaning, and for referring to things the reader has already learned about. Illustrations are good at showing what things look like and their relative size. This can save words and illuminate the words that remain.

Whether you are commissioning illustrations from graphics professionals or drawing them yourself, you may like to consider:

- illustrations in **exploded-view** format (useful for self-assembly products as they show how the item is put together)

- illustrations showing **enlargements** of particular parts so that readers can focus on the relevant point easily

Other important considerations include:

- the **position** of the illustration relative to the text – ideally readers should be able to refer to it as they read

- the **angle of view** from which an object is presented – this should clearly show the parts concerned or the action to be taken

- keeping objects to **scale**

- ensuring that any **typesetting** included in the illustration will be legible if scaled down to fit the document.

6 Test with a panel of typical users

This is the most important rule, because users' performance is the key. Give the draft instructions, and any product associated with them, to a focus group of typical readers—preferably not your own colleagues who will know too much about the product. Watch them trying to use the instructions. Don't intervene unless asked or unless there is danger. Observe any false moves they make. Discuss with them how they got on. Ask them about any misinterpretations. Redraft the instructions in the light of what you find. Test again if possible.

Business Plans

A business plan is a detailed plan setting out the objectives of a business over a stated period, often three, five, or ten years. It may be drawn up for various reasons, perhaps because the business has passed through a bad period or because there has been a major change of policy. For new businesses it is an essential document for raising capital or loans. The plan should provide detailed figures for as many of the objectives as possible; it must also outline the strategy

and tactics it intends to use in achieving these objectives. For a group of companies the business plan is often called a **corporate plan**.

A business plan is a more specialized form of the standard report or proposal, and most of the points about style and so on made in the earlier section apply here. However, the content requirements of such a plan are unusually specific.

It would usually be expected to provide information about:

- The nature, objectives, and (if appropriate) the history of the business

- The personnel employed (or to be employed)

- The products or services to be sold in relation to the market

- The prospective premises

- The equipment required

- A forecast of the sales, year by year, or month by month (as appropriate), for three, five, or ten years

- A financial summary explaining the source of funds, any expected setting-up expenses, and running expenses for the whole period in question. There should be a detailed cash-flow projection covering at least three years in detail and a further two years in outline

- A forecast of the profitability of the enterprise

The business

The following details should be given:

Personal details. For the founder, proprietor, partners, directors, or other instigators of the business, state each person's name, address, age, and profession if it is relevant to the business. Some details of their background and experience should also be given.

Structure of the business. State whether the business is or will be set up as a sole trader, a partnership, or a limited company.

Description of the business activities.
Describe the product or service the business
will offer for sale and to what extent (if at
all) it will manufacture the product.

Commencement date. State the date on
which trading will start (for a new business)
and why this date has been selected.

Objectives. State what the business is expected to achieve in general terms of sales
and profitability, referring to the more detailed analysis later in the report.

History of the business. A new business
will probably have no history; however,
something should be said about how it
came into being. A restructured business
or a business seeking new capital will have
a history and you should give this here, pay-
ing special attention to any mergers or
takeovers.

Personnel

State the number of employees (other than
directors, partners, founders, etc.) For all
senior personnel give names, ages, qualifications, position within the company, and
salary. If no staff are currently employed
but some will be required for the business
to trade, state the numbers you propose to
recruit and their salaries as accurately as
possible. A plan of staff requirements over
the full period, together with any further
recruitment or redundancies this may involve, should also be given. If this requires
considerable detail, present the information as an appendix.

The products or services in relation to the market

Product or service details. Provide details
of all products and the prices at which you
propose to sell them. Explain your pricing
policy, taking into account the price and
quality of competitive products or services.

Market details. State the nature of the market; whether it is growing, declining, static,
or seasonal. Give brief details of any market
testing you have undertaken and profiles of
intended customers. If substantial orders,
or letters stating an intent to place substantial orders, have been received, attach

copies. State if any market research has
been undertaken.

The competition. Give the names of
your major competitors, their pricing policy, strengths, weaknesses, location, etc.
Explain how your company's products or
services will be better than those of your
competitors and state any other ideas you
may have about overcoming competition.

Proposed marketing methods. Give details
of how you plan to market your products or
services and the cost of doing so. Include in
your budgeted expenditure a figure for advertising. If advertising and PR are important to your sales plan, give details in an
appendix.

Suppliers. Give details of your principal
suppliers as well as alternative sources of
supply. Give a brief account of the advantages you see in using the chosen supplier.
If you have any letters from suppliers that
could be of interest to a possible backer, attach copies.

The premises

Property type. State whether the premises
of both offices and any manufacturing or
storage units will be leased or bought. If
the premises are to be leased, state the
length of the lease, whether there is an option to renew, the present rent, and the frequency of rent reviews. Mention should
also be made of who bears responsibility
for internal and external repairs. If you own
the premises, state the purchase price and
when they were bought. If a valuer's report
has been obtained for either leasehold or
freehold property, enclose a copy with the
plan. If the property is freehold, state its
written-down value (i.e. the value given in
the balance sheet after the usual deductions
for depreciation have been made). With
both leasehold and freehold property state
the amounts payable to the local authority
in rates.

Specifications. State the overall size of the
premises and how it is (or is to be) subdivided, e.g. production space, storage space,
retailing space, office space. If appropriate,
supply a plan.

Equipment required

If the business manufactures or intends to manufacture its products, it may be useful to give a brief outline here of the process involved.

Manufacturing equipment. Give details of any equipment you already own, including purchase price, depreciation, and current value. Also give financial details of any manufacturing equipment currently hired, leased, or borrowed. Add a note about the cost of servicing the equipment, mentioning any guarantees.

General trading equipment. Give details of any equipment you have bought for general trading purposes, e.g. cash tills or company vans, including the depreciation, present value, and purchase price. Mention any such items you have leased or borrowed, stating the rent paid and terms of leasing.

Equipment on hire purchase. Give details of any equipment you are currently buying on hire purchase, the date and terms of the contract, and the amounts already paid.

Equipment required. Give details of all equipment that you intend to buy, either to begin trading or to increase existing production. State the prices, leasing arrangements, and source of funds.

Sales forecasts

Your business plan should state how sales are to be achieved, with details of the distribution channels (i.e. wholesalers and retailers) involved. Any fees payable to agents or discounts made to bulk buyers should be stated: a breakdown of the sale price in the form of a pie chart is often useful. Provide a detailed forecast of sales either on a monthly basis, if this is feasible, or on a quarterly or annual basis if this is more appropriate. The sales forecasts should be projected as far into the future as possible—certainly three years but longer if a sensible forecast can be made. These figures will form the basis of the all-important cash-flow projections (see below).

Financial summary

The financial summary of a new business will consist of three documents:

(i) a statement of the **source of funds**

(ii) a **cash-flow projection** for at least three years

(iii) a **projection of profits** for at least three years

For a restructured business or a business seeking new capital the supporting documents should also include:

(iv) copies of the balance sheets and profit and loss accounts for at least the past three years

Source of funds. This explains how the business has raised, or intends to raise, finance for the period in question. For an existing business, set out the capital structure of the company, i.e. the shares, loan stock, etc. which make up the organization's capital, together with any debt. The long-term debt may consist of debentures, while the short-term debt may be in the form of bank loans. For a new business, outline the intended capital structure together with a list of shareholders, stock and debenture holders, etc.

For a business seeking new capital, state your requirements precisely and explain what form of security you can offer.

Cash-flow projection. This sets out all the expected payments and receipts over the period in question; it is probably the most important part of the whole business plan. If the plan is to be credible, it is essential that the cash-flow projection should not contain any estimates that cannot be substantiated as fair and likely. For a convincing business plan, the cash-flow projection might cover the first three years in detail and the next two years in less detail. If an outline projection for ten years can be provided, the picture becomes increasingly credible.

Projection of profits. Give an estimate of your expected profits over at least three years. This should be realistic, even if it shows that the venture is unlikely to be profitable in its initial year (or two).

Section 8: Public Speaking

Spoken presentations to an audience come in a variety of forms. For example:

- a company sales team offering a range of goods or services to a potential client
- a college lecture
- an after-dinner speech or toast

All, however, have these key features:

- one or more speakers presenting information and ideas
- a clearly defined primary purpose (and probably two or three lesser ones)
- an audience with a range of expectations and needs

This Section shows you how to prepare a speech with these key features in mind and how to deliver it with confidence and authority. Although most of what is said here applies to any kind of speech, the main emphasis is on work-related presentations. Certain other types of speech have special requirements and these are considered separately at the end of the Section.

Preparing the Speech

Whatever the form or occasion of your speech, the key to success is intelligent preparation. Without this, the event may be hopelessly disorganized. Even professionals can and sometimes do fail to make proper preparation, whether out of overconfidence, lack of time, or even laziness. Most of us have been present at a poorly prepared speech—one that tried to cover too much ground in the time, for instance, or one that was poorly structured and degenerated into a kind of rambling chat. More disastrous still, we might recall a learned talk made farcical by the lecturer's inability to operate a projector, or a speech received in embarrassed silence owing to the speaker's misguided idea of humour.

All of these mistakes could have been avoided. We cannot all be brilliant, witty, or elegant public speakers, but anyone can turn in a polished and professional performance—if they want to. The key is in the organization.

Think of your purpose

Begin by thinking about *why* you are making the speech. It may be:

- to inform
- to persuade
- to entertain
- to meet and get on with your audience

Frequently it will be a mixture of some or all of these.

To inform. Most talks provide information of some kind, often considerable amounts of it. It is not uncommon for members of an audience to go away with the feeling that 'there was a lot of good stuff there, but it was far more than I could take in at one sitting'. With this in mind, it is valuable to break 'information talk' down into different kinds:

- straight facts (data)

  While these are undoubtedly important, they are often the most difficult to digest. A string of unrelated figures, dates, names, and events is very difficult for most of us to remember, so the speaker has to provide as much help as possible by putting such data into contexts, patterns, and pictures.

- stories

  People find stories much easier to remember. There are two reasons for this. First, a story has its own built-in pattern, and patterns make facts easier to remember; and secondly, stories fulfil a very primitive need in human beings—the desire to 'know what happens next' is strong in almost everybody.

- descriptions and explanations

  Descriptions of what things or people look like are easy to remember in the same way that stories are. More often, however, it is necessary to explain the functioning of organizations, machines, or institutions. Here it is important to make sure that the description creates clear patterns to help the audience visualize what is being described, for example by using images or analogies.

To persuade. Many business presentations have as their chief purpose to persuade the audience to do something: buy your product, sign up for a different way of doing things, agree to a particular course of action. The same is obviously true of a political or polemical speech. Even apparently factual presentations such as a college lecture may involve persuasion: for example, the lecturer may wish to persuade students to take a subject more seriously than they currently do, or to open their minds to a new and challenging way of thinking.

To entertain. Sometimes—as in the case of an after-dinner or best man's speech—the speaker's main aim may be to entertain. Even when it is not the primary aim of a presentation, however, it is very often an important secondary aim. If you can entertain your audience it often makes your primary aim of informing or persuading very much easier.

To meet and get on with your audience. Occasionally the primary purpose of a presentation may be to meet and get on with the members of the audience; for example, a new manager may set up such a meeting with those he or she will be working with. Any address to a new audience must have this as a secondary aim, especially if you are dealing with potential clients; and if your talk is to people whom you meet on a regular basis—students or members of your company—then you need to keep in mind your continuing relationship with them.

Much of this is fairly obvious, but it is important to be aware of all your purposes in making a presentation and not just the primary or most obvious one.

Think of your audience

Remember that the audience sees the whole event as a package that begins when they arrive and ends when they leave. Everything that happens between those

two times is part of the presentation as far as they are concerned. This may make the preparatory need to think of your audience appear rather daunting, but if it is approached step by step it need not be.

Where they are now. The starting point should be a clear idea of 'where the audience are now'—that is, what they currently know and understand about the subject matter of the talk:

- their theoretical knowledge
- their practical knowledge
- their intelligence
- their level of education
- the terminology they are confident about handling
- how quickly they can pick up new ideas
- their concentration span

This information may not be easy to establish and you may have to make assumptions and deductions about it. Remember, too, that your audience may contain a wide range of experience, education, and expectations.

Their expectations. The audience have come for a reason. They may be enthusiastic volunteers bursting to hear your words, or they may be unwilling conscripts who can think of many things they would rather be doing. More likely they will be somewhere between these two extremes. Whatever their attitude to the event, they will have a bundle of expectations and hopes about it. Students at a lecture, for example, may well be there because it is a compulsory part of their course. If it takes place first thing on a Monday morning, some, at least, may be unwilling conscripts. This lack of enthusiasm will be tempered by a willingness to learn and a belief that the lecture could be useful—if only to help them pass one of the modules on the course.

If you have delivered a presentation on the same subject once or more in the past it is very tempting to churn out exactly the same material again. This can, however, lead to a dull and uninspiring performance. The subject matter may not be new to you, but it is to this particular audience, and it is important to assess them and their needs afresh each time and to adapt your material accordingly.

Their practical needs. It is also important to remember the practical needs of your audience. The following may all need to be considered:

- How you will arrange the seating so that everyone can see without straining, everyone can hear, and the participants are in the best relationship with you and with each other.

- Where you will place yourself. Do you require a lectern, a chair, or any other furniture? Do you want to be able to move around?

- Do you need a microphone and loudspeakers and, if so, how should these be placed?

- Where you will place a screen and projector(s), flipchart, or whiteboard.

- What lighting (or blackout) do you need?

All this requires thought and preparation. If you are operating on home ground, this is more straightforward, but even if you are a visiting speaker, most of these points can be organized in advance. At the very least you should make sure that you have a clear idea of the type of room in which you will be speaking and the likely size of the audience.

Their intellectual needs. You should already have some idea of this, having considered the list of points under 'Where they are now'. What you need now is a strategy for making your talk as effective as possible. This should include:

- the **order** in which you present material

- the **communication aids** you will use:
  - visual aids such as projection, charts, and the use of a whiteboard
  - audio or video tape or film
  - verbal aids such as stories and anecdotes, images and analogies, and mnemonics
  - handouts

- the use of **rhythm** and **variety** to keep your audience interested and alert

Their personal needs. Consider also the personal needs of your audience. If a speech or presentation goes on too long, without opportunities for the audience to relax physically and mentally, then it will become increasingly ineffective. In the course of a long session there should be periods for such relaxation: chances for a chat, to stretch your legs, have a coffee, and so on. Make allowances for the time of day or night and think about where your speech comes in the schedule. Will your audience be fresh and attentive, or will they have already sat through two or three speakers? An audience before lunch is subject to different distractions from those that make the minds of an audience wander after lunch.

Putting the speech together

How you research, structure and write your speech will depend on the particular circumstances, but there are a number of general rules which apply to most situations.

Content. What you put in your speech will depend on three variables:

- what you would like to include
- how much time you have
- how much your audience can absorb

This may seem obvious, but people often forget that these three generally pull in conflicting directions and so try to include more material than is really possible. This may result in the audience being detained for longer than envisaged, or in the presentation only covering part of the intended ground. It is always better to err on the side of caution when deciding how much material to include.

At the same time, you don't want to appear poorly informed or to be left flailing by a tricky question. This means that it is a good idea to prepare as much material as you can, even though some of it will not be used on the day. If the speech is designed to persuade, for example, make sure that you have information in reserve to refute any objections that might be raised from the floor. A sound background knowledge should give you confidence and authority. Speakers are often most persuasive when they give the impression that they have not used every argument or fact at their disposal.

To decide what should go into the speech itself, sort your material into three categories:

- what must be discussed
- what should be discussed
- what could be discussed

The main body of the speech should be built round the first two categories; the third category should be kept in reserve to be used if needed. Experienced speakers generally choose a structure with a good deal of flexibility, so that material can be added or dropped on the day as time allows and the situation requires.

This leads to the general question of **priorities**. Here it is as well to be realistic. Much of what you have to say will be forgotten soon after you have said it, and frequently the things that are remembered are not necessarily the most important. An audience may come away from a speech remembering two or three jokes but forgetting the three or four key points the speaker made.

You should have a small number of key points that you consider it is essential your listeners should take away with them at the end of the presentation. The main part of your speech should be devoted to making sure that these key points are understood and remembered.

More detailed information that you want your audience to retain should be communicated in the presentation (preferably using whatever aids are available), but should also be distributed in the form of a handout.

Ordering. A number of factors will help you decide on the order in which material is presented. First and most obviously:

- the logic of the subject

  Frequently there isn't a lot of choice; the subject matter will largely dictate the ordering.

- the logic of learning and understanding

  It is essential to move from the known to the unknown, and from basic concepts to more complex issues.

- the need for variety

  Wherever possible the strictly logical order should from time to time be broken in order to provide variety.

You should also be aware of the natural rise and fall of an audience's attention level during a speech, and try to work with rather than against this. Research has shown that an audience often requires a minute or two to settle down; they are then very receptive for three or four minutes, but attention subsequently falls until the closing three or four minutes of the speech. Many professional speakers structure their speeches to begin with a short preamble, then summarize the main points of the speech in the peak receptive period, elucidate these points, draw conclusions, and recap on the central points in the last minutes.

Some experienced speakers suggest writing the closing section first, as this helps to focus the speech on the main points and provides a target to work towards.

The following are all good hints:

- Try to start with a bang—a lively and memorable statement or question to compel the listeners' attention.
- Give yourself a little time to size your audience up, to develop some rapport, before launching into the main substance of your speech. If the occasion is one which allows a to-and-fro of questions between speaker and audience, it is helpful to warm them up and find out about them by questioning them about their experience of the subject and what they hope to gain from the presentation.
- Make the structure of your speech clear early on. An audience feels much more comfortable if they know where they are throughout.
- After the detailed presentation of each key point allow time to recap not just that point but its relationship to what has gone before. This not only helps to clarify the material but also reinforces the listeners' sense of the structure of the whole presentation.
- End memorably, summing up what has been said and then giving the audience something extra to take away with them.

Jokes, quotations, and anecdotes. These are all good devices for getting and keeping an audience's attention, but all should be used with care.

If you are intending to use quotations, be sure that you get them right, that they are absolutely appropriate, and that the audience will understand their relevance. Inappropriate literary quotations merely look pompous and misquotations and wrong attributions can make a fool of the speaker.

If you intend to use a joke, be sure that you know how to tell it—especially how to get the timing right. A good rule is never to use a joke or a humorous quotation unless you find it funny yourself. If you can make the audience laugh they are likely to warm to you and to your cause. If the joke falls flat or you muff it, you may have lost them for good. Be careful, too, that your jokes do not offend or victimize members of the audience.

Even if you are good at telling jokes and stories, it is important not to get carried away. Unless you are a professional comedian, it is unlikely that you have been invited to speak primarily to make the audience laugh. This applies to convivial occasions such as after-dinner speeches as well as to more sober and businesslike ones.

Anecdotes and stories can add variety to a speech, but they must be pithy and to the point. Stories are riskier than jokes because they take longer to tell. If a one-liner falls flat, the speaker can usually move quickly on without too much damage; this is more difficult after a long and involved story that elicits only groans.

For more on the use and misuse of humour, see the paragraphs below on the after-dinner speech and the best man's speech.

Should you write it all out?

Giving a speech can be a worrying prospect. Faced by nerves about the audience's reaction and anxiety not to miss out anything important, some speakers resort to reading a fully written-out text. Such occasions are rarely a success. A reader finds it difficult to engage with an audience in the way that an unscripted speaker can. When you read, your eyes are, much of the time,

turned down towards your script and thus away from the audience. You do not make eye contact and cannot be properly aware of the way in which your listeners are responding to your words.

On the other hand, it is very difficult to sustain a speech of any duration without some kind of written prompt. It is too easy to lose the thread of your discourse and either flannel, or be led down some tempting but irrelevant by-road. So it is a question of what form of written preparation to make.

A popular solution is to use a set of **prompt cards**, about the size of postcards, on which the main points of the speech are written. Each card is numbered and one key point to be made is written on each, with any additional details that it is important to remember. It is preferable to write on only one side of each card so that after you have used it you can turn it over to indicate that it has been used.

The other advantage of this system is that if you find you are running short of time, you can quickly skip over cards carrying less important points and move on to the more important topics. It is even possible to mark on the cards the approximate time at which you should reach that point so that you have a check on how things are progressing.

Alternatively, if you are using an overhead projector, it is possible to use your transparencies as the basis of a set of prompt cards. You simply keep the transparencies in their box, interleaved with sheets of white paper, each of which carries a summary of the main points you wish to make here. Integrating notes with pictures is even more straightforward if you decide to project images from a computer display (see p 261).

Even if you decide to use one of these methods, it can be a good idea to write the whole of your presentation out in full beforehand. This is a good way of ensuring that all the details and arguments are fully worked out. A full text can also provide reassurance—you know that you have a worthwhile speech to deliver and that you are now unlikely to lose your way or dry up completely.

The danger is that written prose and speech are different. If you read written prose aloud it sounds like a reading and not a speech. One solution is to read the speech aloud as you prepare it—and then right through, preferably more than once, after you have finished writing. If you find yourself stumbling anywhere, try altering the phrasing or the rhythm of the sentence. Choose simple, working, lively words. Avoid long involved sentences and self-conscious rhetorical flourishes.

It can also be very useful to time yourself as you read.

Ideally, once you have written the whole speech out and practised reading it, you should have the confidence to ignore it. The key points can now be transferred to prompt cards. Alternatively, use the speech itself as a series of prompts. Type it out using good spacing and a fairly large typeface, on one side of the paper only. Go through it and underline the key phrase or phrases on each page in red. Then, on the day, use these to talk directly to the audience, only referring to the script to remind yourself of the points you wish to make. If you have spent some time working on what you want to say, you may be surprised just how much of your original phrasing and detail you remember without having to make lengthy references to the typescript.

Delivering the Speech

Finding confidence

In order to deliver your speech effectively, it is important that you seem confident, relaxed, and in charge of the situation. This will come far more easily if you have prepared carefully for the occasion in the various ways suggested.

Even if you do feel a touch of stage fright, try hard not to let this show. Avoid nervous body language such as fiddling, scratching, or rubbing your hands together. A confident outward bearing will help you to take control of your audience and this will boost your inner confidence. The key is to adopt an upright easy posture, to relax your muscles, and to breathe deeply. Remember that a little nervous tension is to be expected and try to work with it; properly managed, it will make your delivery more alert and lively.

Whatever you do, avoid a weak self-deprecating beginning. Never apologize in advance for inadequacies you have no intention of displaying.

Talking to your audience

If your listeners do not feel that you are talking to them personally, then they might just as well have stayed at home and listened to a tape recording of your talk. What gives a live presentation its interest is just that: it is live. The audience are hearing it as it happens, and *how* it happens is affected by the way they respond, or it should be.

So speak to them directly. Look at them—not at the back of the room (a common habit among novices). If an audience feels that you are avoiding looking at them, they may assume that you are not personally convinced by what you are saying; however, direct eye contact with members of the audience can appear confrontational. By looking at people's ears or shoulders you can give an impression of personal contact without appearing too challenging. This also has the effect of making the speech appear more personal—the members of the audience feel that they are being spoken *to* rather than *at*.

Another good tip is to locate one or two friendly faces in the crowd, people whose eyes—or, even better, their smiles—tell you that they are favourably disposed towards you. Remember where they are so that from time to time you look at them and address remarks to them personally. That does *you* some good, by boosting your confidence. The rest of the time your attention should be divided fairly evenly between your other listeners. Let your eyes move over the audience as you speak, focusing briefly on individuals and addressing that part of your speech to them, before moving on again. The purpose of this is that every member of the audience should feel that your words are intended for them personally.

Dealing with interruptions and questions.
Speakers sometimes invite the audience to interrupt them to ask questions or even to challenge what is being said. This can be a useful way of engaging with your listeners and providing a lively discourse. It has a number of disadvantages, however. For one thing, your audience do not know what you are going to say and so may ask questions that will be answered later. Secondly, it can drag you away from the sequence of points you wish to make down a number of blind alleys. And it is an invitation to the bore, the crank, and the attention-seeker to monopolize your attention, to the irritation of everyone else present.

It is generally better to offer one or more slots for questions and discussion at moments in the presentation selected by *you*. If people interrupt without being invited to, you can then ask them, politely, to hold their fire until you reach the chosen moment. If they insist, then try to deal with the point briefly and then move on to your next point. For advice on dealing with hostile interruptions, see p 262.

Question-and-answer sessions can be tricky to handle. The rest of the time you are, or should be, firmly in control; here you are to some extent at the mercy of events. Begin by allocating a set period of time – even if you are actually prepared to spend longer than the stated time on questions. That way if one person threatens to monopolize the session you can point out that others, too, have questions they wish to ask and the time is limited—and then hope that someone else *does* have a question!

Things that have to be read. Any text that your audience can see needs careful handling. If you project a text, you must allow sufficient time for it to be read—and some people are slow readers. Some speakers get round this by reading the text aloud, but audience members may find this irritating. On the other hand if the projected text is at the limits of legibility because of the size of the room, then it is advisable to read it out.

The question of handouts is more complicated. The trouble is that if you distribute handouts before or during your talk, people tend to read them and not listen to what you are saying. So unless there is a good reason to do otherwise, only distribute them at the end of the presentation. It is also helpful to advise your audience that you will be doing this, and to tell them roughly what the handout contains, so that listeners are saved the trouble of taking unnecessary notes. (Also, during the presentation, when you refer to important details it is helpful to say, 'Those details are in the handout which you will receive at the end.')

Using your voice

After inadequate preparation, poor voice production is probably the most common cause of ineffective public speaking. The voice is flawed if:

- it is weakly supported by breath
- it is husky and toneless or has a pinched, strident quality
- it is unresonant and difficult to hear at the furthest reaches of the audience

A speech can also be ruined by sloppy or monotonous diction.

Breath. Control of breath is the foundation on which voice is built. Tone should be balanced on a sufficient and steadily controlled supply of breath. Too much inhaled air fogs the tone; too little weakens supply and tone, and makes assured phrasing impossible.

If you wish to improve your breath control, there are various books of exercises for actors and singers that may be useful.

Tone. Most of us are sensitive to vocal quality; a harsh, shrill tone is offensive to our ears. Voices under stress are particularly prone to distortion. Teachers with weak class-control tend to have voices unnaturally pitched, squeezed, and forced in their vain attempts to quell a noisy class.

Little can be achieved without relaxation. Anxiety tightens the muscles which control the free passage of air. When we yawn we (involuntarily) loosen the muscles of the throat, opening wide the arch at the back, so a series of wide, sustained yawns, each ending with a contented sigh, can do much to help. Try also to loosen the neck and shoulder muscles by shrugging and gentle head-rolling. Taking a series of deep slow breaths before speaking can also help with relaxation.

Resonance. In its passage from lungs to mouth breath passes through the 'reeds' of the vocal cords causing them to vibrate and create sound waves. These are amplified by cavities in the head and the great cavity of the mouth, which is the chief resonator and amplifier.

To obtain good tone the voice must be focused well *forward*. Incorrect placing produces a muffled, unresonant tone. There are books which recommend useful exercises to achieve forward production, but there is no substitute for constant practice. Humming is a simple, effective way of reinforcing the natural resonance created within the nasal cavities. The rapid repetition of the word 'amo*ng*'—with emphasis on the final sound—will help to strengthen a lazy palate.

Although these are useful tips, serious or persistent problems in any of these areas may need the attention of a qualified voice coach. The voice is an instrument easily damaged by misuse.

Diction. Diction is the process of cutting and shaping sound into articulate speech in its two main divisions—vowels, which gives speech its musical quality, and consonants, which give it clarity.

It is important to realise that good diction has nothing to do with 'talking posh'. Whatever his or her natural accent the speaker should concentrate upon:

- A firm shaping of words so that they are cleanly begun and properly finished

- An unforced delivery

- An effective arrangement of the words into sense-groups

- Sufficient variation of pace and inflexion to avoid monotony

- Imaginative and emotional involvement so that meaning, colour, and vitality are communicated

- Competent projection of the voice over the whole speaking area

The speaker must be aware that prose has a natural rhythm of its own and that its free flow is important. Avoid falling into bad habits such as promoting the indefinite article *a* into 'ay' instead of 'uh'. This mangling of the neutral vowel sound impedes the free flow of rhythm and causes the phrase to sound stilted and unnatural.

Try to be aware always of the dominant words in phrases or sentences and don't waste time placing stress on unimportant ones. If heavy stress is given indiscriminately in an attempt to make everything equally important, meaning is confused and delivery made ridiculous.

A discriminating use of inflexion gives charm and variety to language, but beware of the 'soaring' inflexion, a sudden leap up for no discernible reason and without relevance to the sense. It is used in a self-conscious attempt to be musical.

Communication aids

A brilliant speaker can communicate effectively without using aids, and a disastrous one can make a bad presentation even worse by mismanaging them. Most of us fall somewhere between these extremes and need to make effective use of the best aids available.

Each aid has its particular advantages and problems.

Whiteboard. For quick ad hoc use, the modern successor to the school blackboard has a lot of advantages. Particular uses include:

- Building up a summary of key points as you proceed with the speech.

- Collecting ideas from participants in a brainstorming session.

- Demonstrating links between ideas collected in this way.

- Quickly showing the spelling of important technical terms and names.

Its disadvantages are:

- Permanence: once you have written something up, it stays there until you remove it.

- Not everyone can write neatly and clearly on a whiteboard.

- The amount of space is limited so you may have to remove important material to make way for more.

- When you write on it you have to turn away from your audience, so talking and writing require careful management.

- In some work spaces the whiteboard is fixed and not easy for everyone to see clearly.

Flipchart. One step on from the whiteboard, the flipchart can be used for the same purposes, but has a number of advantages:

- There is no need to erase unwanted material; you simply flip to the next sheet.

- Important material, including diagrams, can be prepared in advance.

- Even when you want the apparent spontaneity of writing up new material as you speak, it is possible to 'cheat' by writing a small pencil version of your text in one corner of the sheet beforehand, as a memory-jogger. Alternatively, the main lines of a diagram can be lightly pencilled in to guide your drawing.

The main disadvantages of a flipchart are that you have to turn away to write on it, and that in a large space it may not be easy to see.

Overhead projector. The overhead projector or OHP is a widely used—and misused—aid. When it is used well, it has several important advantages:

- It puts the image where everyone can see it easily.

- Transparencies can be used for a wide range of pre-prepared material from quite lengthy texts to complex diagrams involving several different colours.

- Transparencies can be prepared using a normal computer printer. There are specialist computer presentation programmes to help you do this and many word-processing programmes and business packages also facilitate transparency preparation.

- Empty and pre-printed transparencies can be written on without the speaker having to turn away from the audience.

- Transparencies can be overlaid so that a complex diagram or text can be built up stage by stage.

- You can mask a transparency, only revealing its contents a bit at a time, a useful way of focusing the audience's attention.

- Once a set of transparencies has been prepared for a presentation it can be stored and reused.

The main problems arise from inefficient use of the projector. Common mistakes include:

- Faulty alignment of the projector and screen. This leads to the 'keystone' effect, in which the top of the projected area is considerably wider than the bottom and as a result text and graphics are distorted and partly out of focus. Either the projector needs to be raised, or the screen needs to be angled to avoid this.

- Faulty focusing.

- Text or diagrams that are too small to be comfortably read.

- Mismanagement of transparencies so that they are badly aligned, or get knocked onto the floor.

These can, of course, be overcome, but this requires preparation, practice, and thought.

Slide projector. The slide projector is a somewhat more specialized aid than the OHP, over which it has a small number of advantages which can be very important:

- The image projected is of a higher quality.

- It is better for projecting detailed pictures and photographs.

- Images and sound can be coordinated into a comprehensive and complex audiovisual programme.

On the other hand, to use a slide projector effectively you need a darkened room and you need to make sure that you are proficient at using it, or have an operator who is. (Focus, in particular, can be tricky—and it helps if you get the slides the right way round!)

Projecting from a computer display. This allows for a wide range of text, still images, and even video clips to be integrated into a complete programme that has been prepared in advance, but which can still be controlled by the speaker. Owing to the flexibility and convenience of this method, it seems likely that the older forms of projection will fall into disuse as the technology becomes more widely available. The chief advantages are:

- Computer projection avoids all the fiddle and inconvenience of slides or transparencies (it also removes the worry that these could get into the wrong order).

- It is possible to preview the whole of your presentation on screen, so that you see exactly what the audience will see. Changes to the structure or detail of the presentation can be made without too much work.

- It is possible to have your prompt notes displayed on your computer monitor beside the relevant images (you will see the notes but your audience will not).

- Images stored on a computer can be refined or manipulated in almost any way you choose. During the presentation itself you can write or draw on the projected images; you can also highlight or zoom in on details as required.

- Photographs or graphics used in the presentation can be printed and used in handouts.

- Computer-based presentations can be used in online meetings or broadcast on the Internet.

- They are particularly useful to salesmen or other who have to travel. As long as a suitable projection system is available,

the whole presentation can be made from a laptop computer with no other equipment.

Whatever method(s) you use, it is very desirable to arrive in plenty of time so as to check that everything is working properly. It is also wise to have a backup of some kind in case the worst happens.

Some Other Types of Speech

So far we have concentrated on work-based presentations that are intended mainly to inform or persuade (usually some mixture of the two). There are, however, some other types of speech that have different purposes and requirements.

The political speech

This is perhaps the best example of public speaking as persuasion. There are two clear requirements: to refute the opposition's case and to advance your own. It is partisan (seldom objective), controversial, and unsparing. It may be derisive, persuasive, indignant, and many other things. In practice, it is often far too long and too vocally monotonous to retain interest for long.

Points to bear in mind:

- Read what the opposition have written and listen to what they have said on radio and television or in public. Unless you have studied their claims it is difficult to deal intelligently with them.

- Read and remember anything injudicious they may have written or said in the past; this can often provide a cheap but effective debating point.

- Prepare your 'attack' with dramatic technique; leave the most telling points to the end and make that memorable. A good speech never fizzles out.

- Do not try to slay too many dragons at once. Better short and telling than long and diffused. Avoid common abuse but do not hesitate to use sardonic humour if it is appropriate.

- In putting your own case look to the past if you must but concentrate on the future. Most people are more concerned with what may happen to them than with what has. Have some hopeful thoughts to offer; have an alternative strategy which your hearers may be persuaded to consider. It is not enough to promise this and that: say *how* you think your strategy could be carried out to everyone's benefit. Anticipate objections; have answers ready; be direct.

- Keep vocabulary simple and sentences short. In the age of the spin doctor and the soundbite old-fashioned oratory has (perhaps sadly) lost most of its power and appeal.

- Do not condescend or imply that those with whom you disagree are morons, and never use belligerent, hand-chopping gestures to armour-plate violent language.

- Unless you are a very experienced speaker, don't try to argue with hecklers: you are unlikely to emerge with your dignity enhanced. If an interruptor scores a point off you, it can damage your authority and leave you feeling flustered. On the other hand, if you put the heckler down you can end up looking like a bully and lose the audience's sympathy. It is usually unwise to take a stance against a member of the audience unless it is apparent that the audience already feels hostile towards that individual. Best of all, refuse to rise to the bait and rely on the chairperson to restore order.

The would-be politician is apt to develop irritating mannerisms – head-wagging, a throwing-up of the eyes at the end of a statement, a sudden surge of volume on an upward inflexion for the sake of emphasis. For their own good, such speakers should be filmed occasionally and made to watch the result.

The after-dinner speech

This is perhaps the purest example of a speech made simply to entertain. Being spoken on a social occasion, it must be amiable, relaxed in presentation, and *brief*. It should be a welcome part of the evening's entertainment, not an ordeal for speaker and audience alike. The speaker should aim for directness and spontaneity, but behind this seemingly impromptu delivery there should be very careful and thorough preparation.

In these circumstances, a speaker who is nose-deep in notes *cannot* communicate effectively. It is enough to have a few headline notes printed clearly on a postcard and placed unobtrusively on the table. A quick glance will prompt the memory without distracting the audience.

Because the company have so many things to distract *them* – things to nibble, to drink, to fidget with – it is particularly important that the speaker avoids fidgeting with his or her glasses, handkerchief, cutlery, and the like. An audience fascinated or irritated by such antics is not attentive to the speech.

The after-dinner speaker has even more need of a strong, compelling opening than most and this should be planned with some imagination.

At dinners the tables are often arranged to suit the waiters rather than the speaker, and some tables are on difficult sight-lines. This can tempt the speaker to address himself exclusively to the better-placed tables. Avoid this. No one likes to feel excluded.

It is a delusion to suppose that a speech cannot be entertaining unless it provokes frequent gales of laughter. Indeed, the would-be comic who keeps up a stream of jokes and stories can be a great trial. The best speeches are often those which elicit a smiling response from the audience. This demands wit rather than broad humour, and a nice degree of timing.

The formal toast

On very formal occasions a toastmaster is sometimes engaged to organize the evening's events and call upon the speakers in a formal, established manner. He or she will have been given a list of the guests who are to speak and will have been told who is to propose the toasts and who will reply, and in what order.

The toastmaster calls upon speakers in a formula which the speaker is expected to imitate exactly. *My lords, ladies and gentlemen,* the toastmaster may begin, or *Mr President, distinguished guests…pray silence for…who will propose the toast…* The speaker will then ·

repeat the toastmaster's salutation word for word and propose the toast. When this has been done the toastmaster repeats the toast, the company stand, and all drink. The ritual salutation is repeated in turn by the person who will reply to the toast.

The toasts begin with the service of coffee; in the UK the loyal toast comes first in two simple words: *The Queen.*

Guests who are to reply to the toast to themselves, or to the institutions they represent, are rightly aggrieved if the proposer rambles on about something quite irrelevant, turning to the proper subject only at the end. Care must be taken to keep everyone in good humour as a host should.

If you are replying to the toast it is wise to note a few of the proposer's remarks and refer briefly to them, if only to prove that you were listening. Thank your host courteously, say that you are honoured by the invitation (never that you don't know why you were asked) and that you have enjoyed the hospitality, offer a brief anecdote (preferably humorous) about yourself, and make agreeable comments upon the body which has invited you.

No toast, proposed or replied to, should occupy more than three minutes.

The wedding speech

Traditionally, the order of speeches is as follows:

(i) A toast to the bride and groom, usually proposed by the bride's father or another relative or friend of the family.

(ii) A reply by the groom on his wife's behalf and his own. This must express gratitude to those who have worked to make the day so memorable—especially his new in-laws. Before closing, he should thank the guests for their presents and for coming, perhaps mentioning by name anyone who has come an unusual distance. The groom finishes by proposing a toast to the bridesmaids.

(iii) By convention the best man replies on their behalf, with suitably flattering comments. Usually, however, this is the merest peg on which to hang a series of teasing re-

marks and stories about the groom. Here it is important not to get carried away – although a few jokes at the groom's expense will be expected, these should be clearly affectionate: anything that might cause real offence should be left out, however funny. Risqué jokes or references to former girlfriends are better used up on the stag night. It is also considered bad taste to make even the mildest joke at the expense of the bride or her mother. There is, of course, one perfectly safe target for humour – yourself.

As with the after-dinner speech, it is better to limit yourself to two or three genuinely funny and apposite jokes. It is also a good policy to put your best joke – or the one you feel most confident about – right at the start. A good response here will probably ensure further laughs throughout the speech; it will also do much for your confidence. Remember that your audience will probably be in a mellow and appreciative mood, ready to laugh at anything at all amusing as long as it is clearly well meant. But don't try to boost your own confidence with Dutch courage – one or two drinks may help to relax you, but more could lead to disaster. The speech should close with another toast to the bride and groom; it should not have exceeded five or six minutes in length.

Although these are the speeches decreed by tradition, variations from the set pattern are now quite common. In particular, the bride and the chief bridesmaid may wish to speak for themselves, rather than to be spoken for in this way. It is not unheard of for the best 'man' to be a woman.

Informal presentations

Retirement, promotion, leaving the district, and getting married are among the reasons for such presentations. They are small-group occasions, usually held at lunch-time or after office hours. They should not be dismissed lightly. A retirement presentation is particularly important to the person concerned. It marks a separation after many years from habit, custom, and colleagues. The speech on such an occasion must have warmth and dignity and it should never be laboured.

All the speeches in this category should be friendly and *comfortable*. Notes should never be used.

Talking to the young

Regrettably, many speakers talk to young people as if they belonged to a separate branch of humanity. Children of primary-school age can make a wonderful audience if a few simple facts are remembered.

The subject-matter should be appropriate to their age and present understanding. It should be practical rather than abstract and it should involve their imaginations. It will be enhanced by the use of good visual aids and models. The talk should be given at a moderate pace and with lively inflexions and an effective use of pause. Humour – if it is not sophisticated – is appreciated and the atmosphere should be friendly and relaxed.

However, it is most unwise to allow shouted interruptions and questions, cat-calls, and the like. There may be a few unruly children and these must be treated firmly. It is fatal to try to be one of them in manner or idiom; they will regard you with contempt.

Speaking to secondary-school children and young students allows a more sophisticated vocabulary, though simplicity should still be regarded as important. Visual and sound aids are valuable and notes may be used unobtrusively.

Discourage domination of question-time by one or two extrovert characters. It is foolish to assume that quiet listeners have nothing useful to say; draw them out when you can. Be patient with the occasional crass remark or apparently silly question. These sometimes arise out of self-consciousness: it is not always easy to join in.

Section 9: World English

World English – or World Englishes?

'World English' is a topic commonly debated in language circles and now discussed in daily newspapers—but what is meant by the term? There seem to be several distinct interpretations:

- It is used to mean the core English vocabulary, that part of the language common to all English speakers, over which there can be no dispute—the vocabulary and grammatical structures which are common to English wherever it is spoken. (Some might call this **standard English**.)

- 'World English' is sometimes interpreted as referring to an artificially sanitized form of English for international use, purged of all regional quirks and peculiarities. This 'World English' is perhaps understood as being used among second-language speakers, possibly with a theoretical mid-Atlantic neutrality. (An alternative term might be **International English**.)

- Finally, there is the understanding of the term that will be reflected in the discussion that follows. 'World English' is understood here as a collective term for all the different varieties of English worldwide, for the sum of the core vocabularies, or central word-stocks, of each English-speaking region—including England. In this sense it is probably clearer to use the term **World Englishes** rather than 'World English'.

How did the World Englishes develop? How do the several varieties of English differ? Is there any one form of English that is 'better' than the others? These are among the questions dealt with in the following pages.

The Family of Englishes

The geographical spread of English is unique among the languages of the world,
throughout history. Countries using English as either a first or a second language are located on all six inhabited continents, and the total population of these countries amounts to about 49% of the world's population.

Whereas the English-speaking world was formerly seen as a hierarchy of parent (Britain) and children ('the colonies'), it is now viewed rather as a family of varieties. The English of England, the original source of all the World Englishes, is itself seen as one of the 'family' of world English varieties, with its own peculiarities and its own distinctive vocabulary.

This awareness that English consists of a family of different varieties is not a new phenomenon, but goes back to the early 19th century. Published in 1808, John Jamieson's *Etymological Dictionary of the Scottish Language* recognized that there was a difference between the Scottish variety of English and the English of England. John Bartlett's *Dictionary of Americanisms* appeared in 1848, acknowledging that a distinct variety of English had arisen across the Atlantic. And the huge, multivolume *Oxford English Dictionary* (1884-1928) documented not just British English words, but also words from the varieties of English found in Australasia, the Caribbean, Asia, Africa, and North America.

During the 1980s and 1990s the information available on the major regional varieties of English increased dramatically. Five large, specialized dictionaries were published, providing detailed records of regional Englishes: *The Australian National Dictionary* (1988); *A Dictionary of South African English on Historical Principles* (1996); *A Dictionary of Caribbean Usage* (1996); *The Canadian Oxford Dictionary* (1997); and *The Dictionary of New Zealand English* (1998).

The Role of English

The English language has an increasingly influential position in the world, but accurate statistics are difficult to provide. It is impossible to give a satisfactory answer to the question 'How many countries use English as their first language?' as the definition of 'first language' differs from place to place, according to each country's history and local circumstances. The following examples illustrate the complexities:

- Australia, Botswana, the Commonwealth Caribbean nations, Gambia, Ghana, Guyana, Ireland, Namibia, New Zealand, Uganda, the United Kingdom, the United States, Zambia, and Zimbabwe have English as either statutory or *de facto* official language—but it is often the second or third language of the majority of citizens.

- In Cameroon and Canada, English shares official status with French, as does English and each main local language in the Nigerian states.

- In Fiji, English is the official language with Fijian; in Lesotho with Sesotho; in Pakistan with Urdu; in the Philippines with Filipino; and in Swaziland with Siswati.

- In India, English is an associate official language (after Hindi), and in Singapore English is one of four statutory official languages.

- In South Africa, English is the major language of communication—but it is just one of 11 official languages.

In all, English has official or special status in at least 75 countries (with a combined population of two billion people). It is estimated that one out of four people worldwide speak English with some degree of competence.

Where, When, and How Did World Englishes Develop?

The English language took root as English settlements were established: in the Middle Ages in southern Ireland and south-west Scotland; in the 17th and 18th centuries in North America, the Caribbean, and northern Ireland; and in the 18th and 19th centuries in Australasia and Africa.

A widely differing range of contexts and histories affected the development of these varieties of English. It is difficult (and dangerous!) to generalize about the varieties: each variety of English has developed its own particular characteristics according to the circumstances encountered in the different regions. Colonization patterns, demography, and politics have all played a role.

Factors which shaped the varieties of English

From the time at which each new area was colonized and the settlers were separated from their mother country (i.e. at various times from the early 17th century until the late 19th century), the English spoken there began to evolve its own characteristic form.

Isolation reinforced the differences developing in each region, and meant that the regional Englishes increasingly differed both from each other and from British English. Certain vocabulary items tended to remain in use in a colony after they vanished from British English because of the isolation of the colony from the mother country. For example, the older word *faucet* (*tap* in British English) survived in American English, as did the use of *guess*, meaning 'think, imagine', as in *I guess so*. *Bioscope* (a word for the cinema dating from the early 1900s in Britain) and *geyser*, meaning 'water-heater', lived on as common terms in South African English. In Bangladesh, India, and Malta, the word *Stepney* is still used for a spare wheel.

The **dialect** of the area of Britain from which the settlers originated had an impact upon the vocabulary of the new settlement. Australasian English retains British regional words such as *chook* (reflecting the northern English pronunciation of *chuck*) meaning 'chicken'; *dunny* (a shortening of *dunnikin*) meaning 'lavatory'; *larrikin* (perhaps from *larack* 'to lark about') meaning 'ruffian'; and *pikelet* meaning a type of drop scone. South African English reflects words of Scottish origin in areas such as law and education (*advocate* meaning 'barrister'; *janitor* meaning 'school caretaker'; *honours degree* meaning a higher degree between a bachelor's and a master's degree), and also in general vocabulary (*to stay* meaning 'to reside'; *timeous* meaning 'timely').

The **regional British accents** of the original settlers affected the pronunciation of the English developing in the new settlements. The settlers' level of education determined how 'standard' or 'extreme' their regional accents were when they arrived, and thus partly determined the shape of the colonial accent. In the United States it is suggested that Irish and West Country accents played a part, while in South Africa it is the mixture of London, North Country, and Scottish accents among the British settlers of 1820 to which some attribute the distinctive local accent. The characteristic accents of American, Australian, and South African English all result from the blending of different British regional accents into one comparatively uniform new accent.

The **indigenous languages** encountered in each new colony by English-speaking colonists invariably had an impact upon the English developing there. In some colonies (for example the American states, Australia, and New Zealand), there were initially no powerful competing languages; in others (for instance the eastern provinces of Canada and the Cape Colony of South Africa) numerically strong languages such as French and Dutch vied for supremacy with English. In almost all areas, early colonists borrowed names for unfamiliar flora, fauna, topography, and culture from the languages they encountered in their new homes. Thus new words entered English—words such as *Inuit, mesa, moccasin, racoon, pueblo*, and *wigwam* (North America); *cheetah, gymkhana, juggernaut, mogul* (South East Asia); *aardvark, apartheid, commando, impala, spoor* (southern Africa); *boomerang, kangaroo, kiwi, kookaburra, wombat* (Australasia); and *gumbo, mumbo-jumbo, voodoo, yam* (West Africa, often via the West Indies).

The **relative size of the English settlement** was significant in determining the type of English that developed there. In areas where English settlers were heavily outnumbered, pidgin varieties of English often developed alongside the more standard variety—forms of English unintelligible to English speakers elsewhere in the world. (**Pidgin English** is the name given to a makeshift language based on English but containing a high proportion of words from other languages, and having a simplified grammar and a limited vocabulary.) There are many forms of pidgin English, spoken as second languages in order to make communication possible. Some pidgins developed into **creoles**, the first languages of certain regions. Some of the creole languages based on English are Krio (Sierra Leone), Gullah (South Carolina and Georgia in the United States), Tok Pisin (Papua New Guinea), and the creoles of the Caribbean.

In some regions, such as on the South Asian subcontinent, and in Hong Kong, Singapore, and Malaysia, English was the administrative language, the language of government and education—but it was always the second language of the local people. In these varieties of English there was bound to be considerable borrowing of vocabulary, as well as grammatical and phonological interference, from the first language.

The new English-speaking communities have filled gaps in vocabulary, not only by borrowing and by loan translation from the languages they encountered, but also by **the creation of new English words and phrases** (as is the case in any language community). For example, Australians have created new words by adding the suffixes *-o* or *-ie*, such as *arvo* ('afternoon'), *smoko* ('work break'), and *barbie* ('barbecue'). New Zealanders coined the term *chateau cardboard* for 'wine in a box', and Indian English has generated the terms *cousin brother* and *cousin sister* for male and female cousins. In Nigeria, a person who moved from one political party to another was given the name *decampee*; and South African English created *monkey's wedding* ('alternating or simultaneous sunshine and showers') and *bundu-bashing* ('travelling through the bush').

In summary, the differing circumstances in which the Englishes developed meant that each variety had the potential to differ considerably from the others in a variety of aspects.

A Complex Interrelationship

The linguist Braj Kachru uses concentric circles to illustrate his concept of how the Englishes differ from one another, and of the relationships between them, as follows:

- The **inner circle** (English as first language): Australia, Canada, Ireland, New Zealand, UK, USA

- The **outer circle** (English as second language): Bangladesh, Ghana, Hong Kong, India, Kenya, Malaysia, Nigeria, Pakistan, Philippines, Singapore, Sri Lanka, Tanzania, Zambia

- The **expanding circle** (English as foreign language): China, Egypt, Indonesia, Israel, Japan, Korea, Nepal, Saudi Arabia, Taiwan, the former Soviet republics

(South Africa is a special case: because it has a significant first-language community of English speakers, a much larger second-language community, and a huge number of people approaching English as a foreign language, it can be said to fit into all three circles.)

Other linguists apply different yardsticks to compare the varieties to each other, such as the national or official status of English, the use of the language in education, or the degree of divergence from 'international' standard English in the region.

The World Englishes sometimes share features in an unpredictable way: for example, New Zealand and South Africa both use a now dated expression, *hang of a* (+ adjective or adverb) to mean 'extremely (adjective or adverb)'; both say *in the dogbox* ('in disgrace') while others say *in the doghouse*. South Africa and Australia both use the word *donga* ('gully, depression'), but Australians, having borrowed the word during the South African War of 1899-1902, have added the extra sense 'makeshift dwelling'. Canada and South Africa both use *bachelor* to refer to a flat or apartment consisting of only one room. Jamaica and South Africa both use *yard* to mean an area containing a number of houses.

British and American influence often co-exist in the regional Englishes; for example, South Africa is 'British' in influence, yet follows American English in using *pants* to mean 'trousers' and *pantyhose* for what the British call *tights*.

Summary

The concept 'World Englishes' encompasses a wide range of variables, both political and linguistic. First, the political:

- English fulfils a variety of roles worldwide: it can be national language, official language, administrative language, language of communication, second language, or third (or even fourth) language.

- The forms taken by English worldwide range between standard English at the one end of the spectrum and pidgin English at the other. Many varieties fall somewhere between the two extremes.

- The position held by English may be unassailable, as in the United Kingdom, New Zealand, or Australia, or it may be challenged by other languages, as in Quebec (Canada), South Africa, and (increasingly) the United States.

- While English may be important as the language of commerce, education, and government, it is not always the first language of the majority of citizens of a country. This sometimes leads to a reaction against English as an elitist 'colonial' language—or to demands that the local variety of English be recognized as 'standard'. Reactions to English can be ambivalent: it can be aspired to and yet resented.

Secondly, the linguistic:

- Some English words originated in a regional variety, but are now assimilated into the wider vocabulary of English, with their regional origins no longer recognized—as *budgerigar* (Australia), *bungalow* (South Asia), and *trek* (South Africa). Other words (for example *bluey*, *chotapeg*, *donga*, from the same three regions), while important in their own variety, are rarely used or understood elsewhere.

- Some English words, now archaic or dialectal in Britain, survive in general use only in one of the former British possessions.

- Some regional words are general English words to which new meanings have been assigned.

- Some regional words are borrowed from other languages with which English has come into contact; some are loan translations from these languages; and some are entirely new words or phrases, created in the region.

- One word can mean many things throughout the English-speaking world. For example, a *Dolly Varden* is a frilly dress or a large elaborate hat in Britain, a Californian trout in North America, a cake in the shape of a doll wearing a crinoline dress in Australia, and a draped dressing-table in South Africa! Conversely, one object can be given many different names worldwide (for example, the shoes known as *gymshoes*, *plimsolls*, *sneakers*, and *tackies*).

- Some words describe cultural or topographical phenomena found only in one region (*boomerang*, *haka*, *teepee*). Other words describe something known everywhere but not given a name elsewhere—for example, *Scotch call*, the name in South Africa for a message given to someone by allowing the telephone to ring twice before ringing off.

The Future?

What will happen to English during the next century? Is English splitting into many different fragments, or is it tending to become more standardized because of international use?

There are powerful factors causing divergence between the varieties of English. This is particularly true at a time when there is an established or growing national confidence in the former British colonies, and a pride in the particular characteristics of the local varieties of English. Similarly, although rapidly increasing numbers of people aspire to learn English, they are often being taught by teachers who do not themselves have a good command of the language. Do these factors mean that English will fragment into hundreds of mutually unintelligible languages? Or, with the worldwide influence of the Internet, and of American global broadcasters such as CNN, is it likely that English will become more homogeneous, and perhaps more influenced by American English?

It seems likely that both divergence and convergence will take place. The use of English as the major language of communication worldwide is a great asset in international politics, business, education, and the media. Speakers of English (whether first-language or not) learn to use two 'dialects'—one with their own community, and one in the international context. When communicating with people from other parts of the world, they possess the intuitive ability to suppress words from their regional variety that might not be understood. In international politics, business, and education, in the media, and on the Internet, it is likely that English will remain mutually intelligible because of the constant interaction (electronic and otherwise) between the Englishes of various parts of the world, and the value of English as lingua franca.

At the same time, it also seems likely that mutually unintelligible forms of English will increasingly develop as the language is taught and learned in areas of the world which are isolated from contact with first-language speakers. For example, English is used in Africa as the language of communication between people of different language groups who have absolutely no contact with English speakers, and this can lead to the development of pidgin varieties with numerous borrowings from one or more of the local languages.

Whereas one can only speculate on likely trends, the one certainty is that the English language will continue to change in the future, and to respond in dynamic and unpredictable ways as its use increases across the world.

Further Reading

There are many interesting, informative, and readable books covering the topic of World English, including:

Crystal, D. (1995): *The Cambridge Encyclopedia of the English Language*—Cambridge: Cambridge University Press

McArthur, T. (1998): *The Concise Oxford Companion to the English Language*—Oxford: Oxford University Press

Trudgill, P. and Hannah, J. (1985): *International English: a guide to varieties of Standard English* London: E. Arnold

The following publications provide more detailed analyses:

Goerlach, M. (1991): *Englishes: Studies in Varieties of English, 1988-94*—Amsterdam: John Benjamins

— — (1995): *More Englishes: New Studies in Varieties of English, 1988-94*—Amsterdam: John Benjamins

— — (1998): *Even more Englishes: Studies, 1996-7* Amsterdam: John Benjamins

McArthur, T. (1998): *The English Languages* Cambridge: Cambridge University Press

Schneider, E. (1997): *Englishes Around the World* (Vol. 1, General Studies, British Isles, and America; Vol. 2, Caribbean, Africa, Asia, Australasia) Amsterdam: John Benjamins